THE CRIMINALIZATION OF MIGRATION

MCGILL-QUEEN'S REFUGEE AND FORCED MIGRATION STUDIES
Series editors: Megan Bradley and James Milner

Forced migration is a local, national, regional, and global challenge with profound political and social implications. Understanding the causes and consequences of, and possible responses to, forced migration requires careful analysis from a range of disciplinary perspectives, as well as interdisciplinary dialogue.

The purpose of the McGill-Queen's Refugee and Forced Migration Studies series is to advance in-depth examination of diverse forms, dimensions, and experiences of displacement, including in the context of conflict and violence, repression and persecution, and disasters and environmental change. The series will explore responses to refugees, internal displacement, and other forms of forced migration to illuminate the dynamics surrounding forced migration in global, national, and local contexts, including Canada, the perspectives of displaced individuals and communities, and the connections to broader patterns of human mobility. Featuring research from fields including politics, international relations, law, anthropology, sociology, geography, and history, the series highlights new and critical areas of enquiry within the field, especially conversations across disciplines and from the perspective of researchers in the global South, where the majority of forced migration unfolds. The series benefits from an international advisory board made up of leading scholars in refugee and forced migration studies.

1 The Criminalization of Migration
Context and Consequences
Edited by Idil Atak and James C. Simeon

The Criminalization of Migration

Context and Consequences

EDITED BY IDIL ATAK AND JAMES C. SIMEON

McGill-Queen's University Press
Montreal & Kingston · London · Chicago

© McGill-Queen's University Press 2018

ISBN 978-0-7735-5445-0 (cloth)
ISBN 978-0-7735-5446-7 (paper)
ISBN 978-0-7735-5563-1 (ePDF)
ISBN 978-0-7735-5564-8 (ePUB)

Legal deposit fourth quarter 2018
Bibliothèque nationale du Québec

Printed in Canada on acid-free paper that is 100% ancient forest free
(100% post-consumer recycled), processed chlorine free

This book has been published with the help of a grant from
the Canadian Federation for the Humanities and Social Sciences,
through the Awards to Scholarly Publications Program, using funds
provided by the Social Sciences and Humanities Research Council of
Canada. Funding has also been received from Ryerson University and
York University.

We acknowledge the support of the Canada Council for the Arts,
which last year invested $153 million to bring the arts to Canadians
throughout the country. Nous remercions le Conseil des arts du
Canada de son soutien. L'an dernier, le Conseil a investi 153 millions
de dollars pour mettre de l'art dans la vie des Canadiennes et des
Canadiens de tout le pays.

Library and Archives Canada Cataloguing in Publication

The criminalization of migration : context and consequences / edited by
Idil Atak and James C. Simeon.

(McGill-Queen's refugee and forced migration studies ; 1)
Includes bibliographical references and index.
Issued in print and electronic formats.
ISBN 978-0-7735-5445-0 (cloth). – ISBN 978-0-7735-5446-7 (paper). –
ISBN 978-0-7735-5563-1 (ePDF). – ISBN 978-0-7735-5564-8 (ePUB)

1. Refugees – Government policy – Canada. 2. Human rights – Canada.
3. Emigration and immigration law – Canada. I. Atak, Idil, editor II. Simeon,
James C., editor III. Series: McGill-Queen's refugee and forced migration
studies ; 1

HV640.4.C3C75 2018   305.9'06914   C2018-903628-1
                                                 C2018-903629-x

---

This book was typeset by True to Type in 10.5/13 Sabon

Contents

Protecting the Human Rights of Migrants as Part of a Long-Term Strategic Vision on Mobility and Diversity

François Crépeau

The paradox of current migration policies is illustrated by the number of deaths at sea or in deserts. The suffering of so many is a symptom of systemic failings, despite sustained investment in "securitizing" borders. Such policies also speak to how states respond to difference and diversity.

As long as the drivers of migration – violence and poverty as push factors, labour needs as pull factors – remain, people will move through porous borders. As is well illustrated in this collection, unless we egregiously violate the human rights of migrants, "sealing" the border is a fantasy. Resisting mobility is inefficient and costly. Governing it is a better option.

Yet, we must understand the individual trajectories and policy dynamics at work. A considerable number of employers are actually calling for more exploitable migrants to come. Migrants are responding to the opportunities of such labour markets and would not come otherwise. By not properly regulating labour markets, by providing very limited opportunities for low-wage migrants in the form of mostly precarious migration statuses that subject them to human rights and labour rights violations, "we" are at least co-responsible for undocumented migration, which we then criminalize.

Moreover, electoral democracies do not know how to "represent" migrants. They are the best system we have ever invented for governing ourselves, but they have a structural limit: if one is not represented, one's rights are not respected, protected, and promoted in the political system. Nationalist populist politicians continue to affirm that migrants steal jobs, create insecurity, or change our values – all assertions that have been proven wrong by social sciences – and to affirm this with total impunity, since most mainstream politicians are not taking the electoral risk of picking a fight in favour of persons who are politically non-existent.

There are no easy solutions. Mobility and diversity create complex issues that require long-term vision, sophisticated policies, targeted investments, and nuanced discourses. Up to now, with a few exceptions, we have been treated to none of the above, when we urgently need strong integration policies, efficient equality and anti-discrimination mechanisms, effective action against hate speech, access to justice for all, and the active promotion of diversity at all levels.

We need to change our collective mind-set. States must accept that they all are involved in migration, as destination, transit, and home countries – most often at the same time. Migrants will come, no matter what, because of push and pull factors.

Prohibitions and repressive policies, without regular migration channels for asylum seekers and much-needed low-wage migrants, do not change anything with regard to push and pull factors, and only entrench smuggling operations and underground labour markets, resulting in more deaths at sea and more human rights violations. The testimonies collected in this volume show the toxic, counterproductive, and unsustainable nature of repressive measures when no appropriate official mobility option is offered. On migration issues, as for the regulation of drugs and alcohol, we must choose the path of harm-reduction rather than zero-tolerance policies. The proper governance of mobility must mean legalization, regulation, and taxation for most migrants.

The only way to actually reduce smuggling is to take over the mobility market by offering regular, safe, accessible, and affordable mobility solutions, with all the identity and security checks that efficient visa regimes can provide.

As Kenneth Roth, head of Human Rights Watch, said in September 2015: "if there is a crisis, it is one of politics, not capacity."[1] We are facing a crisis of political leadership. There is no getting out of a crisis unless one provides a post-crisis vision. A long-term strategic vision for mobility policies is needed, just as it is for energy, environmental, public transit, industrial, or other policies. Politicians will need to delineate a long-term, human rights-based strategic mobility and diversity policy vision, with precise timelines and accountability benchmarks, to give meaning and direction to the actions currently taken.

The main axis of this long-term vision should be the elimination of precariousness in the status of migrants, in order to empower them to fight for their rights, whatever the context: labour market, housing, health care, education, or anti-terrorism.

Long-term substantial and collectively shared resettlement policies would go a long way toward responding to the needs of refugees, alleviating the responsibilities of transit countries, and reassuring host populations that this migration is properly governed.

For migrant workers, destination countries should recognize their real labour needs, and facilitate regular migration channels for labour at all wage levels, through many smart visa options.

The idea is not to diminish border controls, but to increase them and make them more effective. Offering most foreigners easy access to appropriate travel documents, such as visas for resettlement, visits, family reunification, work, or studies, would allow states to concentrate their deterrence efforts on the minute percentage of foreigners who really need to be excluded. One key condition, however: we need a sharp increase in the respect of labour conditions in favour of *all* workers, and the repression of exploitative employers and recruiters.

With target 10.7 of the 2030 Agenda for Sustainable Development, states agreed to "facilitate" migration and mobility in the next fifteen years. This means easing mobility – lowering barriers to migration – and governing it better. It does not mean open borders, but a coordinated increase of smart visa and non-visa avenues for migrants at all skill levels and for the resettlement of refugees.

The current negotiation of the UN Global Compact on Migration could be the opportunity to initiate a fifteen-year "agenda," complementary to the 2030 Agenda for Sustainable Development, with benchmarks and accountability mechanisms. The Zero Draft[2] of this Global Compact has positively surprised most observers, as the human rights and labour rights of migrants are at the core of the document. One hopes that the momentum will not be lost during the negotiations themselves.

There is a silver lining. Mobility will eventually come to be celebrated, thanks to the groundwork done by civil society, the vigilance of the judiciary, improved media reporting, welcoming cities, mobile technologies, the diverse and mobile business community, the openness of the youth toward mobility and diversity, and the admirable resilience and courage of migrants themselves.

This volume shows the deep impact of the multiple negative facets of the criminalization of migration. The warping effect of repressive policies (such as policies aimed at creating a "hostile environment" for undocumented migrants) on, for example, refugee status determination processes, the well-being of children and persons with disabilities or illnesses, and the separation of families is clear and cannot be termed "unintended consequences" anymore.

States will need to understand that decisions about human beings – their life, their family links, their future – should not be taken only according to abstract rules, contrary to decisions about goods, services, or capital, but also according to their specific circumstances. This means implementing the principle that is at the root of all human rights, Immanuel Kant's categorical imperative: "Act in such a way that you treat humanity, whether in your own person or in the person of any other, never merely as a means to an end, but always at the same time as an end."[3] One should apply a social work model of case management to welcoming migrants, supporting them in finding the best place for their integration, and providing them with services tailored to their situation: schooling, access to the labour market, language courses, health care, etc. The cost of welcoming migrants is not an expense, but an investment that will produce a remarkable return, if well governed.

The last part of this volume opens avenues of reflection in how to be creative in the development of less rudimentary and brutal mobility policies, benefiting migrants and receiving countries alike.

François Crépeau, OC, FRSC, AdE, Fellow of the Trudeau Foundation
Villers-la-Ville, 27 April 2018

NOTES

1 Kenneth Roth, "The Refugee Crisis That Isn't." Human Rights Watch,
   3 September 2015, https://www.hrw.org/news/2015/09/03/refugee-crisis-isnt.
2 "Global Compact for Safe, Orderly and Regular Migration, draft rev. 1,"
   Global Compact for Migration, 26 March 2018, https://refugeesmigrants.un
   .org/sites/default/files/180326_draft_rev1_final.pdf.
3 Immanuel Kant, *Grounding for the Metaphysics of Morals*, 3rd ed., trans. James
   W. Ellington (Cambridge: Hackett, 1993), 30.

Preface

We live in an ever-globalized reality where the national and world communities are confronted with ever-escalating crises that are more apparently interconnected: protracted armed conflict, predominantly of the non-international variety or civil wars, and the accelerating use of extreme violence such as terrorism; climate change in the form of higher-than-average temperatures due to unrelenting carbon emissions and deforestation; the rapid depletion of nonrenewable resources combined with the relentless pollution of our planet's natural resource endowment; and ever-increasing human mobility with the availability of relatively inexpensive transportation systems such as public air, rail, and coach travel. The number of people on the move has been estimated by the United Nations to be 258 million people in 2017.[1]

The United Nations High Commissioner for Refugees' (UNHCR) "Global Trends: Forced Displacement in 2017" report states that 68.5 million people were forcibly displaced in 2017.[2] This was again a record level of the number of people who had been forcibly displaced primarily due to "persecution, conflict, and generalized violence."[3] Astonishingly, 68 per cent or more than two-thirds of these forcibly displaced people came from only five countries: the Syrian Arab Republic, Afghanistan, South Sudan, Myanmar, and Somalia.[4] All of these countries, sadly, have been embroiled in protracted armed conflict for years.

The other shocking statistic in the UNHCR's 2017 report is that more than half of the world's forcibly displaced people (52 per cent) are children, under eighteen years of age.[5] These statistics underscore one of the most challenging crises of our time: the seemingly ever-growing numbers of forcibly displaced persons in the world, more than half of whom, unconscionably, are children – in addition, it has been estimated that 80 per cent of the world's refugees are women and children. However, despite these glaring and, frankly, highly disturbing statistics, the world's states are not, with a few notable exceptions, welcoming asylum seekers. Indeed, as US president Donald Trump has amply demonstrated,[6] most states are aggressively trying to restrict the flow of refugees in their countries. Perhaps most troubling of all was President Trump's "zero tolerance" family separation policy that affected thousands of Central American asylum seekers at the US-Mexico border when their children were taken away from them and dispersed across the United States.[7] Following an international uproar, this abhorrent policy was finally reversed, by executive order, on 20 June 2018, but not before it had unleashed confusion and chaos throughout the US immigration system.[8] Suffice it to say, all states have committed to supporting the United Nations High Commissioner for Refugees in his efforts to protect refugees and all those seeking asylum. Individually, states are also committed to the doctrine of the Responsibility to Protect their people, and, collectively, they have a Responsibility to Protect each other's people from the severest forms of international harm that can be perpetrated against them.[9]

It is in this global context that this volume was conceived, in preparation for the theme of the Canadian Association for Refugees and Forced Migration Studies (CARFMS) annual conference that was being planned for Ryerson University in 2015. Following this successful conference, the coeditors decided to pursue an edited volume consisting of a number of papers that had been presented at the conference. This was the genesis of the present volume, but it quickly evolved to include a number of others who were not at this conference, but who wanted to be included in this first Canadian volume dedicated to the criminalization of migration, a growing field of study internationally.

The volume is comprised of twelve chapters, a foreword, an introduction, and conclusions. The chapters are divided into four parts, with three chapters in each part. Some of the most outstanding scholars and practitioners in the field of refugee and forced migration studies were gracious enough to make a contribution to this edited volume. The volume breaks new ground in a number of areas that deal with the criminalization of migration, or "crimmigration," as well as the way forward for the "decriminalization" of migration through the advancement of the human rights of migrants. We hope that this edited volume will be a welcomed addition to the literature on this subject and that it will help spur new research and stimulate new ideas, and approaches for the protection and the advancement of the human rights and human dignity of refugees and other forced migrants.

A publication project of this nature requires the commitment and dedication of a number of people in order to come to fruition. First and foremost, we should like to thank all of the contributors who agreed to join us on this publication project. It was a long process that took a number of years to realize from conception to completion and all of the contributors should be thanked for their patience and fortitude. Secondly, we should like to thank McGill-Queen's University Press (MQUP) and their staff, who immediately saw the potential for this publication and marshalled the manuscript through the peer-review and editorial board approval process and through various other stages of the publication production process. They were always cheerful, understanding, and helpful at every step in the completion of this volume and for this we are deeply grateful. We should also like to express our gratitude to the anonymous peer reviewers, who took the time to read our entire manuscript on several occasions and provided their valuable comments and suggestions for how each of the contributions to this volume could be improved.

We are also greatly honoured by the fact that our edited volume was selected by professors Megan Bradley and James Milner as the first publication in the McGill-Queen's Refugee and Forced Migration Studies series.

Thirdly, we should like to thank the Social Sciences and Humanities Research Council of Canada, which supported this project. We also thank both Ryerson University and York University for their publication grants in support of the production of this volume. We are also mindful of the fact that the book was supported by a publication grant from the Canadian government's Canada Council for the Arts, who were generous in their financial support for seeing this volume into print. Fourthly, we should like to thank all of our colleagues on the executive of the CARFMS, particularly the members of the 2015 CARFMS Annual Conference Committee for their support of this publication project. The 2015 CARFMS annual conference was, as noted, instrumental in initiating this volume and CARFMS, as a whole, sustained this publication project throughout. Fifthly, we would like to acknowledge and thank our colleagues at our universities and within our respective units – the Department of Criminology in the Faculty of Arts, Ryerson University; and the School of Public Policy and

Administration in the Faculty of Liberal Arts and Professional Studies, York University – for all of their support and encouragement in
the completion of this edited volume. Finally, we should like to thank
all those who are working in the field of refugee and forced migration
studies and who are advocating on behalf of world's most vulnerable
people, the refugees and other forced migrants, who have been forced
to leave their homes to protect their lives and their security and who
are seeking a decent and respectable life. It is their courage and commitment to the protection and the advancement of the human rights
of all migrants that has given us the inspiration, energy, and encouragement to produce this volume for the advancement of their cause,
but also everyone else's, in the hope of creating a better world for all.

Professor James C. Simeon
Clare Hall and the Lauterpacht Centre for International Law
University of Cambridge
Cambridge, United Kingdom
July 2018

Professor Idil Atak
Department of Criminology
Faculty of Arts
Ryerson University
Toronto, Ontario, Canada
July 2018

NOTES

1 United Nations, "International Migration Report 2017," United Nations
  Department of Economic and Social Affairs, 2017, 4, accessed 6 July 2018,
  http://www.un.org/en/development/desa/population/migration/publications
  /migrationreport/docs/MigrationReport2017_Highlights.pdf.
2 United Nations High Commissioner for Refugees, "Global Trends: Forced
  Displacement in 2017," UNHCR, 2018, 2, accessed 6 July 2018,
  http://www.unhcr.org/5b27be547.pdf.
3 Ibid.
4 Ibid., 3.
5 Ibid.
6 Jonathan Blitzer, "The Trump Administration's Hard Line on Refugees
  Comes Under Fire," *New Yorker*, 1 May 2018, accessed 6 July 2018,

https://www.newyorker.com/news/daily-comment/the-trump-administrations-hard-line-on-refugees-comes-under-fire.

7 Tamsin McMahon, "Parents Separated from Their Children by Trump's 'Zero Tolerance' Policy Ask: 'Will I Ever See My Children Again?'" *Globe and Mail*, 1 July 2018.

8 Sarah Almukhtar, Troy Griggs, Karen Yourish, "How Trump's Policy Change Separated Migrant Children from Their Parents," *New York Times*, 20 June 2018; "Trump Ends His Policy of Family Separations with Executive Order – As It Happened," *Guardian*, 9 July 2018.

9 United Nations Office on Genocide Prevention and the Responsibility to Protect, Responsibility to Protect, accessed 6 July 2018, http://www.un.org/en/genocideprevention/about-responsibility-to-protect.html.

THE CRIMINALIZATION OF MIGRATION

The Criminalization of Migration: Context and Consequences

Idil Atak and James C. Simeon

What is obvious to any casual observer today is that governments are inclined to keep forced migrants out of their countries, rather than to welcome them in. This is perhaps most evident in the case of President Donald Trump and his efforts to ban Muslims from certain countries from entering the United States.[1] But it is also evident in the European Union's initiatives to stop the refugee flows from Turkey and Libya.[2] The situation in Canada has changed dramatically with the election of a Liberal government under the leadership of Prime Minister Justin Trudeau.[3] Nonetheless, despite the significant changes in a number of key areas of migration policy, not everything that the former Conservative Government had introduced has been changed or altered with respect to Canadian migration and refugee protection policy.[4] This edited collection, accordingly, addresses the timely and topical issue of the criminalization of migration and questions of how to advance the protection of forced migrants. It examines how the criminalization of migration is impacted by its context and how this shapes the consequences, whether intended or unintended.

The idea of this edited collection emerged following the Eighth Annual Conference of the Canadian Association for Refugee and Forced Migration Studies/ Association canadienne pour les études sur les réfugiés et les migrations forcées (CARFMS/ACERMF) that was held at Ryerson University in Toronto, from 13 to 15 May 2015. The conference took place in the aftermath of the United Nations (UN) High-level Dialogue on International Migration and Development (in October 2013), which called on states to address international migration through a comprehensive and balanced approach, recognizing the roles and responsibilities of countries of origin, transit, and destination in promoting and protecting the human rights of all migrants.[5] It seems, however, that very few states chose to take up the challenge of adopting a "comprehensive and balanced approach" to international migration. Forced migration related to crises such as protracted internal armed conflicts and political unrest have continued to grow, exacerbated by climate change, natural disasters, and other human-made crises such as growing disparities in wealth, rising rates of poverty, and greater inequalities within and across societies.[6]

According to the United Nations High Commissioner for Refugees (UNHCR), 68.5 million people were forcibly displaced in 2017, compared to 33.9 million in 1997.[7] Protracted armed conflicts, like those in Syria, Somalia, Sudan, Iraq, and Afghanistan, to name but a few, have caused large refugee outflows, are lasting longer, and are pushing the number of refugees in the world steadily upward, from 10.4 million in 2012 to 25.4 million in 2017.[8] In addition, a growing number of migrants who are in precarious socioeconomic and legal situations are becoming increasingly marginalized and victimized in several states around the world. These problems were recently acknowledged in the New York Declaration for Refugees and Migrants, adopted by the UN General Assembly on 19 September 2016, which reaffirmed the political will to protect the rights of refugees and migrants. World leaders also agreed in New York City to work on two global compacts (the Global Compact on Refugees and the Global Compact for Safe, Orderly and Regular Migration), to be adopted in 2018. This comprehensive framework will include a set of common principles and guidelines on the treatment of migrants in vulnerable situations. It also aims to achieve a more equitable sharing of the burden and responsibility for hosting and supporting the world's refugees.[9] These positive developments, largely on an international scale, belie the actions and measures undertaken by states to criminalize migration. President Trump's decision to pull the US out of these negotiations exemplifies this trend.[10]

Against this background, this collection aims to explore one of the main challenges migrants are facing: the criminalization of migration, or "crimmigration," which involves the increasing use of criminal law in immigration matters, the criminalizing of public discourse, and other policies and practices that stigmatize migrants and refugees, and/or diminish their rights in Canada and abroad.[11] In fact, over the past decades, countries in the Global North have resorted to criminal law measures to deter and to punish migrants in irregular situations. Criminal penalties have been imposed on forced migrants, including refugees, for entering or staying in a country in an irregular manner, or using false documents, or for unauthorized employment. Detention has not only become increasingly common but pervasive. Transport companies, employers, and other persons who come into contact with or try to help irregular migrants, such as health professionals, humanitarian workers, landlords, family members, and friends, have also become the targets of criminal sanctions.[12] Asylum systems have become stricter, especially for refugee claimants arriving in destination countries with the help of smugglers.

The criminalization of migration has generated intense interest from academics, researchers, practitioners, the media, and the public. The work published in this field describes and critically examines the following general topics:

- "crimmigration" as a legal process that involves the integration of criminal law processes, categories, and techniques into immigration control, and the use of criminal law enforcement strategies, or administrative sanctions that mimic criminal ones, on migrants for immigration violations;[13]
- the social, political, economic, and discursive construction of the criminality of certain groups of immigrants, and local, national, regional, and international immigration enforcement strategies and mechanisms;[14]
- the intended objectives and unintended consequences of the criminalization of the immigration and refugee processes, including the violation of migrants' human rights;[15] and
- the current dynamics of forced migration and the criminalization of migration, along with a consideration of possible future challenges in this area and its likely prospects.[16]

The broad range of issues covered by this edited collection on a number of specific themes related to the criminalization of migration in Canada and abroad is a welcome addition to the existing work in this area.

DISTINCT FEATURES AND OVERARCHING THEMES
OF THIS COLLECTION

The collection's main aim is to contribute to the debates on the criminalization of migration and the processes of that criminalization. These processes are centred on how immigration and refugee law has become infused with the substance of criminal law, through both negative political, media, or public discourses against targeted populations and an increased reliance on criminal law to enforce immigration statutes.[17] Violations of immigration law carry greater criminal consequences than ever before, without, however, the implementation of procedural protections germane to criminal law within immigration law settings. In addition, the criminalization of migration involves the expansion of law enforcement and correctional powers, thereby enhancing the government's power of discretion to decide who may be excluded from the territory and from membership in society.[18] The criminalization of migration is a powerful conceptual tool that conditions the public's view of migrants, and especially refugees, and how migrants are treated by public officials upon their arrival and while they are residents within a state's territory.

This is the first full-length edited collection that treats migration in Canada using the conceptual tool of the criminalization of migration to examine this subject matter in detail. It strives to deepen our understanding of this process, which is prevalent in Canada and abroad. In line with the above-mentioned global trends, the Conservative government of Stephen Harper (2006 to 2015) tightened considerably Canada's asylum and migration policies. The country had increased immigration detention, strengthened border controls, and enhanced its international cooperation in the fight against irregular migration. Under this Conservative government, asylum policy was, indeed, one of the most contentious issues.[19] After the arrivals off the west coast of Canada in 2009 and 2010 of two ships, the MV *Ocean Lady* and the MV *Sun Sea*, which carried, respectively, 76 and 492 Sri Lankan Tamil asylum seekers, the government underwent a complete overhaul of the asylum system, with the passage of the Balanced Refugee Reform Act in 2010 and the Protecting Canada's Immigration System Act in 2012.[20] As an illustration, the new Designated Foreign National (DFN) regime allows the Minister of Public Safety to designate individuals who arrive to Canada with the help of a smuggler, in a group of two or more, and mandates the detention of DFNs aged sixteen and over.[21]

In addition to mandatory detention, this regime provides for repressive measures such as circumscribed procedural rights for refugee claimants who arrive as a part of a smuggling event and deferred integration and family reunification for refugees. Such refugees are, in other words, directly penalized on account of their mode of arrival. This regime has only been used once since it entered into force in 2012. Hence, it illustrates how the invocation of criminal law in cases of immigration offences serves mostly as a deterrent. Policies such as the DFN regime are also based on the erroneous assumption that if deterrents are made severe enough, people will change their behaviour.[22] However, such policies have shifted the government's approach from humanitarianism and protecting refugees to control through punitive policies. They also prove to be a violation of Canada's commitments to refugees, including Article 31 of the *Convention Relating to the Status of Refugees* (the Refugee Convention),[23] which enjoins states not to impose penalties on refugees who enter or are present in their territory without authorization on account of their illegal entry or presence, provided they present themselves without delay to the authorities, and show good cause for their illegal entry or presence.

As shown in this example, recent legislative and policy changes deal with novel and complex subject matter that has not been adequately studied or understood within Canada. The collection intends to fill this knowledge gap by drawing attention to the increasing use of criminal law measures to manage migration, the negative stereotyping and criminalizing of migrants and refugees in the dominant public discourse, and other public policies and practices.

This collection also provides insights on the criteria and conditions pertaining to the exclusion of refugees and immigrants from the host society for reasons of security, criminality, or abuse of the refugee system.[24] The threat of terrorism has been confronted with increased security practices and border controls, especially after the terrorist attacks against the US on 11 September 2001. Concerns about abuse of the refugee determination system and the entry of terrorists and international criminals have justified the implementation of restrictive policies in Canada and abroad.[25] Security is, undoubtedly, a legitimate criterion in the selection process of immigrants and a well-established ground for excluding those refugees who represent a threat to the nation.[26] As Section 3 of the Immigration and Refugee Protection Act (IRPA) puts it, Canada's immigration policy aims to protect the health and safety of Canadians and to maintain the security of Canadian society. The same provision states that Canada strives "to promote international justice and security by denying access to Canadian territory to persons, including refugee claimants, who are security risks or serious criminals."[27] As well, the 1951 Refugee Convention allows signatory states to deny protection to persons who have engaged in international or municipal criminal activity or serious non-political crime abroad, or who have taken actions contrary to the purposes and principles of the United Nations.[28] One may be deemed ineligible to claim refugee status if the obligation to protect his or her human rights is outweighed by the need to protect the safety of the Canadian public.[29] The reasoning behind the exclusion is that serious criminals should not evade prosecution of and punishment for their crimes by seeking refugee status. Indeed, the exclusion of those who have committed crimes of a significant magnitude helps preserve the integrity of the international refugee protection regime.[30] Canada plays a leading role in setting standards for the interpretation of these exclusion clauses of the Refugee Convention. However, most concepts that form elements of these exclusion clauses are still in flux, and their interpretation varies from one country to another. As highlighted in this collection, this situation underscores the need for some guidance from the highest national courts in order to avoid too much fragmentation of this important area of refugee law.

The other distinctive features of this collection are its focus on the repercussions of criminalization on the immigration and asylum systems, and the situation of migrants settling in Canada and other host countries in a global context of the so-called migration crisis. The criminalization of migration has, in part, been a policy response to the rising number of irregular migrants, which is considered to be a threat to sovereignty, public welfare, and national security. Joanna Parkin notes that "there is a wide consensus among scholars that the criminalization of migration has intensified in Western Europe in the last three decades, echoing the situation in the United States."[31] Irregular migration is a complex issue that lacks a globally accepted definition. It encompasses movement or activities that occur outside of the regulatory frameworks of the source, transit, or receiving state. This includes persons who arrive without authorization, overstay visas, remain as a rejected asylum seeker, or engage in unauthorized work. Irregular migration is considered to be linked to restrictive policies in labour migration and forced migration.[32] The phenomenon has recently attracted considerable political and media attention in Canada following the sudden increase in illegal border crossings after the US presidential elections. From January to October 2017, 15,100 people crossed the land border *via* the US to claim asylum in Canada, in defiance of the 2004 Canada-US Safe Third Country Agreement (STCA) – another legal instrument to manage asylum movements, barring most third-country nationals in the US from making an asylum claim at a Canadian land border.[33] By comparison, authorities intercepted 4,225 migrants between 2011 and 2016. Strikingly, almost 70 per cent of asylum claimants who illegally cross the US border into Canada were granted asylum.[34] Thus, the majority of those who cross the border illegally, and who are portrayed in the political discourse as "bogus refugees" or "illegal migrants," have in fact a well-founded fear of persecution in their home countries and are in need of international protection.[35] The STCA illustrates how restrictive immigration and asylum policies can push asylum seekers to resort to illegal ways to reach safety and thereby construct their irregular status. In effect, the fewer the avenues provided for international protection, the greater the incentive for engaging in irregular migration.

This process is also at play for migrant workers. Alessandro De Giorgi argues that the current model of "prohibitionist governance of migratory movements" started to emerge in the mid-1970s, particularly in Europe, when most industrialized European countries imposed a virtual ban on labour immigration in reaction to rising unemployment rates, economic stagnation, and the unfolding of a broad crisis of the industrial economy.[36] In a globalizing world, demand for both high- and low-skilled migrant workers in northern economies has grown.[37] However, immigration controls have been developed at the nation-state and supranational levels, creating a disjuncture between economic and political interests regarding immigration, in what Hollifield et al. call the "liberal paradox" of "open" markets and "closed" political communities.[38] Legal immigration has become more difficult and is increasingly limited to the privileged few.[39] The fact that migrants are unable to migrate regularly, while there are underground labour markets for the labour force in almost all countries, is actually creating more irregular migration and constitutes a major incentive for criminal organizations to provide their services to circumvent border controls.[40]

The situation is exacerbated by the security logic that has dominated states' responses to mixed migration movements. Mixed migration is a term used to describe the phenomenon whereby asylum seekers move alongside different categories of persons, including economic migrants, across international borders, usually in an irregular manner, using the same channels or routes and means of transport, often with the assistance of migrant smugglers.[41] The UNHCR acknowledges that mixed migratory movements include persons who may have international protection needs.[42] Nevertheless, as illustrated in the above-mentioned arrivals of Tamil asylum seekers in Canada, states usually treat these persons as security threats and/or "bogus refugees." The repressive measures they deploy to deter and punish such arrivals have contributed to the criminalization of migrants, who are portrayed as criminals or accomplices of smuggling rings, and therefore deserving of the penal treatment they receive.[43]

Today, despite the existence of a sophisticated international human rights and refugee protection framework, states continue maintaining national sovereignty through restrictive migration regimes. A significant number of forced migrants endure human rights violations. This became obvious in 2015 during the European "refugee crisis," when the majority of European states reacted to the spontaneous arrival of more than one million forced migrants, mostly from war-torn Syria, by closing their borders and erecting fences. Germany has shown remarkable leadership in opening its borders to more than a million migrants during 2015. Canada's resettlement of refugees is another example of leadership in humanitarianism. More than 26,000 Syrian refugees were resettled in Canada in less than six months from 2015 to 2016, thanks, notably, to a successful private sponsorship program.[44] These examples show that more solidarity with refugees and with the countries in the Global South that are currently hosting them is possible. Nevertheless, they remain the exception. The number of resettled international protection beneficiaries continues to be alarmingly low. In 2016, a total of 189,300 refugees were admitted for resettlement in thirty-seven countries, which represented less than 1 per cent of refugees in the world.[45] In 2017, this number dropped to 102,800. In 2016, the six wealthiest countries in the world, which between them account for almost 60 per cent of the global economy, hosted less than 9 per cent of the world's refugees.[46] Five countries that together constitute less than 2 per cent of global GDP – Turkey, Jordan, Pakistan, Lebanon, and South Africa – provide shelter to almost half of the world's refugees.[47] In contrast, the EU member states relocated just 20,869 refugees – 13,973 from Greece, 6,896 from Italy – as of 9 June 2017, out of 160,000 promised under a settlement scheme agreed to in 2015. By June 2017, the Czech

Republic, Hungary, and Poland had not yet relocated a single refugee, in breach of their legal obligations stemming from the EU decision, and are facing infringement procedures.[48]

Migratory controls have also proven to be counterproductive. Border cooperation diverts migration movements but does not stop them in a lasting manner. Such policies have the effect of driving further underground attempts to reach destination countries and making forced migrants' journeys even more dangerous. The International Organization for Migration (IOM) estimates that over the last two decades, more than 60,000 migrants have died trying to reach their destinations – and this only includes deaths for which there is some record.[49] Critical analyses of US border control policies have shown that increased restrictiveness has also had the unexpected result of turning temporary migrant workers into permanent settlers, thereby increasing irregular migration, due to the high risks of repeated border crossing.[50]

There is, therefore, an urgent need to foster a better understanding of the causes of these "crises" in order to promote constructive ways to tackle them. This collection questions a crisis-led policy model followed by various governments. The notion of "crisis" has two distinctive features. It denotes a condition of disruption or instability, or a danger, affecting an individual, group, community, or whole society. It also leads to a decisive change, as the imminence of disruption or danger points to a need for immediate action and triggers fundamental transformation.[51] De Genova and Tazzioli discuss how in Europe, alarmist reactions to the unauthorized movements of people have largely served to justify new "emergency" policies and the deployment of new means of control.[52] Several chapters in this collection highlight how "the crisis narrative" has exacerbated the criminalization of migration.

The collection offers unique insights into how the criminalization of migration has impacted refugees and other forced migrants in Canada and elsewhere. Building on recent legal, policy, program, and advocacy initiatives, it facilitates the identification and sharing of realistic strategies for a more effective harmonization of security with human rights.

In addition to its distinctive focus on the Canadian context and situation, this collection also differs from existing publications and research by its legal, comparative, historical, and interdisciplinary approach. Individual chapter contributions are situated within a par-

ticular context that moderates in various subtle ways the consequences that ensue within each state and at the societal level, and/or
within regional configurations, including Europe, North America,
and Middle East. The in-depth contextual comparative analysis with
other jurisdictions, such as the European Union, the Middle East, the
United Kingdom, and the US, provides a set of lessons and best practices. It helps appraise the effectiveness of Canadian policies and practices, and their impact on human rights. This international, comparative, and historical approach also illuminates important theoretical
questions pertaining to the criminalization of migration and the promotion of migrants' belonging in host societies.

ORGANIZATION OF THE COLLECTION

This edited collection comprises twelve chapters organized into four
key areas that array context and consequences: Part 1: The Criminalization of Migration and Its Intended and Unintended Consequences;
Part 2: The Criminalization and the Exclusion of Refugees in Canada
and Abroad; Part 3: Crimmigration Responses to "Migration Crises":
Historical and Comparative Perspectives; and Part 4: Criminalizing
Refugees and Other Forced Migrants: Current Dynamics, Future Challenges, and Prospects. Each key area comprises a range of specialized
topics written by Canadian and international experts. The collection
draws on the professional experiences and disciplinary perspectives of
diversely situated practitioners and scholars with considerable experience within their discipline or profession, including law and legal
theory, criminology, history, migration studies, political science, public
policy and administration, journalism, geography, and sociology.

Part 1 offers an in-depth discussion of the process of the criminalization of migration and its consequences. Graham Hudson (chapter
1) examines how and why crimmigration is used to frame constitutional challenges in Canada. Drawing on the role of analogy in both
the construction of and challenges to crimmigration, he argues that
the state misuses analogies between crime and migration, and criminals and migrants to rationalize the imposition of disproportionately
harsh measures on noncitizens. Hudson expresses concerns about the
lack of robust constitutional norms applicable within immigration
proceedings in Canada. Even though there are formal differences
between criminal proceedings and immigration proceedings, he
notes that the interests and values at stake in some immigration pro-

ceedings should be considered equal to, if not more important than, those at stake in criminal proceedings. Using three examples of crimmigration in Canada – protracted and indefinite detentions, inadmissibility on grounds of serious criminality, and deportation to face human rights abuses pursuant to danger opinions – Hudson explores how analogy provides a jurisprudential and rhetorical basis for arguing that constitutional norms largely developed in the context of criminal law ought to be applied in some immigration law settings. His chapter serves as a plea for decision makers to employ criminal law doctrine to help impose constitutional constraints on the government when it comes to immigration proceedings. Migrants, after all, are entitled to constitutional guarantees as much as anyone else in Canada.[53]

Angus Grant (chapter 2) deals with subsection 37(1)(*b*) of IRPA, which renders a person inadmissible to Canada and denies access to refugee determination procedures if he or she has, in the context of transnational crime, engaged in activities such as people smuggling, trafficking in persons, or money laundering.[54] The author refers specifically to the treatment of the asylum seekers on board the MV *Ocean Lady*, which arrived unauthorized off the west coast of Canada in 2009. As one of the defence lawyers who pleaded the case before the Supreme Court of Canada (SCC), Grant recalls that the government criminally prosecuted those thought to be the primary organizers of the voyage. He also notes that the government alleged that *anyone* aboard the ships who in *any way* may have facilitated the voyage was inadmissible to Canada because such a person would have engaged in the organized criminal act of people smuggling. The government also intervened in virtually all of the passengers' refugee claims, urging the Immigration and Refugee Board (IRB) to reject their cases, on either credibility grounds or based on one of the Refugee Convention's exclusion clauses. The author remarks that the frequency of the Canada Border Services Agency's (CBSA) intervention in these cases represented a clear departure from the Canadian government's typical approach to refugee status determination, in which ministerial participation in individual refugee claims is relatively rare. He explains how the government concentrated border control powers within the executive branch to deter future arrivals through punitive measures and to minimize, as much as possible, obligations arising under international refugee law. Grant goes on to examine how section 117 of the IRPA was found unconstitutional by the SCC in 2015, on the grounds that it could be used to prosecute humanitarian organizations, family members of asylum seekers, or even asylum seekers themselves. His chapter points to the overbroad nature of some exclusion provisions and the important role of IRB decision makers in clarifying the scope of these provisions.

Similarly, Julie Kaye (chapter 3) discusses how Canadian anti-trafficking responses have contributed to the construction of restrictive immigration policies, while also supporting broader notions of border securitization and the ongoing precariousness of trafficked persons. Kaye contends that restrictive policies limit legal migratory avenues, particularly for marginalized and gendered populations, without reducing demand for cheap, exploitable, and precarious labour. Although Canada has developed sophisticated anti-trafficking responses with the adoption in 2012 of a National Action Plan, Kaye notes that many structural and social factors continue to restrict migrants' ability to report instances of human trafficking. Using the situation of foreign workers, such as working as exotic dancers, construction workers, and live-in-caregivers, she analyses how anti-trafficking efforts fail to protect the rights of migrants, even in clear-cut instances that meet the criminal definitions of trafficking in persons. Kaye also delves into the gendered assumptions embedded in such policies. She discusses, for instance, how Canada's National Action Plan actually includes measures aimed at restricting the migration of girls and women to Canada. Further, Kaye examines how the CBSA, when implementing the anti-trafficking provisions, often fails to consider the nuanced circumstances that can lead trafficking victims and other criminalized migrants to be in violation of immigration laws. By emphasizing a "crime and security approach," notes Kaye, anti-trafficking discourses and policies contribute to the reproduction of the power differentiation in which human trafficking is rooted.

The contributors in part 2 of the collection focus on a legal analysis of the exclusion of forced migrants and refugees. Nancy Weisman's contribution (chapter 4) deals with the decision of the SCC in *Ezokola v. Canada (Citizenship and Immigration)*,[55] which articulated a new test to be applied in Canada for complicity in Article 1F(a) of the Refugee Convention. Weisman points out that *Ezokola* is the first decision in which the SCC has provided guidance regarding where to draw "the line between association and complicity." In the ruling, the Court notes that the former test for complicity had "inappropriately shifted its focus towards the criminal activities of the group and away from the individual's contribution to that criminal activity." Weisman offers an in-depth analysis of the decision that replaced the previous test for complicity, the "personal and knowing participation" test, with a "contribution-based approach." This means that complicity is established when there are "serious reasons for considering" that the claimant "voluntarily made a knowing and significant contribution to the crime or criminal purpose of the group alleged to have committed the crime." Weisman expands on these three key elements, namely, that the contribution of the person must be "voluntary," "knowing," and "significant," which, she reckons, points to the complexity of the new complicity test, making it potentially challenging for the courts to apply. Since the release by the SCC of *Ezokola* in 2013, there have been several cases in which the Federal Court has had the opportunity to interpret and apply the new "contribution-based" complicity test. Some of these cases are examined by Weisman, who suggests that since the SCC did not provide concrete examples in which these factors may arise, it will be left to the Refugee Protection Division (RPD) and the Refugee Appeal Division (RAD) of the IRB, and to the Federal Court (Canada) and the Federal Court of Appeal, which will review the RPD and the RAD decisions, to further refine and adapt the new complicity test for exclusion from refugee protection to particular situations.

The new complicity test is considered a positive development by Lorne Waldman and Warda Shazadi Meighen (chapter 5), who agree that the decision in *Ezokola* has allowed the exclusion clauses to be applied in an increasingly cautious manner. Their contribution focuses, in particular, on the standard of proof, which, they argue, is another problematic area regarding exclusion analysis. This standard is crucial, according to Waldman and Shazadi Meighen, especially because in most cases there will be little direct evidence, aside from that which emanates from the person concerned, as to the role he or she played in an international crime. Using a comparative analysis, the authors draw attention to two problems in this respect: first, the threshold is lower than the criminal law standard of proof, which is "proof beyond a reasonable doubt." As a result, in certain circumstances a refugee claimant can be excluded for crimes that would not meet the evidentiary threshold required for criminal conviction. Second, although the test for complicity in the UK mirrors the one set out in *Ezokola*, the evidentiary standard of "balance of probabilities" in the UK is higher than the standard in Canada. Given the consequences of exclusion,

Waldman and Shazadi Meighen argue that decision makers have a duty to refrain from a finding of exclusion on anything less than clear and convincing evidence. Their legal analysis suggests that in the absence of an evidentiary standard of a balance of probabilities, like that in the UK, there may well be numerous cases in which people are excluded on less than convincing evidence. According to the authors, the risk that Canada continues to run with its current standard of proof for exclusion, that of "serious reasons for considering," is that refugee claimants can be penalized and excluded for criminal acts under immigration legislation for which they would not be subjected to conviction under the criminal law itself.

In the last chapter of part 2, Joseph Rikhof (chapter 6) highlights the complexity of interpreting the exclusion clauses of the 1951 Refugee Convention and the evolving nature of the case law in different countries. He discusses how tribunals and courts are giving meaning to the concepts contained within the exclusion clauses. The questions they address include: What is a serious crime? What is a political crime? What is the impact of foreign convictions? How broad is the notion of complicity? Rikhof outlines how in various countries the reasoning used to conclude that a crime should be considered serious has been different. According to Rikhof, the most common approaches vary from examining the maximum penalty, which could be imposed for a particular crime in the criminal legislation, to what penalty would likely be imposed if a person would be tried by a criminal court, while, more recently, a third approach, developed originally in Canada, has been gaining popularity in common law countries. This approach, he remarks, uses a number of factors to determine whether a crime is serious, such as a penalty indicated in the criminal legislation, the actual possible sentence as well as possible mitigating and aggravating circumstances. Rikhof underlines that this complexity results in divergent interpretations. To give an example, some countries consider that Article 1F(b) of the Refugee Convention applies to capital or grave crimes without utilizing a more detailed methodology, while other countries examine the maximum penalty which could be imposed for a particular crime in the criminal legislation or what penalty would likely be imposed if a person would be tried criminally. The author further shows that the application and interpretation of Article 1F(b) has been progressively harmonizing.

Part 3 of the collection discusses, from historical and comparative perspectives, state responses to the recent "migration crises" in

Europe, Canada, the Middle East, and in the US. It points to the crisis narrative as one of the principal drivers for the criminalization of migrants. This narrative has become prominent in the political and media discourse in the Global North and draws mainly on the irregular arrivals of large groups of forced migrants perceived as a threat.[56] Petra Molnar (chapter 7) examines the criminalization of Syrian refugees in Turkey and Jordan. Syrians, as she reminds, are not considered "refugees" under Turkish law as this country ratified the 1951 Refugee Convention with a geographical limitation. Consequently, they are only entitled to temporary protection and are expected to resettle in a third country. Molnar argues that the denial of a secure legal status is part of the strategies deployed by authorities to compel refugees to leave Turkey. The exclusionary legal framework, coupled with ongoing social marginalization and increasing vulnerability to labour and sexual exploitation, exacerbates, according to her, the precarity of the Syrian refugee population in this country. Molnar also discusses how Syrian refugees may be criminalized, detained and deported from Jordan by virtue of having a communicable disease, such as tuberculosis or HIV/AIDS. These policies illuminate more subtle mechanisms of population control employed by States, which mix hardline policies of detention and deportation with denial of the rights to residency, employment, public education, or health care. Similarly, restrictions to obtaining identity documents and driver's licences make life unliveable for Syrian refugees so that they may exercise their "choice" to return to Syria. In addition, Molnar's research shows how some refugees are more reluctant to register and continue to work in the informal economy of the host country without the ability to seek resettlement in a third country. She notes that the implementation of hard-line policies of detention and deportation only creates more unaccounted and unregistered refugees who are likely to remain in the host country indefinitely. This is an alarming finding for the social and economic cohesion of host countries such as Turkey, especially when one considers that 70 per cent of Syrian refugees in this country live in urban centres and one-third of all Syrian refugees in this country are believed not to be registered.[57]

Galya Ben-Arieh's (chapter 8) analysis of the US asylum system reveals a trend that is similar to Europe and the Middle East in terms of the proliferation of prohibitive asylum policies. Referring to the surge in Customs and Border Protection (CBP) apprehensions of Central American women and children asylum seekers along the Southwest border of the US in mid-2014, the author explains how the expedited removal program prevented many would-be asylum applicants from accessing the refugee status determination system. She emphasizes how refugees who arrive at the border are detained and how the administration has accelerated deportation before they have the chance to pursue asylum claims. Ben-Arieh recalls that there has been a progressive shift toward restrictive asylum policies in the US, for instance, the 1996 Illegal Immigration Reform and Immigrant Responsibility Act, which created a one-year time limit on applying for asylum, as well as narrower grounds for which asylum could be granted. The Act also removed the right to work for people whose asylum applications are pending and introduced a policy of mandatory detention. It provided for the expedited removal process through which the US Customs and Border Protection was granted authority to screen asylum seekers at the point of entry and make an initial assessment of whether an asylum seeker has a "credible fear" of persecution if returned to his or her home country. Ben-Arieh notes that it is now up to the discretion of the individual immigration officer to decide how to pose questions about fear in the interview. If no fear is explicitly expressed and their documents are otherwise invalid for entry, the asylum seeker is summarily removed. She critiques that the US administration has developed a four-prong policy to deter spontaneous border crossings, including an agreement with Costa Rica for that country to serve as a temporary host for Central Americans waiting to be processed for refugee status. Ben-Arieh further argues that government agents use managerial discretion and informal practices and rulemaking to create an overall restrictive legal institution of refugee law.

In his account of the migration across the North Atlantic world between 1845 and 1855, Dan Horner (chapter 9) explains how the arrival of over one million Irish migrants, who fled from famine and social upheaval, was perceived by the media and politicians as "a remarkable financial and social burden" and a threat to the social fabric in Liverpool, Boston, and Montreal, and how this narrative justified harsh measures against Irish migrants. Horner's chapter also reminds us that the scale of the current forced migration movements is not unprecedented: in April 1847 alone, 150,000 migrants landed in Liverpool, a city with a population of roughly 350,000 at the time. Yet, as Horner reminds us, states reacted by adopting border control policies as a deterrent. In 1819, remarks the author, the US federal government adopted the Passenger Act, which placed restrictions on immigration into the country by dictating how many passengers each ship could carry into the country. In the 1820s and 1830s, taxes were levied on ships depending on how many immigrants were on board, and captains had to provide local officials with detailed manifests outlining the identities of each passenger. As well, the Poor Law Removal Act in Britain allowed the authorities in Liverpool to force Irish migrants who were relying on public relief to return to their native land. By the end of 1847 roughly 15,000 migrants had been deported. Horner recounts how populist political leaders played to the anxieties of the voting public, promising restrictive measures on immigration. They did so through processes that amounted to the gradual criminalization of migration – adopting harsher quarantine measures and easing the path to deportation. Another deterrent used by authorities was the socioeconomic marginalization of forced migrants. The author concludes that the response to the Irish famine migration crisis in three different host jurisdictions demonstrates a willingness to marginalize migrants and strip them of their rights in order to placate an anxious and politically engaged public. He suggests that, in many ways, this response bears a close resemblance to the policies being adopted again in countries across North America and Europe today.[58]

Part 4 of the collection deals with the topic of criminalizing refugees and other forced migrants from a perspective of lessons learned, with a view to identifying challenges and future prospects. It critically analyzes the "root causes" of some of the past criminalizing experiences, as well as good practices such as Canada's private sponsorship of refugees program and the role of cities in countering the criminalization of migrants. Peter Goodspeed (chapter 10) compares Canada's response to the current Syrian refugee crisis with its response to the Indochinese refugee crisis of 1979 to 1980, in order to examine the broad transitional forces that have shaped Canada's reactions to refugees over four decades. He recalls that from 1979 to 1980, not only the government but also tens of thousands of individuals, families, churches and neighbourhood groups in Canada rallied to resettle refugees from Vietnam, Laos, and Cambodia. Among the 60,000 Indochinese refugees resettled, approximately 26,000 were government assisted and 34,000 were privately sponsored.[59] As pointed out by Goodspeed, Operation Lifeline and other nongovernment organizations had allowed for the private sponsoring of thousands of refugees thanks to the remarkable leadership by politicians and the active involvement of Canadian citizens. The author further explains that the creation in 2014 of Lifeline Syria, a Toronto-based private sponsorship initiative, was inspired by the success of Operation Lifeline. This time again, retired civil servants, former politicians, social workers, academics, resettlement workers, and former activists from the Indochinese refugee crisis were involved in the implementation of Lifeline Syria, which aimed to recruit, train, and assist private sponsors to support Syrian refugees to be resettled as permanent immigrants in the Greater Toronto Area.[60] Today, many Western countries consider replicating Canada's private refugee sponsorship program.[61] As Goodspeed suggests, at a time when governments are reluctant to assume new responsibilities for refugees, Canada offers a template for civil society to take a lead.

The penultimate chapter discusses challenges relating to irregular migration. As Charity-Ann Hannan and Harald Bauder recall, Canada, the US, and the UK implemented immigration laws that criminalize the employment of irregular migrants through employer sanctions. These laws aim to deter employers from hiring irregular migrants in order to encourage migrants to return to their countries of citizenship. Hannan and Bauder argue that these laws are ineffective, as they are disconnected from the root causes of irregular migration. In a globalizing world, demand for both high- and low-skilled migrant workers in northern economies has grown. However, legal immigration has become more difficult and is increasingly limited to the privileged few. The "liberal paradox" of "open" markets and "closed" political communities[62] has been a major driver of irregular migration. Against this background, the authors contend that the criminalization of irregular migration through employer sanctions, in conjunction with stricter enforcement practices, have unintentionally created an environment that enables employers to exploit irregular migrants based on their lack of legal status. Unequal access to employment insurance, healthcare, social services, and driver's licenses, they note, further aggravates irregular migrants' vulnerable position in Canadian labour markets. As a concrete measure to grant safety to this population, Hannan and Bauder examine the "sanctuary city" policy – a designation that mandates cities to provide irregular migrants with access to city services without fear of being reported to immigration enforcement authorities. While this is a positive step, the authors remark that irregular migrants' access to workers' employment and labour rights remains, however, restricted, if not impossible,

since these matters fall under federal, provincial, and territorial jurisdictions in Canada and federal and state jurisdictions in the US. Finally, Hannan and Bauder outline policy changes required at the provincial level to provide employment and labour rights protection to
migrant workers in an irregular situation.

Finally, Judith Gleeson (chapter 12) discusses the criminalization of
migration in Europe, in particular in the UK, and highlights the
impact of this process on the human rights of migrants. She provides
insights into how irregular entry into the European Union, particularly by sea, began to increase sharply during the Arab Spring in 2010
and the uprisings in North Africa over the following three years, culminating in a civil war in Syria. The pressures have been particularly
heavy in Greece and Italy, which were not well resourced, administratively or financially, to cope with the situation. Gleeson recalls that the
majority of the EU member states reacted by closing their borders to
stem the migration movement. Further, she notes, the EU authorized
military interventions against migrant smugglers in the Mediterranean whereas the European Border and Coast Guard Agency, also
known as Frontex (the European Agency for the Management of
Operational Cooperation at the External Borders of the Member
States of the European Union), picked up the pace of its interdiction
operations.[63] In addition, the national asylum procedures across
Europe have become stricter, including with the introduction in
many countries of fast track or accelerated processing, and swift
deportations. The author refers to the situation in the UK, which no
longer gives "indefinite leave to remain" to recognized refugees and
considerably reduced access to benefits. The chapter also examines
stricter common asylum policies at the EU level. Gleeson critiques
notably the European Commission's reform proposals, published in
July 2016, which involves repressive measures against asylum seekers.
She contends that these types of measures are divisive and contrary to
the human rights of asylum seekers.

DIVERSE THEORETICAL PERSPECTIVES
AND METHODOLOGICAL APPROACHES

The criminalization of migration in Canada and abroad, context and
consequences, is explored in this collection from a number of conceptual and theoretical perspectives. Central to the collection and
within each of the chapters is the interplay between the context,

whether in Canada, the US, the UK, or elsewhere, of the criminalization of migration and its consequences, often times entirely unintended. This helps to illuminate how the criminalization of migration
is mediated by the context of each particular situation within a jurisdiction and its intended and unintended consequences.

In addition, it is important to note that all the contributors to the
collection adopt, to varying degrees, a legal perspective. For instance,
Grant, Hudson, Waldman, Shazadi Meighen, Rikhof, Weisman, Molnar, and Gleeson conduct their analysis from a decidedly legal perspective, while others take more of a social, political, economic, and
legal perspective, such as Kaye, Horner, Hannan, and Bauder. Still others take more of a theoretical and philosophical legal perspective on
the topic, like Hudson, Ben-Arieh, and Goodspeed. Most of the contributors, if not all, also adopt a comparative analytical approach to
consider their topic, particularly evident in the contributions from
Hudson, Waldman and Shazadi Meighen, Rikhof, Horner, Molnar,
and Hannan and Bauder. As well, a number of others take a predominantly historical approach to their topic, like Horner, Goodspeed,
and Gleeson. Using a variety of legal approaches and perspectives,
combined with a comparative and/or historical approach, should
yield greater reliability and accuracy in their findings and conclusions, but even more, further, perspicacious insights into the structures and processes of the criminalization of migration.[64]

This collection illuminates important theoretical questions pertaining to the criminalization of migration and the promotion of
migrants' human rights. As an example, Ben-Arieh (chapter 8) examines the institutional crisis in the border enforcement practices and
refugee status determination processes for Central American women
and children as an *interactional* legal process between government
agents, decision makers, lawyers, claimants, and advocates. Ben-Arieh
draws on Lon Fuller's theory of law as an interactional process. As
she puts it, this leads us to examine the legal institution, the informal practices, rule making, managerial direction, and discretion in
administrative processes that serve to maintain a restrictive national
asylum system.

Another example is Hudson's (chapter 1) use of the analogy as a
theoretical framework. He argues that both the state and the courts
draw on this concept. The former notably misuses analogies between
crime/migration and criminals/migrants to rationalize the imposition
of disproportionately harsh measures on noncitizens. According

to Hudson, the few effective constitutional challenges witnessed in Canada in recent years have also rested on analogical arguments: lawyers in these cases have been able to demonstrate similarities between how certain immigration measures and practices affect the interests underpinning specific rights protected in the Canadian Charter of Rights and Freedoms and how criminal measures impact these same interests. He reflects on how analogy supports judicial recognition of the unconstitutionality of these practices.

As well, Molnar (chapter 7) refers to the "theory of attrition though enforcement" and suggests that it can easily be adapted to policies of deterrence, detention, and deportation regarding Syrian refugees in Turkey and Jordan, where many Syrian refugees live a precarious existence without access to meaningful work, social services, or community cohesion. As explained by Molnar, attrition through enforcement also comes up in debates on irregular migration in the US, where conditions are made expressly unliveable for irregular migrants in order to spur mass self-deportations. This theory highlights how the state in its quest to regulate migrant populations employs both hardline as well as discretionary policies to disempower migrants.

The contributions in this collection are based on different research methods and approaches, including qualitative and quantitative analysis. Ben-Arieh (chapter 8) draws out insights from her experience as a pro bono legal volunteer (the use of action research and the participant observer method) in the Artesia Pro Bono Project, serving on the ground for a week in August 2014. The study is based on observation of the email correspondence among the volunteer lawyers, the testimony of the lawyers, asylum decisions, advocacy reports, media coverage, government memos, and executive policy. Likewise, Molnar (chapter 7) offers an analysis of the fieldwork (qualitative research based on formal and informal interviews) she conducted in Turkey and Jordan on behalf of the International Human Rights Program (IHRP) based at the University of Toronto's Faculty of Law. The author draws on the results of forty-five interviews with fifty-one people conducted in May and June 2015, in Turkey and Jordan, including lawyers, doctors, and frontline practitioners working with NGOs and INGOs, and Syrian refugees in both countries. Another example of empirical qualitative research is Kaye's (chapter 3) analysis of fifty-six one-on-one conversational interviews, three group interviews, and two focus groups that explores the perspectives of frontline workers, government officials, and law enforcement. These interviews, notes

Kaye, fostered a better understanding of the role of anti-trafficking in the context of border securitization while employing an intersectional lens to examine migrants' precarity in relation to trafficking.

Further, several chapters adopt a comparative approach to the issues discussed. As an illustration, Rikhof (chapter 6) examines the jurisprudence in a comparative manner in over a dozen countries to tease out possible overarching principles with respect to the issues pertaining to Article 1F(b) of the 1951 Refugee Convention. He offers a comprehensive analysis of the jurisprudence in Australia, Belgium, Canada, France, Germany, the Netherlands, New Zealand, the United Kingdom, and the United States, the countries with the largest number of refugee protection exclusion decisions.

Another example is Horner's chapter (chapter 9), which adopts an international historical comparative approach to examine the "root causes" of the Irish mass displacement to the United Kingdom, United States, and Canada. The chapter illustrates how archival research can provide useful insights into the management of "migration crises" in the past, while, at the same time, offering a new basis of historical comparison for how states are currently handling the present "migration crisis."

It is noteworthy that some contributions constitute first-hand accounts of the topics examined, as they are written by refugee lawyers or decision makers, and are directly informed by the professional experiences of their respective authors. For example, in Chapter 10, Goodspeed, a founding board member and volunteer with Lifeline Syria, shares his first-hand experience with and insights into Canada's current private sponsorship of refugees program.

This collection makes a contribution toward filling a knowledge gap by offering a comprehensive, legal, interdisciplinary, and comparative evaluation of the criminalization of migration and refugees, both within Canada and abroad. It sheds light on some of the social, legal, policy-oriented, and theoretical questions related to the general theme of the protection of migrants' rights within a particular contextual environment with their own pending consequences, that are more often than not unintended. As well, the collection sets out a series of lessons learned and best practices. As such, it fosters a rethinking of both the role that the state plays in the process of migration and the political ramifications of changing social and cultural attitudes towards migrants. Some of these lessons learned and best practices are discussed in the conclusions.

While this introductory chapter frames the global context and dimensions of the major theme of this edited collection, the criminalization of migration, given the peculiar context and the resulting consequences, the conclusions provide a further detailed summary of the subject and situate it more centrally within the context of the Global North. Each of the contributions to this edited collection provides lessons learned and examples of the best practices of how to counter the prevailing trend of the criminalization of migration. The most promising avenues in this regard are identified under five broad rubrics: (1) a new framework to deal with the root causes of forced migration, (2) strategic litigation, (3) political leadership that is prepared to develop innovative policies that are grounded in the protection of the fundamental human rights of migrants, (4) the progressive development of a new "international migration regime" that is premised on the protection of the human rights of migrants, and (5) a vigilant and active civil society movement. Drawing on these avenues, the conclusions map the way forward with respect to the effective protection of the human rights of migrants through the "decriminalization of migration." Again, navigating the way forward to the decriminalization of migration requires a mindfulness and consideration of the particular context in order to help ensure the appropriate consequences to the greatest extent possible.

Finally, we believe that this thematic collection by its very nature will engage a wide range of audiences and will be of interest not only to academics and students, but also to practitioners, policy makers, community organizations, migrant communities, and other social groups. It will stimulate public discussion, which is an especially important outcome in light of a relative lack of public debate about the nature, causes, and consequences of the criminalization of migration and its attendant effects on fostering belonging and integrating newcomers into society. We hope that this collection will help contribute to an effective protection policy for all those who are fleeing persecution and the denial of their human dignity.

NOTES

1 Sabrina Siddiqui, Lauren Gambino, and Oliver Laughland, "Trump Travel Ban: New Order Targeting Six Muslim-Majority Countries Signed," *Guardian*, 6 March 2017, https://www.theguardian.com/us-news/2017/mar/06/new-trump-travel-ban-muslim-majority-countries-refugees; "POTUS v the

Constitution: A New Spin on Why the Travel Ban is Unconstitutional," *Economist*, 28 April 2017, https://www.economist.com/blogs/democracy inamerica/2017/04/potus-v-constitution; Ariane de Vogue, "Supreme Court Allows Parts of Travel Ban to Take Effect," CNN, 27 June 2017, http://www .cnn.com/2017/06/26/politics/travel-ban-supreme-court/index.html; and *Donald J. Trump, President of the United States, et al. v. International Refugee Assistance Project, et al.* No. 16–1436 (16A1190), 4th Circuit, and *Donald J. Trump, President of the United States, et al., v. Hawaii et al.* No. 16–1540 (16A1191), 9th Circuit, (582 US), 26 June 2017, https://www.supremecourt .gov/opinions/16pdf/16-1436_l6hc.pdf.

2 Patrick Kingsley, "Refugee Crisis: What Does the EU's Deal with Turkey Mean?" *Guardian*, 18 March 2016, https://www.theguardian.com/world /2016/mar/18/eu-deal-turkey-migrants-refugees-q-and-a; "EU Policies Put Refugees at Risk: An Agenda to Restore Protection," Human Rights Watch, 23 November 2016, https://www.hrw.org/news/2016/11/23/eu-policies-put-refugees-risk; "EU Leaders Ink Deal to Stem the Flow from Libya," Al Jazeera, 3 February 2017, http://www.aljazeera.com/news/2017/02/eu-leaders-ink-deal-stem-refugee-flow-libya-170203151643286.html; and "Germany, Italy Float EU Mission to Stop Migrants in Southern Libya," *Deutsche Welle*, 14 May 2017, http://www.dw.com/en/germany-italy-float-eu-mission-to-stop-migrants-in-southern-libya/a-38834301.

3 David Ljunggren and Anna Mehler Paperny, "Justin Trudeau Tweets Messages of Welcome as Trump Travel Ban Sets In," *Global News*, 28 January 2017, http://globalnews.ca/news/3212041/justin-trudeau-refugees-donald-trump-travel-ban; and Joe Friesen, "Syrian Exodus to Canada: One Year Later, a Look at Who the Refugees are and Where they Went," *Globe and Mail*, 25 January 2017, https://www.theglobeandmail.com/news/national /syrian-refugees-in-canada-by-the-numbers/article33120934.

4 Idil Atak, Graham Hudson, and Delphine Nakache, "The Securitization of Canada's Refugee System: Reviewing the Unintended Policy Consequences," *Refugee Survey Quarterly* 37, no. 1 (2018): 1. See also Stephanie Levitz, "Federal Liberals Postpone Overhaul for Refugee System Reform: Report," *Global News*, 15 May 2017, https://globalnews.ca/news/3451117 /federal-liberals-postpones-overhaul-for-refugee-system-reform-report, and "Refugee Determination System," Canadian Council for Refugees, accessed 16 July 2017, http://ccrweb.ca/en/refugee-reform.

5 "Member States have unanimously adopted a Declaration that calls for the respect of human rights and international labour standards, reiterates the commitment to fight human trafficking and strongly condemns manifestations of racism and intolerance." General Assembly of the United Nations, "High-Level

Dialogue on International Migration and Development: 'Making Migration Work,'" (High Level Meetings of the 68th Session of the General Assembly, 3–4 October 2013), http://www.un.org/en/ga/68/meetings/migration.

6 Jean-Marie Guéhenno, "Conflict Is Key to Understanding Migration," International Crisis Group, 13 May 2016, https://www.crisisgroup.org/europe-central-asia/conflict-key-understanding-migration; United Nations, "Issue Brief #2: Addressing drivers of migration, including adverse effects of climate change, natural disasters and human-made crises, through protection and assistance, sustainable development, poverty eradication, conflict prevention and resolution," 1 May 2017, https://refugeesmigrants.un.org/sites/default/files/issue_brief_ts2_final.pdf.

7 United Nations High Commissioner for Refugees (UNHCR), "Global Trends: Forced Displacement in 2017," 19 June 2018, http://www.unhcr.org/5b27be547.pdf.

8 UNHCR, "Global Trends," 2.

9 United Nations General Assembly, "New York Declaration for Refugees and Migrants," (Resolution A/RES/71/1, 3 October 2016), http://www.un.org/en/development/desa/population/migration/generalassembly/docs/globalcompact/A_RES_71_1.pdf.

10 Patrick Wintour, "Donald Trump Pulls US out of UN Global Compact on Migration," *Guardian*, 3 December 2017, https://www.theguardian.com/world/2017/dec/03/donald-trump-pulls-us-out-of-un-global-compact-on-migration; and Rick Gladstone, "U.S. Quits Migration Pact, Saying It Infringes on Sovereignty," *New York Times*, 3 December 2017, https://www.nytimes.com/2017/12/03/world/americas/united-nations-migration-pact.html.

11 Juliet Stumpf, "The Crimmigration Crisis: Immigrants, Crime, and Sovereign Power," *American University Law Review* 56, no. 2 (2006): 367.

12 Ian Johnson, "Human Smuggling and Trafficking Is a Big Business in Canada," CBC News, 29 March 2012; "Human Trafficking and Smuggling," Department of Homeland Security, U.S. Immigration and Customs Enforcement, last updated 18 August 2017, https://www.ice.gov/factsheets/human-trafficking.

13 See, for example, Stumpf, "Crimmigration Crisis"; Elspeth Guild, "Criminalisation of Migration in Europe: Human Rights Implications" (issue paper, Council of Europe Commissioner for Human Rights, Strasbourg, 2010); Mark Provera, "The Criminalisation of Irregular Migration in The European Union" (CEPS Paper in Liberty and Security, no. 80, 2015); and Ana Aliverti, "Making People Criminal: The Role of the Criminal Law in Immigration Enforcement," *Theoretical Criminology* 16 (2012): 417.

14 Yolanda Vázquez, "Constructing Crimmigration: Latino Subordination in a 'Post-Racial' World," Cincinnati Law Research Paper Series, *Ohio State Law Journal* 76 (2015): 600; Alessandro De Giorgi, "Immigration Control, Post-Fordism, and Less Eligibility: A Materialist Critique of the Criminalization of Immigration Across Europe," *Punishment and Society* 12, no. 2 (2010): 147–67; and Catherine Dauvergne, *Making People Illegal: What Globalization Means for Migration and Law* (Cambridge: Cambridge University Press, 2009).

15 Thomas Spijkerboer, "The Human Costs of Border Control," *European Journal of Migration and Law* 9, no. 1 (2007): 127–39; James C. Hathaway, "The Human Rights Quagmire of 'Human Trafficking,'" *Virginia Journal of International Law* 49 no. 1 (2008): 1–27; Asha Kaushal and Catherine Dauvergne, "The Growing Culture of Exclusion: Trends in Canadian Refugee Exclusions," *International Journal of Refugee Law* 23 no. 1 (2010): 58; Alissa R. Ackerman and Rich Furman, "The Criminalization of Immigration and the Privatization of the Immigration Detention: Implications for Justice," *Contemporary Justice Review* 16 no. 2 (2013): 251–63; and Rachel Kronick and Cécile Rousseau, "Rights, Compassion and Invisible Children: A Critical Discourse Analysis of the Parliamentary Debates on the Mandatory Detention of Migrant Children in Canada," *Journal of Refugee Studies* 28 no. 1 (2015): 9.

16 Stephen Castles, "Confronting the Realities of Forced Migration," Migration Policy Institute, 1 May 2004, https://www.migrationpolicy.org/article /confronting-realities-forced-migration; and Elena Fiddian-Qasmiyeh, Gil Loescher, Katy Long, and Nando Sigona, eds., *The Oxford Handbook of Refugees and Forced Migration Studies* (Oxford: Oxford University Press, 2014).

17 "Defining Crimmigration Law: Part I," Crimmigration: The Intersection of Criminal Law and Immigration Law, 17 September 2015, accessed 16 July 2017, http://crimmigration.com/2015/09/17/defining-crimmigration-law-part-1; and César Cuauhtémoc and García Hernández, *Crimmigration Law* (Chicago: ABA Publishing, 2015).

18 Alissa R. Ackermann and Rich Furman, "The Criminalization of Immigration and the Privatization of the Immigration Detention: Implications for Justice," *Contemporary Justice Review: Issues in Criminal, Social, and Restorative Justice* 16, no. 2 (2012), 251–63; and Joanna Parkin, "The Criminalization of Migration in Europe: A State-of-the-Art of the Academic Literature and Research," CEPS Paper in Liberty and Security in Europe, no. 61, Centre for European Policy Studies, October 2013.

19 Sula Sidnell-Greene, "Bill C-24 and the Ongoing Criminalization of Migra-

tion in Canada," *Shameless*, 30 October 2015, http://shamelessmag.com/blog/entry/bill-c-24-and-the-ongoing-criminalization-of-migrants-in-canada; Us Man and Nadia Saad, "Criminalizing Refugees: The Case Against Bill C-31," *rabble.ca*, 23 April 2012, http://rabble.ca/news/2012/04/criminalizing-refugees-case-against-bill-c-31; Karine Côté-Boucher, "Bordering Citizenship in 'an Open and Generous Society': The Criminalization of Migration in Canada," in *The Routledge Handbook on Crime and International Migration*, eds. Sharon Pickering and Julie Ham (New York: Routledge, 2015); and Scott Watson, "The Criminalization of Human and Humanitarian Smuggling," *Migration, Mobility and Displacement* 1 no. 1 (2015): 39–53.

20 Petra Molnar Diop, "The 'Bogus Refugee': Roma Asylum Claimants and Discourses of Fraud in Canada's Bill C-31," *Refuge: Canada's Journal on Refugees* 30, no. 1 (2014): 67–80; Peter Showler, "The Bogus Refugee Myth," No One is Illegal, 12 August 2009, https://noii-van.resist.ca/the-bogus-refugee-myth; and Eric Neumayer, "Bogus Refugees? The Determinants of Asylum Migration to Western Europe," *International Studies Quarterly* 49, no. 3 (2005): 389–409.

21 Immigration and Refugee Protection Act, 2001, s. 55.

22 Ana Aliverti, "Making People Criminal: The Role of the Criminal Law in Immigration Enforcement," *Theoretical Criminology* 16, no. 4 (2012): 426.

23 *Convention Relating to the Status of Refugees*, 189 U.N.T.S. 150. The Convention entered into force on 22 April 1954.

24 Estibaliz Jimenez, "La criminalisation du trafic de migrants au Canada," *Criminologie* 46, no. 1, (2013): 131–56.

25 Anastassia Tsoukala, "Turning Immigrants into Security Threats: A Multi-Faceted Process," in *Security, Insecurity and Migration in Europe*, ed. Gabriella Lazaridis (Farnham: Ashgate Publishing, 2011): 179–95.

26 James C. Simeon and Sarah Singer, "Armed Conflict, Terrorism and Asylum: Global Solutions for Global Problems?" *RLI Blog on Refugee Law and Forced Migration*, Refugee Law Initiative, 1 November 2017, accessed 26 December 2017, https://rli.blogs.sas.ac.uk/2017/11/01/armed-conflict-terrorism-and-asylum-global-solutions-for-global-problems.

27 Immigration and Refugee Protection Act (IRPA) 2001, s. 3(1)(h) and s. 3(2)(g) and (h).

28 Article 1(F).

29 UNHCR, Standing Committee, Note on the Exclusion Clauses, EC/47/SC/CRP.29, 30 May 1997.

30 UNHCR, "Guidelines on International Protection: Application of the Exclusion Clauses – Article 1F of the 1951 Convention Relating to the Status of Refugees," HCR/GIP/03/05, 4 September 2003.

31 Parkin, "Criminalisation of Migration," 61.

32 Idil Atak, *L'européanisation de la lutte contre la migration irrégulière et les droits humains: Une étude des politiques de renvois forcés en France, au Royaume-Uni et en Turquie* (Brussels: Bruylant, 2011).

33 Canada-U.S. Safe Third Country Agreement, 2002; Nicholas Keung, "Refugee Board's Plea for Assistance with Growing Backlog Ignored," *Toronto Star*, 22 March 2017, https://www.thestar.com/news/immigration /2017/03/22/refugee-boards-plea-for-assistance-with-growing-backlog- ignored.html.

34 Immigration and Citizenship Canada, "Asylum Claimants Processed by Canada Border Services Agency (CBSA) and Immigration, Refugees and Citizenship Canada (IRCC) Offices, January 2011 - October 2017," accessed October 13, 2017, https://www.canada.ca/en/immigration-refugees-citizenship /services/refugees/asylum-claims/processed-claims.html; and Nicholas Keung, "New Data Show 69% of Illegal Border-Crossers Are Being Granted Asylum," *Toronto Star*, 19 October 2017.

35 Sean Rehaag and Sharry Aiken, "It's Time to Abolish the Inhumane Canada-U.S. Deal on Asylum Seekers," The Conversation, 9 May 2018, accessed 10 May 2018, https://theconversation.com/its-time-to-abolish-the-inhumane- canada-u-s-deal-on-asylum-seekers-96107.

36 Alessandro De Giorgi, "Immigration Control, Post-Fordism, and Less Eligibility: A Materialist Critique of the Criminalization of Immigration across Europe," *Punishment and Society* 12, no. 2 (2010): 147–67.

37 Stephen Castles and Mark J. Miller, *The Age of Migration: International Population Movements in the Modern World* (Macmillan: Basingstoke, 2009).

38 James F. Hollifield, Valerie F. Hunt, and Daniel J. Tichenor, "The Liberal Paradox: Immigrants, Markets and Rights in the United States," *SMU Law Review* 6, no. 1 (2008): 67–98.

39 Alice Bloch and Milena Chimienti, "Irregular Migration in a Globalizing World," *Ethnic and Racial Studies* 34, no. 8 (2011): 1,271–85.

40 Frank Düvell, "Paths into Irregularity: The Legal and Political Construction of Irregular Migration," *European Journal of Migration and Law* 13, no. 3 (2011): 275–95.

41 Ryszard Cholewinski and Patrick Taran, "Migration, Governance and Human Rights: Contemporary Dilemmas in the Era of Globalization," *Refugee Survey Quarterly* 28 no. 4 (2009): 1–33.

42 UNHCR, "Refugee Protection and Mixed Migration: A 10-Point Plan of Action," 1 January 2007, http://www.unhcr.org/protection/migration /4742a30b4/refugee-protection-mixed-migration-10-point-plan-action.html.

43 Heather Scoffield, "Stopping Human Smuggling Risks Penalizing Legitimate Refugees, Experts Say," *Globe and Mail*, 14 October 2010,

https://www.theglobeandmail.com/news/politics/stopping-human-smug-
gling-risks-penalizing-legitimate-refugees-experts-say/article1214925; Organisation for Economic Co-operation Development (OECD), "Can We Put an
End to Human Smuggling," Migration Policy Debates, no. 9, OECD, December 2015, https://www.oecd.org/migration/Can%20we%20put%20an
%20end%20to%20human%20smuggling.pdf; and Citizenship and Immigration Canada (CIC), "New Measures to Crack Down on Human Smuggling,"
accessed 4 August 2016, http://www.cic.gc.ca/english/refugees/reform-
smuggling.asp.

44 "#WelcomeRefugees: Key Figures," CIC, accessed 5 November 2016,
http://www.cic.gc.ca/english/refugees/welcome/milestones.asp. The number
of Syrian refugees who arrived in Canada from 4 November 2015 to 30
October 2016 was 33,723, along with 25,229 being processed.

45 UNHCR, "Global Trends."

46 Oxfam, "A Poor Welcome from the World's Wealthy," 18 July 2016,
https://www.oxfam.org/en/research/poor-welcome-worlds-wealthy.

47 Peter Sutherland, "Migration Fact vs. Migration Fiction," *Project Syndicate*, 6
August 2016, https://www.project-syndicate.org/commentary/migration-
fact-and-fiction-by-peter-sutherland-2016-08.

48 European Commission, "European Agenda on Migration: Commission
Calls on All Parties to Sustain Progress and Make Further Efforts," press
release, 13 June 2017; and Aria Bendix, "EU Takes Legal Action Against
Czech Republic, Hungary and Poland," *Atlantic*, 24 June 2017, https://www
.theatlantic.com/news/archive/2017/06/eu-takes-legal-action-against-czech-
republic-hungary-and-poland/530241.

49 International Organisation for Migration (IOM), *Fatal Journeys Volume 2:
Identification and Tracing of Dead and Missing Migrants* (Geneva: IOM, 2016).

50 ² Reinhart Koselleck and Michaela Richter, "Crisis," *Journal of the History of
Ideas* 67 no. 2 (2006): 357–400.

51 Nicolas De Genova and Martina Tazzioli, eds. "Europe/Crisis: New Keywords of 'the Crisis' in and of 'Europe,'" *Near Futures Online* 1, no. 1 (2016):
1–45.

52 Stephen Castles, "Why Migration Policies Fail," *Ethnic and Racial Studies* 27
no. 2 (2004): 205–27; Douglas S. Massey and Karen A. Pren, "Unintended
Consequences of US Immigration Policy: Explaining the Post–1965 Surge
from Latin America," *Population and Development Review* 38 no. 1 (2004):
1–29.

53 *Singh v. Minister of Employment and Immigration*, [1985] 1 SCR 177, 1985
CanLII 65.

54 IRPA section 37(1), "Organized criminality," states: "A permanent resident or

a foreign national is inadmissible on grounds of organized criminality for ... (b) engaging, in the context of transnational crime, in activities such as people smuggling, trafficking in persons or laundering of money"; *B010 v. Canada (Citizenship and Immigration)*, [2015] 3 SCR 704, 2015 SCC 58 (CanLII), par 2.

55 *Ezokola v. Canada (Citizenship and Immigration)*, [2013] 2 SCR 678, 2013 SCC 40 (CanLII).

56 Petra Molnar, "The Boy on the Beach: The Fragility of Canada's Discourses on the Syrian Refugee 'Crisis,'" *Contention: The Multidisciplinary Journal of Social Protest* 4 no. 1–2 (2016): 67–75; Alessandro Spena, "The Injustice of Criminalizing Irregular Immigration," *Border Criminologies* blog, University of Oxford Faculty of Law, 29 October 2013, https://www.law.ox.ac.uk /research-subject-groups/centre-criminology/centreborder-criminologies /blog/2013/10/injustice; and Alison Gerard and Sharon Pickering, "Crimmigration: Criminal Justice, Refugee Protection and the Securitisation of Migration," in *The Routledge Handbook of International Crime and Justice Studies*, eds. Heather Y. Bersot and Bruce A. Arrigo (Routledge: London, 2013).

57 Ahmet Içduygu, "Syrian Refugees in Turkey: The Long Road Ahead," Migration Policy Institute, April 2015, http://www.migrationpolicy.org/research /syrian-refugees-turkey-long-road-ahead.

58 Patrick Kingsley, "Ban Ki-Moon Attacks 'Increasingly Restrictive' EU Asylum Policies," *Guardian*, 28 April 2016, https://www.theguardian.com/world /2016/apr/27/austria-set-to-bring-in-stringent-new-law-on-asylum-seekers; Médecins Sans Frontières (MSF), "Migration: European Policies Dramatically Worsened the So-called 2015 'Refugee Crisis,'" 19 January 2016, http://www.msf.org/en/article/migration-european-policies-dramatically-worsened-so-called-2015-%E2%80%9Crefugee-crisis%E2%80%9D.

59 Michael M. Molloy and James C. Simeon, eds. "The Indochinese Refugee Movement and the Launch of Canada's Private Sponsorship Program," *Refuge: Canada's Journal on Refugees*, Special Issue, 32, no. 2 (2016).

60 Lifeline Syria, http://lifelinesyria.ca.

61 Maria Teresa Rojas and Alyssa Ross, "How Private Sponsorship Programs Could Help Resettle Refugees," Open Society Foundations, 16 December 2015, https://www.opensocietyfoundations.org/voices/how-private-sponsorship-programs-could-help-resettle-refugees; and Citizens UK, "Private Sponsorship," accessed 10 November 2016, https://www.refugees-welcome.org .uk/sponsorship.

62 James Frank Hollifield, *Immigrants, Markets and States: The Political Economy of Post-War Europe* (Cambridge, MA: Harvard University Press, 1992).

63 Frontex: European Border and Coast Guard Agency, "Types of Operations: Sea," accessed 10 November 2016, http://frontex.europa.eu/operations/types-of-operations/sea; and Niels Frenzen, "EUNAVFOR MED-Six Months Report: No Indication of Refugee Protection Plan for EU Operations Within Libyan Territorial Waters and No Report of Human Trafficking," *Migrants at Sea*, 23 February 2016, https://migrantsatsea.org/tag/maritime-interdiction.

64 "Crimmigration or the criminalisation of migration and irregularity are reflected in many countries' social, political and legal agendas." Maria Joao Guia, "Immigration, Crime, and Crimmigration: The Ongoing Management of Irregular Migration," *Border Criminologies*, 15 July 2016, https://www.law.ox.ac.uk/research-subject-groups/centre-criminology/centreborder-criminologies/blog/2016/07/immigration-crime.

PART ONE

The Criminalization of Migration and Its Intended and Unintended Consequences

1

The (Mis-)Uses of Analogy: Constructing and Challenging Crimmigration in Canada

Graham Hudson

I am a philosopher, so I get confused by what others find obvious.[1]
One of the things that confuses me is what it means to say that migration has been "criminalized." These days, the term of art used to describe this process is "crimmigration."[2] As a neologism, this term is still in the process of being fleshed out, but theorists generally use it to describe the imbrication, blurring, or even fusion of criminal law and immigration law. Juliet Stumpf offers a compelling account of crimmigration as an ironic interplay of legal form and function: despite being covered by familiar and distinct legal forms, criminal law and immigration law share the common function of implementing and rationalizing sovereign power consistently with exclusionary conceptions of social membership. In particular, the sovereign uses both as a means of rationalizing authoritative "choices about who should be members of society: individuals whose characteristics or actions make them worthy of inclusion in the national community."[3]

One possible example of this blurring in Canada is criminal prosecutions of persons (chiefly migrants) who have violated particular provisions of the Immigration and Refugee Protection Act (IRPA),[4] for example, for human trafficking, or fraud. But it is not self-evident that there is any blurring of immigration and criminal law going on here. Parliament may criminalize any form of behaviour it wishes, subject to certain constitutional constraints. Making some forms of migration or related activities criminal does not require it to set foot outside the conceptual or institutional boundaries of criminal law. Similarly, Parliament can detain and deport noncitizens for a wide variety of reasons, without once setting foot outside of the conceptual apparatus of immigration law. While difficult to square with our commitment to humanitarianism, human rights, and the rule of law, so-called criminalized measures can be justified on the grounds of other principles and purposes of immigration law, which ultimately come down to state sovereignty. Again, short of constitutional and, to a lesser degree, international constraints, Parliament is free to make engagement in certain criminal activities a criterion of inadmissibility.[5]

But there is something instructive here. That the validity of each of these measures can be demonstrated by reference to the concepts and categories of each field of law is precisely the problem. The forms and procedures of familiar law spread a thin but opaque veneer of legitimacy over what is, in fact, the unjustifiable expansion of executive power. Facades of legitimacy are presented to diverse audiences, modified somewhat to suit the distinctive values, beliefs, and predispositions of each. But the form of argument is more or less the same, resting as it does on analogies between criminals/migrants and crime/migration. As in other countries, the government in Canada has systematically stigmatized migrants as dangerous and/or deceitful, while some forms of migration – most notably, irregular migration – are described as wrongful and harmful. The conclusion presented is that harsh measures of social and territorial exclusion are both necessary and justified.

One strategy of resistance popular in the litigation strategies of American constitutional lawyers is to turn this language on itself, specifically by describing harsh measures as "punitive"[6] – punishment being a contested term. Stumpf relates punishment to the dual power "to exact extreme sanctions and … to express society's moral condemnation."[7] Reference to extreme sanction implies the arbitrary or unfettered sovereign power, which is seemingly characteristic of crimmigration. Yet, expressions of moral condemnation convey a paradoxical process of justification, suggesting a latent political or possibly legal limit on sovereign power. Crimmigration theorists are keenly aware that the notion of punishment carries a distinctive moral significance, drawing as it does from philosophical and institutional justifications for criminal law power. To the extent that shades of such power enter the realm of immigration law, invoking the language of punishment opens the door for legal and moral constraints to follow.

At the least, it forces juridical actors to confront the empirical and normative implications of impugned measures.

And so it seems that crimmigration is less a descriptive term than a rhetorical starting point for arguing that legal constraints germane to criminal law ought to be applied when (quasi-)criminal power is employed in immigration settings. Analogy is again the key to this argument: if the state deploys criminal power across institutional and normative divides, we may rightly insist that the human rights impacts of executive power in criminal and immigration settings are similar either in kind or degree. From this starting point, we may conclude that rights that normally are coupled to criminal law proceedings ought to be applied in whole or in part to criminalized immigration proceedings. But this strategy seems to presuppose two things: first, that rights germane to criminal law should be applied only when immigration consequences are punitive, which tends to mean inordinately harsh, exceptional, or, in Stumpf's language, "extreme" in nature. But why should we think some constitutional rights are "naturally" bound within criminal law? And what about the constitutional qualities of ordinary, unexceptional, or non-punitive immigration consequences that nonetheless cause harm and suffering? Second, it presumes that the substance of immigration law is inadequate to contend with sovereign power. Immigration materials are sidelined in favour of criminal laws that, it should be recalled, carry their own weighty historical and political baggage. In either case, effective resistance to crimmigration is conditional on (tacitly) accepting some of its most pernicious premises.

The purpose of this chapter is to reflect on the role of analogy in the construction of, and challenges to, crimmigration, in Canada. I argue, first, that the state misuses analogies between crime/migration and criminals/migrants to rationalize the imposition of disproportionately harsh measures on noncitizens. I remain agnostic about whether these measures are, to some degree, objectively or inherently "penal" or "punitive" in nature. I do so for practical reasons: the government and courts strongly deny the penal consequences of immigration measures – no matter how tightly cloaked they may be in the language of criminality. This denial impedes the generation of understanding among participants to legal discourses about the nature and the consequences of criminalized measures.[8]

Consequently, my second and primary aim is to reflect on what to do about criminalized measures in the context of denial, avoidance, and ambiguity. Referring to recent case law, I suggest that the few recent and effective constitutional challenges we have witnessed in recent years have rested on analogical arguments. Lawyers in these cases have been able to demonstrate similarities between how certain immigration measures and practices affect the interests underpinning specific Charter rights and how criminal measures and practices impact these same interests. This approach avoids the need to prove the punitive or penal nature of impugned measures, while at the same time affirming that certain constitutional rights doctrines are not bound to criminal law, even if they have developed largely in that context for historical and ideological reasons. I do wonder, however, about the implications of this approach, which includes the risk that immigration consequences that lack an arguable similarity to criminal consequences may be taken even less seriously by our courts in the years to come.

I start the chapter by exploring the historical uses to which constitutional lawyers in Canada and the United States have put key concepts associated with crimmigration, including the notion of punishment and its Canadian analogue: irreparable harm. I hypothesize that this strategy responds to the tendency of judges to treat criminal consequences as generally more worthy of constitutional interventions than immigration consequences. In the second section, I explore how analogy provides a jurisprudential and rhetorical basis for enhancing the scope and applicability of constitutional norms to immigration settings, without having to prove that some immigration measures are objectively punitive or (quasi-)criminal in nature. Practically, this strategy will work best when there are conspicuous similarities between immigration consequences and criminal consequences. But analogical arguments of this sort logically can and morally ought to be extended to so-called ordinary immigration consequences. In the final sections, I explore three interconnected examples of crimmigration in Canada: protracted/indefinite detentions, inadmissibility on grounds of serious criminality, and deportation to persecution and/or torture. I reflect on how analogy has been or may be used in each instance to end manifest injustices.

CRIMMIGRATION, "PUNISHMENT," AND THE CANADIAN CONSTITUTION

As I noted in my introduction, crimmigration is conventionally understood to include the blurring or fusion of functional, normative, and discursive barriers between criminal law and immigration law. Writing in the American context, Teresa Miller observes that crimmigration involves two related practices.[9] First, it includes the use of criminal or quasi-criminal measures in the realm of immigration law. She cites as an example the deportation of noncitizens for having committed certain classes of designated criminal offences. As with many others, Miller sees this practice as punitive, which implies that the administrative machinery of immigration law is used to perform criminal law functions, in the absence of procedural and substantive protections that might otherwise constrain executive power.[10] A similar provision in Canada is section 36 of the IRPA, which renders noncitizens "inadmissible" on grounds of serious or ordinary criminality. Second, Miller argues that crimmigration involves the creation of free-standing criminal offences for the violation of immigration law provisions. Examples of the latter would, in Canada, include human smuggling and misrepresentation.[11]

Miller notes that crimmigration involves a process in which criminal law and immigration law "converge at points to create a new system of social control that draws from both immigration and criminal justice, but it is purely neither."[12] I understand her to mean there has been an expansion of executive power that is exercised under the auspices of each field of law, but which transcends the constraints internal to each. One term for this form of merged power is punishment, which Stumpf defines as extreme sanction and moral condemnation; that is, the state-based imposition of suffering in response to perceived wrongdoing. As with Stumpf, Miller's concern seems to be that the power to punish noncitizens has escaped legal constraints that, we are invited to presume, were relatively effective beforehand and which, again presumably, should be expanded to cover this new political space. It is worth following this line of reasoning further.

In criminal law, punishment is justified by reference to formal (sentencing) goals or purposes, including retribution, deterrence, rehabilitation, and incapacitation, as well as to the deontological and consequentialist theories that underpin them. It is also justified by reference to procedures that ensure a strong link between attributions of criminal responsibility and demonstration of moral fault or blameworthiness. Of course, we know that these justifications obscure a wide range of extraneous, extra-legal motives, structures, and social processes and, ultimately, the instrumental, if not vindictive, targeting of particular individuals and groups. But still, the process of justification provides an opportunity to hold the executive to account – to ideals it has set for itself – and in any event remains a vital field of contestation.

Immigration law lacks these institutional qualities because officials by and large do not consider detentions, deportations, and exclusion to be punitive. This raises the question of what is served by insisting that there is truly something punitive about criminalized measures. The answer seems to be twofold. First are the doctrinal constraints that require lawyers to make this claim in order to persuade judges to apply constitutional protections – a claim I will defend shortly. Second is the ambivalent orientation to the role of law as an antidote for sovereign power, which we glimpse (imperfectly) in the criminal context. After all, the need to tailor arguments to the doctrinal and ideological dispositions of judges is only necessary if one considers constitutional litigation a worthwhile form of contestation. And whatever may be its many demerits, the institution of punishment in criminal law provides us with language, norms, and shared understandings about how we may contest sovereign power in immigration consequences. The link between criminal law and immigration law is fundamentally analogical: perceived similarities between criminal and immigration abuses support inferences about how the constraints and principles historically used to challenge criminal abuses can and ought to be applied to similar immigration abuses.

This process of analogical reasoning is evident in American constitutional litigation – and for good reason, too. In the United States, core constitutional norms relating to procedural fairness are practically unavailable to immigration proceedings or practices, unless one can demonstrate that proceedings are "punitive" in character.[13] The Supreme Court of the United States has, on occasion, recognized the punitive qualities of deportation – at least when it is used as a consequence of conviction for a criminal offence.[14] In the 1889 case of *Chae Chan Ping v. United States*,[15] it held, as our own Court did, that deportation proceedings are "civil" and not criminal in nature. Curiously, in the intervening years, courts have extended due process rights to a wide range of administrative settings, including those concerned with government employment, contracts, and benefits.[16] Yet, courts steadfastly refuse to expand due process rights to immigration proceedings unless there is a patently criminal quality to them. In the 2010 case of *Padilla v. Kentucky*,[17] for example, the Supreme Court considered the constitutionality of allowing deportations when claimants did not receive adequate legal advice about the immigration consequences of a guilty plea. Deciding the case on another ground, the Court stated in obiter that it is "'most difficult' to divorce the penalty from the conviction in the deportation context."[18] There have been smatterings of similar views over the years. In *Fong Haw Tan v. Phelan*, decided in 1948, the Court went so far as to say that "deportation is a drastic measure and at times the equivalent of banishment or exile."[19] Judges, albeit often in dissent, have compared deportation and banishment as early as 1893.[20]

The response to the *Padilla* decision in the United States has been powerful and promising.[21] Lawyers, advocates, and academics have renewed efforts, begun in at least the 1990s, to persuade judges to conceive of certain, more draconian detention and deportation practices as criminal or at least quasi-criminal in nature. So conceived, robust constitutional norms officially restricted to criminal proceedings would be officially applicable within immigration proceedings that lack basic procedural protections.[22]

Although seemingly necessary in the US, emphasis on punishment is not as necessary or common in Canada. Our Supreme Court has repeatedly stated that "deportation is not imposed as a punishment"[23] and is "not concerned with the penal consequences of the acts of individuals."[24] It affirmed this principle in the 2007 case of *Charkaoui v. Canada (Citizenship and Immigration) (Charkaoui I)*,[25] noting that the deportation of a noncitizen may not "in itself" breach the Charter, but may raise constitutional issues if accompanied by separate and "irreparable" harms, such as prolonged detention or deportation to torture – a point I will return to shortly.[26] Most recently, in the 2017 case of *Tran v. Canada (Public Safety and Emergency Preparedness)*,[27] the Court insisted that deportation consequent to criminal convictions are not "criminal or penal" in nature.

The reason for this position is that Canadian constitutional norms are notionally as applicable to immigration law as any other field of law. Section 7 of the Charter, for example, protects the right to life, liberty, and security of the person and the right not to be deprived thereof except in accordance with principles of fundamental justice.[28] The Court's position has regularly been that the threshold for the applicability of a charter right relates to the "interest at stake" and not the formal nature of the proceeding that threatens that interest.[29]

A cardinal principle in section 7 jurisprudence is that as the risk of a deprivation of life, liberty, or security increases, so too must the quality and fairness of procedural protections. This means that such elements of a fair trial as knowing the case against you, being able to respond to that case, and having decisions made on the basis of the facts and law move in lockstep with the substantive impact of a decision. In *Singh v. Minister of Employment and Immigration*,[30] the Court decided that refugee claimants are entitled to an oral hearing at least when issues of credibility arise, precisely because getting decisions wrong can lead to deportation to face persecution. In *Suresh v. Canada (Minister of Citizenship and Immigration)*,[31] the court analogized deportation-to-torture with extradition to capital punishment, the latter of which arose in the case of *United States v. Burns*.[32] The Court reasoned that, just as extradition is normally acceptable, so too is deportation. But in *Burns*, the Court held that section 7 prohibits extradition to face capital punishment. In like kind, it ruled in *Suresh* that section 7 is fully engaged in the context of deportation when there is some sort of irreparable harm at play, including the risk of torture.

And here we see the crack in the Court's overall logic about the strength of constitutional protections: immigration decisions only attract constitutional scrutiny if a claimant can demonstrate some sort of "irreparable harm" over and above the removal – the constitution does not recognize immigration consequences simply, without reservation. Over time, courts have expanded the definition of what counts as "ordinary" consequences, excluding all but the gravest human rights abuses from constitutional consideration. In *Boio v. Canada (Citizenship and Immigration)*,[33] the Court decided that section 7 is "not engaged at the stage of determining admissibility to Canada" and that the benefit of the Charter "is typically engaged" only during the actual removal stage.[34] In *Febles v. Canada (Citizenship and Immigration)*,[35] it expressly denied the applicability of the Charter to decisions about whether a person should be excluded from refugee status under Article 1(E) and (F) of the Refugee Convention.

The Court reasoned that persons who are denied the right to a fair admissibility hearing or the right to claim refugee status can always apply for a pre-removal risk assessment (PRRA) and "a stay of removal to a place if he would face death, torture or cruel and unusual treatment or punishment if removed to that place."[36] Notice, however, that this list of human rights abuses is under-inclusive, excluding as it does persecution. In the baffling case of *Peter v. Canada (Public Safety and Emergency Preparedness)*, the Federal Court found that section 7 of the Charter is not even applicable to legislation that removes the right to claim protection from persecution. In the view of Justice Annis, removal to persecution "does not expose the applicant to irreparable harm, in the sense that if the decision of the removals officer is overturned, the applicant is prevented from being readmitted to Canada."[37] No consideration was given to the fact that protection from persecution is an international right, perhaps because Justice Annis was unduly confident in the quality of inadmissibility and exclusion determinations – an issue I will return to below. The Federal Court of Appeal overruled this decision on the grounds that it was premised on insufficient factual foundations.[38] But it declined to pronounce on the substantive issues, meaning that the constitutionality of this portion of the removal process remains unsettled.

The notion of irreparable harm is in some ways the Canadian equivalent to the notion of punishment in American courts. As our courts have defined it, irreparable harm includes extreme, grave, or exceptional human rights abuses, but does not include "ordinary" immigration consequences: a broad class that ranges from the break-up of family or community relationships to persecution. This raises the question of how to persuade judges to take these harms more seriously. On the one hand, one could invoke language of punishment and criminalization. But I worry that some conceptions of punishment as "extreme sanction" will reinforce the tendency of judges to scrutinize only exceptional measures and outcomes, hinging the applicability of the Charter to some criminal or quasi-criminal quality. On the other, if judges already are receptive to the language of criminalization and indifferent to certain classes of suffering, analogies between immigration consequences and criminal consequences may be a useful starting point for highlighting that a much broader range of interests and values than are currently recognized deserve constitutional protection.

CHALLENGING CRIMMIGRATION: THE ROLE OF ANALOGY

Analogies are a distinctive form of logical reasoning that support the drawing of inferences from one particular case or situation to another particular case or situation. In the context of common law, analogical reasoning occurs whenever a court "draws on similarities or dissimilarities between the present case and previous cases which have no precedential weight in the case at hand."[39] Analogies are often misunderstood as tools that highlight similarities between the inherent qualities of two objects. Analogies actually frame similarities between two discrete sets of relationships. The form of analogy is as follows: A is to B as C is to D. Put another way, analogy is a resemblance of relationship and not a relationship of resemblance.[40]

In the context of common law, analogies are used to demonstrate that the relationship between the facts and law in one case or situation is similar to the relationship between the facts and law in another. From these readily recognizable similarities, we may then infer that there is a further hidden, typically more abstract similarity: namely, that the decision arrived at in an earlier case is more or less a good decision in a present case. In this way, analogies frame the discovery of new or unfamiliar ideas, relationships, and properties.

An important aspect of legal analogies is that the analogized case is not binding on a decision maker; this distinguishes analogies from precedents. In theory, precedents do not so much guide decisions as determine them. A judge must apply a binding rule because it is authoritative; she is not officially free to reject or vary it if she disagrees with the underlying reasoning.[41] Analogies, by contrast, orient judges to the reasoning used by another, which the judge may take, leave, or use in part. If a principle or line of reasoning is persuasive, it does not matter whether it is sourced in another legal field or even another jurisdiction – the value of a decision rests on the merits of the reasoning used.

A good example of analogical reasoning is the 2008 case of *Charkaoui v. Canada (Charkaoui II)*.[42] At issue was whether the Canadian Security Intelligence Service (CSIS) was obligated to retain and to disclose all information on file relevant to a person subject to a security certificate – a rarely used measure that enables the state to detain and deport noncitizens deemed inadmissible for reasons of, *inter alia*, national security and serious or organized criminality. Constitutional principles of disclosure have been defined most expansively in criminal law, and apply in this respect most forcefully to police.[43] The Federal Court of Appeal elected to not apply principles of disclosure to certificate proceedings because this would have "blurred" criminal law standards and administrative law standards.[44] But the Supreme Court took a different view, noting that "[t]he consequences of security certificates are often more severe than those of many criminal charges."[45] In other words, the relationship between criminal charges to an accused is analogous to the relationship between certificate proceedings and a named person. It also took notice of how security intelligence practices increasingly supplement and resemble law-enforcement practices – a point that is all the more salient post-Bill C-51. On the basis of these factual and legal similarities, the Court inferred that principles governing the relationship between police and accused ought to, in good measure, govern the relationship between CSIS and named persons. The result is that CSIS is now obligated to retain and disclose all information on file relevant to a person named in a certificate – subject to some modifications necessary for national security purposes.

This judgement introduces something very important about analogies: they function to help judges develop law in such a way as to realize constitutive principles within a given doctrine and, more generally, a given legal field.[46] Doctrines should exhibit at least some level of internal coherence, whereby adjudicators use intrinsic principles to guide the interpretation and application of specific rules and standards to recurring situations. To the extent that principles and factual scenarios across two or more doctrines, legal fields, or jurisdictions are sufficiently similar, the experiences of decision makers in one setting can help improve the judgement of decision makers in another. If done well, solutions should fit with and further the objectives and principles internal to the doctrinal field that governs the legal problem at hand. Not unlike with migration, "outside" experiences, wisdom, and insights improve the internal quality of doctrine. I hasten to add that this helps explain why domestic courts can and should rely on international and comparative law.[47]

Charkaoui II exemplifies this well. Security certificates are part of administrative law and immigration and refugee law. The former includes jurisprudence on principles of natural justice, while the latter includes principles of respect for humanitarianism and international law. Taken together, these two sets of principles establish the fundamental principle laid down on several occasions that persons subject to serious deprivations of substantive rights, such as deportation to face persecution or torture, are entitled to elevated procedural protections.[48] It is essential to recognize that what were originally principles of administrative law are now ultimately sourced in Charter doctrine.

In like kind, the loss of liberty and the stigma attached to criminal convictions account for robust procedural protections originally sourced in the common law, and now also entrenched in the Charter. Doctrines developed within administrative and immigration law and within criminal law develop separately, but within the bounds of Charter doctrine. It happens that courts generally take criminal consequences more seriously than immigration consequences. But when courts do recognize the impacts of criminalized measures, criminal law doctrine is an obvious source of insight into how shared constitutional principles ought to be interpreted and applied in the context of immigration law.

This account of analogical reasoning explains why conceiving of some immigration measures as punitive is potentially quite powerful. Although by no means conceptually necessary, we tend to associate punishment with criminal law. In this field, punishment is justified by reference to formal goals or purposes, which help guide decisions about just sentences. The most fundamental sentencing principle in Canadian criminal law is proportionality. Section 718.1 of the Criminal Code states that a sentence must be proportionate to the gravity of the offence and the degree of responsibility of the offender. Sentences may be adjusted in light of a list of aggravating and mitigating circumstances related to the offence or the offender. Finally, the justifiability of criminal punishment hinges on the processes of punishment, which ought to rest on respect for rights and the rule of law. Because of the seriousness of punishment and concerns about abuse of the power to punish, procedural protections in criminal law are comparatively robust.

Analogies centred around the theme of punishment help us see both that there are affinities between the impact of some immigration measures on noncitizens and the impact of some criminal measures on offenders, and that criminal law doctrine may help resolve similar problems regarding the rule of law. It is, of course, hard to prove the punitive character of certain immigration measures, in no small part because the state denies that it is punishing migrants. But the appeal of analogies is that one need not prove that certain immigration measures are truly punitive in order to make use of constitutional doctrine that has developed in the context of criminal law. One must simply show that these measures affect the interests underpinning constitutional rights in ways that are similar to how criminal measures affect those same interests. Many constitutional norms relating to a fair trial, for instances, have been developed more fully in the criminal law context due to a mix of historical, cultural, and institutional factors that have shaped the perception that criminal consequences are more serious than immigration consequences. However, these norms are not confined to this field, nor does appealing to such doctrine require us to act as though they are. Criminal law perspectives on constitutional law are valid resources for contending with problems regarding the moral and rule of law that arise in immigration law. Moreover, the use of doctrine across legal fields actually strengthens the purposes and objectives of overarching constitutional norms.

But this is just a point about logic. The practical challenge is that many judges seem to be predisposed against seeing immigration consequences as serious, except in highly securitized settings, such as with security certificates. This predisposition is evident in *Charkaoui II*, in which the Court found that measures of protracted detention and deportation to face the risk of torture or similar abuse are "often more severe" than criminal charges.[49] Yet, migrants face protracted detentions in contexts other than certificates, while the risks associated with deportation are in point of fact not material to certificate proceedings; these issues are only dealt with once someone has already been deemed inadmissible. As I have argued elsewhere,[50] our courts have failed to extend the same procedural protections now available in certificate proceedings to other, functionally equivalent and vastly more common, proceedings.

This highlights one of the problems with analogies: they depend on the perception of similarities between two cases or situations. If one is able to construct, or indeed deny, a similarity, one can justify any number of (in)decisions. We see stark examples of poor analogical argument in the language found in legislative provisions that authorize the protracted detention and deportation of persons who have been convicted of certain crimes. This sort of language has persuaded courts that harsh treatment is justified for reasons relating to crime and border control. But analogies may yet also help judges appreciate how such treatment, and the logic used to justify it, establishes more than sufficient grounds for applying Charter protections commensurate with those that apply to similar criminal measures. I will now examine two examples where analogy can be used, and one example where analogy was used, to challenge the constitutionality of criminalizing measures and practices.

DETENTION, BAIL, AND THE PRINCIPLE OF *HABEAS CORPUS*

The detention of migrants is a growing problem in Canada, as with all Commonwealth countries. The criminalization of migration is nowhere more visible than in the detention of migrants in correctional institutions, which is where a growing number of migrants are detained.[51] For instance, in 2009 and 2010, approximately 570 Tamil asylum seekers arrived in Canada without authorization, aboard the MV *Ocean Lady* and MV *Sun Sea*. The government immediately characterized the arrivals as a serious security threat, alleging the vessels were carrying criminals and terrorists.[52] The Canadian Border Services Agency (CBSA) detained all passengers. The men were initially sent to correctional facilities, while many of the women and children were detained together in detention centres. It is noteworthy that the CBSA, as the agency responsible for the migrant detention regime, is housed within Public Safety Canada, alongside Corrections Canada, the Royal Canadian Mounted Police, and CSIS. The CBSA reports to the Minister of Public Safety and Emergency Preparedness, not the Minister of Immigration, Refugees and Citizenship (IRC).

Parliament has outlined the criteria for continued detention in Division 6 of the IRPA. It has authorized an "officer" (for example, a CBSA officer or immigration officer) to issue a warrant for the arrest and detention of a permanent resident or a foreign national if he or she has reasonable grounds to believe that the person is "inadmissible and is a danger to the public or is unlikely to appear for examination, for an admissibility hearing, for removal from Canada or at a proceeding that could lead to the making of a removal order by the Minister."[53] An arrest or detention may be made without a warrant under the same circumstances, or if the officer is "not satisfied of the identity" of the person (warrantless arrests do not apply to protected persons).[54]

Detentions must be reviewed by the Immigration Division (ID) of the Immigration and Refugee Board (IRB) within forty-eight hours of the detention. A second review is held within the next seven days, while subsequent, periodic reviews must be held at least once every thirty days thereafter.[55] At this stage, the matter would seem to fall back within the purview of the IRC.

Surface comparisons may be made with pre-trial custody and bail provisions. In criminal law, bail is presumptively provided to all accused, unless the Crown can demonstrate, on a balance of probabilities, that he or she is a flight risk or is at risk of reoffending; bail may also be denied if necessary to maintain public confidence in the administration of justice.[56] Similarly, the ID must order the release of a detainee unless the minister establishes, on a balance of probabilities, that the detainee is a danger to the public or a flight risk, or the minister is investigating whether he or she is inadmissible on grounds relating to security, violating human or international rights, serious criminality, criminality, or organized criminality.[57] As with bail, release may be denied if any one of these criteria is established. Finally, the ID must maintain the detention of a foreign national if the minister raises questions of identity.[58] Importantly, once the minister makes the case that detention should continue, the detainee may secure release only if he or she can convince the ID to do so pursuant to a list of supplemental factors that guard against, *inter alia*, unduly long or even indefinite detentions or detentions.[59]

Detainees may not appeal a detention review. If a detainee is dissatisfied with a negative decision, he or she may apply for leave for a judicial review of the decision. This application must be filed within fifteen days of the decision. If leave is granted, the review hearing commences between thirty and ninety days thereafter, and a decision to deny release may only be interfered with if it is unreasonable on a question of fact or incorrect on a question of law. The government may also seek judicial review of a decision to release. Legislation requires that detentions continue until the Federal Court issues a decision (on the leave application or the merits of the case); in this event, detentions are extended well into or over an entire admissibility or refugee determination hearing, the latter of which have been compressed into shortened timelines.[60]

The human rights implications of migrant detention have not escaped the attention of our superior courts. This is interesting for two reasons. First, although provincial courts share with federal courts inherent jurisdiction over constitutional issues arising in the context of immigration law, Parliament has vested the Federal Court with legislative authority over immigration proceedings and issues. Provincial courts have, accordingly, declined to exercise their jurisdiction except in rare cases. Second, superior courts are responsible for the administration of criminal justice, while its judges are responsible for ensuring that the bail system runs smoothly. In *Chaudhary v. Canada (Public Safety and Emergency Preparedness)*,[61] the Ontario Court of Appeal (OCA) took issue with the indefinite detention of migrants. It decided that migrants subject to lengthy or indefinite detentions are constitutionally entitled to apply for the right of *habeas corpus* through superior courts, bypassing the IRPA entirely. This decision was premised on the principle that *habeas corpus* is a constitutional right over which superior courts have inherent jurisdiction.

The OCA decided that the existing detention review regime failed to provide protections that were "at least as broad ... and no less advantageous,"[62] that is, they fell below the bare minimum standard required by the constitution. It was rather pointed in criticizing the IRB and the Federal Court, noting that there had only been one case in which a finding of indeterminate detention was made.[63] This is telling, as one of the claimants in *Chaudhary* had been detained for eight years and eight months. In the view of the Court, this signaled a systemic problem, which it attributed to several factors. First, when it comes to judicial review, neither the ID nor the Federal Court are "tasked with the question of determining whether the immigration detention no longer reasonably furthers the machinery of immigration control."[64] Similarly, the length and expected duration of detention are considered only after the case for detention has been made out by the minister. Given the periodic nature of reviews, this case is made out repeatedly over the course of successive detention review hearings; grounds for detention assume greater persuasive power the more often they are accepted. The OCA decided that in practice, ID members take past decisions to continue detentions as virtual precedent, deviating only when there are "clear and compelling reasons."[65] The Court noted the results of an access to information request that showed that the longer the detention, the less likely a release would be granted – a perverse practice.

Chaudhary is a fine example of analogical reasoning. *Habeas corpus* is not a criminal law principle *per se*; it is a constitutional principle that has been specified in the bail regime, but that applies to any instance of unlawful detention or imprisonment. Consider the words of the court, which states that the legal issues raised in the migrant detention regime:

> do not require the court to have expertise in immigration law. The *habeas corpus* decisions will be made weighing various factors, as well as *Charter* rights and values. These are by and large the same factors that make up the daily fare of the superior courts. The superior courts are closely connected with the administration of criminal justice, and as noted in *Mission*, at para. 57, "when a loss of liberty is involved, the superior courts are well versed in the *Charter* rights that apply."[66]

It is likely that the OCA's decision was influenced by its experience with pre-trial custody and criminal law doctrine. But this passage clearly indicates that the court saw no need to make formal distinctions between immigration law and criminal law, given that the effect of detention on the physical, emotional, and psychological well-being of detainees is similar in both contexts. The IRPA but dimly reflects the principle of *habeas corpus* – one could argue disingenuously. It remains open to the IRB, the Federal Court, Parliament, and soon the Supreme Court to use the principle of *habeas corpus* to fix a broken system.

INADMISSIBILITY ON GROUNDS OF SERIOUS CRIMINALITY

Inadmissibility on grounds of serious criminality is another criminalizing measure of concern. Section 36(1) of the IRPA states that a person is inadmissible on grounds of serious criminality for:

(a) having been convicted in Canada of an offence under an Act of Parliament punishable by a maximum term of imprisonment of at least 10 years, or of an offence under an Act of Parliament for which a term of imprisonment of more than six months has been imposed;

(b) having been convicted of an offence outside Canada that, if committed in Canada, would constitute an offence under an Act of Parliament punishable by a maximum term of imprisonment of at least 10 years; or

(c) committing an act outside Canada that is an offence in the place where it was committed and that, if committed in Canada, would constitute an offence under an Act of Parliament punishable by a maximum term of imprisonment of at least 10 years.[67]

I will focus exclusively on section 36(1)(a), which allows for the deportation of persons already present in Canada and does not distinguish between permanent residents and foreign nationals. Unlike sections 36(1)(b) and (c), it imposes criteria of inadmissibility on persons present in Canada that differ from criteria applied to persons seeking entry. The provision makes no mention whatsoever of the range of impacts that removals may have on persons who have begun, or indeed who are well into, the process of integrating into Canada.

The first step of section 36(1)(a) occurs in a criminal court, when a judge convicts a person of a crime punishable by at least ten years imprisonment, or sentences a person to more than six months imprisonment. This may occur following either a trial or a guilty plea. The imprimatur of a criminal court act triggers a parallel immigration proceeding before the IRB. This second proceeding is *pro forma*, as the IRB only has discretion to confirm inadmissibility; if the conviction and/or sentence meet the criteria set forth in the provision, the IRB must designate the offender as inadmissible.

The noncitizen found inadmissible is now subject to deportation proceedings. The impact of removal has a direct bearing on the fairness (or lack thereof) of inadmissibility proceedings, since deportation can have profoundly negative implications for the substantive rights of affected persons (I will deal with the end stages of removal in the next section). Consequences include not simply deportation to persecution or possibly torture, but the severing of community, employment, and familial bonds. The case of Deepan Budlakoti exemplifies the latter. Budlakoti is a Canadian-born man who never acquired Canadian citizenship. In 2010, he was convicted of weapons trafficking, possession of an illegal firearm, and drug trafficking, and sentenced to three years imprisonment. The government invoked section 36, and has since been attempting to deport him to India – a country he has never visited, where he has never lived, and of which he was never a citizen.[68]

The case of Budlakoti suggests similarities between deportation and banishment from places and spaces one calls "home." Parliament's justification for such harsh measures rests on an impoverished understanding of the reciprocal relationship of obligations between the state and the subjects of its authority – in this case, noncitizens. The reasoning goes that because the IRPA outlines clear, stable, and presumptively fair rules governing the benefits and conditions of immigration, (conscious) violation of one's duties to the state absolves the state of most of its responsibilities to the noncitizen; that is, it justifies removal. But surely there are a core of substantive and procedural rights that cannot be denied under any circumstances, and a larger pool of rights that can only be infringed upon after weighty justification. The language of crimmigration does the work here, signifying subjective fault or knowledge with respect to the underlying offence, and presumably also with respect to the violation of the IRPA. In the case of the commission of serious crimes, the noncitizen displays contemptible disregard for the rights of others and the laws of Canada. We are then invited to accept that criminal fault may be substituted for fault in the immigration realm, making deportation in most cases a proportionate response to be used either in lieu of or in addition to the punishment provided for by criminal law. What is more, since the noncitizen receives a fair criminal process, he or she has been accorded requisite procedural fairness.

There are many ways I could challenge this line of reasoning, including by attacking the claims that the state-criminal relationship may be substituted for the state-migrant relationship, and that the latter relationship determines rights to social membership. The Sanctuary City movements in Toronto, Hamilton, Vancouver, Montreal, and elsewhere could be marshalled to bolster the latter claim that the federal government alone has the authority to grant and revoke membership in our political community. Instead, I will challenge the argument on its own terms, by arguing that our method for designating crimes as "serious" does not adequately delineate "fault," nor, for that matter, is deportation a uniformly proportionate response to whatever level of fault there may be. This is because the IRPA denies both criminal and immigration law decision makers from considering the severity of the offence, the degree of responsibility of the offender, and whether deportation is a proportionate response in consideration of such factors as employment, familial, and community bonds. In short, the supposed procedural fairness afforded during a criminal trial appertains to a decision of criminal guilt and not of whether to deport under any circumstances; this latter decision is actually never subject to meaningful constraints.

Notice that I am here invoking the doctrinal and statutory elements of proportionality in criminal sentencing. But we should remember that proportionality has constitutional foundations, including the tests used in delineating the boundaries of rights in sections 1 and 7 of the Charter. In these contexts, principles of proportionality require that limitations or deprivations of rights, respectively, not be unnecessarily or unreasonably excessive in relation to pressing and substantial legislative objectives or any legitimate government interest.[69] Relevantly, this requires some engagement with the narrative of the reciprocal relationship of responsibility between state and subject, and, of course, the interests of the "community," which ought to be distinguished conceptually from the interests of the state. In all cases, courts do the work of balancing the rights of affected persons, as well as the spectrum of state and nonstate values and interests protected or pursued by a given provision or practice. This takes a lot of work, including carefully assessing the relative weight of the interests of state, community, and the individual in light of a concrete, factual matrix and robust bodies of law.

There is no balancing of interests, either, within section 36(1). Criminal courts do not and at present cannot make fulsome assessments about the immigration consequences of convictions or sentences, or the *future* risk a person poses to Canada. The Court recognized a limited power to consider immigration consequences in the case of *R. v. Pham*, deciding that sentencing judges can consider immigration consequences as "collateral" consequences; that is, the impact a particular sentence has on a particular offender. Collateral consequences is a stop-gap measure, as it falls well short of a fulsome inquiry into whether a sentence (and the immigration consequences thereof) is proportional to the objective severity of the crime and the degree of responsibility of the offender.[70] To this point, the Court further said that immigration consequences "must not be allowed to dominate the exercise or skew the process either in favour of or against deportation. Moreover, it must not lead to a separate sentencing scheme with a *de facto* if not a *de jure* special range of sentencing options where deportation is a risk."[71]

Although somewhat welcome, *Pham* does not address the core problem, which is that at no point does someone consider whether deportation is proportional, or, therefore, justified. The bifurcated nature of the regime is part of the problem. Originating in criminal courts, trial judges focus on the justifiable sentencing range in relation to predominantly criminal law criteria, with immigration consequences standing as mere collateral consequences that can support only minor adjustments to the outer ranges of a sentence. When a file moves to the IRB, the board member has no statutory power to consider the seriousness of the offence or the implications of removal, being tasked only with stamping his or her imprimatur on designations of inadmissibility. The only recourse a noncitizen has to unjust deportation arises at the removal stage, where, short of demonstrating a substantial risk of torture or similar abuse, one's only chance of avoiding deportation is to successfully apply to the minister for permanent residence status on the basis of humanitarian and compassionate (H&C) considerations[72] – a very uncertain, stop-gap process.

The balancing process is skewed on the other end as well. To recall, a "serious" offence is one that carries a maximum punishment of ten years or more (no matter what the actual sentence was), or for which the offender has been punished more than six months. The former will always involve an offence that provides for prosecution by way of indictment and would therefore seem to be serious. Human smuggling, for example, carries a maximum of ten years if treated as an indictable offence. But as with most offences in Canada, human smuggling is a hybrid offence, meaning it may be prosecuted by way of indictment, or summarily. In the latter case, the maximum is two years. According to section 36(3)(a), all offences are to be treated as indictable offences, even if prosecuted summarily. Keep in mind that the choice of a prosecutor to proceed summarily may indicate that he or she does not consider the offence to be (relatively) serious.

This all means that if one is prosecuted for human smuggling summarily or by way of indictment, and is sentenced to less than six months imprisonment, he or she would still be subject to automatic deportation – precisely the same result as if he or she were sentenced to two, five, seven, or ten years. A sentence of less than six months for human smuggling is, by the way, a conceivable scenario. A study on sentencing ranges for the similar (and more serious) offence of human trafficking found that the majority of sentences between 2002 and 2009 ranged from four and a half months to two and a half years.[73] Low sentences like this indicate that the seriousness of an offence from the perspective of criminal justice actors relates not to the maximum punishment Parliament has selected, but to the facts and circumstances of the conduct and the characteristics of the offender.

This regime is draconian. It allows the deportation of noncitizens for engagement in what may well be a minor offence, regardless of whether he or she has strong familial, economic, and community roots in Canada. At no point, save for an H&C application, may a noncitizen apply for a proper balancing of his or her high-priority interests and the government's legitimate interest in deporting bona fide serious criminals. Given the criminalized context of the measure, and how the principle of proportionality is iterated in the sentencing process, criminal law norms can and should be used to guide a Charter challenge.

The Supreme Court has already provided some resources in this regard, and is, in my view, bound by the terms of its own logic to require fundamental changes to the section 36(1)(a) process. In the 2014 case of *Febles*, the Court considered how the term "serious non-political crimes" could be defined vis-à-vis international legal norms and domestic criminal law principles. It stated that crimes punishable by ten years or more may "presumptively" be considered serious, but, recognizing the nature and principles of sentencing, it added that "the ten-year rule should not be applied in a mechanistic, decontextual-ized, or unjust manner."[74] In particular, "a claimant whose crime would fall at the less serious end of the [sentencing] range in Canada should not be presumptively excluded."[75]

Febles did not relate to section 36(1), but the 2017 case of *Tran* does. Here, the Court held that conditional sentences of greater than six-months duration cannot be considered "terms of imprisonment" suffi-cient to trigger section 36(1)(a). This judgement did not rest on the Charter, which the Court reminded does not apply to proceedings that are neither criminal nor penal – a point I could easily contest given the palpable imprint of criminal functionality in this context. Instead, it employed statutory interpretation, concluding that treating condition-al sentences as terms of imprisonment would be absurd, given that such sentences are uniformly considered indicia of non-serious criminal activity in the realm of criminal law. In other words, conditional sen-tences of more than six months signal lower fault and responsibility than sentences of incarceration for terms less than six months. But rest-ing on statutory interpretation, this decision leaves Parliament free to rewrite the IRPA to expressly allow for this "absurd" and unjust result.

The logic of *Febles* and *Tran* ought to be applied with full force to the entire section 36(1)(a) regime via constitutional review. The rote imposition of possibly severe immigration consequences based on hollow "presumptions" of seriousness tied to arbitrary, unjustifiably low sentencing ranges is plainly inconsistent with both judgements, the internal logic of criminal law, and the basic principles of proce-dural fairness. Parliament should revise its definition of serious crim-inality in section 36 to allow for contextualized assessments, by the IRB during section 36(1)(a) inadmissibility hearings, or perhaps even by criminal courts, as was once done in the United States.[76] If per-formed by the IRB, these assessments should take into account the rea-soning of the trial judge on the question of sentencing, including his or her views on aggravating and mitigating factors. This would allow the ID to consider what counts as a serious crime on a case-by-case basis. Parliament should also raise the sentencing threshold from six months to at least two years (if not more) and not treat summary con-victions as though they are indictable offences. The IRB or a sentenc-ing judge should balance the seriousness of the offence with the effect deportation will have, with specific regard to the extent of attachment a noncitizen has to Canada. If deportation is disproportionate, the noncitizen should serve his or her sentence in Canada.

DEPORTATION TO PERSECUTION AND TORTURE

I would like to conclude my review of criminalizing measures by connecting section 36(1) to the deportation process, raising broader questions about deportation to persecution or torture. Section 101(1)(f) of the IRPA states that persons deemed inadmissible on grounds of serious criminality, organized criminality, security, or the violation of international or human rights are ineligible to claim refugee status before the Refugee Protection Division (RPD) of the IRB. Ordinarily, persons subject to removal are entitled to a PRRA, in which an immigration officer assesses whether a person is at risk of either persecution (i.e., is a Convention refugee) or grave human rights abuses, including torture (i.e., is a person in need of protection). However, persons deemed inadmissible on the grounds mentioned above may only ask for a PRRA to screen for a substantial risk of death, torture, or cruel and unusual treatment or punishment; they are not entitled to Convention refugee status. As noted above, the Federal Court recently refused to submit this bar to review under section 7 of the Charter, on the grounds that deportation to persecution does not expose one to "irreparable harm."[77] Meanwhile, section 115(2) allows the Minister of Immigration, Refugee and Citizenship to deport to torture by issuing a "danger opinion," which outlines reasonable grounds for believing that a noncitizen constitutes a danger to the public in Canada or to the security of Canada.

International law governing these situations is based in the 1951 *Convention Relating to the Status of Refugees* (the Refugee Convention)[78] and the 1984 *Convention Against Torture* (CAT).[79] Article 33(2) of the Refugee Convention allows states to deport to face persecution if there are reasonable grounds for believing a person is a "danger to the security of the country in which he is, or who, having been convicted by a final judgment of a particularly serious crime, constitutes a danger to the community of that country."[80] I have already noted that the criteria we use to label one a "serious" criminal is mechanistic and overly broad, allowing for the denial of Convention refugee status and access to a PRRA unless there is a substantial risk of death, torture, or cruel and unusual treatment or punishment. The absence of administrative review of the risk of persecution, absent these additional, irreparable harms, means that one can be deported to face a *de facto* risk of persecution after having been convicted of a summary offence. It is inadequate to defend this state of affairs by insisting there is no

de jure risk of persecution, since claimants are never given the opportunity to make that case. These measures reduce to elaborate avoidance mechanisms and should be remedied.

Deportation to torture is also a serious issue. The CAT imposes a categorical ban on deportation to torture. In a surprising and untenable
judgement, the Supreme Court departed from international law in
the case of in *Suresh*, ruling that Canada may deport persons to face
torture under "exceptional" circumstances.[81] This is to say that there is
a presumption against deportation to torture that the government
may rebut if it demonstrates evidence of a "serious threat to national
security."[82] The Court specified that:

> a person constitutes a "danger to the security of Canada" if he or
> she poses a serious threat to the security of Canada, whether
> direct or indirect, and bearing in mind the fact that the security
> of one country is often dependent on the security of other
> nations. The threat must be "serious", in the sense that it must be
> grounded on objectively reasonable suspicion based on evidence
> and in the sense that the threatened harm must be substantial
> rather than negligible.[83]

The Court was clear that determinations of risk are fact-based, political, and entitled to deference if "the Minister is able to show evidence
that reasonably supports a finding of danger to the security of Canada."[84] Decisions concerning the risk a person poses, as well as whether
that person may be safely removed from Canada, are findings of fact
reviewable on a standard of patent unreasonableness. The Court did
not clarify what counts as an "exceptional circumstance," stating only
that "[t]he ambit of an exceptional discretion to deport to torture, if
any, must await future cases."[85] This decision is clearly inconsistent
with international law and should be revisited – most especially in
light of revelations of Canada's role in extraordinary rendition and
normative developments.[86]

Our courts' tolerance of substantive human rights abuses in the
context of both deportation to persecution and deportation to torture
hinges on their expectation that affected persons will be afforded
robust procedural protections. In the former case, they presume that
inadmissibility and exclusion determinations are soundly made,
though my review of section 36 shows this presumption to be poorly
founded. Decisions about deportation to torture are similarly ques-

tionable. A review of the procedures for issuing and reviewing danger opinions will underline this point.

The first step in this process is a PRRA.[87] The affected person must demonstrate to an Immigration Official (IO), on the basis of written materials, that he or she faces a personalized risk of torture. In the context of deportation to torture, general conditions in a given jurisdiction are not enough; an IO will not find a substantial risk of torture if the risk one faces is no greater than that faced by the average person living in a given jurisdiction – no matter how objectively dangerous a locale may be. Some claimants have been returned to high-risk jurisdictions, such as Somalia and Sri Lanka, precisely on this basis.[88] The example of Somalia is apt. Tellingly, Canadian regulations prohibit the CBSA from personally delivering deportees to Somalia due to the danger involved. Instead, they drop deportees off in neighbouring countries, such as Kenya, and pay a private contractor to fly the person the rest of the way.[89]

If the IO determines there is a risk of torture, the minister or a Ministerial Delegate (MD) is free to either accept this report or reject it. If the MD accepts the report, they may issue a danger opinion, or accept that they cannot remove the person. During this stage, affected parties are not entitled to an oral hearing. All that is required is that the affected person receive disclosure of non-sensitive or non-privileged evidence relied on by the MD; be able to submit written challenges to the relevance, reliability, and sufficiency of disclosed evidence; and be able to submit evidence and make arguments about the risk of torture, as well as (the extent of) the risk he or she poses to the security of Canada. Finally, the minister is obligated to provide the affected person with the reasons for their ultimate decision.[90] The decision to issue a danger opinion may then be judicially reviewed by the Federal Court. I am aware of only one instance in which the Federal Court allowed the government to deport a person to face torture.[91] In all others, the courts have not allowed it.

The real problem lies in the capacity of the IO or the MD to deny the existence of a risk of torture in spite of compelling evidence to the contrary. This has happened in a number of cases concerning deportation to torture. The most well known are *Sogi v. Canada (Minister of Citizenship and Immigration)*,[92] *Mostafa Dadar v. Canada (Minister of Citizenship and Immigration)*,[93] and the case of Jama Warsame.[94] In *Sogi*, the government initially recognized a risk of torture and tried to invoke the *Suresh* exception. After its danger opinion was invalidated by the Federal Court on other grounds, it conducted a second PRRA, this time finding, mysteriously, that there was no risk of torture. It proceeded to deport Mr Sogi, who was subject to extrajudicial physical and mental punishment. In each of these cases, the UN Committee Against Torture assessed the evidence and found that there was a risk of torture. The Federal Court has consistently declined to provide stays of removal while questions of fact are being assessed by the Committee Against Torture.

Courts have seldom intervened when an IO or MD refused to recognize a substantial risk of torture. This is because the Supreme Court has instructed courts to intervene only if a danger opinion is "unreasonable," that is, was made "arbitrarily or in bad faith, it cannot be supported on the evidence, or the minister failed to consider the appropriate factors."[95] So long as a decision is reasonable, it does not matter that it was wrong. Not having time to critique the jurisprudence on standards of review, I will say only that decisions about the risk of torture should be subject to stringent oversight or review. The former would involve having decisions made by a tribunal during the course of a full and fair oral hearing, and not by an executive officer on the basis of written materials. The RPD is the obvious candidate here; even persons designated as inadmissible on grounds of security or criminality should be entitled to have their claims considered carefully and in the context of procedural fairness and adversarial challenge. Alternatively, the decisions made during PRRAs should be appealable to or reviewable by an independent and impartial tribunal. This is the approach used in the United Kingdom in the case of torture, albeit with its own problems.[96]

CONCLUSION

I started the chapter confused about what crimmigration entails. To a degree, I am still confused – and I suspect others are, too. The literature on crimmigration describes it as the cooperation and even the fusion of criminal law and immigration law. This dynamic raises all sorts of normative problems. Immigration lawyers and scholars tend to regard crimmigration as an instance of the government using criminal law to coerce, threaten, and govern (vulnerable) populations in ways that are inconsistent with the humanitarian and human rights commitments required of it by international and statutory law. Criminal law theorists, by contrast, see it as a perversion or distortion of criminal law, which has been made subject to the utilitarian, security-laden, and extra-penal objectives of immigration law.[97] Still others see it as having opened up an interstitial space that inheres somewhere between and beyond each field, in which principles internal to each field of law fail to adequately constrain sovereign power.

So much is fine. However, immigration lawyers and scholars further this process of convergence, perhaps paradoxically, by presupposing that criminalized measures have an objective or demonstrable penal or punitive quality to them. By invoking punishment or its analogue as a condition of constitutional rights, they give credence to doctrine that constructs faulty, hierarchical divisions between two fields of law that are, in truth, subsumed under one field of constitutional law. Among the questions this raises are: how can one distinguish between a criminalized and an ordinary measure in a nonarbitrary way, how can one justify in jurisprudential terms the application of criminal law doctrine in immigration law settings, how can one distinguish between criminal law doctrine and constitutional law developed in the context of criminal law, and, most importantly, will this approach ultimately diminish the perceived seriousness of immigration consequences that cannot be (readily) compared with criminal consequences. In challenging crimmigration, I worry we may well reify its most pernicious premises.

I do not have all the answers to these questions. But a fruitful base for further exploration is analogy – the rhetorical basis upon which crimmigration is constructed and, it seems, with which it can be most effectively challenged. The few examples we have of successful constitutional challenges to harsh measures have tended to rest on analogy. While not logically necessary to justify judicial interventions, analogies have been practically necessary to persuasively convey the high priority interests and values at stake. The advantage of analogy is that the one invoking them need not prove a measure is punitive in nature; one must not entertain the spurious claim that somehow the constitution does not apply in immigration law unless there is a criminal or penal quality to a proceeding. Analogies remind us that criminal law, immigration law, and any other legal field are not closed systems, but rather that each is part of a larger body of constitutional law, the principled development of which requires the integration of its many constituent elements.

As rhetorical mechanisms, analogies have the added advantage of possessing a distinct logical form and discursive quality that is conducive to persuasion. In our case, they help judges appreciate that at least certain classes of immigration consequences are worthy of being taken seriously – sadly, this is no simple task. But while those who invoke analogies may reject hierarchical distinctions between criminal and immigration consequences, my review of Canadian jurisprudence suggests that analogies work because judges continue to ascribe to this binary thinking. The fact is, analogies are most effective when they make use of prior beliefs and the willingness or capacity of decision makers to see similarities. In this way, analogies are only capable of supporting rather conservative inferential leaps and are rarely if ever transformative. For this reason, I cannot help but wonder if analogies feed the very source of our initial problem: the tendency of our courts to situate "ordinary" immigration proceedings at the very margins of our constitutional terrain.

NOTES

1 I cannot remember where I heard this quote, but admit it is not mine.
2 The term was coined in Juliet Stumpf, "The Crimmigration Crisis: Immigrants, Crime, and Sovereign Power," *American University Law Review* 56, no. 2 (2006): 367–419. Other important works in crimmigration theory include: Juliet Stumpf, "Doing Time: Crimmigration Law and the Perils of Haste," UCLA *Law Review* 58 (2011): 1,705; Stumpf, "The Process Is the Punishment in Crimmigration Law," in *The Borders of Punishment: Criminal Justice, Citizenship, and Social Exclusion*, eds. Katja Franko Aas and Mary Bosworth (Oxford: Oxford University Press, 2013); Jennifer M. Chacón, "Managing Migration Through Crime," *Columbia Law Review Sidebar* 109 (2009): 135–48; Stephen H. Legomsky, "The New Path of Immigration Law: Asymmetric Incorporation of Criminal Justice Norms," *Washington and Lee Law Review* 64 (2007): 469; Allegra M. McLeod, "Immigration, Criminalization, and Disobedience," *University of Miami Law Review* 70 (2016): 556–84; Allegra M. McLeod, "The U.S. Criminal-Immigration Convergence and Its Possible Undoing," *American Criminal Law Review* 49 (2012): 105–78; David Alan Sklansky, "Crime, Immigration, and Ad Hoc Instrumentalism," *New Criminal Law Review*, 15, no. 2 (2012): 157–223; Efrat Arbel, "Between Protection and Punishment: The Irregular Arrival Regime in Canadian Refugee Law," in *Extreme Punishment: Comparative Studies in Detention, Incarceration, and Solitary Confinement*, eds. Keramet Reiter and Alexa Koenig (London: Palgrave Macmillan UK, 2015); and Sharryn Aiken, David Lyon, and Malcolm Thorburn, "Introduction:

'Crimmigration, Surveillance and 'Security Threats': A Multidisciplinary Dialogue," *Queen's Law Journal* 40, no. 1 (2014): 1–11.

3 Ibid., 397.

4 Immigration and Refugee Protection Act, SC 2001, ch. 27, http://laws.justice.gc.ca/eng/acts/i-2.5.

5 International constraints include: *Convention Relating to the Status of Refugees* ("Refugee Convention"), 28 July 1951, 189 UNTS 150, Can. TS 1969/6 (entered into force 22 April 1954, accession by Canada 2 September 1969), Arts. 1F, 33(2); and *Convention Against Torture and Other Cruel, Inhuman or Degrading Treatment or Punishment* ("Convention Against Torture"), 10 December 1984, 1465 UNTS 85, Can. TS 1987 No. 36.

6 *Padilla v. Commonwealth of Kentucky*, 559 US 356 (2010).

7 Stumpf, "Crimmigration Crisis," 410.

8 I rely here on a "dialogical" conception of argumentation as an *ideally* fair, inclusive, and principled process geared towards the generation of shared understandings, and eschew the use of political, social, and ideological power to distort this process. See Frans H. van Eemeren, *Advances in Pragma-Dialectics* (Amsterdam: Vale Press, 2002); Frans H. van Eemeren, Rob Grootendorst, and A. Francisca Snoeck Henkemans, *Argumentation: Analysis, Evaluation, Presentation* (Mahwah, NJ: Lawrence Erlbaum Associates, 2002), 182–83; and Brant B. Burleson and Susan L. Kline, "Habermas' Theory of Communication: A Critical Explication," *Quarterly Journal of Speech* 65, no. 4 (1979): 412–28.

9 Teresa A. Miller, "Citizenship and Severity: Recent Immigration Reforms and the New Penology," *Georgetown Immigration Law Review* 17, no. 4 (2003): 619.

10 Ibid., 621.

11 Immigration and Refugee Protection Act, SC 2001, ss. 117(1), 127.

12 Miller, "Citizenship and Severity," 618.

13 For a small selection of commentaries, see Christopher N. Lasch, "'Crimmigration' and the Right to Counsel at the Border Between Civil and Criminal Proceedings," University of Denver Legal Studies Research Paper, no. 14-42, *Iowa Law Review* 99 (2014): 2,131–60, http://ssrn.com/abstract=2442124; and Peter L. Markowitz, "Deportation Is Different," Cardozo Legal Studies Research Paper, *University of Pennsylvania Journal of Constitutional Law*, no. 308 (2010): 1,299–361, http://ssrn.com/abstract=1666788.

14 For a detailed historical analysis of this issue, see Peter L. Markowitz, "Straddling the Civil-Criminal Divide: A Bifurcated Approach to Understanding the Nature of Immigration Removal Proceedings," *Harvard Civil Rights-Civil Liberties Law Review* 43, no. 2 (2008): 289–351, http://ssrn.com/abstract=1015322.

15 *Chae Chan Ping v. United States* 130 US 581 (1889) (9 S.Ct. 623, 32 L.Ed. 1068).

16 See, for example, *Goldberg v. Kelly*, 397 US 254 (1970), 62; *Greene v. McElroy*, 360 US 474, 360 US 496-497 (1959), 180; *Morrissey v. Brewer*, 408 US 471, 408 US 481 (1972), 71–5,103.

17 *Padilla v. Kentucky*, 559 US 356 (2010).

18 Ibid., 1481.

19 *Fong Haw Tan v. Phelan*, 333 US 6 (1948), para. 4.

20 *Fong Yue Ting v. United States*, 149 US 698 (1893).

21 For a small selection of commentaries, see Christopher N. Lasch, "'Crimmigration' and the Right to Counsel at the Border Between Civil and Criminal Proceedings," University of Denver Legal Studies Research Paper, no. 14-42, *Iowa Law Review* 99 (2014): 2,131–60, http://ssrn.com/abstract=2442124; Markowitz, "Deportation Is Different."

22 Markowitz, "Deportation is Different," 1,307. Markowitz notes that this process is unofficially underway.

23 *Medovarski v. Canada (Minister of Citizenship and Immigration)*, *Esteban v. Canada (Minister of Citizenship and Immigration)*, [2005] 2 SCR 539, 2005 SCC 51, para. 46; *Canada (Minister of Employment and Immigration) v. Chiarelli*, [1992] 1 SCR 711, 1992 CanLII 87 (SCC); *Hurd v. Canada (Minister of Employment and Immigration)*, [1989] 2 F.C. 594 (C.A.), pp. 606–7; *Hoang v. Canada (Minister of Employment and Immigration)* [1990], 13 Imm. LR (2d) 35.

24 *Reference as to the effect of the Exercise by His Excellency the Governor General of the Royal Prerogative of Mercy Upon Deportation Proceedings*, [1933] SCR 269, 1933 CanLII 40 (SCC), p. 278.

25 *Charkaoui v. Canada (Citizenship and Immigration)*, [2007] 1 SCR 350, 2007 SCC 9 (CanLII).

26 Ibid., para. 17.

27 *Tran v. Canada (Public Safety and Emergency Preparedness)*, [2017] 2 SCR 289, 2017 SCC 50 (CanLII), on appeal from *Canada (Public Safety and Emergency Preparedness) v. Tran*, [2016] 2 FCR 459, 2015 FCA 237 (CanLII).

28 *Re B.C. Motor Vehicle Act*, [1985] 2 SCR 486, 1985 CanLII 81 (SCC), para. 30.

29 Ibid., para. 18.

30 *Singh v. Minister of Employment and Immigration*, [1985] 1 SCR 177, 1985 CanLII 65 (SCC).

31 *Suresh v. Canada (Minister of Citizenship and Immigration)*, [2002] 1 SCR 3, 2002 SCC 1 (CanLII).

32 *United States v. Burns* [2001] 1 SCR 283, 2001 SCC 7 (CanLII).

33 *Bo10 v. Canada (Citizenship and Immigration)*, [2015] 3 SCR 704, 2015 SCC 58 (CanLII).

34 Ibid., para. 75.
35 *Febles v. Canada (Citizenship and Immigration Canada)*, [2014] 3 SCR 431, 2014 SCC 68 (CanLII).
36 Ibid., para. 67.
37 *Peter v. Canada (Public Safety and Emergency Preparedness)*, [2014] FCJ No 1132 (QL), para. 296.
38 *Savunthararasa v. Canada (Public Safety and Emergency Preparedness)*, [2016] FCJ No. 173 (QL).
39 Stephen E. Toulmin, *The Uses of Argument* (New York: Cambridge University Press, 1958), 202; Chaïm Perelman and Lucie Olbrechts-Tyteca, *The New Rhetoric: A Treatise on Argumentation* (Notre Dame, IN: University of Notre Dame Press, 1969), 372–74.
40 Perelman and Olbrechts-Tyteca, *New Rhetoric*, 372.
41 Of course, this happens in practice all the time, through such mechanisms as distinguishing or sometimes with no justification offered at all.
42 *Charkaoui v. Canada (Citizenship and Immigration)*, [2008] 2 SCR 326, 2008 SCC 38 (CanLII).
43 *R. v. Stinchcombe*, [1991] 3 SCR 326, 1991 CanLII 45 (SCC); *R. v. La*, [1997] 2 SCR 680, 1997 CanLII 309 (SCC); *R. v. Egger*, [1993] 2 SCR 451, 1993 CanLII 98 (SCC); *R. v. O'Connor*, [1995] 4 SCR 411, 1995 CanLII 51 (SCC).
44 *Charkaoui v. Canada (Citizenship and Immigration)*, [2006], 272 DLR (4th) 175, para. 88.
45 Ibid., para. 54.
46 Grant Lamond, "Analogical Reasoning in the Common Law," *Oxford Journal of Legal Studies* 34, no. 4 (2014): 567–88, http://ojls.oxfordjournals.org/content/34/3/567.abstract.
47 Graham Hudson, "As Good as It Gets? Security, Asylum and the Rule of Law After the Certificate Trilogy," *Osgoode Hall Law Journal* 52, no. 3 (2015): 905–50; and Karen Knop, "Here and There: International Law in Domestic Courts," *New York University Journal of Law and Politics* 32, no. 2 (Winter 2000): 501–36.
48 Prominent examples include *Singh v. Minister of Employment and Immigration*, [1985] 1 SCR 177; *Suresh v. Canada*, [2002] 1 SCR 3, para. 118; and *Charkaoui v. Canada*, [2007] 1 SCR 350. I would even include in this list *Baker v. Canada (Minister of Citizenship and Immigration)*, [1999] 2 SCR 817, 1999 CanLII 699 (SCC).
49 *Charkaoui v. Canada*, [2008] 2 SCR 326, para. 54.
50 Hudson, "As Good as It Gets?"
51 Delphine Nakache, "The Human and Financial Cost of Detention of Asylum-Seekers in Canada," United Nations High Commissioner for Refugees (2011): 24.

52 Canadian Press, "Terrorists or Civilians? MV Sun Sea Passengers Face Scrutiny in Days Ahead," *Waterloo Region Record*, 13 August 2010, http://www.the record.com/sports-story/2565119-terrorists-or-civilians-mv-sun-sea-passengers-face-scrutiny-in-days-ahead.

53 Immigration and Refugee Protection Act, SC 2001, s. 55(1).

54 Ibid., s. 55(2).

55 Ibid., s. 57.

56 Criminal Code, R.SC 1985, c. C-46, ss. 515(1) and 515(10).

57 Immigration and Refugee Protection Act, SC 2001, s. 58(1)(a–c).

58 Ibid., s. 58(1)(d)(e).

59 Immigration and Refugee Protection Regulations, SOR/2002-227, s. 248.

60 For an overview of how the new timelines work, see "Claiming Refugee Protection Under the New System: A Basic Overview," FCJ *Refugee Centre* (2012), http://www.fcjrefugeecentre.org//wp-content/uploads/2012/12/Claiming-Refugee-Protection-Under-the-New-System.pdf.

61 *Chaudhary v. Canada (Public Safety and Emergency Preparedness)*, 2015, 127 O.R. (3d) 401.

62 *May v. Ferndale Institution*, [2005] 3 SCR 809, 2005 SCC 82 (CanLII), para. 40.

63 *Chaudhary v. Canada*, 2015, 127 O.R. (3d) 401, para. 77.

64 Ibid., para. 82.

65 *Canada (Minister of Citizenship and Immigration) v. Thanabalasingham*, [2004], 236 DLR (4th) 329, para. 10.

66 *Chaudhary v. Canada*, 2015, 127 O.R. (3d) 401, para. 102.

67 Immigration and Refugee Protection Act, SC 2001, ss. 36(1)(a–c).

68 Information on Budlakoti's case may be found at http://www.justicefordeepan.org (n.d.).

69 *R. v. Oakes* [1986] 1 SCR 103, 1986 CanLII 46 (SCC); *Canada (Attorney General) v. P.H.S. Community Services Society*, [2011] 3 SCR 134, 2011 SCC 44, para. 133.

70 *R. v. Pham*, [2013] 1 SCR 739, 2013 SCC 15 (CanLII), para. 11.

71 Ibid., para. 16.

72 Immigration and Refugee Protection Act, SC 2001, s. 25.

73 Louis-Philippe Jannard and François Crépeau, "The Battle Against Migrant Trafficking in Canada: Is the Target Organized Crime or Irregular Immigration?" *Our Diverse Cities* 7 (spring 2010): 116–20. http://canada.metropolis.net/pdfs/ODC_vol7_spring2010_e.pdf.

74 *Febles v. Canada*, [2014] 3 SCR 431, para. 62.

75 Ibid., para. 62.

76 Markowitz, "Deportation Is Different."

77 *Peter v. Canada*, 2014, para. 296.

78 Refugee Convention, 1951.

79 *Convention Against Torture*, 1984.

80 Refugee Convention, 1951, Art. 33(2).

81 *Suresh v. Canada*, [2002] 1 SCR 3, para. 78.

82 Ibid., para. 89.

83 Ibid., para. 90.

84 Ibid., para. 85.

85 Ibid., para. 78.

86 Canada, Privy Council Office, "Internal Inquiry into the Actions of Canadian Officials in Relation to Abdullah Almalki, Ahmad Abou-Elmaati and Muayyed Nureddin" (Ottawa: Queens Printer, 2008); and Canada, Privy Council Office, "Report of the Events Relating to Maher Arar: Analysis and Recommendations" (Ottawa: Queen's Printer, 2006).

87 Immigration and Refugee Protection Act, SC 2001, ss. 112–14.

88 For just one of many examples, see *Mohamed v. Canada (Citizenship and Immigration)*, [2011] FCJ No. 1869 (QL).

89 Anna Maria Tremonti, "To No Man's Land: The Story of Saeed Jama's Deportation to Somalia," CBC Radio: *The Current*, 12 May 2015, http://www.cbc.ca/radio/thecurrent/a-story-of-deportation-to-somalia-and-canada-s-voice-at-war-1.2907289/to-no-man-s-land-the-story-of-saeed-jama-s-deportation-to-somalia-1.2907291.

90 *Suresh v. Canada*, [2002] 1 SCR 3, para. 122–23.

91 *Nlandu-Nsoki v. Canada (Minister of Citizenship and Immigration)* 2005 F.C. 17 (CanLII), para. 22.

92 *Sogi v. Canada (Minister of Citizenship and Immigration)*, [2005] 1 FCR 171, 2004 FCA 212 (CanLII).

93 *Dadar v. Canada (Minister of Citizenship and Immigration)*, [2004] F.C. 1381 (CanLII).

94 Jama Warsame v. Canada, HRC Communication No. 1959/2010, UN Doc. CCPR/C/102/D/1959/2010 (2011).

95 *Suresh v. Canada*, [2002] 1 SCR 3, para. 41; *Nagalingam v. Canada (Minister of Citizenship and Immigration)*, [2008] 1 FCR 87 , 2007 FC 229 (CanLII), para. 18.

96 See Special Immigration Appeals Commission Act 1997, Acts of the Parliament of the United Kingdom (1997) c. 68. For an excellent review of the UK system, see Geoffrey Care, "The Judiciary, the State, and the Refugee: The Evolution of Judicial Protection in Asylum – A U.K. Perspective," *Fordham International Law Journal* 28, no 5 (2004): 1,421; and Geoffrey Care, *Migrants and the Courts: A Century of Trial and Error?* (London: Routledge, 2013).

97 Alessandro Spena, "Iniuria Migrandi: Criminalization of Immigrants and the Basic Principles of the Criminal Law," *Criminal Law and Philosophy* 8, no. 3 (2014): 635–57; Alessandro Spena, "A Just Criminalization of Irregular Immigration: Is It Possible?" *Criminal Law and Philosophy* 11, no. 2 (2017): 351–73; and R.A. Duff, Lindsay L. Farmer, S.E. Marshall, Massimo M. Renzo, and Victor V. Tadros, eds. *The Boundaries of the Criminal Law* (Oxford: Oxford University Press, 2010).

2

Treating the Symptom, Ignoring the Cause: Recent People-Smuggling Developments in Canada and Around the World

Angus Grant

It is sometimes said that Moses was the original people smuggler. While the historical accuracy of this claim is open to question, it is certain that, at least since Biblical times, political entities have sought to prevent, control, and regulate the entry of foreigners into their lands. But like the story of Moses, it also seems that there have always been those who – for humanitarian reasons or financial reward, or perhaps both – have assisted others in traversing borders. In recent years, however, the issue of people smuggling and the response of states to it has surged to the top of the newsfeed in media outlets the world over. Notwithstanding the prevalence of the topic, many relatively basic questions continue to be asked, particularly in the context of asylum: What are the rights of asylum seekers who migrate by way of smuggling operations? What obligations do states have to receive them and consider their claims to refugee status? How do these rights and obligations intersect with international legal instruments aimed at combatting people smuggling?

Another question being confronted in a number of different locations is this: How are states to distinguish those who assist refugees in escaping persecution for humanitarian reasons from the smuggling networks that also assist refugees in traversing borders, but often in usurious ways? There are some who see little reason to distinguish the two, noting that human smugglers, while perhaps unseemly, are wrongly conflated with human traffickers, whose actions are inherently exploitative. The result is that the actions of human smugglers who transport asylum seekers to Western countries are distorted and the services they provide are overly vilified. Both smugglers and humanitarians, the argument goes, provide a necessary service to asylum seekers, helping them to pierce the fortress-like domains of countries determined to avoid their international human rights obligations.

Others question the distinction between smuggling and humanitarian assistance to refugees, but from the opposite perspective, noting that facilitating the unauthorized crossing of borders is illegal, regardless of the motive of the person providing the assistance. This view appears to be gaining traction. In Denmark, for example, a seventy-year-old grandmother recently happened upon asylum seekers walking along a country road; she picked them up and drove them to the Swedish border. Consequently, she was charged under the Danish Criminal Code and was convicted of human smuggling. According to the *Washington Post*, hundreds of other Danes currently face similar charges.[1] The *Post* goes on to quote a Danish parliamentarian – Peter Kofod Poulsen – as saying: "These people broke the law ... Human smuggling is not all right – not if it's done by the train company and not if it's done by private individuals."[2]

In a well-publicized case from France, Rob Lawrie, a British citizen, was recently charged with people smuggling for attempting to take a four-year-old Afghan girl from the "squalid" (and now demolished) French migrant camp known as the "jungle" to her family members in Britain.[3] While Lawrie noted that he was simply trying to assist "an innocent little girl who had lost the birth lottery," he also acknowledged that he had made a "mistake" and asked for the mercy of the French courts, where he faced up to five years in prison. The court did appear to recognize Lawrie's noble intentions, and after accepting his guilty plea, sentenced him to a suspended fine.[4]

In this chapter, I first explore another example ·of the smuggling phenomenon, one that arose in Canada in recent years. In 2009 and 2010, two ships, the MV *Ocean Lady* and the MV *Sun Sea*, arrived without authorization off the west coast of Canada carrying, respectively, 76 and 492 Sri Lankan Tamil asylum seekers.[5] The state's response to these arrivals was an aggressive one: the alleged organizers of the operations were prosecuted criminally, while those asylum seekers on board who were alleged to have assisted in the journey, even in relatively minor ways, were subject to immigration inadmissibility proceedings. A finding of inadmissibility in these cases was significant because, under Canadian law, such findings deprive asylum seekers of the right to assert a refugee claim under the 1951 Refugee Convention.[6] While these inadmissible asylum seekers may still submit an application for protection on the basis that they face a risk of torture, a risk to their life, or a risk of cruel or unusual treatment,[7] their rights to seek asylum pursuant to the Universal Declaration of Human Rights[8] or to *any* form of status under the Refugee Convention[9] are permanently extinguished.[10] As such, these cases raised important questions about the sanctity of both the right to seek asylum and the principle of non-refoulement under Canadian law.[11]

The cases were also significant because they explored the role of profit in the conceptualization of people smuggling in domestic law, and the extent to which domestic anti-smuggling legislation has diverged from international instruments on people smuggling, which contain built-in protections for the rights of refugees under the Refugee Convention.[12] In a context of almost unprecedented global movements of refugees across borders, frequently assisted by individuals, aid agencies, and, yes, smugglers, state responses to smuggling events involving asylum seekers are of obvious and pressing relevance internationally. The results of these Canadian cases provide interesting insights into the legal distinctions between criminal smuggling and humanitarian assistance to refugees. They also illustrate the ways in which legislation on people smuggling and preoccupations with border control have eroded state commitments to asylum seekers and the role of state courts in preserving non-refoulement obligations.

Next, I move beyond these cases to briefly touch on Canadian legislative responses to smuggling and point out that such measures, as with others in countries around the world, are little more than an attempt by the states of the Global North to respond to the undesired symptoms of a global refugee crisis by restricting, penalizing, and criminalizing the movement of refugees. It is not, in other words, reflective of an attempt made in good faith to resolve the crisis itself. This, I suggest, is the wrong way to address the problem of people smuggling.

Ultimately, I argue that while states have signed on to binding international law to combat human smuggling, it is important to maintain conceptual clarity in addressing the issue and its underlying causes. Anti-smuggling efforts, furthermore, must be connected to their purpose in a rational manner, recognizing both that global efforts to restrict and obstruct unauthorized migration to the Global North are intimately connected with the demand for smuggling activities, and that state interests in border control must always accede to the right to seek asylum. From these conclusions, I suggest that any legislative initiatives aimed at combatting smuggling by imposing penalties or burdens on asylum seekers, such as those implemented by Canada in recent years, should be reconsidered.

BACKGROUND: THE ARRIVAL OF THE TAMIL SHIPS

The response to the arrival of the *Ocean Lady* in 2009 was reminiscent of previous responses to other boat arrivals in Canada and around the world. Despite the relative infrequency of such arrivals, politicians and various media outlets decried this perceived threat to the integrity of the country's immigration system. After the vessel's arrival, and with reports of another ship – the *Sun Sea* – also en route to Canada, the Canada Border Services Agency (CBSA) went into crisis management mode, issuing a strategic internal memorandum to its employees. Among other instructions, the memo provided that:

- "In terms of port of entry examination, the CBSA will ... demonstrate that the marine people smuggling is serious and poses a significant threat to the *health and safety* of those in Canada."
- "In these cases, the CBSA will be *aggressive* in building evidence and arguing for inadmissibility. The focus will be on the *health and safety* impact for Canada and the exploitation of vulnerable persons which results from the efforts of organized people smuggling."
- "In terms of the approach for refugee determination hearings, they will be dealt with aggressively as well. The CBSA will advise the IRB [Immigration and Refugee Board] that it intends to intervene in each case, however, the IRB's current 84% acceptance rate will be a challenge."
- "Detention is an effective tool against those who circumvent immigration processes. The CBSA will take maximum advantage of this tool, recognizing that there *may* be limitations if no legal grounds to detain exist."
- "Those who are found to be inadmissible and have removal orders issued against them, will be removed to Sri Lanka. The CBSA would be proactive in *working with the Sri Lankan* authorities to obtain timely travel documents."

- "The CBSA continues to work ... to ensure that the *best possible enforcement* outcome is supported to ensure that a *deterrent* for future arrivals is created." (emphasis added)[13]

Upon arrival of the *Sun Sea*, the government of the day implemented the "aggressive" stance set out in the CBSA memo, notwithstanding concerns that doing so would violate Canada's international obligations under the Refugee Convention.[14] The government deployed its response in the three distinct ways, contemplated in the memorandum. First, it criminally prosecuted those thought to be the primary organizers of the voyages. Second, it alleged that *anyone* aboard the ships who in *any way* may have facilitated the voyage was inadmissible to Canada because such a person would have engaged in the organized criminal act of people smuggling. And finally, it intervened in virtually all of the passengers' refugee claims, urging the Immigration and Refugee Board to reject their cases, typically on either credibility grounds or based on one of the Refugee Convention's exclusion clauses. The frequency of CBSA's intervention in these cases represented a clear departure from the Canadian government's typical approach to refugee status determination, in which ministerial participation in individual refugee claims is relatively rare.

Beyond this case-by-case response to the boat arrivals, the government determined that it needed more tools at its disposal. Justified by the assertion that Canada's existing laws were incapable of responding to large-scale (if infrequent) smuggling events, the government set out to create a new scheme of differential treatment for asylum seekers who arrive to Canada in groups.[15] Passed into law in 2012, the new scheme permitted the minister of public safety to designate certain categories of migrants as "Designated Foreign Nationals" (DFNs).[16] Under the new law, once designated, DFNs become subject to a range of measures, including periods of mandatory detention with infrequent review, ineligibility to appeal first-level refugee determinations, and, for those who do obtain refugee protection, ineligibility for permanent residence and family reunification for a period of five years. These legislative changes were reminiscent, albeit in milder form, of the radical legislative reaction in Australia following the so-called Tampa Affair of 2001.[17] Canada did not excise portions of its territory to effectively "warehouse refugees," as did Australia. Nevertheless, the response in both countries reflected essentially the same impulse: to concentrate border control powers within the executive, to deter future arrivals through punitive measures and to minimize as much as possible obligations arising under international refugee law.[18]

While these new Canadian measures were not considered in the *Sun Sea* and *Ocean Lady* litigation and have not, to date, been contested in the courts, they appear to be inconsistent with the Refugee Convention, most notably its provisions related to freedom of movement (Article 26), non-penalization (Article 31), and naturalization (Article 34).[19]

LITIGATION

As mentioned above, in response to the boat arrivals, the Canadian government engaged in a varied litigation strategy involving criminal prosecutions, immigration inadmissibility proceedings, and refugee claim interventions. The main criminal proceedings involved a prosecution of the alleged organizers of the *Ocean Lady* vessel under section 117 of the Immigration and Refugee Protection Act (IRPA), which at that time provided that: "No person shall knowingly organize, induce, aid or abet the coming into Canada of one or more persons who are not in possession of a visa, passport or other document required by this Act."[20]

Section 117 of the IRPA gives effect to Canada's obligations to criminalize migrant smuggling pursuant to the *Convention against Transnational Organised Crime* (UNCTOC) and, more specifically, the UNCTOC's supplementary protocol, the *Protocol against the Smuggling of Migrants by Land, Sea and Air* (Smuggling Protocol).[21] This said, it is clear that the Canadian provision, like equivalent provisions in other jurisdictions,[22] is significantly broader than the definition of migrant smuggling set out in Article 3 of the Smuggling Protocol: "'Smuggling of migrants' shall mean the procurement, in order to obtain, directly or indirectly, a financial or other material benefit, of the illegal entry of a person into a State Party of which the person is not a national or a permanent resident."

Most notably, the Canadian provision contains no "material benefit" component, meaning that at least in theory, any assistance provided to migrants in securing illegal entry into Canada may constitute a criminal offence. In the litigation that ensued, the parties agreed that the plain scope of section 117 would cover, for example, two refugee claimants travelling together and providing "mutual assistance" to each other – perhaps a mother fleeing her country of origin with her infant daughter to escape the spectre of genital mutilation – and the humanitarian who, for no profit or personal gain, assists them in their flight from persecution to come to Canada to make a refugee claim.[23] Because the ambit of the provision clearly goes beyond the government's objective of preventing human smuggling, the defendants argued at trial that section 117 was overbroad and a violation of constitutionally protected rights to life, liberty, and security of the person, pursuant to section 7 of the Canadian Charter of Rights and Freedoms.[24] In this the trial court agreed, but the ruling was later reversed on appeal. The defendants appealed the matter to the Supreme Court of Canada.[25]

At the same time, the government also initiated removal cases against several former *Sun Sea* passengers – not for having masterminded the venture, but because of their assistance during the voyage. According to the persons brought before these proceedings, the plan prior to embarking on the journey was for the ship to be crewed by Thai seaman. Upon boarding the (by all accounts unfit) vessel, however, the crew promptly quit, leaving the passengers, many of whom had paid upwards of C$40,000 for the voyage, in a quandary. Determined to proceed with the trans-Pacific crossing, the organizers enlisted passengers to assist with various activities, from charting the course to cooking to collecting rain water. These activities ultimately resulted in allegations that the enlisted passengers had themselves engaged in the act of people smuggling. In defence of their actions, the appellants asserted that the provision at issue in these cases – section 37 of the IRPA – was not intended to apply to asylum seekers who merely assisted in their own flight from persecution, and such an interpretation would violate the non-penalization provisions in the Refugee Convention. They also argued that in their case, such an inadmissibility provision would be, as with the criminal sanctions in the other proceedings, unconstitutionally overbroad.

In two consolidated appeal proceedings, the Federal Court of Appeal concluded that it was reasonable for immigration decision makers to define people smuggling by relying on the above-described criminal prohibition, meaning that in this context as well, the Canadian definition of people smuggling contained no "material benefit" or profit component.[26] As mentioned above, upon finding that someone is inadmissible for organized criminality (which includes people smuggling),

that person is automatically rendered ineligible to obtain refugee status.[27] While they may still receive temporary protection against removal
to torture or to cruel or unusual treatment, their eligibility for refugee
status under the Refugee Convention, and the corresponding entitlement for permanent resident status for those found to be Convention
refugees, is immediately and permanently extinguished.[28] The appellants argued that the more limited form of protection for which they
would be eligible was not the same as refugee protection: they faced a
higher burden of proof, and protection was simply not available for several forms of persecution not contemplated under the temporary protection regime.[29] As such, the appellants argued that the regime leaves
refugee claimants open to the possibility of refoulement.

The parties sought leave to appeal their cases to the Supreme Court
of Canada.[30] As in the criminal proceedings, leave was granted and
the matters were heard together in February 2015. In two separate sets
of reasons, the Supreme Court ruled against the Canadian government and granted the appeals.

THE SUPREME COURT DECISIONS:
DEFINING PEOPLE SMUGGLING IN CANADIAN LAW

Criminal Proceedings

With respect to the criminal proceedings, the Supreme Court found
that, taking both legislative history and international law into consideration, the parliamentary objective of section 117 of the IRPA was
merely to combat people smuggling. Given that the actual scope of
the provision clearly captured, and criminalized, a much broader
ambit of activity – humanitarian aid to undocumented entrants,
mutual assistance among asylum seekers, and assistance to family
members were the examples cited by the Court – it was overly broad,
and as such was contrary to the principles of fundamental justice. In
arriving at this conclusion, the Court implicitly rejected a key argument advanced by the government: that a broad approach to smuggling is justified because the integrity of immigration law demands
that the state, and only the state, be permitted to determine questions
of admission.

In granting the appeal, the Court also considered the argument that
the broad criminal prohibition could remain constitutionally com-

pliant through the proper application of prosecutorial discretion. Leave it to the government, the argument went, to distinguish between the lofty humanitarian and the nefarious smuggler. In firmly rejecting this argument, the Court concluded that laws that clearly infringe core legal guarantees cannot be made lawful on the hope and assumption that government officials will make the "right" prosecutorial choices. The Court stated (paragraph 74):

> Ministerial discretion, whether conscientiously exercised or not, does not negate the fact that s. 117(1) criminalizes conduct beyond Parliament's object, and that people whom Parliament did not intend to prosecute are therefore at risk of prosecution, conviction and imprisonment. So long as the provision is on the books, and so long as it is not impossible that the Attorney General could consent to prosecute, a person who assists a family member or who provides mutual or humanitarian assistance to an asylum-seeker entering Canada faces a possibility of imprisonment. If the Attorney General were to authorize prosecution of such an individual, despite s. 117's limited purpose, nothing remains in the provision to prevent conviction and imprisonment.[31]

Rather than striking the provision in its entirety, however, the Court opted to "read it down" as being not applicable to persons who assist asylum seekers for humanitarian reasons or for reasons of mutual aid or family assistance. Given that the accused in the litigation were those alleged to have actually masterminded the *Ocean Lady* operation, for a profit, the prosecutions in these cases would proceed.[32] What should categorically not happen, the Court concluded, are criminal prosecutions of those who assist refugees for no material benefit.

Inadmissibility Proceedings

In also granting the inadmissibility appeals, the Court found that section 37 of the IRPA applied only to people who act to further illegal entry of asylum seekers in order to obtain, directly or indirectly, a financial or other material benefit in the context of transnational organized crime. Acts of humanitarian and mutual aid (including aid between family members) do not, contrary to the government's assertions, constitute people smuggling under the IRPA's inadmissibility provisions.

Read in its ordinary and grammatical sense, the Court found that section 37 clearly indicates that it only applies to acts of illegally bringing people into Canada where such acts are connected to transnational organized criminal activity.

In arriving at this conclusion, the court rejected the government's contention that limiting the people smuggling provision to those circumstances involving a material benefit to the smugglers fails to catch operations undertaken for other illicit purposes, such as sexual exploitation or terrorism. Other inadmissibility provisions, the Court noted, are available to address these situations, most notably those found in sections 34 to 36 of the IRPA relating to, respectively, security, human rights violations, and serious criminality.

In an intriguing, if not entirely fleshed out, passage, the court also appeared to find that Article 31 of the Refugee Convention, which mandates that states refrain from imposing penalties against refugees on account of their illegal entry, also applies to refugees who assist others in seeking asylum. According to the Court, the law recognizes that refugees often flee in groups and work together to enter a country illegally. In this context, Article 31(1) of the Refugee Convention does not permit a state to deny refugee protection to refugees solely because they have aided others in entering illegally in an unremunerated, collective flight to safety.[33] The court then concluded on this issue as follows:

> The wording of s. 37(1)(b), its statutory and international contexts, and external indications of the intention of Parliament all lead to the conclusion that this provision targets procuring illegal entry in order to obtain, directly or indirectly, a financial or other material benefit in the context of transnational organized crime. To justify a finding of inadmissibility against the appellants on the grounds of people smuggling under s. 37(1)(b), the Ministers must establish ... that the appellants are people smugglers in this sense. The appellants can escape inadmissibility under s. 37(1)(b) if they merely aided in the illegal entry of other refugees or asylum-seekers in the course of their collective flight to safety.[34]

Given the above findings, the Court found it unnecessary to consider fully the appellants' constitutional challenge, which was raised as an alternative argument in the event that the Court found that section 37 did capture more than profit-seeking smuggling activity. However, in briefly addressing the issue, the Court further provided that the Charter arguments were of "no assistance" to the appellants because section 7 of the Charter is not engaged in respect of inadmissibility determinations. It is only later in the removals process that someone's protected interests under section 7 of the Charter are "typically engaged."[35]

Since the Supreme Court's decisions in these cases, subsequent proceedings have tended to focus not on whether a material benefit is a necessary element of people smuggling allegations – it clearly is – but rather on what precisely constitutes a material benefit. Is extra food on a voyage defined by food shortages a benefit bringing someone's actions within the people smuggling criteria? What about a reduction in the fees associated with a voyage? While the situation remains somewhat unsettled, these are the questions that Canadian tribunals are now confronting.[36]

OBSERVATIONS:
WHAT CAN WE LEARN FROM THESE CASES?

Several observations may be made about the above Canadian cases. The first and most obvious issue that the cases illuminated is the simmering tension between state objectives to criminalize and penalize irregular migration and the rights of refugee claimants to seek protection under the Refugee Convention. It is important at this point to underscore that the UNCTOC and its corresponding protocols are not, at least principally, human rights instruments. Instead, they are enforcement mechanisms aimed at coordinating international approaches to combat human trafficking, people smuggling, and other forms of organized crime.[37] Furthermore, the protocols explicitly provide that they represent minimum standards; states are permitted to go beyond the requirements of the instruments to combat organized crime as they see fit.[38] However – and this is where the tension lies – these mechanisms also explicitly provide that they are only meant to target *smugglers* and not those being *smuggled*. Article 5 of the Smuggling Protocol provides: "Migrants shall not become liable to criminal prosecution under this Protocol for the fact of having been the object of conduct set forth in article 6 of this Protocol."

The Protocol is also explicit that its terms are not intended to diminish from any rights accruing under international law, including the rights of refugees under the Refugee Convention. Article 19 of the Smuggling Protocol, for example, states: "Nothing in this Protocol shall affect the other rights, obligations and responsibilities of States and individuals under international law, including international humanitarian law and international human rights law and, in particular, where applicable, the 1951 Convention and the 1967 Protocol relating to the Status of Refugees and the principle of non-refoulement as contained therein."

As with all international legal instruments, the final text of the Smuggling Protocol was a function of compromise, reflected in the Protocol's Article 6(4), which, notwithstanding the above rights-oriented provisions, provides that: "Nothing in this Protocol shall prevent a State Party from taking measures against a person whose conduct constitutes an offence under its domestic law."

The task for the Canadian Supreme Court was, at least in part, to wade through this quagmire of seemingly contradictory language and resolve the tension between the interests of the state and the rights of asylum seekers. On the one hand, the government argued that the absence of any mention of material benefit in the smuggling provisions of the IRPA, taken together with Canada's right to go beyond the terms of the Smuggling Protocol, evinced and justified a parliamentary objective to implement a more expansive anti-smuggling regime. Genuine refugees remain authorized to engage in irregular migration in order to seek safety under both Canadian law and the Refugee Convention, the government maintained, but they were legitimately prohibited from assisting others in the process.[39]

On the other hand, the fallout of this regime – which includes ineligibility of refugee claimants to access a determination under the Refugee Convention – presented what seemed to be a clear conflict with Article 19 of the Smuggling Protocol and, more worrisome, opened the door to the possible expulsion of refugees to situations of persecution, known in refugee law as refoulement.

The cases also arose in an international context in which states have frequently and increasingly sought to avoid assuming obligations to refugee populations by limiting the arrival of asylum seekers, achieved through sophisticated processes of visa controls and interdiction practices.[40] As a result, asylum seekers must increasingly rely on assistance to exercise their fundamental right to seek asylum from persecution. In particular, advocacy organizations such as the Canadian Council for Refugees argued that the potential penalization of humanitarian workers who provide assistance to asylum seekers would have a chilling effect on them, forcing asylum seekers even further into the hands of exploitative human smugglers who operate wholly outside national and international law.[41]

Considering the recent surge in refugee flows and thinking back to the Danish and French examples referred to at the beginning of this chapter, the Court's decisions in these cases are likely to be of significant interest to advocates and state courts in many countries. Of particular interest in this respect was the Court's emphatic rejection of an approach to people smuggling that equally criminalizes refugees who engage in mutual assistance, humanitarian aid providers, and actual people smugglers. Instead, the Court adopted an interpretation of Canadian law that is, for the most part, harmonious with both the Smuggling Protocol and the Refugee Convention.[42] This said, it is somewhat unfortunate that the Court opted to read down, rather than strike down the legislative provision that it found to be unlawful. The latter would have required Parliament to re-draft its people smuggling prohibitions in language that clearly complies with both international and domestic law.

LEGISLATIVE CHANGE, THE TARGETING OF ASYLUM SEEKERS, AND A WAY FORWARD

Unlike the Supreme Court decisions discussed above, there is a clear dissonance between the legislation adopted by the Canadian government following the arrival of the MV *Sun Sea* and the above-mentioned international instruments. Recall that Canada's new DFN regime creates a system of mandatory detention, deferred integration and family reunification of refugees, and circumscribed procedural rights to refugee claimants who arrive as a part of a smuggling event. Such refugees are, in other words, directly penalized on account of their mode of arrival. This is not only a clear violation of Article 31 of the Refugee Convention, it is also contrary to the already enforcement-oriented Smuggling Protocol. Moreover, the government of the day did not even attempt to justify the DFN regime on any empirically based data related to Canadian security – indeed it could not, as no such data exists. Rather, the government unapologetically suggested that such legislation was necessary for the primary purpose of deterring other would-be asylum seekers from seeking access to Canada in similar ways.[43] The perversity of this rationale jumps off the page: the Canadian Parliament passed legislation to deter people from exercising rights that Canada has specifically obligated itself to observe, protect, and help implement.

But Canada is not alone in this perversity. Indeed, the promulgation of the DFN regime is really just a microcosm of what has gone wrong globally in the realm of both anti-smuggling regulation and refugee protection – from Australian offshore refugee processing to the prosecutions in Europe of those who have assisted refugees.[44] The bottom line is that Western states lament and try to deter human smugglers even as they have created an international regime that leaves asylum seekers with little alternative but to engage their services in order to find protection. We chastise refugees for behaviour that, if we are to be honest, we would all likely replicate if faced with a similarly impoverished set of choices. Ultimately, however, states must recognize that the problem of people smuggling is merely a symptom of the larger problems of widespread displacement, closed borders to the Global North, and a broken international refugee protection regime.[45] As one Italian refugee advocate recently put it, the refugee crisis, the response of Northern states and the multitude of deaths on the Mediterranean are, at their core, "the fruit of a sick relationship between the north and the south of the world."[46]

Recall for a moment that the average duration of protracted refugee situations around the world is over a quarter century – twenty-six years.[47] Recall further that the global refugee resettlement regime is essentially a lottery – less than 1 per cent of refugees are resettled every year. Finally, recall that the overwhelming majority of refugees remain in the Global South – over 85 per cent – either in camps or in urban areas, where they often live in destitution with limited rights to work or to go to school and little hope for the future.[48] In these circumstances, it simply comes as no surprise that refugees frequently make the difficult decision to take perilous journeys in the hope of a brighter future. It is similarly unsurprising that there are those who will seek to benefit from this desperate demand.

But all of this need not be the case. As several commentators have noted – most notably Alexander Betts[49] and James Hathaway[50] – the global community already has the tools at its disposal to address the global refugee crisis and, indirectly, to alleviate the problem of people smuggling. Part of the solution is embedded in the Refugee Convention itself which, throughout its preamble, specifically calls on signatories to cooperate in the orderly protection of refugees, and with the UNHCR to help coordinate these international efforts.

Beyond the general framework of the Refugee Convention, specific and considerably larger commitments are required from states in the Global North. These commitments, moreover, must take on at least a couple of forms. First, greater financial support must be provided to the states of the Global South that receive the vast majority of the world's refugees to assist with local integration. Second, the Global North must dramatically increase the number of refugees in situations of protracted risk that it resettles. I am not the first to suggest that adopting such measures would greatly undercut the global demand for migrant smuggling.

This approach, however, requires something that is currently in short supply: political will. While the international community has in the past responded to large-scale refugee crises, most notably during the nascent era of modern refugee law after the Second World War, there does not appear to be at present a similar degree of international resolve to address the current crisis. "Between words and deeds," one journalist recently commented, "there is a sea."[51] This is lamentable.

However, there would appear to be a way forward, one that also emanates from Canada, though which has nothing to do with the aforementioned DFN regime. On the contrary, I refer here to the decision of the current government to ramp up its refugee resettlement program and, more generally, to re-engage with, and lead, efforts to address the global refugee crisis.[52] Ironically, in doing so, the current government has probably done more to combat human smuggling than the criminalization-oriented agenda and aggressive enforcement tactics of the previous one. Notwithstanding the current government's more receptive approach to refugee resettlement, it is not impervious to the kinds of pressures that can arise in the face of increasing arrivals. Indeed, as the numbers of undocumented arrivals crossing illicitly into Canada from the United States increased significantly in Canada in early 2017, pressure mounted on the government to address the situation, resulting in at least one new people smuggling prosecution.[53]

CONCLUSION

In this era, in which thousands of people are traversing borders and seeking asylum, and hundreds more are acting to assist them for both remunerative and humanitarian reasons, it is crucial to have a clear sense of the legal, political, and moral issues at play.

The Canadian Supreme Court's decisions explored at the beginning of this chapter are helpful in sorting through the complex entanglement of domestic and international law with respect of people smuggling. At the very least, they reinforce the idea that, absent clear legislative language to the contrary, refugees who mutually assist one another in their flight from persecution are not engaging in unlawful activity, nor are those who assist them for humanitarian reasons. Bringing the analysis back to a question posed at the beginning of this chapter, the decisions convey a strong normative claim: that countries should consider and distinguish the motives of those who assist asylum seekers. While states may criminalize assistance to refugees for material gain, they should refrain from doing so in other contexts.

This is a useful judicial contribution, particularly in light of people smuggling prosecutions taking place in numerous countries around the world, bringing as it does conceptual clarity to the very different contexts of humanitarian assistance to refugees and extra-legal smuggling operations contemplated by the UNCTOC. They also help to dispel the stigma attached to asylum seekers who travel with the assistance of smugglers.

That said, the decisions alone will not provide much assistance to the millions of people who remain in need of protection, and, as such, it will do little to stem the tide of human smuggling networks. Just as criminalization and enforcement efforts have done little to limit drug trafficking, they have similarly failed to prevent human smuggling events. Entrenched political conflicts have created a seemingly endless stream of refugees, and in such circumstances, where there are people whose very lives depend on escape, there will always be people to facilitate this movement. To adopt the language of liberal economics, the demand for safety, when it arises, is a powerful one that will always be met by suppliers of one kind or another. There is a very clear line, furthermore, between the actions of Northern states to prevent refugee movements and the emergence of smuggling networks; marginalized asylum seekers are pushed into ever more marginalized positions, forcing them to risk their lives in the process of trying to save them.

This is why in the second part of this chapter I argued that neither liberal jurisprudential pronouncements on human smuggling nor enforcement-oriented legislative initiatives aimed at punishing those involved in smuggling operations are likely to have an effect on the smuggling industry. What is needed, rather, is a thoughtful reconsideration of the system of international refugee protection, one that will provide meaningful protection and alternatives to the world's refugees, and, in the process, greatly diminish demand for the grim option of human smuggling.

NOTES

1 Griff Witte, "Denmark, a Social Welfare Utopia, Takes a Nasty Turn on Refugees," *Washington Post*, 11 April 2016, https://www.washingtonpost.com /world/europe/denmark-a-social-welfare-utopia-takes-a-nasty-turn-on-refugees/2016/04/11/a652e298-f5d1-11e5-958d-d038dac6e718_story.html.

2 Ibid.

3 See Adam Lusher, "Ex-Soldier Who Smuggled Afghan Girl out of Calais Refugee Camp Spared Jail," *Independent*, 14 January 2016, http://www.independent.co.uk/news/uk/home-news/rob-lawrie-former-sol-dier-who-smuggled-afghan-girl-out-of-calais-refugee-camp-spared-jail-a6813121.html.

4 Ibid.

5 Petti Fong, "76 Illegal Migrants Found on Ship Seized off B.C.," *Toronto Star*, 18 October 2009, https://www.thestar.com/news/world/2009/10/18 /76_illegal_migrants_found_on_ship_seized_off_bc.html.

6 *Convention Relating to the Status of Refugees* ("Refugee Convention"), 28 July 1951, 189 UNTS 150, Can. TS 1969/6 (entered into force 22 April 1954).

7 Pursuant to section 97 of Canada's Immigration and Refugee Protection Act (IRPA), SC 2001, ch. 27.

8 *Universal Declaration of Human Rights*, GA Res. 217 (III), UN GAOR, 3rd Sess., Supp. No. 13, UN Doc. A/810, 1948, Art. 14.

9 Refugee Convention, 1951.

10 See the combined effect of sections 101(1)(*f*) and 112(3) of the IRPA.

11 The principle of non-refoulement, codified at Article 33 of the Refugee Convention, requires that no state "shall expel or return ('refouler') a refugee in any manner whatsoever to the frontiers of territories where his life or freedom would be threatened on account of his race, religion, nationality, membership of a particular social group or political opinion." This obligation is incorporated into Canadian law at section 115(1) of the IRPA.

12 See in particular the *Protocol against the Smuggling of Migrants by Land, Sea and Air, supplementing the United Nations Convention against Transnational Organized Crime* ("Smuggling Protocol"), 15 November 2000, 2241 UNTS 507 (entered into force 28 January 2004).

13 The memorandum was obtained through an Access to Information Request,

ATIP Request A-2013-03486 (10 September 2013), accessed 16 July 2017, http://ccrweb.ca/en/sun-sea-cbsa-strategy.

14 Most notably the concern that inadmissibility findings in relation to refugee claimants would deprive such claimants of the right to a hearing into their claim to refugee status.

15 Infrequent is actually an understatement. As Neve and Russell note, the number of people who have arrived in Canada as a part of a marine smuggling event is "not even a drop in the bucket" compared to the number of individual asylum seekers who arrive by other means. See Alex Neve and Tiisetso Russell, "Hysteria and Discrimination: Canada's Harsh Response to Refugees and Migrants Who Arrive by Sea," *University of New Brunswick Law Journal* 62 (2011): 37–46. Neve and Russell continue (at 40): "Taking a ballpark estimate of 25,000 refugee arrivals per year in Canada over those twenty-five years, the 1500 who have arrived on these eight ships reflect just over 1/5 of 1%, .2% of the total. It is as many as would otherwise arrive over the course of just three weeks in any one of those twenty-five years."

16 The designation process has been incorporated into the IRPA at section 20.1(1).

17 Irene Khan, "Trading in Human Misery: A Human Rights Perspective on the Tampa Incident," *Pacific Rim Law and Policy Journal* 12 (2011): 9.

18 For a recent comparison of the Australian and Canadian legislative responses to smuggling events, see Luke Taylor, "Designated Inhospitality: The Treatment of Asylum Seekers Who Arrive by Boat in Canada and Australia," *McGill Law Journal* 60 (2015): 333.

19 These basic rights enumerated in the Convention guarantee, for example, that refugees and asylum seekers be permitted to move freely within their country of refuge, that they not be penalized on account of their mode of entry into the country, and that, as much as possible, they be afforded a pathway to citizenship or some other comparable status.

20 IRPA, s. 117.

21 *Convention against Transnational Organized Crime*, 15 November 2000, 2225 UNTS 209; Smuggling Protocol, 2000.

22 See, for example, the Australian Migration Act 1958 (as amended), No. 62, s. 233A, and the United States Title 8 USC ss. 1324(a)(1)(A)(i) (alien smuggling) and ss. 1324(a)(1)(B)(i) (providing increased penalty where an offence is committed for financial gain).

23 The case was of particular concern to several refugee advocacy organizations because of its implications for refugees travelling in groups, but also because it raised the spectre of criminalizing certain forms of advocacy commonly undertaken by them.

24 In *Singh v. Minister of Employment and Immigration*, [1985] 1 SCR 177, the
    Supreme Court of Canada affirmed that all people physically present in
    Canada are entitled to the protections contained in the Canadian Charter
    of Rights and Freedoms. While refugee claimants have no constitutional
    right to remain in Canada, the Court further concluded that they do have
    the right to have their claims determined in accordance with the principles
    of fundamental justice.

25 *R. v. Appulonappa*, [2015] 3 SCR 754, 2015 SCC 59 (CanLII).

26 *Boio v. Canada (Citizenship and Immigration)*, 2013 FCA 87 (CanLII); and
    Canada (Public Safety and Emergency Preparedness) v. J.P., 2013 FCA 262
    (CanLII).

27 Pursuant to sections 101(1)(*f*) and 112(3) of the IRPA.

28 The narrower form of protection available to those found inadmissible is set
    out at section 97 of the IRPA. While all refugee claimants are eligible to seek
    protection under section 97, it is only inadmissible claimants who are prevent-
    ed from obtaining permanent resident status upon a positive finding of risk.

29 Under Canadian law, the standard of proof to establish a well-founded fear
    of persecution is that of a "reasonable chance," see *Adjei v Canada (Minister
    of Employment and Immigration)*, [1989] 2 FCR 680, 1989 CanLII 5184 (FCA).
    The standard used under section 97 of the IRPA is the balance of probabili-
    ties. And because section 97 only affords protection against the most severe
    forms of human rights violations, there is a wide band of mistreatment –
    cumulative acts of discrimination or persistent police harassment, for exam-
    ple – that amounts to persecution but is not accounted for in respect of
    those found inadmissible.

30 *Boio v. Canada (Citizenship and Immigration)*, [2015] 3 SCR 704, 2015 SCC 58
    (CanLII).

31 *R. v. Appulonappa*, 2015.

32 Indeed, at present, one of the alleged masterminds of the *Sun Sea* voyage has
    been convicted of people smuggling offences. Three others were acquitted.
    As of 26 June 2017 new trials had been conducted in respect of those
    accused of spearheading the *Ocean Lady* voyage and a verdict is pending.
    See Canadian Press, "Supreme Court Jury Finds Man Guilty of Smuggling
    Tamil Migrants to Canada," CBC, 27 May 2017, http://www.cbc.ca/news
    /canada/british-columbia/supreme-court-jury-finds-man-guilty-of-smuggling-
    tamil-migrants-to-canada-1.4134810.

33 *Boio v. Canada*, 2015, para. 63.

34 Ibid., para. 72.

35 Ibid., para. 75. While perhaps beyond the scope of this chapter, the finding
    that the Charter rights of people subject to admissibility proceedings are

only engaged at what is essentially the removals stage of the process is, even in *obiter*, a potentially far-reaching conclusion worthy of exploration in its own right.

36 See, for example, *Handasamy v. Canada (Public Safety and Emergency Preparedness)*, 2016 FC 1389 (CanLII); *Appulonappar v. Canada (Citizenship and Immigration)*, 2016 FC 914 (CanLII); and *Gechuashvili v. Canada (Citizenship and Immigration)*, 2016 FC 365 (CanLII).

37 Andreas Schloenhardt and Hadley Hickson, "Non-Criminalization of Smuggled Migrants: Rights, Obligations, and Australian Practice Under Article 5 of the Protocol against the Smuggling of Migrants by Land, Sea, and Air," *International Journal of Refugee Law* 25 (2013): 41.

38 Anne Gallagher and Fiona David, *The International Law of Migrant Smuggling* (New York: Cambridge University Press, 2014), 366.

39 Section 133 of the IRPA defers charges against refugee claimants related to their own illegal entry pending the outcome of their claims, in conformity with Article 31 of the Refugee Convention.

40 See, for example, Attila Ataner, "Refugee Interdiction and the Outer Limits of Sovereignty," *Journal of Law and Equality* 3 (2004): 7; and, more recently, Rachel Landry, "The 'Humanitarian Smuggling' of Refugees: Criminal Offence or Moral Obligation?" (Refugee Studies Centre, Working Paper Series No. 119, 2016).

41 See the factum of the Canadian Council for Refugees: http://www.scc-csc.ca/WebDocuments-DocumentsWeb/35388/FM040_Intervener_Canadian-Council-for-Refugees.pdf.

42 See *Boio v. Canada*, 2015 and *R. v. Appulonappa*, 2015.

43 The government's own legislative summary of the bill that created the DFN regime stated: "A key objective of Bill C-4 is to deter large-scale events of irregular migration to Canada, particularly where these involve human smuggling." See Parliament of Canada, "Legislative Summary of Bill C-4: An Act to Amend the Immigration and Refugee Protection Act, the Balanced Refugee Reform Act and the Marine Transportation Security Act," Library of Parliament Research Publications, 30 August 2011, https://lop.parl.ca/About/Parliament/LegislativeSummaries/bills_ls.asp?source=library_prb&ls=C4&Parl=41&Ses=1.

44 The examples themselves being but a small illustration of the criminalization of migration within Europe. For a comprehensive examination of the kinds of penalties imposed on migrants and those who assist them in the EU, see "Criminalisation of Migrants in an Irregular Situation and of Persons Engaging with Them," European Union Agency for Fundamental

Rights, 2014, http://fra.europa.eu/sites/default/files/fra-2014-criminalisation-of-migrants-o_en_0.pdf. See in particular part 2 of the paper: *"Délits de solidarité"* – Criminalisation of Persons Engaging with Migrants in an Irregular Situation.

45 In making this point, I do not suggest that people smuggling is unproblematic. Existing as it does in a domain of almost total lawlessness, the smuggling phenomenon will almost inevitably produce highly problematic situations, none more disturbing than recent reports of refugees having organs harvested by smugglers in repayment of their debts. See Elsa Vulliamy, "Refugees Who Cannot Pay People Smugglers 'Being Sold for Organs,'" *Independent*, 4 July 2016, http://www.independent.co.uk/news/world/europe/refugee-crisis-sold-for-organs-people-smugglers-trafficker-a7119066.html. The point remains, however, that in looking to solve the scourge of people smuggling it is important to begin by examining its root causes.

46 Mattathias Schwartz, "The Anchor," *New Yorker*, 21 April 2014, 78.

47 United Nations High Commissioner for Refugees (UNHCR), "Global Trends: Forced Displacement in 2015," UNHCR, 20 June 2016, http://www.unhcr.org/statistics/unhcrstats/576408cd7/unhcr-global-trends-2015.html.

48 Ibid.

49 Alexander Betts, *Protection by Persuasion: International Cooperation in the Refugee Regime* (Ithaca, NY: Cornell University Press, 2009).

50 See James Hathaway and Alex Neve, "Making International Refugee Law Relevant Again: A Proposal for Collectivized and Solution-Oriented Protection," *Harvard Human Rights Journal* 10 (1997): 10; and, more recently, James C. Hathaway, "A Global Solution to a Global Refugee Crisis," *Open Democracy*, 29 February 2016, accessed 16 July 2017, https://www.openglobalrights.org/global-solution-to-global-refugee-crisis.

51 Schwartz, "The Anchor," 85.

52 See, for example, Nicholas Keung, "Canada 'an Inspiration' on Syrian Refugee Resettlement," *Toronto Star*, 29 March 2016, https://www.thestar.com/news/immigration/2016/03/29/canada-an-inspiration-on-syrian-refugee-resettlement.html.

53 "Canadian Woman Faces Human Smuggling Charges," BBC News, 20 April 2017, http://www.bbc.co.uk/news/world-us-canada-39646504.

3

Anti-Trafficking and Exclusion: Reinforcing Canadian Boundaries through Human Rights Discourse

Julie Kaye

Human trafficking is widely understood as a threat to national security and a violation of human rights. However, rather than enhance the ability of migrants to exercise their rights, responses to trafficking have heightened insecurity for migrants of precarious status, including increasing criminalization at the border. On the heels of the Cold War, anti-trafficking discourses and responses underwent a marked resurgence into public consciousness. At that time, trafficking, for many, "*meant* prostitution."[1] In particular, anti-trafficking garnered substantial attention through widely circulated images of the figure of the "Natasha," the archetypal trafficking victim:[2] women portrayed as having been coerced, deceived, and moved from the former Soviet Union and Eastern Bloc.[3] In Canada, a threat assessment by the Royal Canadian Mounted Police (RCMP) specifically associated trafficking with women "recruited from Eastern European countries for non-sexual work but were later forced to dance in strip clubs and even provide sexual services."[4] In this context, anti-trafficking efforts were initially focused on identifying – and making it easier to identify – gendered constructions of victimization and "at risk" bodies by reinforcing enforcement mechanisms of Canadian border securitization.

In turn, anti-trafficking measures have particular implications for the reproduction of national hierarchies,[5] wherein Canada emphasizes its position as "a good, helpful nation," while "maintaining a particular gendered and raced neocolonial identity."[6] Building on existing critical examinations of anti-trafficking responses, this chapter discusses how Canadian anti-trafficking responses problematically contribute to the construction of restrictive immigration policies while supporting broader notions of border securitization and the ongoing invisibilization of precarity. The chapter also explores the gendered assumptions embedded in such restrictive policies. It includes an analysis of fifty-six one-on-one interviews, three group interviews, and two focus groups that explored the perspectives of frontline workers, government officials, and law enforcement.[7] The chapter demonstrates the ongoing criminalization of migrants that is reproduced in spite of – and at times through – rights-based efforts at interventions. It traces conceptions of human trafficking in Canada in order to examine restrictions placed on the temporary migrant worker program, especially those limiting the movement of people working in sex industries. The chapter also draws on the well-known case of human trafficking, occurring in Hamilton, Ontario. Although the case challenged gender assumptions of victimization, the response further points to processes whereby immigration policy restrictions are justified through anti-trafficking discourses. Far from fostering belonging, such restrictions result in ongoing forms of criminalization and insecurity for migrants facing precarity and reinforce the policing of migrant communities.

ANTI-TRAFFICKING, TRANSNATIONAL CRIME, AND HUMAN RIGHTS

In 2000, the United Nations *Protocol to Prevent, Suppress and Punish Trafficking in Persons, especially Women and Children* (the UN Protocol)[8] cast human trafficking alongside arms dealing and the drug trade as one of the leading forms of transnational criminal activity.[9] The UN Protocol, adopted in Palermo, Italy, was situated under the *United Nations Convention against Transnational Organized Crime*. The UN Protocol, as Suchland highlights,[10] could logically have been situated under previous international trafficking declarations or conventions on forced labour and human rights. However, the transnational crime placement points to the carceral response embedded in the UN Protocol, which conflated humanitarian intervention with enforcement-based intervention. This approach assumes state benevolence in relation to precarious migrants. At the same time, the core elements of the UN Protocol remained purposefully ambiguous.[11] Thus, since this time, enforcement-based responses to human trafficking as well as widespread awareness-raising initiatives have multiplied, while anti-trafficking discourses are relied upon to justify a variety of political agendas.[12]

The UN Protocol provided a contested international framework for understanding human trafficking. It has come to underpin national anti-trafficking policies, including the promotion of restrictive national boundaries, such as tough-on-crime approaches to migrant smuggling that are proclaimed as appropriate responses to trafficking.[13] As Anderson identifies,[14] national boundaries are "imagined" in a context of global economic relations that produce and reproduce structural forms of inequality[15] and differential freedom of movement.[16]

From a transnational crime perspective, human trafficking is understood as a threat to state sovereignty and national security. Responses to human trafficking emphasize enhanced border controls and restrictive immigration policies.[17] In particular, by constructing the "other"[18] in terms of a potential risk and threat to the nation-state,[19] human trafficking discourses help to facilitate the realization of exclusion. In foregrounding the role of individual traffickers and organized criminal networks, advocates of human rights approaches and efforts against "modern-day slavery"[20] emphasize legal mechanisms to mitigate the illicit activity of trafficking. For instance, Shelley[21] argues that organized crime groups have modified their activities to include the profit-making opportunities associated with human trafficking in response to heightened flows of labour across international borders. From this perspective, heightened border security is required to monitor and interrupt the proliferation of transnational criminal activities.

In a similar way, anti-trafficking discourse constructs migrating subjects as "at risk" and in need of intervention and control.[22] By assuming state neutrality or even state benevolence, such approaches underestimate the role played by a continuum of labour "unfreedom" in the global capitalist political economy.[23] In particular, structural inequalities assume a differentiation of rights, which is realized through migrant labour market reforms and redesigned immigration policies.[24] By emphasizing a crime and security approach, anti-trafficking discourses facilitate such policy shifts and thereby contribute to the reproduction of the power differentiation in which human trafficking is rooted.

Thus, while reinforcing territorial boundaries in response to perceived threats,[25] restrictive policies limit legal migratory avenues, particularly for marginalized and gendered populations, without reducing demand for cheap, exploitable, and precarious labour.[26] To supplement global labour supplies, a growing number of people, especially women, rely on "alternative circuits."[27] These can include a variety of legal and illegalized cross-border migrations in which women move voluntarily or on a spectrum of unfreedoms[28] to resource governments, other public infrastructure, and contractors, as well as traffickers. In this context, restrictive policies limit access to the benefits associated with secure membership in a national community, such as social services, employment, and a voice in political matters.[29]

Although early representations of women deceived into sexual forms of exploitation in Canada continue to pervade the public consciousness, anti-trafficking responses have come to assume a far broader mandate, emphasizing international and internal movements in sex work and non-sexual forms of labour as well as the trafficking of organs.[30] In particular, Canada's prostitution legislation, the Protection of Communities and Exploited Persons Act, was designed to harmonize with counter-trafficking legislations. Chuang refers to this widening conflation of legal concepts under the rubric of human trafficking as "exploitation creep."[31] In spite of a growing mandate, anti-trafficking responses have thus far maintained an emphasis on trafficking as an aberration within global capitalist relations, and enforcement-based policies as the prominent solution to trafficking. In this way, Canadian anti-trafficking responses continue to render invisible the role of Canadian policy in the production of varying forms of exploitation and contexts ripe for exploitative practices. As O'Connell Davidson notes, far from constructing political alliances among varying groups of migrants, anti-trafficking policy "inspires and legitimates efforts that divide a small number of 'deserving victims' from the masses that remain 'undeserving' of rights and freedoms."[32] In part, such divisions include various forms of border securitization and the criminalization of migrating bodies.

In 2002, Canada enacted laws to criminalize the trafficking of persons through the Immigration and Refugee Protection Act (IRPA). Section 118 of IRPA prohibits deliberately organizing the entry into Canada of one or more persons through the use of force, threats, fraud, deception or any other form of coercion.[33] Portrayed as important for identifying and prosecuting human traffickers, the IRPA, however, offers no provision for people victimized by human trafficking. In 2005, anti-trafficking legislation was adopted in the Criminal Code to include both "international" trafficking (i.e., trafficking from international contexts) and "domestic" trafficking (i.e., trafficking within Canadian borders).[34] Although narrower in scope, some law enforcement representatives suggest the IRPA provides a less onerous framework with which to charge traffickers than the Criminal Code legislation.[35] Moreover, border controls are demonstrably ineffective mechanisms for protecting the rights of migrants in general and trafficked persons in particular. For example, Hanley et al.[36] draw attention to the relationship between "precarious status," legislated under the IRPA, and broader experiences of labour trafficking. Since the IRPA offers no provisions for people victimized by human trafficking, trafficked persons are left vulnerable to criminalization or deportation, or having to endure the abusive situation.[37] At the same time, provisions for trafficked persons, such as Temporary Resident Permits (TRPs), are unable to address their underlying precarity and have the potential to further isolate them.[38] Although temporary permits allow for a period of reflection, they necessitate identification within law enforcement structures and rely on officials interpreting a person's experience as fitting the contested trafficking definition. For precarious migrants rejected from this process and facing exploitative practices, there is little to no recourse. With these limitations in mind, reflecting on human trafficking from a broader human rights perspective encourages us to work toward a framework that will not only protect trafficked persons but address the widespread precarity that results in migrants facing exploitative practices.

From a foreign policy standpoint, the promotion of international anti-trafficking protocols and the adoption of anti-trafficking legislation in Canada are framed as both a matter of human rights and of crime control. However, in doing so, anti-trafficking responses direct resources and attention towards identification and intervention on behalf of *victims* of trafficking, while reproducing and at times reinforcing the structural context in which trafficking emerges.[39] In the words of Suchland, "today's anti-trafficking apparatus is largely focused on locating, identifying, and categorizing 'victims of trafficking.' Indeed, human trafficking is only legible when a victim is identified or can claim that she was enslaved by force, fraud, or coercion."[40] As a result, anti-trafficking in Canada has led to both additional monitoring and enforcement of national boundaries, while also maintaining a complaints-based system wherein responses to trafficking are only available to people willing and able to bring forward their experiences to authority structures. Such a system has the potential to further exacerbate deportations and threats of deportation facing precarious migrants.

Specifically, the process of adopting the National Action Plan to Combat Human Trafficking, released in 2012, exemplifies the exclusionary emphasis of Canada's anti-trafficking initiatives. Frontline workers consulted in the formulation of the plan indicate that certain recommendations were out of step with the realities that they themselves perceived and in line with broader efforts of border securitization. In the words of one frontline worker:

> One of the [proposed] recommendations was that we should have more stringent immigration procedures and policies *for women entering Canada alone*. It was totally uninformed, it was just like, 'this will fix it,' and we were just like, 'we would like to state our concern with this,' and I don't know if it has been revised … My concern is that people go, 'oh yeah, that will do, we are dealing with it: pass.' It is kind of frightening if something like that can even get in there. (frontline worker, Calgary, 11/10, emphasis added)

In the end, the national plan does emphasize some exclusionary measures aimed at restricting the migratory movements of girls and women, including voluntary movements. Specifically, the plan states: "those who are likely to be at-risk [of trafficking] include persons who are socially or economically disadvantaged, such as some Aboriginal women, youth and children … who are in protection, as well as girls and women, who may be lured to large urban centres or who move *or migrate there voluntarily*" (emphasis added).[41]

In this, discourses on the precarity of low-wage migrant workers, including instances of trafficking, emphasize unscrupulous employers and depend on migrant complaints, thereby eliding the role of nation-states in fostering planned precarity. Yet, as a result of restrictive policies and programs, migrant workers with precarious status – including temporary migrant workers in low-wage jobs in the primary agriculture and live-in caregiver streams of the Temporary Foreign Worker (TFW) program – face significant difficulties in exercising their rights. This differentiation of rights and privileges occurs alongside a growing reliance on the remittances of migrant workers – not only to supplement household incomes but also to help finance public infrastructure, such as roads and schools, and supplement public revenues.[42] Despite such dependencies, in the name of anti-trafficking, a number of Western countries, including Canada, have adopted policies that dissuade legal migratory routes[43] and fail to protect the rights of migrant workers with precarious immigration status.[44] In this way, anti-trafficking discourses serve as a "moral reform arm" of anti-immigrant politics, which, alongside global capitalism, encourages the free mobility of capital, yet increasingly restricts the mobility rights of migrant labourers.[45]

In this context, anti-trafficking advocates hoping to extend boundaries through anti-trafficking discourse and responses argued for a human rights approach to address human trafficking. From this standpoint, many anti-trafficking advocates were especially critical of the role played by the Canada Border Service Agency (CBSA) in criminalizing trafficked and potentially trafficked persons by emphasizing border control efforts. Frontline service providers, law enforcement representatives, and government officials all suggest an unwillingness on the part of the CBSA to recognize the experiences of trafficked persons and to consider the nuanced circumstances that can lead trafficked persons and other criminalized migrants to be in violation of immigration laws. For example, as one provincial government representative suggests: "[CBSA] don't want to admit that we have got trafficking in this country. They see everybody as trying to break in illegally, queue jumping and that kind of stuff, so they never have taken this issue seriously ... They just want to deport. So that's really unfortunate because they are huge gatekeepers and could make a huge difference" (provincial government representative, British Columbia, 01/11). While some indicate that the CBSA is unaware of, or unwilling to consider, the experiences of trafficked persons, others indicate that the CBSA is aware of human trafficking but is dominated by an enforcement-based approach that limits a more nuanced examination of the narratives of those in violation of immigration policies. In the words of one frontline service provider: "CBSA is aware of trafficking, but they are probably less intent on prosecuting it because their approach is to detain, interview, deport. They don't even get to what is the story of this person" (frontline worker, Vancouver, 01/11).

Similarly, former and current law enforcement personnel indicate that the CBSA emphasizes exclusionary practices to the extent that border securitization is creating more insecurity for trafficked persons and migrants in general:

We would look at them as being in violation of the Act, overstaying, misrepresenting the purpose of why they are here, take them
into custody and proceed with removal processes ... I have never
received, in the 14 years that I was with the CBSA, I never received
any formal training on what constituted human trafficking ... We
don't look at the nuances of why they are in violation of the Act.
Technically, yes, they are in violation of the Act, but why are they
in violation of the Act? ... I know personally for myself, I am
responsible for removing dozens upon dozens of people that were
victims of trafficking and we dealt with them as immigration vio-
lators and removed them." (former law enforcement officer,
national, 12/10)

Of note, the official is only discussing cases that narrowly fit into
a trafficking framework, which has further implications for the criminalization of those who fall outside such "victim" labels. According
to a current law enforcement representative, training and awareness
have improved among frontline border security officials; however,
the emphasis on enforcement approaches above migrant rights per-
sists: "They are aware of the issue [of human trafficking], but how
they handle it hasn't progressed" (law enforcement officer, national,
12/10). This raises the question of whether further training and education on anti-trafficking for border security and specialized law
enforcement units with protocols for the detection of human trafficking would advance the rights of trafficked persons. Moreover,
what effect might this have on the broader community of precarious
status migrant workers?

Although some frontline service providers working with migrants
with precarious status argue that border security needs to address anti-
trafficking, many conclude that anti-trafficking responses lend themselves to an emphasis on exclusion-based policies, and thereby
become a mechanism of crime control and border security. Service
providers in an Alberta-based examination of responses to trafficking
of migrant women, in particular, identify the complexity of navigating a criminalizing system from a rights-based standpoint. As one service provider discusses:

[It is] hard to navigate programs and information that do exist,
[there is] so much to think about. Immigration law, status, vulnerability ... Are they safe getting help, or if they leave the situation

they're in will they no longer be sponsored? Will they have to leave the country? How do they fit into existing legal categories or definitions, or even supportive (i.e. victims accessing support) categories and programs? (information specialist, legal support agency, Northern Alberta, as cited in Kaye 2016)[46]

As the respondent identifies, there is "so much to think about," including negotiating the challenges arising from the system mandated with responding to human trafficking, and the reinforcement such responses provide to pre-determined categories of whether victimized people are considered legal or able to access support. Although law enforcement and criminal justice comprise the primary institutions mandated with anti-trafficking responses,[47] advocates argue that the ability to partner with such formal organizations is restricted given the many structural and social factors that restrict migrants from being able to report exploitation and abuse, including trafficking. Thus, migrants navigating fears of deportation, job loss, family separation, being sent back to a place they wished to migrate from, and a limited ability to exercise their human rights remain in situations of precarity in spite of and at times as a result of increasing attention and expanding responses to human trafficking. As one service provider indicates: "And we know it doesn't always work out for women – [they] may be deported, their children may be ordered to stay here, but they are deported. Things, situations happen and rightfully cause fear in women to come forward (program manager, social service agency, Northern Alberta, as cited in Kaye 2016)."[48] Thus, anti-trafficking policies claiming to prevent or respond to human trafficking are perceived to create more insecurity for trafficked persons. As a national law enforcement representative indicates, "I think the main concern tends to be that these laws were not written with the victim at the core. The purpose is to address the crime. It's crime oriented, it's to stop trafficking ... And I don't know if that's going to change anytime soon."[49] As this suggests, an over-emphasis on interrupting the activities of individual traffickers or organized criminal groups encourages the adoption of more restrictive border control measures. In turn, this leads to the reproduction of differential access to global labour markets, as trafficked persons and migrants with precarious status face heightened risk of criminalization and restricted migratory options.

ANTI-TRAFFICKING IN CANADA
AND RESTRICTING MOVEMENT

In spite of concerns about the link between anti-trafficking and border securitization, anti-trafficking responses in Canada have led to
more restrictive immigration reforms. By way of example, this section examines the role of anti-trafficking discourses in leading to
changes in the IRPA through the adoption of clauses in the omnibus
crime bill (Bill C-10) in March 2012.[50] Drawing on anti-trafficking
discourses, these amendments enabled the withdrawal and refusal of
visas issued to exotic dancers under the TFW program and, at the discretion of immigration officials, the pre-emptive restriction of foreign nationals from working in Canada if they are believed to be "at
risk" of exploitation. Such exclusion on the basis of *perceived risk* and
gendered constructions of vulnerability warrant attention in their
own right, especially since the restrictive measures have so far only
been applied to restricting visas for exotic dancers and not for workers in other temporary employment sectors in which documented
cases of labour trafficking have occurred, such as live-in caregivers
or construction workers. While this section points to such political
constructions, the focus of this analysis remains on the use of anti-
trafficking discourses to shape exclusionary immigration policies,
such as restricting migration through amendments to the visa program used by migrant dancers.

Since the implementation in 1978 of Canada's temporary work permit process, foreign exotic dancers have participated in the cross-border movements facilitated by the program.[51] Typically, temporary
work permits must be obtained overseas by demonstrating a job offer
and a validation of the offer by Human Resources Development
Canada (HRDC).[52] Temporary employment offers are validated when
employers obtain a positive labour market opinion by reasonably
demonstrating a shortage of qualified Canadians or permanent residents available to recruit, train, and fill the position. However, in the
case of exotic dancers, the requirement to obtain a work permit overseas and the employment validation from HRDC was exempted. The
exemption was implemented because the initial cross-border movements in the 1970s and 1980s primarily involved "Canadian and U.S.
women engaging in an informal stripper exchange program."[53] However, in the early 1990s, the source regions supplying exotic dancers to

Canada shifted to countries in Eastern Europe and Asia.[54] It was in this context that concerns of human trafficking entered the public discourse, with anti-trafficking discourses suggesting that the special exemption of the program used by migrant dancers reflected the state's complicity in facilitating human trafficking. In turn, this led to public discussions about restricting the program.

However, alongside a shift in workplace standards in the countries supplying exotic dancers to Canada, workplace standards were also changing in Canada in the 1990s with the institutionalization of lap dancing as an industry standard.[55] This resulted in a declining supply of Canadian dancers, which facilitated industry claims of labour shortages.[56] As a result, in 1998, the then-minister of HRDC, Pierre Pettigrew, classified foreign dancing as a job to be monitored for shortages, which, in effect, eliminated the need for individual labour market opinions. While in appearance this facilitated a streamlined entry of exotic dancers into Canada "to serve the economic interests of the private sector," Citizenship and Immigration Canada (CIC) relied on legal devices to restrict the movement of exotic dancers.[57] Specifically, CIC denied employment authorizations based on the qualifications presented by the applicants. For instance, as Macklin highlights, the Federal Court upheld a CIC decision that an applicant who "only had experience topless dancing"[58] lacked the necessary qualifications for "nude dancing" in Toronto (see *Silion v. Canada*).[59] Applicants were also rejected based on the assumption they would only enter the exotic dancing industry in Canada if their circumstances overseas were extremely dire, which meant they would pose a risk of not wanting to return to their home countries, in violation of the temporary design of the program.

Despite the already constrained flow of exotic dancers to Canada, a political scandal led to further calls to cancel the visa program available to migrant dancers. In 2004, Immigration Minister Judy Sgro was alleged to have been in a conflict of interest over the issuing of a visa on behalf of a migrant dancer who worked on her re-election campaign. The scandal led to the resignation of Minister Sgro and to a renewal of criticism surrounding the visa program and its implications for the role of the state in human trafficking.[60] As a result, the requirement to have a job offer validated was applied to the exotic dancer program, and the number of work permits issued and extended dramatically declined: 342 permits and extensions were granted in 2004, while only six were granted or extended in 2010.[61] Measures to further restrict and/or eliminate the program were proposed between 2007 and 2010; however, they gained little footing until the Conservatives won a majority in May 2011.

The omnibus crime bill, Bill C-10, which was introduced on 20 September 2011 and received royal assent on 13 March 2012, amended the IRPA with the stated intention of addressing international forms of human trafficking. In particular, clauses 205 to 208 of Bill C-10 "give immigration officers discretion to refuse to authorize foreign nationals to work in Canada if, *in the opinion of the officers,* the foreign nationals are *at risk* of being victims of exploitation or abuse" (emphasis added).[62] The bill proposed to address the problem of human trafficking by excluding the migratory movements of the visa applicants. In doing so, the measure restricted freedom of movement without addressing the root cause of the presupposed "risk" or the motivating factors leading to the visa request. Thus, while the policy potentially limits cases of exploitation through this specific visa program, it expands other forms of insecurity where "at risk" people use or are forced to use alternate, illegalized routes of entry and/or face the constraints associated with precarity.

In addition to Bill C-10, further measures to eliminate the exotic dancer visa program were advanced with the passing of Bill C-38, the omnibus budget that received royal assent on 29 June 2012. Building on the program restrictions implemented in 2004, provisions in Bill C-38 drew on anti-trafficking discourses to grant immigration officials the power to invalidate existing visas issued to exotic dancers, refuse new applications to the program, and prohibit people with open work visas from working in the adult entertainment industry. Announcing the new measures, Diane Finley, then-minister of human resources and skills development, indicated: "Through collaborative partnerships and preventative action, these new measures will further strengthen Canada's National Action Plan to Combat Human Trafficking."[63] The measures are in step with the National Action Plan (NAP).

Towards this end, then-minister of citizenship, immigration and multiculturalism Jason Kenney announced the new measures to be implemented with the passing of Bill C-38 by building on this discourse of suspected risk: "The government cannot in good conscience continue to admit temporary foreign workers to work in businesses in sectors where there are reasonable grounds to *suspect a risk* of sexual exploitation" (emphasis added).[64] The minister further pointed to a

2010 report in which the RCMP worried that escort agencies, brothels, and massage parlours were connected to human trafficking and sexual exploitation."[65] The RCMP report does refer to the involvement of organized crime with connections to convicted traffickers in facilitating the entry of women from the former Soviet states to Canada to work in massage and escort services. Specifically, the RCMP threat assessment associated strip clubs with human trafficking of foreign nationals to Canada, citing "investigations conducted in the 1990s" that found "strong indications that women were recruited from Eastern European countries for non-sexual work but were later forced to dance in strip clubs and even provide sexual services."[66] Since human trafficking legislation was not in place at the time of the investigations, the RCMP report argues that anecdotal stories alongside investigations pointing to circumstances consistent with human trafficking needed to be considered in lieu of numerical data.[67] However, the report goes on to contradict discourses connecting human trafficking with the exploitation of foreign nationals in exotic dancing industries. Specifically, according to the report, more recent investigations in Ontario, Quebec, and the Atlantic regions all concluded that in clubs offering sexual services, "human trafficking complaints were mostly unfounded ... [T]hough foreign workers were indeed located in the clubs, investigations determined that these subjects were engaged *voluntarily* as exotic dancers" (emphasis added).[68] As a result, the report concluded: "Overall, investigations so far have not been able to substantiate the trafficking of foreign nationals in exotic dance clubs but this possibility has not been ruled out."[69] Conversely, the report suggests that interprovincial trafficking of Canadian citizens is an "increasing trend."[70] Nonetheless, by connecting the migratory movements of women, including voluntary migrations, to the risk of human trafficking, anti-trafficking discourses presented the restrictive measures as a preventative strategy to address the victimization of foreign nationals exploited in exotic dancing industries.

Despite scarce evidence connecting human trafficking to the exotic dancer visa program, abolishing the program has, in effect, prevented potential cases of international human trafficking from occurring through the specific use of exotic dancer visas. However, in doing so, the restrictive measures limit the legal migratory options for predominantly migrant women, criminalize the experiences of women who continue to work once their visas are declared invalid, and fail to address the structural constraints and constructed precarity at the core of all forms of human trafficking and related exploitations. Moreover, excluding women from accessing legal migratory options fails to address the socioeconomic realities of the migrants, the motivations behind their migrations, and mobility rights in general. In doing so, the measures contradict a primary purpose of the UN Protocol: "to protect and assist the victims of such trafficking, with full respect for their human rights" (Article 2(b)).[71]

ANTI-TRAFFICKING, CRIMINALIZATION, AND DEPORTATION

In Canada, approximately a dozen convictions have occurred under the Criminal Code's trafficking in persons legislation.[72] All but one of these were categorized as sex trafficking. Yet, a number of recent trafficking cases point to the exploitation of precarious labour and, especially, the precarity created by temporary migrant worker programs. For example, in 2012, the RCMP charged three people for trafficking sixty-three migrant workers who arrived from Poland and the Ukraine on student visas and were threatened with deportation for their labour with Kihew Energy.[73] The owners of the company pled to lesser charges and had to pay a fine of $215,000, which represented a small portion of the approximate $1,000,000 that was profited through the exploitation of migrant labour.[74] In 2014, human trafficking charges were laid against Jennilyn Morris in Edmonton for the exploitation of seventy-one migrant workers through the Demot Cleaning Company.[75] The human trafficking charges were dropped, but Morris was sentenced to two and a half years in prison for related charges under the IRPA.[76]

There are far too many examples of migrant women and those working in sex industries facing criminalization and deportation as a result of anti-trafficking responses.[77] The *R v. Domotor* case, for example, demonstrates how anti-trafficking responses equally fail to protect the rights of migrants even in clear-cut instances that meet the criminal definitions of trafficking in persons. In this case, restrictive measures in Canada led to the deportation of a trafficked person's family, despite concerns of significant "risk" posed by the trafficking network in the family's country of origin. As this narrative exemplifies, notions of perceived risk are unidirectional. In other words, such notions are employed to restrict migration into Canada, yet they are not similarly adopted when removal orders are concerned. Thus,

enforcement-based identification of a potential victim of human trafficking can be used to restrict entry into Canada, yet identification as
a victim of trafficking provides no sustainable legal right to remain in
Canada, which further highlights the failure in law to provide such
rights to trafficked persons and the restricted ability of trafficked persons to exercise their rights.

On 6 October 2010, the RCMP laid nine charges of human trafficking and fraud against Ferenc Domotor following a ten-month investigation initiated by the self-reporting of a Hungarian Roma migrant
worker.[78] An additional nine charges associated with the case were
laid on 7 September 2012, making it Canada's largest human trafficking case to date. According to the RCMP, the trafficked persons were
recruited from Hungary with promises of "steady work, good pay and
a better life."[79] Upon arrival, the trafficked persons had their documents withheld and were told they had to sleep on the basement floor
with a number of other hired workers.[80]

The case fit the prototypical image of human trafficking in transnational criminal activities. It involved a large-scale organized crime operation, including widespread criminal and fraud schemes, as well as
the use of significant threats and violence in order to coerce. Moreover,
compared to other cases of trafficking, the willingness of the trafficked
persons to cooperate with police and the availability of physical evidence helped lead to criminal charges and, ultimately, convictions
under the Criminal Code's anti-trafficking legislation.[81] Significantly,
the trafficked persons were "coached to file false Refugee Claims as
well as social assistance," benefits that would eventually be appropriat-
ed by the traffickers.[82]

The case shaped debates over the right to claim asylum and the perceived threat of asylum seekers abusing the refugee system in Canada,
with the prevailing anti-trafficking discourse suggesting that situations like this one could be prevented through immigration reforms.
At the time, Minister Jason Kenney was quoted as saying "The government has tried but so far failed to stem the tide of Roma coming
into Canada and abusing its refugee system ... [T]he flood of asylum-
seekers is "highly organized" and not at all spontaneous. More worrisome is the evidence of human trafficking involved in these cases."[83]

By connecting the now politicized influx of Roma refugee
claimants to the abuses of the refugee system and the "highly organized" criminal network responsible for the Hamilton human trafficking case, the minister presented human trafficking as a threat to

national security and restrictive immigration reform as an appropriate response. Although those advocating the prevailing anti-trafficking discourses cited the experience of the Hungarian labourers in their justification for more restrictive immigration policies, these policies led to the deportation of the family of one of the key witnesses in the case: Tibor Baranyai.

The deportation of Baranyai's wife and stepdaughter occurred despite fears they would be targeted for reprisals. According to a victim impact statement, at least one of the families of a person victimized by the case had previously been subjected to threats and intimidation by the network affiliated with the traffickers:

My family has been threatened many times in Hungary. They promised them money if they told them where I was. My family suffered a lot because of it. I have so much guilt because of what they did to my family, and because of what happened to my family back home. [They] visited my family home in Hungary many times, they surrounded my family and they intimidated them so they would tell them where I was. My parents wouldn't allow my siblings to go to school because they were afraid for their safety. My father couldn't fall asleep because he was afraid that [they] will break-in in the middle of the night, and that something serious will happen to my family members. Every night he tried to sleep with a huge piece of metal next to his bed, for protection, in case someone does break in ... If for some reason me and my family have to go back to Hungary one day I am sure that we are going to be harmed seriously, in short period of time. (victim impact statement)[84]

Before 1 July 2012, those in Canada who had been issued a pre-removal order were rarely removed from Canada without being given the opportunity to receive a pre-removal risk assessment (PRRA).[85] However, with the passing of more restrictive immigration policies, failed refugee claimants now have at least a one-year waiting period before being eligible for a PRRA[86] and are likely to be deported from Canada within that year, making the PRRA effectively unavailable to refugee claimants who have received a negative decision.[87] Since Baranyai's wife and stepdaughter had been issued a failed refugee claim prior to the marriage, border security had limited legal options for considering the evolving narrative of the migrants involved. Thus, despite the changing circumstances and potential risk created for the family of this trafficked person, they were deported back to Hungary.

Baranyai argues that, in the absence of a risk assessment and recognition of the potential danger faced by the family members, he was victimized not only by the traffickers, but also by the criminal justice system in Canada: "I want to say I feel used. The traffickers used me for my labour, Canada used me as a witness to get a prosecution. But both Canada and the traffickers would deny me the basic thing I need as a human: to be loved, to love, and be supported by a family that I can see and touch. You would deny those I love safety."[88]

The altering of the PRRA clause offers one example of how migrants living in precarity are limited in exercising their rights in relation to their evolving contexts. Moreover, the case points to the reality that in spite of claims to protect trafficked persons from the potential harms of deportation,[89] trafficked persons are not provided with sustainable legal rights to remain in Canada and deportations continue to occur even when criminal definitions of trafficking are met.

Although the *R v. Domotor* trafficking case challenges the idealized conceptions of trafficking and the gendered assumptions of trafficking interventions, by reinforcing the boundaries of the state, anti-trafficking and corresponding "tough on crime" policies have created significant challenges for some migrant workers in Canada, and especially for migrant women and those migrating in sex industries who, in a context of restrictive policies and precarious immigration status, face heightened forms of insecurity.

CONCLUSION

Paralleling the international rise of human trafficking onto the "global agenda of high politics,"[90] the considerable attention afforded to human trafficking and anti-trafficking responses in Canada shows no sign of decline. New policies, response models, networks, and advocacy groups continue to emerge across the country. In spite of a sustained critique, anti-trafficking discourses have shaped Canadian immigration policies, leading to changes that emphasize border control, enforcement, and securitization. By framing human trafficking as a violation of human rights that involves a potential threat to national security, the existing immigration system reinforces the dichotomous categories of "deserving victim" and "complicit criminal." In turn, Canadian anti-trafficking discourses validate the perceived sovereignty and benevolence of the nation-state to protect the rights of "victims" while pre-emptively restricting and/or criminalizing those migrants who fall outside the bounds of a legitimized victim narrative, including refugee claimants, asylum seekers, migrants with criminalized or precarious status, and trafficked persons.

Anti-trafficking discourses were also employed to established exclusionary boundaries that restrict migratory movements on the basis of perceived risk. However, restricting migratory movements without addressing the complex motivations underlying the desire to move, limits the legal options available to migrants. Meanwhile, such approaches create space for criminalizing migrants and deporting "at risk" migrants, while simultaneously failing to address the exploitative contexts that underlie instances of trafficking. In turn, by restricting migration, such approaches reinforce the authority of the state to limit movement and establish differential access to protections associated with membership. In a context in which global dependence on migratory labour continues to intensify, restricting the movements of labouring bodies reinforces existing forms of structural inequality and perpetuates the insecurity of migrants, including migrants victimized by human trafficking.

NOTES

1 Jo Doezema, *Sex Slaves and Discourse Masters: The Construction of Trafficking* (London: Zed Books, 2010): 163.

2 See, for example, Victor Malarek, *The Natashas: Inside the New Global Sex Trade* (Canada: Viking Canada, 2003).

3 Jennifer Suchland, *Economies of Violence: Transnational Feminism, Postsocialism, and the Politics of Sex Trafficking* (Durham: Duke University Press, 2015).

4 "Human Trafficking in Canada," Royal Canadian Mounted Police (RCMP) Criminal Intelligence and Human Trafficking National Coordination Centre, March 2010, http://publications.gc.ca/collections/collection_2011/grc-rcmp/PS64-78-2010-eng.pdf.

5 Julie Kaye, *Responding to Human Trafficking: Dispossession, Colonial Violence, and Resistance Among Indigenous and Racialized Women* (Toronto: University of Toronto Press, 2017).

6 Leslie Ann Jeffrey, "Canada and Migrant Sex Work: Challenging the 'Foreign' in Foreign Policy," *Canadian Foreign Policy* 12, no. 1 (2005): 33–48. For similar discussions, also see Ratna Kapur, "The 'Other' Side of Globalization: The Legal Regulation of Cross Border Movements," *Canadian Women Studies*

22, no. 3–4 (2003): 6–15; Rachel Parrenas, *Servants of Globalization: Women, Migration, and Domestic Work* (Palo Alto: Stanford University Press, 2001); Nandita Sharma, "Travel Agency: A Critique of Anti-Trafficking Campaigns," *Refuge* 21, no. 3 (2003): 53–65; and Rutvica Andrijasevic, *Migration, Agency and Citizenship in Sex Trafficking* (New York: Palgrave Macmillan, 2010).

7   Data was collected between October 2010 and February 2011. Of note, this chapter is part of a broader project on responses to human trafficking in the context of settler colonialism in Canada (see Kaye, *Responding to Human Trafficking*). Portions of the broader work are reproduced here for the purpose of specifically discussing the role of anti-trafficking in the context of border securitization. The chapter also relied on research in Alberta that employs an intersectional lens to examine migrant precarity in relation to trafficking (see Julie Kaye and Bethany Hastie, "The Canadian Criminal Code Offences of Trafficking in Persons: Challenges from the Field and Within the Law, *Social Inclusion* 3, no. 1 [2015]: 88–102).

8   According to the UN Protocol, trafficking in persons refers to: "the recruitment, transportation, transfer, harbouring or receipt of persons, by means of the threat or use of force or other forms of coercion, of abduction, of fraud, of deception, of the abuse of power or of a position of vulnerability or of the giving or receiving of payments or benefits to achieve the consent of a person having control over another person, for the purpose of exploitation. Exploitation shall include, at a minimum, the exploitation of the prostitution of others or other forms of sexual exploitation, forced labour or services, slavery or practices similar to slavery, servitude or the removal of organs." See also "Trafficking in Persons," United Nations Office on Drugs and Crime (UNODC), 2007, http://www.unodc.org/documents/human-trafficking/HT_GPATleaflet07_en.pdf.

9   Kamala Kempadoo, "Introduction: From Moral Panic to Global Justice: Changing Perspectives on Trafficking," in *Trafficking and Prostitution Reconsidered: New Perspectives on Migration, Sex Work, and Human Rights*, eds. Kamala Kempadoo, Joyti Sanghera, and Bandana Pattanaik, vii–xxxiv (Boulder, CO: Paradigm Publishers, 2005); and Maggy Lee, *Trafficking and Global Crime Control* (Thousand Oaks, California: Sage, 2011).

10 Jennifer Suchland, *Economies of Violence: Transnational Feminism, Postsocialism, and the Politics of Sex Trafficking* (Durham: Duke University Press, 2015).

11 Anne Gallagher, "Human Rights and the New Protocols on Trafficking and Migrant Smuggling: A Preliminary Analysis," *Human Rights Quarterly* 23, no. 4 (2001): 975-1004.

12 Jyoti Sanghera, "Unpacking Trafficking Discourse," in *Trafficking and Prostitution Reconsidered: New Perspectives on Migration, Sex Work, and Human Rights*,

eds. Kamala Kempadoo, Joyti Sanghera, and Bandana Pattanaik, (Boulder, Colorado: Paradigm Publishers, 2005).

13 Julietta Hua, *Trafficking Women's Human Rights* (Minneapolis: Minnesota: University of Minnesota Press, 2011); Doezema, *Sex Slaves and Discourse Masters*; Anne Gallagher, *The International Law of Human Trafficking* (Cambridge: Cambridge University Press, 2010); Kempadoo, "Introduction: From Moral Panic to Global Justice"; Ann Jordan, "The Annotated Guide to the Complete UN Trafficking Protocol"; and NSWP: Global Network of Sex Work Projects, http://www.nswp.org.

14 Benedict Anderson, *Imagined Communities: Reflections on the Origin and Spread of* Nationalism (New York: Visco, 2006).

15 Maria Mies, *Patriarchy and Accumulation on a World Scale: Women in the International Division of Labour*, 6th ed. (New York: Zed Books, 1998); and Robert H. Wade, "Is Globalization Reducing Poverty and Inequality?" *World Development* 32, no. 4 (2004): 567–89.

16 Lee, *Trafficking and Global Crime Control*.

17 John Morrison and Beth Crosland, "The Trafficking and Smuggling of Refugee: The End Game in European Asylum Policy?" (UN High Commissioner for Refugees, working paper no. 39, 2001), http://www.unhcr.org/3af66c9b4.html; Sharma, "Travel Agency"; and Lee, *Trafficking and Global Crime Control*.

18 Postcolonial and anticolonial thinkers, such as Gayatri Spivak, have long critiqued the discursive power of representations of the "other" in colonial development discourses. See Gayatri Spivak, "Can the Subaltern Speak?" in *Marxism and the Interpretations of Culture*, eds. C. Nelson and L. Grossberb (Urbana, IL: University of Illinois Press, 1988): 271–313.

19 Barbara Adam and Joost Van Loon, "Introduction: Repositioning Risk: The Challenge for Social Theory," in *The Risk Society and Beyond: Critical Issues for Social Theory*, eds. Barbara Adam, Ulrich Beck, and Joost van Loon (London: Sage, 2000); and Ashley Bradimore and Harald Bauder, "Mystery Ships and Risky Boat People: Tamil Refugee Migration in the Newsprint Media," *Canadian Journal of Communication* (2011): 637–61.

20 Kevin Bales, *Understanding Global* Slavery (Berkeley: University of California, 2004); and Benjamin Perrin, *Invisible Chains: Canada's Underground World of Human Trafficking* (Toronto: Penguin Group, 2010).

21 Louise Shelley, *Human Trafficking: A Global Perspective* (Cambridge: Cambridge University Press, 2010).

22 Claudia Aradau, "The Perverse Politics of Four-Letter Words: Risk and Pity in the Securitisation of Human Trafficking," *Millennium Journal of International Studies* 33, no. 2 (2004): 251–78; and Julia O'Connell Davidson, "New

Slavery, Old Binaries: Human Trafficking and the Borders of 'Freedom,'"
Global Networks 10, no. 2 (2010): 244–61.

23 Leah Vosko, *Managing the Margins: Gender, Citizenship, and the International Regulation of Precarious Employment* (Oxford: Oxford University Press, 2009); and Genevieve LeBaron, "Unfree Labour Beyond Binaries," *International Feminist Journal of Politics* 17, no. 1 (2015): 1–19.

24 Nandita Sharma, *Home Economics: Nationalism and the Making of 'Migrant Workers' in Canada* (Toronto: University of Toronto Press, 2006).

25 Jef Huysmans, *The Politics of Insecurity* (Abingdon: Routledge, 2006).

26 Zygmunt Bauman, *Globalization: The Human Consequences* (New York: Colombia University Press, 1988); Suzanne Williams and Rachel Masika, "Editorial," in *Gender and Development* 10 (2002): 2–9; Saskia Sassen, "Women's Burden: Counter Geographies of Globalization and the Feminization of Survival," in *Feminist Post Development Thought: Re-Thinking Modernity, Post Colonialism, and Representation*, ed. Kriemild Saunders (London: Zed Books, 2002), 89–104; and Kapur, "The 'Other' Side of Globalization."

27 Sassen, "Women's Burden."

28 LeBaron, "Unfree Labour Beyond Binaries."

29 Alison Brysk, *People Out of Place: Globalization, Human Rights, and the Citizenship Gap* (New York: Routledge, 2004).

30 "National Action Plan to Combat Human Trafficking," Public Safety Canada, 2012, https://www.publicsafety.gc.ca/cnt/rsrcs/pblctns/ntnl-ctn-pln-cmbt/ntnl-ctn-pln-cmbt-eng.pdf.

31 Janie A. Chuang, "Exploitation Creep and the Unmaking of Human Trafficking Law," *American Journal of International Law* 108, no. 4 (2014): 609–49.

32 O'Connell Davidson, "New Slavery, Old Binaries," 245.

33 According to Section 118 of IRPA, "(1) No person shall knowingly organize the coming into Canada of one or more persons by means of abduction, fraud, deception or use or threat of force or coercion ... (2) For the purpose of subsection (1), *organize*, with respect to persons, includes their recruitment or transportation and, after their entry into Canada, the receipt or harbouring of those persons." Immigration and Refugee Protection Act (SC 2001, c. 27), http://laws-lois.justice.gc.ca/eng/acts/I-2.5.

34 Kaye's *Responding to Human Trafficking* troubles the construction of this split between "international" and "domestic" in the context of settler colonialism in Canada. In terms of the Criminal Code, Section 279.01 states, "(1) Every person who recruits, transports, transfers, receives, holds, conceals or harbours a person ... or exercises control, direction or influence over the movements of a person ... for the purpose of exploiting them or facilitating

their exploitation is guilty of an indictable offence ... No consent to the activity that forms the subject-matter of a charge under subsection (1) is valid. Criminal Code (RSC, 1985, c. C-46), http://laws-lois.justice.gc.ca /eng/AnnualStatutes/2010_3/page-1.html.

35 Julie Kaye, John Winterdyk, and Lara Quarterman, "Beyond Criminal Justice: A Case Study of Responding to Human Trafficking in Canada," *Canadian Journal of Criminology and Criminal Justice* 56, no. 1 (2014): 23–48.

36 Jill Hanley, Jacqueline Oxman Martinez, Marie Lacroix, and Gal Sigalit, "The 'Undeserving' Undocumented? Government and Community Responses to Human Trafficking as a Labour Phenomenon," *Labour, Capital, and Society* 39, no. 2 (2006): 78–103.

37 Jacqueline Oxman Martinez, Jill Hanley, and Fanny Gomez, "Canadian Policy on Human Trafficking: A Four-Year Analysis," *International Migration* 43, no. 4 (2005): 7–26.

38 Kaye and Hastie, "Criminal Code Offence of Trafficking in Persons."

39 Kaye, *Responding to Human Trafficking*; and Jennifer Suchland, *Economies of Violence*.

40 Suchland, *Economies of Violence*, 3.

41 "National Action Plan to Combat Human Trafficking," Public Safety Canada.

42 Sassen, "Women's Burden"; Philip McMichael, *Development and Social Change: A Global Perspective*, 4th ed. (Thousand Oaks: Pine Forge Press, 2012).

43 Hua, *Trafficking Women's Rights*; Kapur, "The 'Other' Side of Globalization"; and Yvon Dandurand, *Human Trafficking: Exploring the International Concerns, Nature, and Complexities*, eds. Benjamin Perrin, Philip Reichel, and John Winterdyk (Boca Raton, Florida: CRC Press, 2012).

44 Hanley, Martinez, Lacroix, and Sigalit, "The 'Undeserving' Undocumented?"

45 Sharma, *Home Economics*.

46 Julie Kaye, "Intersections of Race, Class, and Gender in Human Trafficking in Alberta: An Environmental Scan," Government of Alberta, Ministry of Human Resources, 2015, http://www.actalberta.org/wp-content/uploads /2017/04/intersections.pdf.

47 Kaye, Winterdyk, and Quarterman, "Beyond Criminal Justice."

48 Kaye, "Intersections of Race, Class, and Gender."

49 Kaye and Hastie, "Criminal Code Offence of Trafficking in Persons."

50 The following sections are reproduced from a broader theoretical discussion in Kaye, *Responding to Human Trafficking*.

51 Audrey Macklin, "Dancing Across Borders: "'Exotic Dancers,' Trafficking, and Canadian Immigration Policy," *International Migration Review* 37, no. (2): 454.

52 This department has since been expanded and renamed to Employment and Social Development Canada.

53 Audrey Macklin, "Dancing Across Borders," 467.

54 Ibid.; and "Legislative Summary of Bill C-10," Library of Parliament: Parliamentary Information and Research Services," 2012, http://www.parl.gc.ca/Content/LOP/LegislativeSummaries/41/1/c10-e.pdf.

55 Bekki Ross, "Striptease on the Line: Investigating Trends in Erotic Entertainment," in *Making Normal: Social Regulation in Canada*, ed. Deborah Brock (Toronto: Nelson, 2003), 146–75.

56 Audrey Macklin, "Dancing Across Borders."

57 Ibid.

58 Ibid., 478.

59 *Silion v. Canada (Minister of Citizenship and Immigration)*, 1999 CanLII 8608 (FC).

60 Editorial, *Globe and Mail*, 2 December 2004.

61 "Legislative Summary of Bill C-10," Library of Parliament.

62 Ibid., 146.

63 National Action Plan to Combat Human Trafficking, Public Safety Canada, 2012, https://www.publicsafety.gc.ca/cnt/rsrcs/pblctns/ntnl-ctn-pln-cmbt/index-en.aspx.

64 Adrian Morrow, "How Hungarian Criminals Built a Slave Trade in Ontario, *Globe and Mail*, 2 April 2012, updated 26 March 2017, https://www.theglobeandmail.com/news/national/how-hungarian-criminals-built-a-slave-trade-in-ontario/article4097573.

65 Ibid.

66 "Human Trafficking in Canada," RCMP.

67 Ibid.

68 Ibid., 19. See also Jeffrey, "Canada and Migrant Sex Work; Leslie Ann Jeffrey and Gayle MacDonald, "'It's in the Money, Honey': The Economy of Sex Workers in the Maritimes," *Canadian Review of Sociology and Anthropology* 43, no. 3 (2006): 313–27; and Cecilia Benoit and Frances Shaver, "Critical Issues and New Directions in Sex Work Research," *Canadian Review of Sociology and Anthropology* 43, no. 3 (2006): 243–52.

69 "Human Trafficking in Canada," RCMP.

70 Ibid., 20.

71 "Trafficking in Persons," UNODC.

72 "Human Trafficking in Canada," RCMP; see, generally, United Nations Office on Drugs and Crime Research Database; and "Trafficking in Persons Report 2012," US Department of State, https://www.state.gov/j/tip/rls/tiprpt/2012. See also *R. v. Nakpangi* 2008 OJ No 6022 (guilty plea); *R v. St Vil*, [2008] OJ

No 6023 (QL) (guilty plea); *R v. Urizar* 2010 JCQ L-017.10 (upheld on appeal, 2013 QCCA 46) (verdict by judge); *R v. Estrella* 2011 OJ No 6616 (QL) (verdict by jury); *R v. AA* 2012 OJ No 6256 (QL) (upheld on appeal, 2013 OJ No 3192 [QL]) (verdict by jury); *R v. Byron* 2013 ONSC 6427, [2013], OJ no 5396 (verdict by judge); *R v. Domotor, Domotor, and Kolompar*, [2012] OJ No 3630 (Ont SCJ) (guilty plea); and the cases of Emerson (guilty plea) (see RCMP, 2010, 25); Vilutis (guilty plea) (see RCMP 2010, 25); and Lennox (guilty plea) (see RCMP 2010, 26).

73 Kaye and Hastie, "Criminal Code Offence of Trafficking in Persons."
74 "Conviction Obtained in Human Trafficking and Human Smuggling Investigation," *The Trustline*, 10 October 2012, https://thetrustline.wordpress.com/2012/10/10/conviction-obtained-in-human-trafficking-and-human-smuggling-investigation.
75 *R. v. Morris*, 2016 ABQB, 150593093Q1.
76 Paula Simons, "Edmonton Entrepreneur's Shocking Business Secret? Exploiting Foreign Workers, *Edmonton Journal*, 20 May 2016, http://edmontonjournal.com/opinion/columnists/paula-simons-edmonton-entrepreneurs-shocking-business-secret-exploiting-foreign-workers.
77 See, for example, Kaye, *Responding to Human Trafficking*; "Asian Sex Workers Facing Arrests and Violence in Canada," NSWP: Global Network of Sex Work Projects, 4 Feburary 2016, http://www.nswp.org/news/asian-sex-workers-facing-arrests-and-violence-canada; Catherine McIntyre, "Migrant Sex Workers Caught up in Ottawa Sting Facing Deportation, Further Exploitation," *National Post*, 13 May 2015, http://nationalpost.com/news/canada/migrant-sex-workers-caught-up-in-ottawa-sting-facing-deportation-further-exploitation-activists; and "Collateral Damage: The Impact of Anti-Trafficking Measures on Human Rights Around the World," Global Alliance Against Traffic in Women (GAATW), 2007, https://www.iom.int/jahia/webdav/shared/shared/mainsite/microsites/IDM/workshops/ensuring_protection_070909/collateral_damage_gaatw_2007.pdf.
78 "Human Trafficking in Canada," RCMP.
79 Ibid.
80 "Human Trafficking: Victim Impact Statements," *Hamilton Spectator*, 2009, https://www.scribd.com/document/84688173/Human-Trafficking-Victim-impact-statements; and Morrow, "How Hungarian Criminals Built a Slave Trade."
81 Although, charges under IRPA related to this form of trafficking in the Criminal Code legislation provide a higher threshold, including more substantial repercussions.
82 "Human Trafficking in Canada," RCMP.

83 Sarah Boesveld, "Editorial," *National Post*, 22 April 2012.

84 "Human Trafficking," *Hamilton Spectator*.

85 For a discussion of this clause, see Rekha McNutt, "Pre-Removal Risk
    Assessments (PRRA)," Caron and Partners LLP, 19 January 2016, http://www
    .caronpartners.com/immigration-blog/2016/1/19/pre-removal-risk-
    assessments-prra.

86 This waiting period has increased to thirty-six months for failed claimants
    from "a designated country of origin."

87 Ibid.

88 Boesveld, "Editorial."

89 "National Action Plan to Combat Human Trafficking," Public Safety
    Canada.

90 Lee, *Trafficking and Global Crime Control*, 1–2.

PART TWO

The Criminalization and the Exclusion of Refugees in Canada and Abroad

4

Recent Jurisprudential Trends in the Interpretation of Complicity in Article 1F(a) Crimes

Nancy Weisman

"Criminal responsibility does not fall solely upon direct perpetrators of crime. A murder conviction, for example, can attach equally to one who pulls the trigger and one who provides the gun. Complicity is a defining characteristic of crimes in the international context, where some of the world's worst crimes are committed often at a distance, by a multitude of actors."[1] So begins the decision of the Supreme Court of Canada (scc) in *Ezokola v. Canada (Citizenship and Immigration)*, which rearticulated the test to be applied in Canada for complicity in Article 1F(a) crimes, such as crimes against humanity and war crimes, to those claiming refugee protection under the United Nations *Convention Relating to the Status of Refugees* (the Refugee Convention).[2] It is instructive to review the Federal Court decisions over the five years after the *Ezokola* decision was released, in 2013, which have interpreted and adapted the legal test for complicity set out by the scc in this important decision. While the scc, in setting out its new test, provided a comprehensive guide to the concept of complicity in crimes against humanity, it is the Federal Court, in its judicial review of decisions of the Immigration and Refugee Board of Canada (IRB), that will determine the scope of the new test in relation to particular fact situations.

THE SCC DECISION IN *EZOKOLA*

People who come to Canada and claim refugee protection must prove to the Refugee Protection Division (RPD) of the IRB that they are either a Convention refugee or a person in need of protection, pursuant to section 95(1)(*b*) of the Immigration and Refugee Protection Act (IRPA).[3] However, section 98 of the IRPA provides that those who fall within the Article 1F(a) exclusion clause of the Refugee Convention are excluded from refugee protection in Canada if there are "serious reasons for considering that [they have] committed a crime against peace, a war crime, or a crime against humanity."[4] The SCC noted that "the *Refugee Convention's* commitment to refugee protection is broad, but not unbounded. It does not protect international criminals."[5] Put more directly, the SCC said that "those who create refugees are not refugees themselves."[6]

The SCC noted that it is not necessary to distinguish between principals, aiders and abettors, or other criminal participants when considering exclusion under Article 1F(a), since persons may be excluded from refugee protection for international crimes through a variety of modes of commission.[7] Hence, a person may have "committed" crimes against humanity in the context of Article 1F(a) even if they were not directly responsible for "pulling the trigger" or committing the actual act of torture; rather, they can be found to be complicit in such acts, and therefore excluded from refugee protection. However, a person is not complicit in crimes against humanity merely through "guilt by association."[8]

The decision in *Ezokola* is the first time that the SCC has provided guidance regarding where to draw "the line between association and complicity," asking the important question, "when does mere association become culpable complicity?"[9] The Court noted that it needed "to determine what degree of knowledge and participation in a criminal activity justifies excluding secondary actors from refugee protection."[10]

To understand the decision of the SCC in *Ezokola* it is necessary to set out the relevant facts and review briefly the judicial history of the case. Rachidi Ekanza Ezokola began working for the government of the Democratic Republic of Congo (DRC) in 1999 and worked in various ministries.[11] He was eventually assigned to the Permanent Mission of the DRC to the United Nations and "represented the DRC at international meetings and UN entities."[12] He acted in various capacities at the UN and "led the Permanent Mission of the DRC and spoke before the Security Council regarding natural resources and conflicts in the DRC."[13] He resigned in 2008 because, he says, he did not want to serve in a corrupt and violent government, and as a result he received threats from DRC intelligence and then fled to Canada and claimed refugee protection with his wife and children.[14]

The issue faced by the RPD when adjudicating his refugee claim was whether Ezokola had "committed" crimes against humanity in the context of Article 1F(a), not because he had personally committed the crimes against humanity committed by the government of the DRC during the time that he represented it at the UN, but whether as a result of that activity he was "complicit" in those crimes and as such should be excluded from refugee protection. Based on the existing Canadian case law of the Federal Court and the Federal Court of Appeal at the time, the RPD found him complicit in the crimes against humanity committed by those in the DRC acting on behalf of the government and excluded him from refugee protection.[15]

The Federal Court disagreed with the finding of the RPD and "determined that an individual cannot be excluded under art. 1F(a) merely because he had been an employee of a state whose government commits international crimes. Complicity requires a nexus between the claimant and the crimes committed by the government."[16] On appeal to the Federal Court of Appeal, the appellate court rejected this "new test" put forward by the Federal Court as being too narrow and reaffirmed its own jurisprudence, holding that "a senior official may, by remaining in his or her position without protest and continuing to defend the interests of his or her government while being aware of the crimes committed by this government demonstrate 'personal and knowing participation' in these crimes and be complicit with the government in their commission."[17]

The SCC allowed the appeal, and while it acknowledged that "senior officials *may* be held criminally responsible for crimes committed by their government" in such circumstances, this will not always be the case, since "[c]omplicity arises by contribution."[18] Hence the Court replaced the existing test for complicity by the Federal Court of Appeal in *Ramirez v. Canada (Minister of Employment and Immigration)*, the "personal and knowing participation test," with a "contribution-based approach to complicity."[19] The SCC set out the new test for complicity as follows: "an individual will be excluded from refugee protection under art. 1F(a) for complicity in international crimes if there are serious reasons for considering that he or she voluntarily made a knowing and significant contribution to the crime or criminal purpose of the group alleged to have committed the crime."[20]

It is noteworthy that while this new test does not require a link to a particular crime, there must at least be a link between the person and the criminal purpose of the group.[21] Hence, there need not be evidence that the person's activities are linked to a particular crime committed, but there must at least be evidence that the person made a knowing and significant contribution to the criminal purpose of the group alleged to have committed the crime. The Court described this new approach to complicity as requiring "a nexus between the individual and the group's crime or criminal purpose."[22]

The reason given by the SCC to reformulate the test for complicity is that the existing test had "been overextended to capture individuals on the basis of complicity by association."[23] While it is beyond the scope of this paper to review the reasoning underlying the Court's conclusions in the reformulation of the complicity test, it is important to note that the Court expressed a need "to bring Canadian law in line with international criminal law, the humanitarian purposes of the *Refugee Convention*, and fundamental criminal law principles."[24]

The question, then, is what type of activity and what degree of participation would satisfy the "contribution-based" test for complicity? Does there have to be evidence that the person was present during the commission of the crimes against humanity? Must the person have contributed tangibly to the crimes in question? And what degree of knowledge of the crimes must the person have possessed during the commission of the crimes? The SCC stated that someone "can be complicit without being present at the crime and without physically contributing to the crime ... [T]o be excluded from the definition of refugee protection, there must be evidence that the individual knowingly made at least a significant contribution to the group's crime or criminal purpose. Passive membership would not be enough."[25]

To further clarify its new test that "there must be serious reasons for considering that the claimant has voluntarily made a significant and knowing contribution to the organization's crime or criminal purpose,"[26] the Court elaborated on three key elements: namely, that the contribution of the person must be "voluntary, significant, and knowing." And, to assist in the application of these elements to a particular fact situation, the Court set out a series of additional factors that may be considered, namely: "(i) the size and nature of the organization; (ii) the part of the organization with which the refugee claimant was most directly concerned; (iii) the refugee claimant's duties and activities within the organization; (iv) the refugee claimant's position or rank in the organization; (v) the length of time the refugee claimant was in the organization, particularly after acquiring knowledge of the group's crime or criminal purpose; and (vi) the method by which the refugee claimant was recruited and the refugee claimant's opportunity to leave the organization."[27] While the purpose of setting out these factors was to assist the RPD in applying the new complicity test to a refugee claimant's particular fact situation, the SCC felt it necessary to caution decision makers that "the focus must always remain on the individual's contribution to the crime or criminal purpose."[28] It would be contrary to the SCC decision to find complicity in a crime based solely on the application of the factors without ultimately determining whether the person "voluntarily made a significant and knowing contribution to the organization's crime or criminal purpose."

As to the "voluntariness" of the person's contribution to the organization's crime or criminal purpose, the Court said that it is necessary to "consider the method of recruitment by the organization and any opportunity to leave the organization. The voluntariness requirement captures the defence of duress."[29] A person's participation may not be seen as voluntary if there was evidence the person "was coerced into joining, supporting, or remaining in the organization."[30] However, the SCC did not state that evidence of coercion in these circumstances would always negate a finding of complicity; it merely stated that this is one factor to consider when considering voluntariness. The Court also stressed the importance of considering whether the person had the opportunity to leave the organization, as well as their specific resources to enable that exit, but emphasized that "the factors discussed ... should be relied on only for guidance."[31] Since the SCC did not provide concrete examples in which these factors may arise, it is left to the RPD and the Federal Court, which will judicially review the RPD decisions, to further refine and adapt the new complicity test to particular fact situations.

As to the "significant" aspect of the person's contribution to the organization's crime or criminal purpose, the Court cautioned that "given that contributions of almost every nature to a group could be characterized as furthering its criminal purpose, the degree of the contribution must be carefully assessed."[32] Related to this, the Court, once again, emphasized that the "contribution does not have to be 'directed to specific identifiable crimes' but can be directed to 'wider concepts of common design, such as the accomplishment of an organisation's purpose by whatever means are necessary including the commission of war crimes.'"[33] The Court goes on to state that this falls in line with international criminal law, as well as being consistent with section 21(2) of the Canadian Criminal Code,[34] "which attaches criminal liability based on assistance in carrying out a common unlawful purpose."[35] However, it is highly likely the scc did not intend to narrow "significant" contribution in the complicity test to the Criminal Code definition of common intention for parties to offences under section 21 of the Criminal Code, since the Court reaffirmed the need when interpreting Article 1F(a) to "look beyond the bounds of Canadian criminal law" to international criminal law.[36]

In providing further guidance regarding the "significant contribution" element of the complicity test, the Court noted that "[t]he size of an organization could help determine the likelihood that the claimant would have known of and participated in the crime or criminal purpose. A smaller organization could increase that likelihood."[37] In addition to the size of the organization, there must also be a consideration of the nature of the organization. The scc said that "where the group is identified as one with a limited and brutal purpose, the link between the contribution and the criminal purpose will be easier to establish."[38] The Court also noted that "[a] lengthy period of involvement may also increase the significance of an individual's contribution to the organization's crime or criminal purpose."[39] A person's "position or rank in the organization" may also affect the "significance" of a person's contribution, especially if they had "effective control over those directly responsible for criminal acts."[40]

Perhaps the most important factor to consider when assessing if a person's contribution is "significant" are their "duties and activities within the organization." According to the Court, this factor "goes to the heart of a claimant's day-to-day participation in the activities of the organization," and the RPD should "consider the link between the duties and activities of a claimant, and the crimes and criminal purposes of the organization."[41] Even for organizations with a limited and brutal purpose, the scc stressed that "the individual's conduct and role within the organization must still be carefully assessed, on an individualized basis, to determine whether the contribution was voluntarily made and had a significant impact on the crime or criminal purpose of the group."[42] The scc also emphasized the need to assess "the part of the organization with which the refugee claimant was most directly concerned."[43] Often organizations like a military or police force are very large and multifaceted, and the person's involvement in the organization is limited to one department in a specific location, quite separate from the unit involved in crimes. In such circumstances, the Court said that "where only one part of the organization in question was involved in the crime or criminal purpose, a claimant's exclusive affiliation with another part(s) of the organization may serve to exonerate him or her for the purpose of art. 1F(a)."[44]

The final element in the complicity test is that the person must have made a "knowing contribution" to the organization's crime or criminal purpose. The Court said that "[t]o be complicit in crimes committed by the government, the official must be aware of the government's crime or criminal purpose and aware that his or her *conduct* will assist in the furtherance of the crime or criminal purpose."[45] If an organization may be identified as "one with a limited and brutal purpose," the Court said that "a decision maker may more readily infer that the accused had knowledge of the group's criminal purpose and that his conduct contributed to that purpose."[46] The Court also noted that "[a] high ranking individual in an organization may be more likely to have knowledge of that organization's crime or criminal purpose."[47] Also, the longer a period of time that a person has spent in an organization will "increase the chance that the individual had knowledge of the organization's crime or criminal purpose."[48]

Despite this guidance relating to the three elements of a "voluntary, significant, and knowing" contribution, the scc, rather than provide specific examples of when a person's activities may fall within the new complicity test, has left it to the IRB and the Federal Court to apply these concepts to particular fact situations. The Court did note, however, that the former test for complicity, the "personal and knowing participation" test,[49] had "inappropriately shifted its focus towards the criminal activities of the group and away from the individual's contribution to that criminal activity."[50] The Court has been quite clear that mere membership in an organization that has been responsible for the commission of crimes against humanity is not sufficient to establish complicity in those crimes.[51] The Court did give examples of cases in which it believed the approach to complicity in Canadian law had been overextended by excluding people based primarily on their membership in an organization without focussing on their actual activities.[52]

The scc allowed the appeal in *Ezokola* and sent the case back to the RPD to rehear Ezokola's refugee protection claim and to apply the new test for complicity, directing that "[a] detailed assessment is required to determine whether the particular facts of this case establish serious reasons for considering that the *actus reus* and *mens rea* for complicity are present and therefore justify excluding the appellant from the definition of refugee by operation of art. 1F(a) of the *Refugee Convention.*"[53]

THE INTERPRETATION OF *EZOKOLA* IN THE CASE LAW

Since the scc's release of the *Ezokola* decision in 2013, there have been several cases in which the Federal Court has had the opportunity to interpret and apply the new "contribution-based" complicity test. One of the first opportunities of the Federal Court to consider the new complicity test was *Mudiyanselage v. Canada (Citizenship and Immigration).*[54] In that case the RPD had excluded a person, a citizen of Sri Lanka, for being complicit in crimes against humanity on the basis that he had been a police officer in the Sri Lanka Police (SLP) during a period in which the SLP had committed crimes against humanity. He held a mid-level management position in the force.[55] It would appear that the RPD, in finding the claimant complicit, found that the claimant was aware of the human rights abuses committed by the SLP, and by failing to protect the victims of this abuse he was complicit in the crimes committed by others.[56] Since the RPD decision preceded the release of the scc decision in *Ezokola*, the RPD applied the former complicity test of "personal and knowing participation." The Court questioned "whether it is fair and just to set the decision aside because the RPD rendered it on an application of a legal standard ... with respect to complicity under Article 1F(a) that has been "clarified" by the Supreme Court of Canada."[57] The Court decided to return the case back to the RPD for redetermination because "the Supreme Court of Canada's efforts to bring clarity to complicity under Article 1F(a) has the effect of impugning the RPD's decision. This is so because the legal test applied by the RPD has been effectively extinguished as a matter of law."[58] The Court acknowledged that in formulating a new test for complicity the scc made "it clear that an overextended approach to complicity is to be avoided."[59] Though not analyzing whether in fact this had occurred in this case, given that the "overextended approach to complicity" in the form of the old test had been applied by the RPD, the Court determined that it was more appropriate to send the matter back to the RPD to apply the new complicity test.

The next opportunity the Federal Court had to consider the new complicity test was in *Kamanzi v. Canada (Citizenship and Immigra-*

tion),[60] when it reviewed a decision of the RPD made prior to the SCC decision in *Ezokola*. James Mobwano Kamanzi, a citizen of the DRC, was recruited in 1996 as an intelligence agent by a leader of the Alliance des forces démocratiques pour la libération du Congo-Zaïre (AFDL). It was not a salaried post, and instead he received periodic gifts of food, gas, and money. He was tasked with checking information on local affairs and continued this work into 1999.[61] In fact, Kamanzi described himself as the "right hand man" of Masasu, the leader.[62] At issue before the RPD was whether he was complicit in war crimes or crimes against humanity, since he worked as an intelligence officer for one of the main leaders and military commanders of the AFDL, which among other crimes had recruited 10,000 child soldiers in 1996 and 1997.[63] The RPD determined that the claimant's work as an intelligence officer was entirely voluntary. It also found that Kamanzi was aware of the recruitment of child soldiers by the AFDL and, in fact, had testified at the RPD hearing that he had provided intelligence in relation to families that did not want their children to join the AFDL.[64]

The RPD excluded Kamanzi on the basis that he was complicit in war crimes, a decision that was finalized prior to the formulation of the new test for complicity by the SCC in *Ezokola*. At issue for the Federal Court was whether the decision of the RPD could stand in light of the modified complicity test.[65] In upholding the RPD decision the Court applied the "futility doctrine" as set out in *Sivakumar v. Canada (Minister of Employment and Immigration)*[66] that "if no properly instructed tribunal could come to a different conclusion, the decision may be upheld."[67] The Court acknowledged the new complicity test in *Ezokola*, and determined that were the case to be returned to the RPD "with instructions to apply the Supreme Court test of active knowing participation as the basis for complicity, the Board would conclude the matter by having 'serious reasons to consider' that the applicant voluntarily and knowingly participated in the conscription of child soldiers."[68] In coming to this conclusion the Court noted that Kamanzi had provided information about families who did not want their children to join the AFDL, and hence he had been "directly involved in providing Masasu with important intelligence regarding those who opposed the recruitment of child soldiers, which Mr Masasu then acted upon. His personal work thus facilitated the terrible crime."[69] The Court held it would be futile to return the matter to the RPD because if properly instructed the RPD would come to the same conclusion that he had "participated in the war crime of conscripting child soldiers."[70]

Though in *Kamanzi* the Court did not thoroughly analyze the key elements of the new complicity test, namely whether he "voluntarily made a significant and knowing contribution to the organization's crime or criminal purpose," by finding that Kamanzi had participated in the war crime of conscripting child soldiers and by applying the futility doctrine, the Court clearly agreed that the key elements of the new complicity test had been met.

In contrast to *Kamanzi*, the Federal Court refused to apply the "futility doctrine" in *Aazamyar v. Canada (Citizenship and Immigration)*.[71] While in this case the Federal Court was reviewing an officer's decision to reject a humanitarian and compassionate application, as opposed to a review of the decision of the RPD, the comments made by the Court with respect to the test in *Ezokola* are nevertheless instructive. Aazamyar was a citizen of Afghanistan who sought refugee protection in Canada. The RPD, which decided the case prior to the release of the SCC decision in *Ezokola*, excluded him from refugee protection under Article 1F(a) of the Refugee Convention because it found that as a captain in the Afghan Air Force, he was complicit in the war crimes and crimes against humanity committed by that organization. Aazamyar claimed that he was just an instructor who mainly trained civilian pilots. The RPD said that Aazamyar knew or should have known about the crimes the Afghan Air Force was committing and could have fled without repercussions.[72]

The officer whose decision was being reviewed made no mention of the decision in *Ezokola* and instead adopted and quoted from the RPD decision that Aazamyar "knew, or ought to have known, that pilots he trained operated in support of this goal [terrify, maim and kill civilians] and that he is not credible when he alleged that he trained pilots for commercial purposes only."[73] The Court described as troublesome the RPD finding that he "knew, or ought to have known" about the goals of the Air Force, and stated that this finding "appears to be very much like the sort of 'guilt by association' that was rejected by *Ezokola*."[74] Although counsel for the Minister urged the Court to apply the "futility doctrine," as had been done in *Kamanzi*, the Court refused to do so and returned the matter back to be determined in accordance with the decision in *Ezokola*.[75]

In *Moya v. Canada (Citizenship and Immigration)*,[76] the Federal Court determined that the RPD properly applied the decision in

Ezokola and excluded the claimant, a citizen of Peru, from refugee protection based on his complicity in the actions of the Shining Path, an organization responsible for numerous crimes against humanity, including murder, kidnapping, and forcible confinement.[77] While studying in the faculty of chemical engineering at a university in Peru, Moya voluntarily provided two litres of acid meant for making bombs to his professor, who was affiliated with the Shining Path.[78] The RPD, applying the complicity test in *Ezokola*, determined that Moya was complicit in crimes against humanity "because of his significant, voluntary and conscious contribution to the crimes perpetrated by the [Shining Path]."[79] In coming to this conclusion, the RPD rejected the credibility of the claimant's evidence that he had contributed the acid under armed threat of members of the Shining Path.[80] The RPD concluded the following regarding the evidence: the Shining Path is an organization directed to a limited, brutal purpose; though not a member, Moya had contact with the Shining Path; and Moya contributed to the Shining Path's activities because he knowingly gave them chemical material, and in return Moya received free access to university services.[81]

The Court noted that the RPD had conducted a "methodical analysis of each of the non-exhaustive criteria"[82] in *Ezokola*. With respect to the voluntary nature of his contribution to the Shining Path, the RPD rejected the defence of duress raised by Moya for lack of credibility.[83] Regarding the nature of his contribution, the RPD determined that "the contribution of the two litres of acid is a significant contribution, since the bombs made with these chemicals were used to kill people" and that "this material was used to make 'high impact' domestic bombs."[84] Finally, the RPD found that Moya "contributed consciously since he was aware that the use of these chemicals was intended to make deadly bombs ... [H]e knew of the ideology and abuses committed by the [Shining Path] ... [H]e knew that the [Shining Path] was using explosives, in particular to blow up bridges, colleges and town halls."[85] According to the Court, the complicity finding of the RPD, in light of *Ezokola*, was reasonable, and hence it determined that "the Court's intervention is not warranted."[86]

The Federal Court also found that the RPD properly applied the complicity test in *Ezokola* to the facts in *Ndikumasabo v. Canada (Citizenship and Immigration)*.[87] The Court found it was reasonable for the RPD to exclude the claimant, a citizen of Burundi and former civil servant, for being complicit in crimes against humanity. Ndikumasabo had been district chief in an area where massacres had taken place. The Court said that "[t]here is no doubt that the Burundi government, particularly the Ministry of the Interior and the local administrators under its leadership, were complicit in the crimes against humanity committed mainly against the Hutu population in 1972. The documentary evidence reveals that these systematic, generalized crimes were largely perpetrated by people in positions of authority, including in the regional administration."[88] In its assessment of the RPD decision the Court noted that the RPD methodically analyzed the complicity test based on the *Ezokola* factors and the contribution-based test.[89] The RPD had concluded that his actions were voluntary, his contribution to the crime was significant based on his duties and responsibilities, and he had knowledge of the crimes committed.

The Court noted with approval that the RPD analyzed each of the six factors put forward by the SCC in *Ezokola* in order to determine whether the claimant "voluntarily made a significant and knowing contribution to the crimes or criminal purpose of the Ministry of the Interior."[90] The Court said that, given that Ndikumasabo had been the commissioner in certain districts, "it was reasonable for the RPD to conclude that [he] was aware of the government's contributions to the 1972 massacres."[91] It found that given the applicant's duties, including holding meetings and managing centralized data regarding the population in his district, "the RPD reasonably concluded that the applicant ... contributed to facilitating the deployment of trucks making it possible to dig graves to bury thousands of bodies."[92] While his duties were found to be "broad and included agricultural management, market maintenance, literacy, birth records, hygiene, crop distribution to peasants, support to commune administrators and support to the population,"[93] the broadness of his work did not detract from the finding that he was complicit in crimes against humanity. The Court found that, given that he was second in command in the province, the RPD reasonably concluded that he "was aware of the decisions made in his district and ... he did nothing to dissociate himself from the crimes being committed," and that he "continued to occupy this position during the time of the crimes committed in spring 1972."[94]

In a recent decision of the Federal Court, *Habibi v. Canada (Citizenship and Immigration)*,[95] the RPD's complicity finding was not upheld and the case was sent back to the RPD for redetermination. The claimant in *Habibi* had been a police officer in Iran for twenty-eight years, working as a criminal investigation officer, and retired in 2002.[96] The RPD excluded him on the basis that he had "committed a crime" in the context of Article 1F(a).[97] It found that even though there was no evidence of his direct involvement in crimes against humanity, given Habibi's long service and his senior rank in the Iranian police force, which actively supported other security and enforcement agencies, he was aware of actions against the Iranian people and "he would have been involved directly or indirectly through direction to others in acts which have been determined by international law to be 'crimes against humanity.'"[98]

While the RPD did not specifically refer to the test and the six factors to be used as guidance when applying the complicity test in *Ezokola*, the Court said that "[this] fact alone does not make its decision unreasonable."[99] The Court, however, said that even if the RPD understood the complicity test in *Ezokola* – as there were some references to the test – the decision of the RPD "as a whole rests more upon a 'guilt by association' approach to complicity, an approach which was explicitly rejected in *Ezokola.*"[100] The mistake of the RPD in its complicity analysis was that it "should have clearly set its mind to a full and transparent assessment and analysis of the relevancy and weight of the six factors ... The failure to explicitly set out the test and factors for complicity, while in itself not a fatal flaw in the RPD's decision, strongly indicates that the RPD did not reasonably or properly consider the six factors and their respective relevance or weight."[101] While the RPD considered the duties of Habibi as a police officer, it was unable to show how he had "*personally* made a significant and knowing contribution to some crime or crime against humanity."[102] What the Court found problematic was that the reasoning of the RPD resembled guilt by association, a concept that had been categorically rejected by the SCC in *Ezokola.* The flawed reasoning of the RPD was that "Habibi is associated with the national police force, and because the police in turn are associated with other enforcement organizations which committed crimes against humanity, that makes him complicit in those crimes."[103] The Court noted that "[t]here was no evidence before the RPD that Habibi in particular, or other members of the District 8 Police Station in Tabriz, had participated in any abuses or played any role in working with other enforcement agencies."[104] It pointed out that one of the six factors in *Ezokola* is "the size and nature of the organization" and that the Iranian "national police force numbered some 50,000 members during the mid-1980s," yet the RPD did not explain the link between Habibi's work as a police officer and the crimes or criminal purpose of that organization.[105]

While the SCC in *Ezokola* provided the six factors as a guide to assist the RPD in determining whether the new complicity test has been met, without a sufficient analysis of these factors it may be difficult for the RPD to assess whether there are serious reasons for considering that the refugee claimant has voluntarily made a significant and knowing contribution to the organization's crime or criminal purpose. While a systematic analysis of each of the factors is the more prudent approach in assessing complicity, it will still be up to the individual IRB decision maker "to determine which factors are significant" in the context of the particular facts of a case.[106]

One such decision in which the Federal Court determined the decision maker appropriately considered the necessary factors in the context of the complicity test is *Parra v. Canada (Citizenship and Immigration).*[107] In that case, the Federal Court judicially reviewed a decision of the Immigration Division (ID), which determined that the person concerned was inadmissible to Canada under section 35(1)(a) of the IRPA for violating human or international rights by being complicit in crimes against humanity. Parra was a citizen of Colombia and did his mandatory military service with the Twentieth Brigade of the Colombian military, from 1985 to 1986.[108] Upon his arrival in Canada he made a claim for refugee protection, but based on his interview with the Canadian Border Services Agency (CBSA), he was referred to the ID for an admissibility hearing pursuant to section 35(1)(a) of the IRPA. Based on his participation in the Colombian military the ID determined that he had "committed" crimes against humanity as a result of being complicit in such crimes and was therefore inadmissible to Canada.[109]

The Court noted that "[t]here is no dispute between the parties that the 20th Brigade was engaged in the commission of acts that amounted to crimes against humanity during the period the applicant served with the unit."[110] Since there was no evidence that Parra had personally committed crimes against humanity, the issue before the ID was whether he was complicit in the crimes against humanity committed by members of his unit based on his actual duties in the Twentieth Brigade.

The duties of Parra while in the Twentieth Brigade involved "surveying and arresting individuals and bringing them to where he knew they would be interrogated and tortured. This included surveillance of the Fuerzas Armadas Revolucionarias de Colombia [FARC] and paramilitaries by listening to, taping or intercepting communications. The applicant would also secure the areas where more senior officers were interrogating and torturing individuals. The applicant witnessed acts of torture, and some of the victims of torture included members of the civilian population."[111] The question the ID had to consider was whether these activities and level of knowledge were sufficient to find that he voluntarily made a significant and knowing contribution to the organization's crime or criminal purpose, even though there was no evidence that he personally committed any acts of torture.

In contrast to *Habibi*, in *Parra* the ID assessed the six factors identified in *Ezokola* and "the key components of the contribution-based test for complicity" to determine that Parra was complicit in crimes against humanity.[112] The ID found "that while the applicant did not participate in torture, he was aware of it, was close to it, supported it, did not question it, and sought employment with the Columbian (sic) military even after leaving the 20th Brigade at the completion of his compulsory service" and hence his involvement with the Twentieth Brigade constituted a significant and knowing contribution to crimes against humanity.[113]

Regarding the issue of voluntariness, Parra had raised the issue of duress before the ID, which if accepted could have served to negate a finding that he was complicit in crimes against humanity. However, the ID determined that his "actions while serving in the 20th Brigade were voluntary," and the Federal Court found there was a "rational basis" for that finding.[114] The Court ruled that the ID reasonably concluded that Parra was inadmissible to Canada based on its complicity findings.[115]

CONCLUSION

A review of the cases decided by the Federal Court following the decision of the SCC in *Ezokola* makes it clear that this decision has had and will continue to have a significant impact on how cases involving complicity in Article 1F(a) crimes, such as crimes against humanity and war crimes, are analyzed at the IRB. As noted, the SCC reformulated the test for complicity so that it would be in conformity with international law, and in so doing substituted a long-standing test with one that requires that the person's contribution to the crime or criminal purpose of the group to which they belonged was voluntary, significant, and knowing. The Court said a finding of complicity in a crime against humanity does not require that a link be made between the person and a particular crime, but there must at least be a link between the person and the criminal purpose of the group. And, to assess whether the actions of the person were voluntary, significant, and knowing, the Court set out six factors that decision makers should consider when assessing complicity in crimes. While a failure to explicitly list these factors is not necessarily fatal to an IRB decision, the case law demonstrates that a more prudent approach is a systematic analysis of each of these factors in the complicity determination. Despite the SCC providing a comprehensive complicity scheme in *Ezokola*, the Court could not provide for every potential outcome. Hence, the impact of *Ezokola* will ultimately be determined on a case-by-case basis by IRB decision makers, and by the Federal Court, which stands in review of their decisions, through the adaption of the complicity test to particular fact situations.

NOTES

1 *Ezokola v. Canada (Citizenship and Immigration)*, [2013] 2 SCR 678, 2013 SCC 40 (Can LII), para. 1.
2 United Nations, *Convention Relating to the Status of Refugees*, 28 July 1951, 189 UNTS 150, Can. TS 1969/6.
3 Immigration and Refugee Protection Act, SC 2001, c. 27.
4 Ibid., s. 98.
5 *Ezokola v. Canada*, 2013, para. 33.
6 Ibid., para. 34.
7 Ibid., para. 2.
8 Ibid., para. 3.
9 Ibid., para. 4.
10 Ibid., para. 4.
11 Ibid., para. 11.
12 Ibid., para. 12.
13 Ibid., para. 12.
14 Ibid., para. 14.
15 Ibid., para. 15–19.
16 Ibid., para. 20.
17 *Canada (Citizenship and Immigration) v. Ekanza Ezokola*, 2011 FCA 224 (Can LII), para. 72, cited in *Ezokola*, para. 25.
18 Ibid., para. 6–7.

19 Ibid., para. 9.
20 Ibid., para. 29.
21 Ibid., para. 8.
22 Ibid., para. 77.
23 Ibid., para. 9.
24 Ibid., para. 9.
25 Ibid., para. 77.
26 Ibid., para. 84.
27 Ibid., para. 91.
28 Ibid., para. 92.
29 Ibid., para. 86.
30 Ibid., para. 99.
31 Ibid., para. 99–100.
32 Ibid., para. 88.
33 *R. (J.S. (Sri Lanka)) v. Secretary of State for the Home Department*, [2010] UKSC 15, [2011] 1 AC 184, para. 38, cited in *Ezokola*, para. 87.
34 Criminal Code, RSC 1985, ch. C-46.
35 *Ezokola v. Canada*, 2013, para. 87.
36 Ibid., para. 46–47.
37 Ibid., para. 94.
38 Ibid., para. 94.
39 Ibid., para. 98.
40 Ibid., para. 97.
41 Ibid., para. 96.
42 Ibid., para. 94.
43 Ibid., para. 95.
44 Ibid., para. 95.
45 Ibid., para. 89.
46 Ibid., para. 94.
47 Ibid., para. 97.
48 Ibid., para. 98.
49 *Ramirez v. Canada (Minister of Employment and Immigration)*, [1992] 2 FC 306, 1992 CanLII 8540 (FCA).
50 Ibid., para. 27.
51 Ibid., para. 78.
52 Ibid., para. 79.
53 Ibid., para. 103.
54 *Mudiyanselage v. Canada (Citizenship and Immigration)*, 2013 FC 1076 (Can LII).
55 Ibid., para. 2.

56 Ibid., para. 5.
57 Ibid., para. 3.
58 Ibid., para. 6.
59 Ibid., para. 5.
60 *Kamanzi v. Canada (Citizenship and Immigration)*, 2013 FC 1261 (Can LII).
61 Ibid., para. 3–5.
62 Ibid., para. 11.
63 Ibid., para. 7.
64 Ibid., para. 14.
65 Ibid., para. 17.
66 *Sivakumar v. Canada (Minister of Employment and Immigration)*, [1994] 1 FC 433, 1993 CanLII 3012 (FCA).
67 *Kamanzi*, 2013, para. 21.
68 Ibid., para. 25.
69 Ibid., para. 26.
70 Ibid., para. 27.
71 *Aazamyar v. Canada (Citizenship and Immigration)*, 2015 FC 99 (Can LII).
72 Ibid., para. 1–3.
73 Ibid., para. 39.
74 Ibid., para. 40.
75 Ibid., para. 42–45.
76 *Moya v. Canada (Citizenship and Immigration)*, 2014 FC 996 (Can LII).
77 Ibid., para. 4 and 43.
78 Ibid., para. 16.
79 Ibid., para. 23.
80 Ibid., para. 40.
81 Ibid., para. 46.
82 Ibid., para. 46.
83 Ibid., para. 48.
84 Ibid., para. 49.
85 Ibid., para. 50.
86 Ibid., para. 51–52.
87 *Ndikumasabo v. Canada (Citizenship and Immigration)*, 2014 FC 955 (Can LII).
88 Ibid., para. 28.
89 Ibid., para. 33.
90 Ibid., para. 37.
91 Ibid., para. 37.
92 Ibid., para. 37.
93 Ibid., para. 37.

94 Ibid., para. 37.
95 *Habibi v. Canada (Citizenship and Immigration)*, 2016 FC 253 (Can LII).
96 Ibid., para. 3.
97 Ibid., para. 10.
98 Ibid., para. 10.
99 Ibid., para. 18.
100 Ibid., para. 19.
101 Ibid., para. 24.
102 Ibid., para. 26.
103 Ibid., para. 26.
104 Ibid., para. 26.
105 Ibid., para. 25.
106 *Ezokola v. Canada*, 2013, para. 93.
107 *Parra v. Canada (Citizenship and Immigration)*, 2016 FC 364 (Can LII).
108 Ibid., para. 3.
109 Ibid., para. 6–7.
110 Ibid., para. 3.
111 Ibid., para. 4.
112 Ibid., para. 13 and 30.
113 Ibid., para. 12–14.
114 Ibid., para. 23 and 25.
115 Ibid., para. 32.

5

An Analysis of Post-*Ezokola* and *JS* Jurisprudence on Exclusion

Lorne Waldman and Warda Shazadi Meighen

Regardless of the merits of a refugee claim, anyone who has committed certain acts will not be granted refugee status. Article 1F of the 1951 *Convention Relating to the Status of Refugees* (the Refugee Convention) governs the exclusion of claimants from refugee protection (exclusion clause).

The rationale underpinning the exclusion clause is important. Namely, serious criminals should not evade prosecution and punishment of their crimes by seeking refugee status. Indeed, the exclusion of people who have committed crimes of a significant magnitude helps preserve the integrity of refugee law. According to the guidelines of the United Nations High Commissioner for Refugees (UNHCR), Article 1F upholds the principle that "certain acts are so grave as to render their perpetrators undeserving of international protection as refugees."[1] The exclusion clause was also instrumental in facilitating state "buy-in," as it offered reassurance to states that they would not be required to grant refugee status to serious criminals.[2]

The consequences of being excluded under Article 1F, then, are grave. Indeed, the UNHCR, recognizing the serious consequences of Article 1F, commented that the clause should "only be used with great caution."[3] In the 2012 case of *Al-Sirri v. Secretary of State for the Home Department*, the United Kingdom Supreme Court (UKSC) held, fittingly, that Article 1F ought to be "interpreted restrictively and applied with caution."[4] In a similar vein, in *Pushpanathan v. Canada (Minister of Citizenship and Immigration)*, Justice Bastarache of the Supreme Court of Canada (SCC) held "[t]he *a priori* denial of the fundamental protections of a treaty whose purpose is the protection of human rights is a drastic exception to the purposes of the Convention … and can only be justified where the protection of those rights is furthered by the exclusion."[5]

Understanding the ambit of the seminal exclusion clause is important. Once a decision maker finds that someone has committed certain acts, that person *must* be excluded from refugee protection – a decision maker has no discretion in the matter. A determination of the applicable evidentiary standard must then balance the goals of maintaining the integrity of the refugee determination system with the grave consequences of a finding of exclusion. In this regard, Canadian and UK jurisprudence have divergent postures.

Both the Canadian and UK courts apply a similar legal test to the exclusion analysis in their respective leading decisions: *Ezokola v. Canada (Minister of Citizenship and Immigration)*[6] and *JS (Sri Lanka) v. Secretary of State for the Home Department.*[7] However, the leading cases in these two countries have set different evidentiary standards of proof in the application of the exclusion analysis. Canada has adopted a lower standard of proof than has the UK. The respective standards are set out below:

- Canada:
  - Pre-*Ezokola*: personal and knowing participation
    - Evidentiary standard: serious reasons for considering
  - Post-*Ezokola*: voluntary, significant, and knowing contribution to the organization's crime or the criminal purpose.
    - Evidentiary standard: serious reasons for considering
- United Kingdom:
  - Pre-*JS*: personal and knowing participation
    - Evidentiary standard: serious reasons for considering
  - Post-*JS*: voluntary, significant, and knowing contribution to the organization's crime or criminal purpose
    - Evidentiary standard: balance of probabilities

An important question arises as to whether the lower evidentiary standard of proof for exclusion in Canada results in criminalizing acts within the realm of immigration law that the criminal law itself would not encompass. In Canada, the criminal law evidentiary standard is "proof beyond a reasonable doubt." Post-*Ezokola*, the standard of proof for exclusion remains "serious reasons for considering" that the person has engaged in serious crimes that would exclude him or her from refugee status. As a result, in certain circumstances, a migrant can be excluded for crimes that would not even meet the evidentiary threshold required for criminal conviction.

The SCC's divergence in *Ezokola* from the standard of proof set out in *JS*, the leading UKSC case regarding the criminal evidentiary threshold, can criminalize migration in a manner that goes beyond the reach of criminal law itself.

EZOKOLA

In *Ezokola*,[8] the SCC rejected the test for complicity under Article 1F(a) of the Refugee Convention as one that could leave room for guilt by association or passive acquiescence. The Court found that this test violated fundamental principles of domestic and international law. It set out a test for exclusion that requires an evaluation of whether the accused "has *voluntarily* made a *significant* and *knowing contribution* to the organization's crime or criminal purpose."[9] This substantive test is identical to the test formulated by the UKSC in *JS*.[10]

The addition of a clear requirement for the evidence to establish the person knowingly contributed, in a significant way, to the crime or to the organization's criminal purpose has significantly influenced the application of Article 1F(a) by immigration tribunals in both Canada and the United Kingdom. Tribunals in both countries are now required to carefully analyze the actual role played by the person and determine whether the facts establish, to the requisite standard of proof, that the person knowingly and significantly contributed to the crimes, or at least to the criminal purpose, of the organization.

This seminal decision in *Ezokola* overturned a long line of jurisprudence of the Federal Court of Appeal (FCA) dating back to the decision in *Ramirez v. Canada (Minister of Employment and Immigration)*.[11] Prior to *Ezokola*, the test for determining culpability for exclusion under Article 1F(a) was "personal and knowing participation." Under the *Ramirez* test, participation could be inferred based on a person's membership in a "limited, brutal purpose" organization – an organization whose sole purpose was the commission of intentional crimes. The test for complicity did not require the tribunals to consider the specific role played by the person concerned, and, as such, allowed for exclusion even when there was no evidence that the person had actually committed or contributed towards the commission of the crimes.

CANADIAN EVIDENTIARY STANDARD OF EXCLUSION:
"SERIOUS REASONS FOR CONSIDERING"

Article 1F of the Refugee Convention states that the provisions of the Convention shall not apply to any person where there are "serious reasons for considering" that the person has committed the enumerated acts, including:

a) he has committed a crime against peace, a war crime, or a crime against humanity, as defined in the international instruments drawn up to make provision in respect of such crimes;
b) he has committed a serious non-political crime outside the country of refuge prior to his admission to that country as a refugee;
c) he has been guilty of acts contrary to the purposes and principles of the United Nations.

The state has the burden of proving exclusion within the evidentiary rubric of "serious reasons for considering,"[12] but within that framework, states are permitted to choose what the evidentiary standard ought to be, a decision made at the time the Refugee Convention was drafted.[13] As a result of the state-driven choice on the applicable standard of proof, Canadian jurisprudence has been able to set a lower standard than that in the UK. It remains to be seen, however, whether a lower standard has the effect of allowing immigration law to punish people for crimes in a manner in which the criminal law itself does not.

Canadian courts have interpreted "serious reasons for considering" as a lower standard of proof than a balance of probabilities, but one that approximates to "serious reasons to believe." In *Ramirez*,[14] the FCA determined that the term "reasons for considering" in Article 1F of the Refugee Convention did not require proof to a balance of probabilities.

The SCC in *Ezokola* did caution that "[t]he unique evidentiary standard does not, however, justify a relaxed application of fundamental criminal law principles in order to make room for complicity by association."[15] Further, in affirmatively adopting Lord Brown's reasons in the UK case of *JS*, the SCC in *Ezokola* stated its position on the standard of proof for exclusion as follows, at paragraph 101: "'serious reasons for considering' obviously imports a higher test for exclusion than would, say, an expression like 'reasonable grounds for suspecting.' 'Considering' approximates rather to 'believing' than to 'suspecting.'"

Thus, in *Ezokola*, the SCC reconsidered this issue and noted, citing paragraph 39 of the decision of the UKSC in *JS*,[16] that the test was above reasonable grounds to suspect, but below the civil standard of a balance of probabilities. As a result, it did not alter the low evidentiary standard. Interestingly, the SCC did not consider the decision of the UKSC in *Al-Sirri*, which was decided a few months before *Ezokola* was heard and which overruled earlier jurisprudence. In *Al-Sirri*, the UKSC held that the standard of proof was higher than the "reasonable grounds to believe" threshold and applied the balance of probabilities standard.[17] As a result of *Al-Sirri*, the evidentiary threshold in the UK is higher than the Canadian threshold (i.e., less than a balance of probabilities).

In *Ching v. Canada (Citizenship and Immigration)*, the Federal Court affirmed that a decision maker was bound by *Ezokola*, which endorsed a pre-*Al-Sirri* standard, at paragraph 58:

> It is not necessary to consider this authority and to comment further. The decision in *Ezokola* is binding as the Court endorses a pre-*Al-Sirri* standard. I would not wish to suggest that the standard is stronger than "believing", in spite of the decision of the Supreme Court of the United Kingdom that "serious reasons" in section 1F is stronger than "reasonable grounds" and that "considering" is stronger than "suspecting" and even "believing". Rather, it will suffice at this stage to decide that the RPD does not articulate a standard beyond reasonable suspicions. Given the lack of information before the RPD, it is hardly surprising that the Panel could not offer justification, transparency and intelligibility within its decision-making process because it was relying on a different decision-making process. There is no need to seek to apply *Al-Sirri* in this case.[18]

Given the consequences of exclusion, we ought to give thought to whether the standard of proof, as currently articulated in Canadian jurisprudence, is appropriate. Scholars have cautioned that "the duty not to approach exclusion on the basis of less than clear and convincing evidence is a critical safeguard."[19] Further, the Court of Justice of the European Union correctly recognized in *Bundesrepublik*[20] that discharging this burden of establishing exclusion requires an individual assessment rather than decisions based on group guilt. There should be a "meticulous investigation" where exclusion is concerned.[21] Further, the standard of proof in exclusion analysis is especially crucial, in light of the nature of evidence in many exclusion cases.

EVIDENCE IN EXCLUSION CASES

In most cases, there will be little direct evidence, aside from that which emanates from the person concerned, as to the role they played in the intentional crimes. In certain cases, admissions from the person concerned are sufficient to warrant an exclusion finding. In some cases, however, evidence will emanate from the country or agent of persecution, from which the claimant is seeking protection. Within the refugee determination context, this evidence must be carefully evaluated for credibility, taking into account the documentary evidence dealing with the country's compliance with the rule of law. In many cases, however, direct evidence from the person concerned or from the persecutor will not be available; instead, in many cases, the tribunal will be required to review the record and determine whether there is a sufficient basis on which to *infer* that the person concerned made a substantial contribution to intentional crimes.

The task facing tribunals and courts determining exclusion is now more complex under the new test adopted in *Ezokola* and *JS*. To determine whether the person concerned has made a significant contribution, the tribunal must now consider the evidence of the person's activities within the specific organization. The tribunal must also determine whether the evidence, in light of the objective documentary record, is sufficient to conclude that the person made a significant contribution. As exclusion determinations require careful analysis of the evidence, the lower evidentiary threshold in Canada may have a significant impact on the manner in which exclusion is applied.

In order to discern what the evidentiary standard of exclusion ought to be, it is important to carefully consider the common sources of evidence in exclusion cases.

Admissions from the Person Concerned

In some cases, the person concerned will provide sufficient evidence to establish that he or she ought to be excluded. In *Singh v. Canada (Public Safety and Emergency Preparedness)*,[22] for instance, the person concerned was a citizen of India. In that case, the Immigration Division (ID) of the Immigration and Refugee Board (IRB) assessed whether he was inadmissible to Canada due to his complicity in crimes against humanity. The evidence established that the person concerned voluntarily joined the army on 31 October 1984. There was no evidence that he was directly involved in the torture of suspects. However, there was evidence, based on his own admissions, that he had, on several occasions, transported prisoners to detentions centres and that he was aware they would be tortured there. This personal admission was sufficient to establish a knowing and significant contribution. Similar findings have been made in *Parra v. Canada (Citizenship and Immigration)*,[23] *Kamanzi v. Canada (Citizenship and Immigration)*,[24] and *Petrov v. Canada (Citizenship and Immigration)*.[25] In some cases, a person may initially make an admission but later seek to resile from that admission. It is certainly open to the tribunal to accept and rely on the initial statement made if there is evidence that it was made freely and is otherwise credible.[26]

Evidence Emanating from the Country from which the Refugee Has Fled

In many cases, the person concerned will deny any complicity in intentional crimes, and the tribunal must therefore weigh and assess the totality of the evidence and make a determination. If the claimant denies involvement, the tribunal may be presented with evidence that emanates from the country from which the person has fled. The tribunal will be required to consider the evidence adduced and determine whether it is sufficient to meet the evidentiary threshold to find that the person committed war crimes or crimes against humanity.

Jurisprudence, for instance, has held that an arrest warrant against the person concerned can be sufficient evidence to support a finding of exclusion. However, as noted by the FCA in *Legault v. Canada (Minister of Citizenship and Immigration)*,[27] the decision maker must first be satisfied that the warrant is credible and trustworthy. Part of this analysis requires that the tribunal take into consideration whether the material comes from a democratic country that abides by the rule of law. If the tribunal accepts that the warrant is credible, it can be used to sustain a finding that a person committed a crime. In *Legault*, the evidence emanated from the United States, and as a result the Court was prepared to accept that the warrant was credible evidence.

The case of *Xie v. Canada (Minister of Citizenship and Immigration)*[28] dealt with exclusion under Article 1F(b). This case is noteworthy because it illustrates that the tribunal was prepared to infer that the "serious reasons for considering" threshold had been met, based on the subject's unexplained wealth, taken together with the warrant for arrest. The Court did note that the warrant alone might not have been sufficient evidence.

Thus, a warrant for arrest can be used as evidence to support a finding of exclusion in certain circumstances. However, the weight to be given to the warrant and other evidence emanating from a state will depend on whether or not the state respects the rule of law. In *Legault*, the legal system in question was viewed as a democratic one entitled to deference. In *Xie*, the issue was not raised. However, where the evidence shows that the legal system from which the evidence emanates does not respect the rule of law, the tribunal must provide cogent reasons for accepting the evidence that emanates from such a regime as being credible.[29]

Inferential Evidence of Exclusion

Given the consequences of exclusion, the evidence underlying the assessment must be clear and convincing. The state has the burden of proving exclusion.[30] As mentioned earlier, the Court of Justice of the European Union recognized in *Bundesrepublik* that discharging this burden requires an individual assessment rather than decisions based on group guilt.[31] In *Xie* the Court applied the lesser than balance of probabilities standard and inferred from the person's unexplained wealth, together with the arrest warrant, that there was sufficient evidence to meet that threshold. It is doubtful that the same conclusion would be reached if the minister was required to establish the burden of proof on the balance of probabilities standard, set by the UKSC in *JS*. The case of *Xie*, then, highlights the importance of which evidentiary standard one adopts.[32]

Where the minister adduces direct evidence from the state, this evidence must be weighed against the evidence from the person concerned, and the evidentiary standard becomes a key consideration. In *Lai v. Canada (Minister of Citizenship and Immigration)*,[33] the minister called witnesses from China to testify as to the crimes committed by the person concerned. The Federal Court concluded that it was open to the tribunal to accept the *viva voce* evidence of the witnesses. The tribunal had before it *viva voce* evidence of Chinese officials, including the primary investigating officer, and witnesses from China who were called by the minister to provide testimony about what had occurred. The tribunal was required to assess the *viva voce* evidence of the witnesses and the person concerned, together with evidence as to the lack of the rule of law in China, and make a determination as to the credibility of the evidence before it.

The tribunal can draw reasonable inferences based on the evidence about an organization and about general conditions in the country of reference. The inferences must be reasonably open to the tribunal based on the totality of the evidence. The extent to which it can reasonably infer that a person made a significant contribution will depend on the circumstances of the case. Whether the inferences are reasonable will hinge upon the evidentiary standards that apply.

Post-*Ezokola*, there is a clear requirement of connecting the person to intentional crime through a significant contribution to the crime or to the common criminal purpose. As such, the objective evidence must provide the basis for concluding that the "significant contribution" test is met. When it becomes necessary to draw an inference, the evidentiary standard attributed to "serious reasons for considering" becomes critical.

Post-*Ezokola*, in considering whether an inference can be drawn, the tribunal may make reference to six factors:

1 The size and nature of the organization: The smaller size of an organization may justify an inference that the person would have known about or participated in the criminal enterprise. If the group is larger and more heterogeneous, the link will be more tenuous. If the organization has a limited, brutal purpose, it may be easier to infer knowledge and contribution. However, in all cases the person's conduct and role must be carefully scrutinized.[34]
2 The part of the organization with which the refugee claimant was most directly concerned: If only a part of an organization is connected to the commission of crimes, the person's link to another part of the organization might exonerate him or her.[35]
3 The refugee claimant's duties and activities within the organization: This is an important factor and requires the tribunal to consider whether there is a link between the person's duties and the criminal activities of the organization.[36]
4 The refugee claimant's position or rank in the organization: A person of a higher rank is more likely to have knowledge of the

crimes, and may have effective control over those responsible for the crimes.[37]

5 The length of time the refugee claimant was in the organization, particularly after acquiring knowledge of the group's crime or criminal purpose: It may be easier to infer complicity if the person is in the organization for a longer period of time.[38]

6 The method by which the refugee claimant was recruited and the refugee claimant's opportunity to leave the organization: If participation was not voluntary, this will support a finding that there is no complicity.[39]

However, courts in both Canada and the UK have noted that these factors are only for guidance and that in each case an assessment must be made on the facts before the tribunal.[40]

Pre-Ezokola *Jurisprudence*

This section considers Canadian pre-*Ezokola* jurisprudence with a view to determining whether, as a theoretical exercise, based on the facts in pre-*Ezokola* jurisprudence, it would be possible to conclude that the person made a "significant contribution." A review of this jurisprudence reveals that the application of the "personal and knowing contribution" test led to an extremely wide application of exclusion in cases, even where there was no evidence that the person contributed in any significant way to the commission of the crimes or to the common purpose of the perpetrators. In some cases, it is clear that the application of the *Ezokola* test, had the test been legally applicable to the facts of these cases, would have led to another result.

In other cases, there is some evidence that might point towards a finding that the person made a significant contribution, but further evidence would be necessary to determine whether the person ought to have been excluded. The point of this theoretical exercise is to highlight the importance of discerning how broad or narrow the scope of exclusion ought to be.

Any discussion of the pre-*Ezokola* jurisprudence must begin with the first exclusion case in Canada, *Ramirez v. Canada (Minister of Employment and Immigration)*. Ramirez served in El Salvador's army during the civil war. Both sides – the army and the insurgents – committed numerous atrocities. At issue was whether Ramirez ought to be excluded for his role as a soldier in the armed forces. The FCA accepted that there was no direct evidence that Ramirez had personally taken part in international crimes, but found that he had knowledge that crimes were committed. He was excluded based on his role as a soldier despite the lack of direct evidence that he was involved in any crimes. Thus, under the pre-*Ezokola* test, the fact that the army was known to be involved in numerous atrocities, coupled with the appellant's awareness of the atrocities, was sufficient to meet the test. Absent was any assessment as to how the appellant specifically contributed to the crimes. Under the narrower *Ezokola* test, these factual findings would not be sufficient to warrant exclusion. Evidence beyond mere presence at the scene where the crimes were committed would be required. Application of the *Ezokola* test would likely have led to a finding that Ramirez ought not to be excluded, particularly in light of his low rank, short service, limited responsibility, and the lack of any findings that he was involved in or aided in the commission of international crimes.

In *Acevedo Beza v. Canada (Minister of Citizenship and Immigration)*,[41] the Refugee Protection Division (RPD) of the IRB considered the refugee claim of a Guatemalan citizen who served as a military commissioner in the Guatemalan army between 1983 and 1997. At that time, the country was embroiled in a civil war. The documentary evidence showed that the Guatemalan armed forces committed human rights violations during that period. The RPD cited a book in the documentary evidence that noted, "in the early eighties, counterinsurgency policy took the form of state-sponsored terrorism featuring systematic mass destruction, particularly of indigenous communities and organized peasant groups." The report further stated "the ability of perpetrators to commit crimes with impunity has been a constant factor influencing the conduct of the army, police, military commissioners and civil patrol, and has contributed to further violence against the people." The Board found that 0.5 per cent of massacres were committed in the claimant's region, Chiquimula, and eight massacres occurred there during the time that the claimant worked with the military authorities.

Further, the RPD found that "there are serious reasons to believe that the claimant voluntarily and consciously collaborated with military activities and, therefore, that he was complicit in the crimes against humanity that the Guatemalan army was held responsible for by the international community." It held that the claimant "had to know the consequences of his denunciations and, therefore, the army's reprisals." He voluntarily joined the army without trying to get out of it. Although he did not hold a high-ranking position, "his role as informer gave him considerable responsibility, and the information that he provided to his superiors had serious consequences." He "had to have known" that the activities of the paramilitary organization that he belonged to would likely lead to the commission of crimes against humanity. Although he apparently committed no crime himself, the RPD found that "he was complicit through his personal and knowing participation and he shared the same intention as his superiors." It concluded that "the claimant committed crimes against humanity through association" and as such was excluded from protection under Article 1F(a).

The tribunal in this case used the personal and knowing participation test. Notwithstanding this, had the *Ezokola* test been applicable at the time, there is some evidence in this case that might have supported a finding that the person concerned made a significant contribution – namely, the finding that he acted as an informer and the information he passed on had serious consequences within the context of an organization that committed international crimes. Certainly, if there were a clear finding that the claimant had provided information that led to the arrest and torture of persons, this would be sufficient to support a finding that he made a significant contribution to the commission of international crimes.

In *Mpia-Mena-Zambili v. Canada (Minister of Citizenship and Immigration)*,[42] the applicant, a citizen of the Democratic Republic of Congo (DRC), was a legal advisor in the ministries of Justice, Foreign Affairs and Internal Affairs under the leadership of Mobutu. He later became a senior inspector (*chef de poste*) of the migration service (DGM) for Matadi Port and a member of the restricted security committee. Due to a rebellion in Angola, there was a massive influx of Angolans entering the DRC. The Congolese central government gave an order to kill all Angolans who ventured into border towns. The applicant claimed to have unequivocally opposed the decision, proposing instead the creation in border towns of specific Congolese reception structures that would allow Angolans to recuperate and return to their villages in Angola. He later learned that 767 Angolans had been massacred by the Congolese military force, the Forces armées congolaises (FAC). The applicant was arrested not long after for "having opposed a government order at the meeting of the restricted security committee of September 22, 2000. [He] was detained at the central prison …

where he was threatened and beaten, and forced to do hard labour."[43] He eventually escaped, fled to Angola, and was repatriated back to the Congo and placed under house arrest. A week later, he was received by the president, Joseph Kabila, who ordered that the applicant be reinstated to his position as senior inspector of the DGM. His exclusion from refugee protection was based on his failure to disassociate himself from the crimes against humanity committed by DGM agents and his knowledge of these acts.

The Federal Court agreed with the tribunal's finding that there were numerous abuses committed by the DRC government under Kabila senior and junior that met the definition of crimes against humanity. These abuses included extrajudicial killings, disappearances, torture, rape, excessive use of force, bombing civilian populated areas in rebel-held territory, and abuses against religious entities, among other crimes. The applicant himself acknowledged that the DRC government committed serious, inhumane acts against civilians. The Court stated that the applicant "knew full well of the acts of extortion committed by DGM agents ... and of the abuses perpetrated by DGM agents,"[44] even though he claimed he was never aware of any abuses at Matadi Port where he was posted. The Court found that it was "implausible that abuses committed by security forces in DRC, including the DGM, did not taint the agents of this same service at Matadi Port, especially in a context of endemic corruption."[45] The Court faulted the applicant for failing to resign from his position, and even returning to his position within the DGM after having allegedly been arrested on the order of the Ministry of the Interior, under which the DGM belongs. The Court held that it was reasonable for the IRB to find that the applicant had "personal and knowing awareness" of the abuses committed by the Congolese government and the DGM "by reason of the positions he held" and that it was also reasonable to conclude that there were serious reasons for considering that the applicant "personally and knowingly participated in the crimes committed by the Congolese government ... by virtue of the fact that he was complicitous by association in serious crimes against humanity.[46]

Again the adjudicator's failure to find any connection, direct or indirect, between the claimant and any international crimes suggests that this case would not lead to an exclusion finding under the *Ezokola* test, had the test been applicable at the time. The determination in this case was based on the fact that he was complicit by association due to the position he held, an approach the SCC expressly rejected in *Ezokola*.[47]

Mere awareness or knowledge of crimes committed by his government does not suffice for a finding of complicity. In fact, in *Ezokola* the scc cited the *Mpia-Mena-Zambili* decision as an example of an overly broad form of complicity, where the focus has inappropriately shifted "towards the criminal activities of the group and away from the individual's contribution to that criminal activity."[48] A case with similar facts, then, might be decided similarly in the post-*Ezokola* context.

In *Fabela v. Canada (Minister of Citizenship and Immigration)*,[49] the principal applicant was a police officer in Toluca, Mexico, from 1985 to 1998. Having refused to engage in corrupt activities with the police service, he sought refugee protection for fear of his life after he had witnessed police abuse of power and corruption. The IRB excluded the applicant on the basis that he had been a police officer for thirteen years with the Mexican Judicial Police, a group recognized for its corrupt activities, and while he was an officer, he had "personal and (sic) knowledge of the participation in systematic and widespread torture" and false imprisonments.[50] The applicant argued that the crimes perpetrated by the Mexican Judicial Police did not constitute crimes against humanity.

The Federal Court accepted that the Mexican Judicial Police committed crimes of torture and false imprisonment, both of which are crimes against humanity. It found that, "[e]ven if the official purpose of this organization is not the perpetration of those crimes, the evidence suggests that a vast majority of the police officers have participated in such crimes."[51] The fact that the applicant voluntarily joined the police force, achieved a 90 per cent confession rate (50 per cent higher than his colleagues), and was awarded a monetary prize for having enforced the most arrest warrants, were assessed as factors that negatively affected the applicant's case. He was a group chief for numerous years and had officers under his supervision. The Court also found that, although he resigned on two occasions, he returned to his job soon after. The applicant also testified that he was aware of crimes committed by members of the police. The Court held that "it is now widely recognized that a person can be held liable for such crimes as an accomplice, even though the person has not personally perpetrated the acts himself or herself. The tolerance of such crimes is sufficient to be held liable."[52] The Court upheld the Board's ruling that the applicant was excluded under Article 1F(a).

The facts in this case might be sufficient to justify a finding that the applicant committed or at least made a significant contribution to the commission of international crimes, if it were decided in the post-*Ezokola* context. If the evidence in fact supported the finding that "a vast majority" of police officers in the applicant's division participated in such crimes, this evidence – taken together with the applicant's higher than average confession rate, his senior position in the organization, and his many years of service – might have justified an inference that the applicant committed or at least made a significant contribution to the criminal purpose. This is especially likely considering the lower than civil standard of balance of probabilities applied in Canada. It would be difficult to justify an exclusion finding in this case if the *Al-Sirri* standard had been applied – that is, whether it is more likely than not that the applicant committed the crimes.

In *Sivakumar v. Canada (Minister of Employment and Immigration)*,[53] which was decided pre-*Ezokola*, the appellant was a senior member of the Liberation Tigers of Tamil Eelam (LTTE). There was no evidence that he had personally committed any international crimes or that he had ordered others to do so. Sivakumar held senior positions in the organization for a period of approximately ten years, both in the intelligence division and in the military wing. There was, however, no evidence directly linking him to international crimes, although he was aware at one point that the LTTE was summarily executing persons who were determined to be traitors. There was no evidence that he had any role in the killings.

The Court based its finding of complicity on the appellant's senior position in the organization, coupled with his knowledge that the organization had committed international crimes. While the Court applied the wrong test for complicity, the case does raise an interesting question: At what point is it reasonable to infer that the person concerned made a significant contribution to the commission of an international crime, or to the organization's common purpose? If we consider the *Ezokola* factors, we note that Sivakumar held a senior position for a long period. He joined the organization voluntarily. However, the organization was heterogeneous and not all of its activities were directed to the commission of international crimes. Given this context, is it reasonable to draw such an adverse inference from the fact that the person held a senior position within the organization?

No hard and fast rule can be applied to these situations. The entire factual context must be considered. For example, it would be crucial to know the extent of the international crimes committed, whether the applicant was aware that the crimes were going to be committed, whether he acquiesced in any way, and whether he had any command authority over the persons who committed the crimes or assisted the perpetrators or their criminal purpose. An analysis of the entire context might be sufficient to justify an inference that the applicant had made a significant contribution to the crimes or to the criminal purpose of the organization. Evidence simply that the appellant held a senior position would not generally be sufficient to warrant an adverse inference. Application of the standard of a balance of probabilities might provoke this type of inquiry. It is noteworthy that this case is strikingly similar to the fact situation in the UK case of *JS*, as discussed below. Both applicants were members of the LTTE.

Ezokola, then, has gone a long way in addressing the overly broad application of the exclusion clause. These cases highlight how critical the evidentiary tests of exclusion are to the outcome of a case.

Post-Ezokola *Jurisprudence*

Having surveyed how pre-*Ezokola* cases might theoretically be decided in a post-*Ezokola* environment, it is now appropriate to look forward, post-*Ezokola*, in order to discern how the law in this area has actually evolved.

In *Verbanov v. Canada (Public Safety and Emergency Preparedness)*,[54] the ID of the IRB, applying *Ezokola* factors, declined to find a police officer from Moldova complicit in crimes against humanity. Although there was no dispute that such crimes occurred, the tribunal found that the nature of the duties and rank of the person concerned were such that there was no basis to conclude that he had contributed in the commission of crimes while working as a police officer. Similar decisions have been reached in other cases.[55]

The minister appealed this decision.[56] The panel upheld the determination. The panel was concerned that the complicity standard should capture those who directly participate, and not extend to guilt by association. It explained:

According to the evidence, crimes were committed by certain police officers and they could be seen as isolated incidents or, to a certain point, even systematic, and could be considered crimes against humanity. Nevertheless, the panel is of the opinion that the appellant did not discharge its burden of establishing that the respondent is one of the individuals who allegedly committed

those types of crimes or condoned them. The Minister's representative is of the opinion that, even if the respondent did not commit those crimes, he was complicit. In the panel's opinion, on a
balance of probabilities, that is going too far and would effectively
render all police officers or even public servants inadmissible if
they come from a country with high levels of corruption, abuse
and acts of retaliation against the civilian population. Unfortunately, Moldavia and the majority of the former Soviet republics
are in a similar situation, as are many other countries around the
world. The panel is of the opinion that that is not the intention of
the Canadian Parliament, which rather is to crack down on those
who directly participated and make a distinction between mere
association and culpable complicity, as described in *Ezocola* (sic).[57]

In *Murillo v. Canada (Minister of Citizenship and Immigration)*,[58] the
officer found that there were reasonable grounds to believe that the
applicant had committed a war crime or crime against humanity. The
applicant had held various positions in the Nicaraguan army, including aircraft mechanic and flight engineer in the executive squadron,
which was responsible for transportation of the ministers in the Government of Nicaragua and the military commanders.

The tribunal based its decision on the compulsory relocation of the
Miskito population by the government and military commanders,
and determined that this relocation was a crime against humanity and
that the applicant was complicit. The applicant denied having knowledge of any attacks on civilian populations. The application for judicial review was allowed. While the Court noted that knowledge of
crimes against humanity may be inferred in some cases, the Court
found that in this case there was no evidence from which the tribunal
could infer the applicant's knowledge of crimes against humanity.
There was no evidence involving the applicant directly in the compulsory deportation of the Miskitos.

Continuing Low(er) Evidentiary Canadian Standard

As the cases above show, the decision in *Ezokola* has, appropriately,
allowed the exclusion clause to be applied in an increasingly cautious
manner. While *Ezokola* has helped tailor the approach to exclusion,
there are still cases in which, even where there is no direct evidence
implicating an applicant, the low standard of proof of "serious reasons

for considering" has meant that people have been excluded. However, there are still numerous cases in which significant contribution is being inferred from generic evidence; this may not rise to the level of "meticulous investigation" called upon by courts in other jurisdictions.

There is indeed a duty to refrain from a finding of exclusion on anything less than clear and convincing evidence. This duty is the very safeguard upon which the weighty consequences of exclusion can reasonably be buttressed.[59] A cautious approach to exclusion was something that the SCC in *Ezokola* itself prescribed.[60] However, in the absence of an evidentiary standard of a balance of probabilities, like that in the UK, there may well be numerous cases in which people are excluded on less than convincing evidence. The recent case of *Nsika v. Canada (Public Safety and Emergency Preparedness)*[61] is one such post-*Ezokola* example.

In *Nsika*, the ID of the IRB concluded that the person concerned made a knowing and significant contribution to crimes against humanity because of the role he played in the Congolese army. Nsika arrived to Canada in 2007 and made a claim for refugee protection. The issue before the tribunal was whether Nsika was complicit in crimes against humanity. The tribunal noted that Nsika joined the Congolese military in 1991. After six months of training, he was sent to work in the "ZAB" unit – la Zone autonome de Brazzaville – as part of a unit responsible for maintaining security in the Brazzaville area. Toward the end of his term in the military, Nsika held the rank of sergeant and was responsible for his own sub-unit.

Even though the tribunal found that there was no evidence to show Nsika directly committed atrocities as part of the Congolese military, it found he had personal knowledge of the atrocities. The tribunal noted that Nsika's six years of service in the Congolese army was a significant period of time. He only deserted the military in 1998, when the government was overthrown. The tribunal found Nsika complicit, although it did not clearly explain how he had provided a significant contribution to the crimes against humanity committed by the regime. Even though this case existed before *Ezokola*, it is interesting to note that a theoretical analysis of these facts under the *Ezokola* test would mean that such a finding would be unlikely under the standard of a balance of probabilities.

In *Nsika v. Canada*,[62] the tribunal found the opposite in the case of Nsika. Specifically, it held that Nsika's contribution to the military's crime or criminal purpose was voluntary, as he joined on his own volition and stayed with the military for over six years. He could have deserted at any time. The tribunal found and his contribution was significant, as his position within the military was one of authority: he assigned tasks to the members of his unit, and achieved the rank of sergeant. Finally, the tribunal found that Nsika had knowledge of the atrocities committed by the military. The tribunal was of the view that, while his specific unit may not have been directly involved, Nsika *ought* to have had knowledge about the atrocities committed by the Congolese army by virtue of living and working in the affected areas. Moreover, given his position, and the size and nature of the Congolese army, the tribunal found that it was reasonable to conclude that Nsika was fully aware of what was going on.

Nsika argued that there was nothing before the tribunal to link him to a particular crime. However, the tribunal was of the view that there need not be a link to a particular crime; there must only be evidence of complicity between a person and the criminal purpose of the group. This link, according to the tribunal, is established when there are serious reasons for considering that someone has voluntarily made a significant and knowing contribution to a group's crime or criminal purpose.

The decision underscores the need for even more caution in considering exclusion in light of its weighty consequences. It fails to clearly explain how the person concerned made a significant contribution to the crimes committed by the organization. It is difficult to determine based on the evidence set out in the decision how the tribunal came to the conclusion that the person concerned made a significant contribution to the crimes committed. There was no evidence that the group with which he was associated committed or aided in the commission of international crimes. Again, such a finding would be unlikely under the UK standard of a balance of probabilities.

However, it is difficult to ascertain, at least based on the summary of evidence set out in the decision, whether or not the contribution of the applicant was "significant." A number of questions remain unanswered. For example, was there evidence that the bombings actually occurred? If this case had taken place after *Ezokola*, rather than before, a finding subject to a higher evidentiary standard of a balance of probabilities might have prompted a more nuanced and explicit consideration of these questions. This, again, is important, given the power of the exclusion clause.

UK COURTS AND TRIBUNALS

The UK represents a jurisdiction in which the test for complicity mirrors that set out in *Ezokola*. However, the evidentiary standard in the UK is "balance of probabilities," which is higher than the standard in Canada. Any discussion of UK jurisprudence should commence with the leading case, *JS*, decided in the context of Article 1F(a).[63] The UKSC held that "one needs ... to concentrate on the actual role played by the particular person, taking all material aspects of that role into account so as to decide whether the required degree of participation is established." *Ezokola* mirrors this decision on the substantive front.

The UKSC identified a non-exhaustive list of relevant factors to consider in making this assessment:

(i) the nature and (potentially of some importance) the size of the organisation and particularly that part of it with which the asylum-seeker was himself most directly concerned, (ii) whether and, if so, by whom the organisation was proscribed, (iii) how the asylum-seeker came to be recruited, (iv) the length of time he remained in the organisation and what, if any, opportunities he had to leave it, (v) his position, rank, standing and influence in the organisation, (vi) his knowledge of the organisation's war crimes activities, and (vii) his own personal involvement and role in the organisation including particularly whatever contribution he made towards the commission of war crimes.[64]

The facts in *JS* are similar to those in the Canadian case of *Sivakumar*, discussed above. *JS* was a member of the Tamil Tigers (LTTE) for fourteen years. He was involved in both intelligence and combat roles, at one point commanding a platoon of forty-five soldiers. He was second in command in the combat unit of the Intelligence Division and sent to operate clandestinely in Colombo.

As in the case of *Sivakumar*, it is not possible, based on this information, to conclude that the applicant made a significant contribution to the commission of international crimes. There are a number important questions to discern. What international crimes were committed by the LTTE while he was a member? Were any committed by the combat unit during his tenure there? Did JS aid the LTTE when they exploded the suicide bombs in Colombo in October 2006, which killed approximately 100 people? Answers to these and other questions will shed light on whether JS ought to be excluded from protection under the Refugee Convention.[65]

JS was excluded for, *inter alia*, complicity in the LTTE's crimes, under Article 1F(a) of the Refugee Convention. His appeal[66] followed from the UKSC's decision in *JS*, in which the Court ordered a redetermination of the asylum claim, and the secretary of state subsequently dismissed the claim on all grounds. The appeal was heard by a panel of two first-tier tribunal judges, which rejected the secretary's decision to exclude the appellant from refugee protection.

The secretary appealed to the Upper Tribunal on, *inter alia*, the following bases: (a) the panel erred in accepting the appellant's submission that he was not a commander; (b) the panel erred in concluding that the secretary had "imputed" high rank to the appellant, even though the appellant's high rank had been based on the agreed facts before the UKSC and the appellant's own evidence; (c) the panel gave no adequate explanation as to why it found no evidence of his involvement in aiding crimes and gave no explanation regarding why they found that the appellant had no knowledge of the LTTE's commission of crimes in government-controlled territory; and (d) the panel claimed the secretary had not pinpointed the exact crimes that JS had committed, but that doing so would justify the opening of criminal proceedings, whereas the test for exclusion purposes is not a criminal law standard but rather "serious reasons for considering."

In its decision, the Upper Tribunal upheld the panel's findings and ruled in favour of JS. It found that JS's position that he was not a commander was consistent with the statements of agreed facts. The statements referred to the appellant as being the leader of a nine-man combat unit and a forty-five-man platoon. He also became the leader of a mobile unit, with which he was responsible for transporting military equipment and other members of the Intelligence Division. He later became second in command of the combat unit of the Intelligence Division. However, the statement does not specifically refer to the appellant as a "commander," nor make any reference to a particular rank or his seniority. His two former leadership roles were from when he was still a minor.

The Upper Tribunal also held that the panel's finding that "the appellant did not have sufficient knowledge that crimes were being committed [by the LTTE] such as to engage Article 28" was not inconsistent with the agreed statement of facts.[67] It accepted the panel's findings that "when asked to transport military equipment [the appellant] did not know what the equipment was being used for. He never asked questions and was forbidden from discussing his orders with anyone." The extent of his activities and contribution to the LTTE's strategy was "transporting or escorting unidentified agents and military equipment from place to place."[68] Furthermore, the Upper Tribunal agreed that there was "no compelling evidence that he personally participated in or had sufficient knowledge, if any, of the war crimes or crimes against humanity."[69] The Upper Tribunal was satisfied that there were no inconsistencies in JS's evidence before the UKSC and his post-2010 evidence before the tribunal. In any event, the alleged inconsistencies did not serve to establish JS's "knowledge of what the intelligence officers would be doing once they had reached their destination or the intended use of the weapons, such that he could be found to have furthered or contributed to the commissioning of war crimes by his actions."[70] As such, the Upper Tribunal found that the panel did not make an error of law and it rejected the basis of JS's exclusion from refugee protection.

This UK decision, adjudicated on the evidentiary standard of a balance of probabilities, differs from the Canadian case of *Sivakumar*, with a similar factual context. *JS* provides a thoughtful consideration of assessing a person's complicity in crimes against humanity. Indeed, given the mandatory nature of Article 1F and the significant consequences of exclusion, this approach might be warranted.

The *JS* decision has set a standard of proof that is perhaps a better corollary to the nature of the consequence of an exclusion finding. The decision in *R (Polat)*[71] provides an illustration. This case concerns Ali Polat, a Turkish national of Kurdish ethnicity who challenged the decision of the secretary of state for refusing his application for indefinite leave to remain (ILR) in the UK under a special policy known as a "one-off exercise." Asylum-seeking families were granted ILR if they were living in the UK for three or more years, applied for asylum before 2 October 2000, and had at least one dependant under the age of eighteen in the UK. The secretary of state determined that the claimant did not qualify because he had committed a serious non-political crime (under Article 1F(b) of the Refugee Convention) prior to coming to the UK.

In 1996, while in Turkey, the claimant was alleged to have been in possession of a pistol with ammunition. The secretary also concluded that, under Article 1F(c), there were serious reasons for considering that the claimant had committed acts contrary to the purposes and principles of the United Nations. Namely, he was actively involved in the Kurdistan Workers' Party (PKK), a terrorist organization, which was fighting an armed struggle against the Turkish state.[72]

The Court applied the complicity test set out in *JS*. It affirmed the factors expounded by Lord Brown in *JS* and upheld the principle that mere membership in a terrorist organization is not sufficient for an applicant to fall within the scope of Article 1F(c). It found that there was no evidence about the *quality* of the claimant's alleged contribution to acts of terrorism on the part of the PKK, nor to establish that the contribution was "substantial" or "significant."[73] The two central pieces of evidence were both flimsy.

The secretary's conclusion that the claimant encouraged others in the armed struggle against the Turkish state was a single-line statement that lacked particularity. Further, "there was no evidence of physical or logistical support for PKK and its operations and no evidence to support or explain what 'encouragement' means" and as such, this evidence "was not *of itself*" sufficient to establish an Article 1F(c) exclusion for acts contrary to the purposes and principles of the United Nations.[74] The Court held that the second piece of evidence – the claimant's presence at the incident on 2 July 1996 – regarded an incident between the PKK and the Turkish armed forces that did not amount to "terrorist" activity and as such fell outside the scope of Art 1F(c). The Court found that there was insufficient evidence to conclude rationally that there were serious reasons for determining the claimant "voluntarily to have contributed in a significant way to the PKK's ability to pursue its purpose of committing terrorist acts, aware that his assistance would in fact further that purpose."[75] The Court also ruled that neither the evidence nor the secretary's assessment was sufficient to meet the standard for an Article 1F exclusion outlined in *JS*, which requires "an individual assessment of the particular person's circumstances, based on cogent evidence so as to enable the decision maker to reach a careful considered conclusion."[76] The Court suggested that the secretary could and should have made more specific inquiries.

The level of analysis in this case is perhaps warranted given the consequences of the exclusion clause. A lower standard of "serious reasons to believe" in Canada would likely not yield this level of analysis. There are numerous examples of post-*JS* jurisprudence that engage in a nuanced consideration of whether the analysis satisfies the balance of probabilities standard. Some examples include *SK (Zimbabwe),*[77] AA-R *(Iran),*[78] *AN (Afghanistan),*[79] *CM (Zimbabwe),*[80] and *MT (Zimbabwe).*[81]

The decisions in these cases did, at times, result in the exclusion of persons concerned under Article 1F. As such, a further tightening of the evidentiary standard of exclusion in Canada post-*Ezokola* could continue to advance the goals of the exclusion clause, whilst also preserving the integrity of the refugee determination system.

CONCLUSION

The *Ezokola* and *JS* decisions now require the tribunals and courts considering exclusion to carefully review the specific activities and role of the person concerned, viewed together with the objective country conditions, when deciding whether or not there are grounds for exclusion. Between Canadian and UK jurisprudence, this paper considered three different standards of exclusion:

1 Pre-*Ezokola* (Canada): personal and knowing participation
   Evidentiary standard: serious reason for considering
2 Post-*Ezokola* (Canada): voluntary, significant, and knowing contribution to the organization's crime or criminal purpose
   Evidentiary standard: serious reason for considering
3 Post-*JS* (UK): voluntary, significant, and knowing contribution to the organization's crime or criminal purpose
   Evidentiary standard: balance of probabilities.

The analysis above demonstrates that the distinction between the evidentiary threshold in *JS* and *Ezokola* will, undoubtedly, have a significant impact on how the exclusion clauses are applied. In Canada, it will be easier to exclude people because it will be possible to infer by less than civil and criminal standards that a person did contribute significantly to a serious crime. In the UK, the evidence that will be required to meet the evidentiary standard to the balance of probabilities will certainly be more demanding. The decision in *JS* highlights that difference. In it, the Appeals Tribunal declined to apply the exclusion clauses to the claimant due to there being "no compelling evidence that he personally participated in or had sufficient knowledge, if any, of the war crimes or crimes against humanity."[82] On the current UK evidentiary standard of "serious reasons to believe," it is doubtful that a tribunal in Canada will require evidence with the same threshold.

Ezokola has gone a long way in limiting the overreach of decision makers in excluding people. The risk that Canada continues to run with its current standard of proof for exclusion being "serious reasons for considering" is that migrants can be penalized and excluded for criminal acts under immigration legislation for which they would not be subjected to conviction under the criminal law itself. Whether we ought to adopt the more stringent evidentiary standard than the current one of "serious grounds for considering" requires a thoughtful analysis of what the scope of the exclusion clause ought to be. This analysis will need to be guided by what in Canada is considered to be the appropriate balance between maintaining the integrity of the refugee system while keeping in mind the grave and mandatory consequences of a finding of exclusion under the Refugee Convention for a person. The promulgation of the evidentiary standard of a balance of probabilities in the UK case of *JS* provides one sound alternative, which ought to be considered carefully in Canada.

ACKNOWLEDGMENTS

The authors would like to thank Joanna Berry and Steven Blakey for their invaluable research assistance.

NOTES

1 United Nations High Commissioner for Refugees (UNHCR), *Guidelines on International Protection No. 5: Application of the Exclusion Clauses: Article 1F of the 1951 Convention Relating to the Status of Refugees*, HCR/GIP/03/05, 4 September 2003, para. 2.

2 James C. Hathaway and Michelle Foster, *The Law of Refugee Status*, 2nd ed. (Cambridge: Cambridge University Press, 2014).

3 UNHCR, *Background Note on the Application of the Exclusion Clauses: Article 1F of the 1951 Convention Relating to the Status of Refugees*, 4 September 2003, 3.

4 *Al-Sirri v. Secretary of State for the Home Department*, [2012] UKSC 54, [2012] 3 WLR 1263.

5 *Pushpanathan v. Canada (Minister of Citizenship and Immigration)*, [1998] 1 SCR 982, 1998 CanLII 778 (SCC), para. 74.

6 *Ezokola v. Canada (Citizenship and Immigration)*, [2013] 2 SCR 678, 2013 SCC 40 (CanLII), para. 102.

7 *JS (Sri Lanka) v. Secretary of State for the Home Department*, [2010] UKSC 15, [2011] 1 AC 184, para. 38: "Put simply, I would hold an accused disqualified

under article 1 F if there are serious reasons for considering him voluntarily to have contributed in a significant way to the organisation's ability to pursue its purpose of committing war crimes, aware that his assistance will in fact further that purpose."

 8 *Ezokola*, 2013, para. 84.
 9 Ibid., para. 81 and 84.
10 *JS (Sri Lanka)*, 2010. Emphasis added.
11 *Ramirez v. Canada (Minister of Employment and Immigration)*, [1992] 2 FC 306, 1992 CanLII 8540 (FCA).
12 *Ezokola*, 2013, para. 29.
13 UN Ad Hoc Committee on Refugees and Stateless Persons, *Ad Hoc Committee on Statelessness and Related Problems, First Session: Summary Record of the Seventeenth Meeting Held at Lake Success, New York, on Tuesday, 31 January 1950, at 11 a.m.*, 6 February 1950, E/AC.32/SR.17, 9, statement of Mr Henkin.
14 *Ramirez*, 1992; *Mugesera v. Canada (Minister of Citizenship and Immigration)*, [2005] 2 SCR 100, 2005 SCC 40 (CanLII). In *Mugesera v. Canada*, the Supreme Court of Canada described the reasonable grounds threshold in the following terms:

> [114] The first issue raised by s. 19(1)(*j*) of the *Immigration Act* is the meaning of the evidentiary standard that there be "reasonable grounds to believe" that a person has committed a crime against humanity. The FCA has found, and we agree, that the "reasonable grounds to believe" standard requires something more than mere suspicion, but less than the standard applicable in civil matters of proof on the balance of probabilities: *Sivakumar v. Canada (Minister of Employment and Immigration)*, [1994] 1 FC 433 (CA), p. 445; *Chiau v. Canada (Minister of Citizenship and Immigration)*, [2001] 2 FC 297 (CA), para. 60. In essence, reasonable grounds will exist where there is an objective basis for the belief which is based on compelling and credible information.

15 *Ezokola*, 2013.
16 See *Ezokola*, 2013, para. 101.
17 *Al-Sirri*, 2012, para. 75.
18 *Ching v. Canada (Citizenship and Immigration)*, [2016] 1 FCR 507, 2015 FC 860 (CanLII), para. 58.
19 Hathaway and Foster, *Law of Refugee Status*, 2014, 535.
20 *Bundesrepublik Deutschland v. B. and D.* (C-57/09) and (C-101/09), CJEU 2010, para. 16.
21 As argued by the State Secretary for Justice to the Netherlands Parliament in 1997, referred to in Geoff Gilbert, "Current Issues in the Application of

the Exclusion Clauses," in *Refugee Protection in International Law* (Cambridge: Cambridge University Press, 2003), 457, n. 163.

22 *Singh v. Canada (Public Safety and Emergency Preparedness)*, 2014 CanLII 99210 (CA IRB).

23 *Parra v. Canada (Citizenship and Immigration)*, 2016 FC 364 (CanLII).

24 *Kamanzi v. Canada* (Citizenship and Immigration), 2013 FC 1261 (CanLII).

25 *Petrov v. Canada (Citizenship and Immigration)*, 2007 FC 465 (CanLII).

26 See *Navaratnam v. Canada (Citizenship and Immigration)*, 2011 FC 856 (CanLII), para. 15.

27 *Legault v. Canada (Minister of Citizenship and Immigration)*, [2002] 4 FC 358, 2002 FCA 125 (CanLII).

28 *Xie v. Canada (Minister of Citizenship and Immigration)*, [2005] 1 FCR 304, 2004 FCA 250 (CanLII).

29 See also *Canada (Minister of Employment and Immigration) v Satiacum* (1989), 99 NR 171, [1989] FCJ No. 505 (FCA).

30 *Ezokola*, 2013, para. 29.

31 *Bundesrepublik*, 2010, 16.

32 In *Jakobovitz v. Canada* (paragraphs 30 to 32), the Immigration Appeal Division applied *Xie* to find that the existence of an arrest in the US could bolster the probative value of the warrant so as to satisfy the standard of proof. *Jakobovitz v. Canada (Public Safety and Emergency Preparedness)*, 2016 CanLII 90983 (CA IRB).

> 30 Reading the document as a whole, it is clear that it was generated by a competent legal authority in the United States – the Department of Justice – in order to pursue the extradition of the respondent. It outlines the basic facts which supported the return of a sealed indictment and the issuing of an arrest warrant. The credibility of the content of this document is not to be assessed by reading it in the abstract. Its content is to be considered in light of related facts that are not in dispute: that there was enough evidence to convene a grand jury; that it sat for three days; that it in turn found that there was enough evidence to commit the respondent for trial; that it returned an indictment against her and that this in turn led to the issuing of a warrant for her arrest.
>
> 31 That said, there is no doubt that the document is short on detail. Notwithstanding the deficiencies of the document, when I read it in this context I am satisfied that it meets the evidentiary thresholds of credibility and trustworthiness to be able to rely on it as an account of the respondent's role in a scheme of fraud. It is evident that the Request sets

out – albeit sparingly – allegations of the respondent's actions and intent that, when taken together, would constitute the elements of the offences with which she is charged in New York.

32 However, unlike the facts in *Legault*, I do not base my determination on an assessment of these documents alone. In *Xie v. Canada (Minister of Citizenship and Immigration)* the Federal Court of Appeal held that an arrest warrant, when considered in conjunction with the circumstantial evidence of an applicant's unexplained wealth, was sufficient to infer that there were serious reasons to consider that the applicant had committed a serious non-political crime (fraud in that case).

33 *Lai v. Canada (Minister of Citizenship and Immigration)*, [2008] 2 FCR 3, 2007 FC 361 (CanLII).

34 *Ezokola*, 2013, para. 94.

35 *Ramirez*, 1992, para. 95.

36 Ibid., para. 96.

37 Ibid., para. 97.

38 Ibid., para. 98.

39 *Ezokola*, 2013, para. 91.

40 Ibid., para. 100.

41 *Acevedo Beza v. Canada (Minister of Citizenship and Immigration)*, 2006 FC 478 (CanLII).

42 *Mpia-Mena-Zambili v. Canada (Minister of Citizenship and Immigration)*, 2005 FC 1349 (CanLII).

43 Ibid., para. 10.

44 Ibid., para. 40.

45 Ibid., para. 43.

46 Ibid., para. 47.

47 *Ezokola*, 2013, para. 83.

48 Ibid., para. 79–80.

49 *Fabela v. Canada (Minister of Citizenship and Immigration)*, 2005 FC 1028 (CanLII).

50 Ibid., para. 8.

51 Ibid., para. 17.

52 Ibid., para. 19.

53 *Sivakumar v. Canada (Minister of Employment and Immigration)*, [1994] 1 FC 433, 1993 CanLII 3012 (FCA).

54 *Verbanov v. Canada (Public Safety and Emergency Preparedness)*, 2015 CanLII 93747 (CA IRB).

55 *Bajraktari v. Canada (Public Safety and Emergency Preparedness)*, 2014 CanLII 99204 (CA IRB).

56	*Verbanov v. Canada (Public Safety and Emergency Preparedness)*, 2017 CanLII 26478 (CA IRB).

57	Ibid., para. 13.

58	*Murillo v. Canada (Minister of Citizenship and Immigration)*, [2003] 3 FCR 287, 2002 FCT 1240 (CanLII).

59	Hathaway and Foster, *Law of Refugee Status*, 2014, 535.

60	*Ezokola*, 2013.

61	*Nsika v. Canada (Public Safety and Emergency Preparedness)*, 2015 CanLII 97782 (CA IRB).

62	Ibid.

63	*JS (Sri Lanka)*, 2010.

64	Ibid.

65	Ibid., para. 58.

66	Upper Tribunal (Immigration and Asylum Chamber), UKUT AA/10772/2013, 2015.

67	Ibid., para. 35.

68	Ibid., para. 42.

69	Ibid., para. 37.

70	Ibid., para. 38.

71	*R. (on the application of Polat) v. Secretary of State for the Home Department*, [2011] EWHC 3445 (Admin).

72	*KJ (Sri Lanka) v. Secretary of State for the Home Department*, [2009] EWCA Civ 292, United Kingdom: Court of Appeal (England and Wales), 2 April 2009. In paragraph 34 of *KJ (Sri Lanka)*, the Court of Appeal ruled that acts of terrorism, including the deliberate killing or injuring of civilians in pursuit of political objects, constitutes "acts contrary to the purposes and principles of the United Nations."

73	*R. (Polat)*, 2011, para. 97.

74	Ibid., para. 98.

75	Ibid., para. 103.

76	Ibid., para. 100. This standard was specified in paragraphs 38 to 39 of Lord Brown's judgement in *JS*.

77	*SK (Zimbabwe) v. Secretary of State for the Home Department*, [2012] EWCA Civ 807.

78	*AA-R (Iran) v. Secretary of State of the Home Department*, [2013] EWCA Civ 835.

79	*AN (Afghanistan) v. Secretary of the State for the Home Department*, [2015] EWCA Civ 684.

80 *CM Zimbabwe*, [2012] UKUT 00236 (IAC). This case is discussed in
   Satvinder S. Juss, "The Notion of Complicity in UK Refugee Law," *Journal of International Criminal Justice* 12, no. 5 (2014): 1,201–16.
81 *MT (Zimbabwe)*, [2012] UKUT 00015 (IAC).
82 *JS v. Secretary of State for the Home Department*, Appeal No.:
   AA/10772/2013, 9 September 2015, para. 37,
   https://tribunalsdecisions.service.gov.uk/utiac/aa-10772-2013.

6

The Interpretation of Exclusion 1F(b) of the 1951 Refugee Convention Internationally and in Canada

Joseph Rikhof

This article discusses the interpretation of exclusion clause 1F(b) of the *Convention Relating to the Status of Refugees* (the Refugee Convention).[1] Although a person seeking asylum is entitled to protection under this treaty if he or she has "a well-founded fear of being persecuted for reasons of race, religion, nationality, membership of a particular social group or political opinion,"[2] Article 1F sets an exception to this rule by excluding a person if:

a) he has committed a crime against peace, a war crime, or a crime against humanity, as defined in the international instruments drawn up to make provision in respect of such crimes;
b) he has committed a serious non-political crime outside the country of refuge prior to his admission to that country as a refugee;
c) he has been guilty of acts contrary to the purposes and principles of the United Nations.

Because exclusion can have a profound effect on the right of asylum seekers to remain in the country of refuge, it is important that the parameters of the above exclusion grounds are finely drawn to ensure that only persons with a truly criminal background are kept from benefitting from the protection of the Refugee Convention. With such a caveat, objections that have been raised in other contexts with respect to the criminalization of refugee and immigration law, have much less force in the context of exclusion, as the original intention and consensus of the drafters of the Refugee Convention was to prohibit entry and the granting of status to persons who had been involved in universally recognized criminal and nefarious behaviour.

While exclusion grounds (a) and (c) provide, in their text, unifying methods of interpretation of international instruments and principles, no such luxury is provided in ground (b), resulting in tribunals and courts giving meaning to the concepts contained within in it (such as: What is crime? What is a serious crime? What is a political crime? What is the effect of foreign convictions? What does "outside the country of refuge" mean? Do subsequent events affect the determination of criminality? How broad is the notion of complicity?). This has been done based on national context, with limited knowledge and interest in what has happened in other countries. This chapter will examine the jurisprudence in a comparative manner in over a dozen countries to tease out possible overarching principles with respect to the issues pertaining to Article 1F(b). Aspects such as the notion of crime, the meaning of serious crime and political crime, and questions related to the breadth of liability beyond personal involvement and events that occurred after the commission of the crime, known as expiation, will be discussed. Canadian jurisprudence will be given special attention, as it has the most sophisticated case law in some areas that could be of benefit to the larger legal community.

EXCLUSION 1F(B) IN A COMPARATIVE CONTEXT

While the jurisprudence in Australia, Belgium, Canada, France, Germany, the Netherlands, New Zealand, the United Kingdom, and the United States, the countries with the largest number of exclusion decisions, shows some consistency in the use of Article 1F(b) in the abstract, some variations occur in the concrete application of the clause.

The Notion of Crime and the Use of Foreign Convictions

The judiciary of Australia,[3] Canada,[4] and New Zealand[5] were of the view that, for the purposes of this provision, the criminal law of the country of refuge should be the determinative factor for what constitutes a crime. At times in Canada, however, some lip service has been paid to the fact that some crimes, such as corruption or drug trafficking, are also addressed at the international level, which has been seen as bolstering the reliance on the national law in the country of refuge.[6] In this context, an Australian case involving drug trafficking made it clear that the crime had to be in existence in the legislation of the country of refuge at the time of its commission rather than the time of the hearing.[7]

Related to this concept is the role of a foreign conviction in determining whether a crime has been committed. Australian, Belgian, Dutch, and UK tribunals have given deference to foreign convictions if the Article 1F(b) assessment was made on the same facts, and it would be part of the evidence to be considered if the Article 1F(b) examination is used for a different fact pattern.[8] Canadian courts have advised caution when using foreign convictions, which is further explained below in a more detailed discussion of Canadian law.[9] In the US the courts ruled in one case that such a conviction should not be taken at face value.[10] In France, a tribunal refused to exclude a person who had been convicted in his country of origin of aggressive behaviour during public discourse.[11] The difference in opinion could very well have been the result of the country in which the conviction was imposed. If so, more deference would be given to legal systems in which an independent judiciary operates, applying similar rules to the ones used in the country of refuge.[12]

The Issue of Serious Crime

The concept of serious crime raises a number of issues. All countries examined in this chapter have considered serious common crimes, such as murder, torture, assault, rape, drug trafficking, and arson, to fall within the parameters of Article 1F(b). Some countries, such as Canada,[13] the Netherlands,[14] and the US,[15] have specifically indicated that economic crimes such as embezzlement and large-scale theft are also serious crimes. According to a Canadian court, small-scale theft, even if carried out in a habitual fashion, was deemed not to fall within the ambit of Article 1F(b) of the Refugee Convention.[16]

The reasoning used to conclude that a crime should be considered serious has varied from country to country. Some countries (Australia,[17] Germany,[18] and France[19]) state in general that Article 1F(b) applies to capital or grave crimes without using a more detailed methodology.

Other countries examine the maximum penalty that could be imposed for a particular crime in the criminal legislation (such as older Canadian[20] and French cases[21]).[22] They sometimes add that this legislation needs to be reflective of international criminality in that particular area (such as the Netherlands, with respect to cases involving female genital mutilation, rape, and drug trafficking,[23] as well as in Germany[24]). The last approach in this category is examining what penalty would likely be imposed if a person were tried criminally, as happened in New Zealand, where a tribunal came to the conclusion that this sentence should be set at a minimum between eighteen months and two years, and in the UK, where a two-year minimum is set out in the legislation.[25]

A third approach determines if a crime is serious using a number of factors. These include a penalty indicated in the criminal legislation that operates as a presumption of seriousness; the actual possible sentence; as well as possible mitigating and aggravating circumstances that could affect the presumption regarding penalties. This has been used in Australia,[26] Canada,[27] the US,[28] and in some respects France.[29]

The *United Nations Convention against Transnational Organized Crime*[30] provides guidance on serious crime and could result in a consistent approach among countries of refuge. It would therefore be desirable for national courts and tribunals to take this international development into account by having a minimum of four years set as the benchmark for serious crimes, as is done in this treaty.

Apart from the general category of serious crimes set out above, it is worth mentioning some specific application of Article 1F(b) to criminal behaviour, such as the prohibition against people trafficking in some Australian and Belgian cases,[31] the selling of human organs in the US,[32] the scuttling of a ship in New Zealand,[33] child abduction in Canada,[34] organized crime in France,[35] piracy in the Netherlands,[36] and undertaking armed attack missions and preparing for a suicide mission in the UK.[37] In addition, in France, Article 1F(b) has been used frequently to exclude persons who have been involved in the commission of war crimes in civil wars.[38] None of the methodologies used above would have come to a different conclusion in these examples of serious crimes, as in general these activities would occupy the higher range of seriousness in any approach taken to protect the physical integrity of persons, a hallmark for setting high penalties in criminal legislation.

The Interpretation of
"Outside the Country of Refuge"

Another aspect of Article 1F(b), that the activities set out in this exclusion clause have to be committed outside the country of refuge, has been given some judicial consideration in Australia and France. In Australia, the courts have had no problem applying Article 1F(b) to crimes that began outside its borders but continued within Australia – specifically drug trafficking.[39] In France this provision has been applied by tribunals to situations in which the conduct occurred in France but was carried out in support of organizations that committed crimes outside France, even though the highest administrative court had made it clear that Article 1F(b) only applied to acts committed outside the country of refuge.[40]

Influence of Events
That Occurred after the Commission of the Crime

The notion of expiation for reasons of having served a sentence or received a pardon or amnesty has been rejected out of hand in Canada,[41] Germany,[42] the UK,[43] and New Zealand,[44] as well as the Court of Justice of the European Union.[45] France[46] and Belgium[47] have been more equivocal about this issue, although more recent jurisprudence seems to indicate a similar trend.

The *Febles* (2014) decision by the Supreme Court of Canada is illustrative of this approach.[48] While living in the United States, the appellant, Mr. Febles, had been convicted and served time in prison for two assaults with a deadly weapon, in 1984 and 1993. However, the court was of the view that, in spite of having turned his life around after his final release from prison in 1998, he still would fall within the confines of Article 1F(b) because factors such as current lack of dangerousness or post-crime expiation or rehabilitation are not to be considered or balanced against the seriousness of the crime.

Political Crimes and the Issue of Terrorism

With respect to serious crimes and international law aspects, all countries mentioned above have used Article 1F(b) to exclude persons who have been involved in terrorist activities. While the issue of terrorism became more prevalent after the attacks of 9/11, this exclusion clause had been used regularly in most countries before that event as well. There had been little difficulty applying Article 1F(b) to this type of criminal behaviour, even though the courts and tribunals could not rely on an internationally accepted definition.

It is expected that with the most recent developments in international law there will be less of an *ad hoc* approach to activities that have been deemed terrorist. There appears to be an emerging trend at several levels with regard to the elements of terrorism. Whereas the UK House of Lords felt obliged in 1996 to return to a pre-Second World War draft convention for a definition of terrorism,[49] more recently there have been signs of a consensus in the description of this phenomenon. At the international level, the United Nations' draft Comprehensive Convention on International Terrorism has provided a definition of terrorism,[50] as have some European Union documents.[51] It is also worthwhile mentioning that the Special Tribunal for Lebanon[52] has provided a definition of terrorism, based on both conventional and customary international law. At the national level, a number of countries have passed criminal legislation to combat terrorism, which invariably includes a definition as well. All these sources set out two essential elements for a working definition of terrorism: first, the commission of a very serious crime that affects the integrity of persons or property, including infrastructure; and second, that these crimes are carried out in order to intimidate a population or force a government or international organization to do something or refrain from doing something.[53] An approach that could be followed by refugee decision makers if an emerging comprehensive description is brought to bear could provide consistency in asylum proceedings.

The use of Article 1F(b) for terrorism activities has often brought into play the issue of political crimes. All countries have applied the so-called predominance and proportionality test, which was originally developed in international extradition law. This test entails an assessment of the political motivation of the perpetrator. If the reason for engaging in common crimes is predominantly political, in the sense that there is a direct relationship between the offence and the political goal sought, one part of the test is fulfilled. Connected to this part of the test is the context in which the crimes are carried out, in that the more oppressive a state apparatus is or if the crimes are carried out during a civil war, the more likely this leg of the test can be accepted. Conversely, resorting to violent means in a democratic society with a fully independent court system will rarely be considered a political offence, as there are other means in such a society by which to accomplish political objectives. Furthermore, the second requirement of proportionality must be fulfilled, meaning that the violence of the criminal act or the damage caused by it needs to be weighed against the purpose to be achieved. If the result of the crime causes unpredictable or large amounts of damage or harm to victims who have no connection to the object of the attack, this part of the test has not been met.[54]

This test was already enunciated by the UK House of Lords in 1996, and this decision has been used by the highest courts in Canada,[55] New Zealand,[56] the UK itself,[57] the US,[58] and Australia[59] (although in Australia the legislator clarified that the first part of the test would apply only to dominant purposes of the crimes carried out, whereas the High Court had required a lower standard in this regard, namely, a significant purpose[60]). In continental Europe the same test was set out in tribunal and court decisions.[61]

While the abstract test was the same in all countries, at times its application to the cases at hand differed. For instance, when an asylum seeker raised the political purpose for the commission of crimes, the argument was rejected each time in Belgium,[62] Canada,[63] Germany, and the US.[64] It was also rejected in the majority of cases in Australia, France, the Netherlands, New Zealand, and the UK, but was accepted on some occasions in slightly different situations. In Australia, for instance, the High Court was of the opinion that the political views of a person who committed very serious crimes, including murder, for the independence of Khalistan in India were not sufficiently considered, and sent the case back for a rehearing.[65] In France, the political purpose was accepted for a Chechnyan freedom fighter in the civil war against Russia because he carried out his activities within the confines of the rules of war while defending his country and family.[66] In New Zealand the same result was reached for a person who had been fighting for the liberation of Oromo in Ethiopia,[67] as well as for a ship's engineer involved in the transportation of arms on behalf of the Liberation Tigers of Tamil Eelam (LTTE) in Sri Lanka.[68] In the Netherlands, a person who provided information to a party opposed to the Saddam Hussein regime, resulting in the murder of two members of the security apparatus, was found to have acted for a political purpose while adhering to the proportionality principle.[69]

Complicity

While in most cases Article 1F(b) was applied to persons personally involved in serious crimes, there has been little hesitation by the judiciary to extend the reach of this clause to persons who carried out such activities in an indirect fashion. The contours of complicity have been specifically addressed in Australia,[70] Belgium,[71] Canada,[72] Germany,[73] the Netherlands,[74] New Zealand,[75] the UK,[76] and the US.[77] In some instances it was stated that the same complicity principles that apply to Article 1F(a) for the international crimes of genocide, war crimes, and crimes against humanity should be used for Article 1F(b). However, at times the caveat was added that the government was not absolved from the obligation to show that a person who was a member of an organization that had been placed on a prohibited list did indeed support that organization, implying that membership alone is not sufficient to attract Article 1F(b) liability.[78] Germany employed the words "substantial contribution" to describe the level of involvement required for Article 1F(b) activities.[79] In one case, a tribunal in France relied on a number of factors, such as duration and the intensity of the association with a nefarious group, and the manner of disassociation from it, to determine complicity.[80] In Australia, peripheral support functions by crews of ships involved in people smuggling were found not to amount to complicity.[81] An association with a hybrid organization with both a peaceful and a militant faction was considered enough to warrant exclusion in the Netherlands[82] and the US,[83] even though in both situations the association was with the peaceful element of the organization.

This interplay between Articles 1F(a) and 1F(b), regarding extended liability, poses a conceptual dilemma. On one hand, the same word is used in both provisions, but on the other hand, exclusion under Article 1F(a) includes a specific reference to international instruments (meaning international criminal law), which is not the case for 1F(b).

Since Article 1F(b) fulfills a different role than 1F(a) in that it is primarily concerned with individual crimes for which traditional forms of extended liability were envisaged, caution should be exercised in applying forms of liability developed in Article 1F(a). A better source for forms of liability might lie with transnational law, especially the most recent terrorism conventions, such as the *International Convention for the Suppression of Terrorist Bombings*[84] and the *International Con-*

vention for the Suppression of the Financing of Terrorism,[85] as well as the already mentioned *International Convention against Transnational Organized Crime.*[86] These conventions have a large number of ratifications, including by all the countries mentioned in this chapter, and represent the consensus of a large number of states with respect to the extended liability concepts set out in these treaties. For instance, the most recent treaty dealing with organized crime includes the following types of liability: organizing, directing, aiding, abetting, facilitating, counselling, and common purpose.[87] Some of these modes of liability are known in international criminal law, and guidance could be derived from the international jurisprudence. Nevertheless, it is more likely that transnational legal concepts will be interpreted by national criminal courts, since the provisions of transnational treaties are typically implemented in national legislation.

EXCLUSION 1F(B) IN THE CANADIAN CONTEXT

The Concept of Serious Crime

The comparative analysis above has analyzed the Canadian jurisprudence primarily in the context of general propositions with respect to the exclusion ground in Article 1F(b) until the middle of 2011. However, since that time the majority of the cases decided by the Federal Court have dealt with the application of the methodology adopted in the *Jayasekara* case in 2008 by the Federal Court of Appeal.[88] The case stood for the following propositions with respect to the notion of "serious crime":

- There is a strong presumption that any crime for which the equivalent carries a maximum penalty of more than ten years in Canadian criminal law is a serious crime, even though the actual sentence imposed abroad might be less than the maximum penalty.
- Factors such as the elements of the crime, the mode of prosecution, the penalty prescribed, the facts, and the mitigating and aggravating circumstances underlying the conviction should be considered in this context of serious criminality and could rebut this presumption.[89]
- Economic crimes can also be Article 1F(b) crimes.[90]
- The mitigating and aggravating factors should be balanced in a meaningful manner.[91]

The Supreme Court of Canada briefly confirmed this approach of serious crime as follows:

> The Federal Court of Appeal in *Chan* ... and *Jayasekara* has taken the view that where a maximum sentence of ten years or more could have been imposed had the crime been committed in Canada, the crime will generally be considered serious. I agree. However, this generalization should not be understood as a rigid presumption that is impossible to rebut. Where a provision ... has a large sentencing range, the upper end being ten years or more and the lower end being quite low, a claimant whose crime would fall at the less serious end of the range in Canada should not be presumptively excluded. Article 1F(*b*) is designed to exclude only those whose crimes are serious ... While consideration of whether a maximum sentence of ten years or more could have been imposed had the crime been committed in Canada is a useful guideline, and crimes attracting a maximum sentence of ten years or more in Canada will generally be sufficiently serious to warrant exclusion, the ten-year rule should not be applied in a mechanistic, decontextualized, or unjust manner.[92]

The new factor[93] related to the sentencing range has been explored in Federal Court jurisprudence to the effect that potential Canadian sentences should be assessed in this context, for which actual foreign sentences received can be an important consideration.[94]

With respect to the penalty described, a decision maker should not take into account the cumulative effect of the penalties that could be imposed for all the offences committed by a person.[95] On the other hand, a decision maker should not confuse maximum penalties that can be imposed for the commission of an offence with a mandatory minimum sentence, in that the latter has no role to play in the assessment of what constitutes a serious crime.[96]

The Federal Court has held that the mode of prosecution referred to above relates to the choice made by a foreign prosecutor in deciding to proceed in the case of hybrid offences. This choice can be proceeding with either the more serious variation of the offence in question – namely, by way of indictment, or with the less serious manner of laying a charge by using a summary or misdemeanour offence. The implication of a preference in which a prosecutor went ahead with the less serious charge is a factor in favour of the asylum seeker.[97] On the other hand, if an offence is committed outside Canada but the behaviour amounts to a hybrid offence in Canada of which the summary variation has a maximum penalty much higher than other summary offences in Canada, such as the offence of sexual interference, a person can be excluded.[98]

The courts have indicated that the seriousness of an offence is measured by the criminal law in Canada at the time of the refugee determination[99] rather than the time of commission.[100]

Aggravating factors can include habitual criminal conduct as well as possible psychological harm to victims;[101] absconding from the jurisdiction where the crime was committed;[102] and committing crimes after having been given protection in another country.[103]

Mitigating circumstances can include admission of guilt by the claimant, a favourable plea bargain, a troubled childhood,[104] the claimant's age, lack of previous convictions, limited amount of drugs, and the fact that the substance contained methamphetamine as opposed to pure methamphetamine;[105] the claimant's refugee status, and life in a marginalized neighbourhood;[106] and the claimant's addiction to painkillers resulting from an injury occurred during a criminal gang fight, his cooperation with authorities and his role as an instrumental key witness for the Crown as well as the lack of weapons in the drug trafficking offence and that absence of serious injury resulting from the offence.[107]

Although mitigating circumstances are part of the considerations of the decision maker, these circumstances are only relevant if they relate to the commission of the offence at that time and not to issues with respect to the character of the refugee claimant after the event in question. As such, factors such as rehabilitation[108] and the person not posing a danger to the security of Canada after arrival[109] are not to be taken into account. Serving a sentence in the country where the crime was committed is not conclusive either.[110] On the other hand, post-conviction conduct that sheds light on the factors highlighted in *Jayasekara*, such as probation and parole violations related to the offence in question, is relevant for Article 1F(b).[111] However, a full defence such as duress goes beyond being a mitigating factor and instead negates liability under Article 1F(b), if accepted.[112]

The Impact of Foreign Convictions and Charges

A foreign conviction can be relied upon as long as the foreign laws are not so unjust as to be intolerable[113] and there is no challenge to the integrity of the applicant's conviction or the judicial system of the foreign country.[114] However, if the judicial system is allegedly corrupt, a decision maker can go behind the record of conviction.[115] The fact that charges were dismissed in a foreign jurisdiction does not, by itself, mean that a serious crime was not committed, and the decision maker can rely on other evidence, as well as the evidence adduced in the criminal trial that did not result in a conviction, to assess whether exclusion under Article 1F(b) should be applied. Factors with respect to the use of the evidence that led to the dismissal of charges include whether the dismissal was for technical, legal reasons, as well in which country the dismissal took place.[116] On the other hand, in the case of *Mohamad Jawad v. Canada*, for example, an allegation whereby a police report referred to trafficking in drugs but a later criminal conviction was for the reduced charge of possession, combined with a short period of probation, was held not to be a serious offence.[117]

CONCLUSION

Most notions that form elements of Article 1F(b) are still in a considerable amount of flux at the international level, with only the parameters of political crimes having been resolved in a satisfactory manner by national institutions through the use of the predominance and proportionality test.

In common law countries, the criminal law of the country of refuge has been held to be the determinative factor in determining the notion of what constitutes a crime, while this issue has not been addressed so far in continental Europe.

With respect to the relevance of foreign convictions, some countries have had no problem using such convictions to find Article 1F(b) exclusion, while others have been more careful. The difference in opinion could very well stem from the country of origin in which the conviction was imposed. Indeed, more deference would be given to legal systems with an independent judiciary applying rules that are similar to the ones used in the country of refuge.

The reasoning used to conclude that a crime should be considered serious has varied from country to country. The most common approaches range from examining the maximum penalty that could be imposed in the criminal legislation, to examining what penalty would likely be imposed if a person were to be tried by a criminal court. More recently, a third approach, originally developed in Canada, has been gaining popularity in common law countries. This approach uses a number of factors to determine whether a crime is serious, such as a penalty indicated in the criminal legislation, the actual possible sentence, and possible mitigating and aggravating circumstances that could affect the presumption regarding penalties. One area of international law – transnational law – could provide an answer, as a treaty in that area had equated serious crime with a maximum penalty of four years.

While the notion of what constitutes a serious crime outside the country of origin appears obvious, Article 1F(b) has at times been applied in situations in which crimes began outside a country of refuge and continued inside that country, as well as where the conduct occurred within the country of refuge but were carried out in support of organizations that committed crimes outside that country.

The notion of expiation by reasons of serving a sentence or receiving a pardon or amnesty have, in most countries, been found to not be a factor to be taken into account for an Article 1F(b) determination, although in some countries this is only a recent development.

In the majority of cases, Article 1F(b) exclusion has been applied to persons personally involved in serious crimes, but there has been little hesitation by the judiciary in all countries examined to extend the reach of this clause to persons who carried out such activities in an indirect fashion. However, at the moment there is some uncertainly as to what form and which principles of liability should be applied, even though some countries have started to use the extensive jurisprudence developed in Article 1F(a) for this purpose. Again, transnational law might be a better source for Article 1F(b), as some treaties in this field have already provided some guidance.

These issues could still benefit from some guidance from the highest national courts or even international institutions in order to avoid too much fragmentation in the future of this important area of refugee law.

On the other hand, in Canada most of these issues have been resolved by the courts. The notion especially of what constitutes a serious crime has been given the most attention in the last couple of years. This jurisprudence has provided more details to the approach of using aggravating and mitigating factors, as developed by the Federal Court of Appeal in 2008 in *Jayasekara*. In 2014 this development was given new impetus by the recent decision of the Supreme Court of Canada in *Febles*. This has given rise to new litigation with respect to the meaning of the new factor set out in that decision, relating to the sentencing range of criminal offences. It is not yet clear where the Federal Court (and possibly higher courts) will land on this particular question.

While the jurisprudence, both in other countries and in Canada, has waxed and waned in terms of the reach of Article 1F(b), and as a result the numbers of asylum claimants affected by such vicissitudes in the approach taken by the courts, on the whole it would appear that more recently fewer such claimants will be affected by the application of Article 1F(b) than in the past. While the notion of expiation has expanded, it is used in a very small number of cases, while other legal aspects, such as the notions of crime, serious crime, and political crime, which affect far more people, have on the whole been applied less often.

NOTES

1 *Convention Relating to the Status of Refugees* ("Refugee Convention"), 28 July 1951, 189 UNTS 150, Can. TS 1969/6.
2 Refugee Convention, 1951, Art. 1A(2).
3 *Igor Ovcharuk v. Minister for Immigration and Multicultural Affairs* [1998] FCA 1314.
4 *Zrig v. Canada (Minister of Citizenship and Immigration)*, [2003] 3 FC 761, 2003 FCA 178 (CanLII); *Sing v. Canada (Minister of Citizenship and Immigration)*, 2005 FCA 125 (CanLII); *Jayasekara v. Canada (Minister of Citizenship and Immigration)*, [2009] 4 FCR 164, 2008 FCA 404 (CanLII); and *Li v. Canada (Minister of Citizenship and Immigration)*, [2010] 3 FCR 347, 2010 FCA 75 (CanLII).
5 *S. v. Refugee Status Appeals Authority*, CA262/97, New Zealand: Court of Appeal, 2 April 1998.
6 *Kovacs v. Canada (Minister of Citizenship and Immigration)*, 2005 FC 1473 (CanLII); and *Jayasekara v. Canada*, 2009.
7 *"WAT" and Minister for Immigration and Multicultural and Indigenous Affairs* [2002] AATA 1150; and YYMT and Anor and FRFJ and Anor [2010] AATA 447.
8 YYMT and Anor and FRFJ and Anor, 2010, para. 120, in Australia; CCE No. 163.448, 3 March 2016, in Belgium; *AH (Algeria) v. the Secretary of State for*

the Home Department [2012] EWCA Civ 395, para. 16, in the UK; and in the Netherlands, Awb, 12/39765, 4 February 2014; AbRS, 201403749/1/V1, 8 December 2014; Awb, 12/22706, 27 January 2015; and Awb 13/16907, 24 April 2016. Although for an opposite finding in the Netherlands, see Awb 15/3802, 16 February 2016.

9 *Biro v. Canada (Citizenship and Immigration)*, 2007 FC 776 (CanLII); *Arevalo Pineda v. Canada (Citizenship and Immigration)*, 2010 FC 454 (CanLII); and *Ching v. Canada (Citizenship and Immigration)*, [2016] 1 FCR 507, 2015 FC 860 (CanLII).

10 *Abramov v. Ashcroft*, Docket No. 03-71856 (9th Cir. 2004).

11 Frédéric Tiberghien, *La protection des réfugiés en France* (Aix-en-Provence: Presses Universitaires D'Aix-Marseille, 1988), 469.

12 In a slightly different context, the Supreme Administrative Court of Finland, in assessing the criminal process in Finland of a person who was also considered for exclusion, was of the view that neither a criminal conviction nor the filing of an indictment was required to meet the standard of serious grounds for considering in the Refugee Convention, but that if such actions had been taken they were equivalent to this standard, although this might not be the case for a police investigation into such an allegation (KHO:2014:35, 18 February 2014); see also in the Netherlands the case of Awb 14/12590, 10 July 2014; and in Australia the cases of *SRYYY v. Minister for Immigration and Multicultural and Indigenous Affairs* [2005] FCAFC 42, and *VWYJ v. Minister for Immigration and Multicultural and Indigenous Affairs* [2006] FCAFC 1.

13 *Xie v. Canada (Minister of Citizenship and Immigration)*, [2005] 1 FCR 304, 2004 FCA 250 (CanLII); and *Sing v. Canada*, 2005.

14 AbRS 30 December 2009, nr. 200902983/1.

15 *Mahini v. INS*, 779 F.2d 1419 (9th Cir, 1986); *Arauz v. Rivkind*, 834 F.2d 979 (11th Cir. 1987); and *Kenyeres v. Ashcroft*, 538 US 1301 (2003).

16 *Brzezinski v. Canada (Minister of Citizenship and Immigration)*, [1998] 4 FCR 525, 1998 CanLII 9079 (FC).

17 *Minister for Immigration and Multicultural and Indigenous Affairs v. Singh* [2002] HCA 7; *SZJRI v. MIC* [2008] FCA 1090; *Ballibay and Minister for Immigration and Multicultural and Indigenous Affairs* [2002] HCA 7; [2000] AATA 1147; and *SRLLL and Minister for Immigration and Multicultural and Indigenous Affairs* [2002] AATA 795.

18 BverwG 10 C 7.09, 10 February 2010, para. 47; BverwG 10 C 24.08, 24 November 2009, para. 41; and BverwG 10 C 48.07, 14 October 2008, para, 19.

19 Most recently, see CNDA, 27 October 2014, 14016605, M. E.; and CNDA 3 November 2015, 10013998, M.B.

20 *Chan v. Canada (Minister of Citizenship and Immigration)*, [2000] 4 FCR 390, 2000 CanLII 17150 (FCA).

21 Tiberghien, *La protection des réfugiés*, 103–4, 468–69.

22 This is also the approach at the international level with the international *United Nations Convention against Transnational Organized Crime*, which came into force in 2003. It sets the penalty level for serious crimes as four years in Article 2(b).

23 AbRS, 201208875/1/V1, 10 February 2014; Awb 13/12113, 17 September 2013; and AbRS, 201202758/1, 27 September 2013.

24 BverwG 10 C 7.09, 10 February 2010, para. 47; BverwG 10 C 24.08, 24 November 2009, para. 41; and BverwG 10 C 48.07, 14 October 2008, para. 19.

25 RSAA 76157, 26 June 2008, para. 196–200, for New Zealand. For the UK, see *R. (on the application of Polat) v. Secretary of State for the Home Department*, [2011] EWHC 3445 (Admin), para. 73; and *R (ABC a minor) v. Home Secretary* [2011] EWHC 2937 (Admin), para. 35.

26 *FTZK v. Minister for Immigration and Border Protection* [2014] HCA 26, para. 78.

27 *Jayasekara v. Canada*, 2009.

28 *Mahini v. INS*, 1986.

29 CRR, 26 May 2005, 459358, V.; CRR, 28 January 2005, 448119, C.; CRR, 4 April 2005, 487639, N.; and CNDA, 15 January 2009, 594649, R.

30 *United Nations Convention against Transnational Organized Crime*, which states in Article 2(b): "'serious crime' shall mean conduct constituting an offence punishable by a maximum deprivation of liberty of at least four years or a more serious penalty."

31 *SRBBBB and Minister for Immigration and Multicultural and Indigenous Affairs* [2003] AATA 1066, and *SRCCCC and Minister for Immigration and Multicultural and Indigenous Affairs* [2004] AATA 315, in Australia. For Belgium, see CCE No. 151.393, 28 August 2015.

32 *Guo Wang v. Eric Holder*, Docket No. 07-5369-ag (2d Circuit, 2009).

33 *Attorney-General (Minister of Immigration) v. Tamil X and the RSAA*, [2010] NZSC 107, para. 81, 84.

34 *Kovacs v. Canada*, 2005; and *Paris Montoya v. Canada (Minister of Citizenship and Immigration)*, 2005 FC 1674 (CanLII).

35 CNDA, 3 November 2015, 10013998, M. B.

36 Awb 14/9363, 1 July 2014; and Awb 14/12590, 10 July 2014.

37 AA (Exclusion clause) Palestine [2005] UKIAT 00104.

38 CRR, 18 April 1997, 291084, Danso; CNDA, 12 February 2009, 598383, K.; CRR, 8 December 1997, 316623, Brown; CRR, 7 July 1997, 272114, Hamid Husain; CE, 15 May 2000, 190059, Hamid; CRR, 18 May 2006, 548090, Kurta; CRR, 20 October 2005, 537046, T.; CNDA, 15 December 2009,

637456/08017677, S.; CNDA, 15 January 2009, 594649, R.; CRR, 3 May 2007, 586579, J.; CRR, 22 December 2000, 346184, Hatem; CRR, 14 December 2000, 336795, Bolinga; CRR, 20 June 2003, 412882, Mabika Konde; and CRR, 4 April 2005, 487639, N.

39 *Dhayakpa v. Minister for Immigration and Ethnic Affairs*, (1995) 62 FCR 556; *Ovcharuk v. Minister for Immigration and Multicultural and Indigenous Affairs* [2002] HCA 7; *Ovcharuk v. Minister for Immigration and Multicultural Affairs*, 1998; *NADB v. Minister for Immigration and Multicultural and Indigenous Affairs* [2002] FCA 200; and *"WAT" and MIMIA*, 2002.

40 CE, 25 September 1998, 165525, Rajkumar; and CRR, 26 October 2005, 399706, K.

41 *Febles v. Canada (Citizenship and Immigration)*, [2014] 3 SCR 431, 2014 SCC 68 (CanLII).

42 BverwG 10 C 48.07, 14 October 2008, para. 27–30.

43 *AH (Algeria) v. Secretary of State for the Home Department* [2015] EWCA Civ 1003 (relying on the *Febles* case). See also *Ireland, H.O. v. Refugee Appeals Tribunal and Anor* [2014] IEHC 494; and Greece, Council of State, Application No. 1661/2012, 8 May 2012.

44 EC (Sri Lanka) [2017] NZIPT 801021 (relying on the *Febles* case).

45 *Bundesrepublik Deutschland v. B. and D.* (C-57/09) and (C-101/09), CJEU, 2010, para. 100–5.

46 Compare CRR, 14 November 1997, 290466, Can; CRR, 22 January 1999, 322914, Tat; CRR, 26 October 2005, 399706, K.; and CRR, 21 July 2006, 509322, Toskic, with CE, Ofpra c/ M.A., 320910, 4 May 2011.

47 Compare CCE No. 16.779, 30 September 2008, with CCE No. 27.479, 18 May 2009; CCE No. 69.656, 8 November 2011; and CCE No. 118.284 31 January 2014.

48 *Febles v. Canada*, 2014.

49 *T. v. Secretary of State for the Home Department* [1996] AC 742, referring to the League of Nations *Convention on the Prevention and Punishment of Terrorism*, which has the following definition: "'acts' of terrorism mean criminal acts directed against a State and intended or calculated to create a state of terror in the minds of particular persons, or a group of persons or the general public."

50 UN Doc. A/59/895, 12 August 2005, Appendix II, Art. 2.

51 *European Convention on the Suppression of Terrorism*, concluded at Strasbourg on 27 January 1977. There is also the *European Convention for the Prevention of Terrorism*, concluded at Warsaw on 16 May 2005, which does not contain a definition of terrorism but criminalizes extended liability, such as recruitment and training. The source for these two instruments was the Council of

Europe. However, in the context of the European Union, the Council Common Position of 27 December 2001 (which was repeated a year later in the 2002 Council Framework Decision of 13 June 2002 on combating terrorism) on the application of specific measures to combat terrorism provides a more detailed definition.

52 *Interlocutory Decision on the Applicable Law: Terrorism, Conspiracy, Homicide, Perpetration, Cumulative Charging*, STL-II-OI/I/AC/RI76bis, Special Tribunal for Lebanon, Appeals Chamber, 16 February 2011.

53 Joseph Rikhof, *The Criminal Refugee: The Treatment of Asylum Seekers with a Criminal Background in International and Domestic Law* (Delft: Republic of Letters, 2012), 302–4.

54 Geoff Gilbert, *Responding to International Crime*, 2nd rev. ed. (Leiden: Martinus Nijhoff, 2006), 205–28.

55 *Gil v. Canada (Minister of Employment and Immigration)*, [1995] 1 FCR 508, 1994 CanLII 3523 (FCA).

56 *Attorney-General (Minister of Immigration) v. Tamil X*, 2010, para. 81–96.

57 AA (Exclusion clause) Palestine [2005] UKIAT 00104.

58 *McMullen v. INS*, 788 F.2d 591 (9th Cir. 1986); *Efe v. Ashcroft*, 293 F.3d 899 (5th Cir. 2002); *McAllister v. AG of the United States*, 444 F.3d 178 (3rd Cir. 2006); *Chay-Velasquez v. Ashcroft*, 367 F.3d 751 (8th Cir. 2004); *Berhane v. Holder*, Docket No. No. 09-3153 (6th Cir. 2010); and *Annachamy v. Holder*, 686 F.3d 729 (9th Cir. 2012).

59 *MIMIA v. Singh*, 2002.

60 Section 91T of the Migration Act 1958, which was interpreted by YYMT and Anor and FRFJ and Anor, 2010.

61 See, in France: CRR, 9 January 2003, 362645, Altun; CRR, 11 May 2006, 523285, Ucar; CRR, 25 July 2006, 538535, Tagiyev; and CRR, 25 January 2007, 552944, S. In Germany: BverwG 10 C 48.07, 14 October 2008, para. 20; BverwG 10 C 7.09, 10 February 2010, para. 48; and BverwG 10 C 24.08, 24 November 2009, para. 42. In the Netherlands: Awb 02/60920, 19 July 2004; Awb 04/40384, 24 May 2005; Awb 03/26897, 2 July 2004; and Awb 13/24563, 15 July 2014. In Greece: Council of State, Application No. 1661/2012, 8 May 2012.

62 CCE No. 33.720, 3 November 2009.

63 *Gregorio v. Canada (Minister of Citizenship and Immigration)*, 1999 CanLII 7541 (FC); *Taleb v. Canada (Minister of Citizenship and Immigration)*, 1999 CanLII 8014 (FC); *Vergara v. Canada (Minister of Citizenship and Immigration)*, 2001 FCT 474 (CanLII); *Sharma v. Canada (Minister of Citizenship and Immigration)*, 2003 FCT 289 (CanLII); *Zrig v. Canada (Minister of Citizenship and Immigration)*, [2002] 1 FCR 559, 2001 FCT 1043 (CanLII);

Sing v. Canada, 2005; and *Durango v. Canada (Citizenship and Immigration)*, 2012 FC 1081 (CanLII).

64 *Efe v. Ashcroft*, 2002; *McAllister v. AG of the United States*, 2006; *Chay-Velasquez v. Ashcroft*, 2004; and *Berhane v. Holder*, 2010.

65 *MIMIA v. Singh*, 2002.

66 CRR, 25 January 2007, 552944, S.

67 RSAA Appeal No. 71150, 4 March 1999.

68 *Attorney-General (Minister of Immigration) v. Tamil X*, 2010.

69 Awb 02/60920, 19 July 2004.

70 *MIMIA v. Singh*, 2002.

71 CPPR No. 99-0164/W5686, 17 September 1999; and CCE No. 118.284, 31 January 2014.

72 *Gregorio v. Canada*, 1999; *Zrig v. Canada*, 2003 (relying on Australian jurisprudence); *Jaouadi v. Canada (Minister of Citizenship and Immigration)*, 2005 FC 1256 (CanLII); and *Rudyak v. Canada (Minister of Citizenship and Immigration)*, 2006 FC 1141 (CanLII).

73 BverwG 10 C 48.07, 14 October 2008, para. 21; and BverwG 1 C 19.09, 26 October 2010, para. 23.

74 Awb 05/54643, 15 September 2006; as well most recently Awb 16/6954, 7 March 2017; Awb 16/27787, 20 June 2017; and Awb 17/2027, 15 August 2017.

75 RSAA 74273, 10 May 2006; RSAA 71335, 12 September 2000; RSAA 71398, 10 February 2000; and RSAA 70001, 30 April 1997.

76 *Polat v. SSHD*, 2011.

77 *Singh-Kaur v. Ashcroft*, 385 F.3d 293 (3rd Cir. 2004); *Perinpanathan v. INS*, 310 F.3d 594 (8th Cir. 2002); *Khan v. Holder*, 584 F.3d 773 (9th Cir. 2009); *Raghunathan v. Holder*, Docket No. 08-2475, 08-3147 (2nd Cir. 2010); and *Haile v. Holder*, 658 F.3d 1122 (9th Cir. 2011).

78 BverwG 10 C 48.07, 14 October 2008, para. 17–18. This part of the decision was upheld by the Court of Justice of the European Union, from which a preliminary ruling had been requested by the Federal Administrative Court, in the case of *Bundesrepublik Deutschland v. B. and D.*, 2010, para. 87–99.

79 BverwG 10 C 48.07, 14 October 2008, para. 21. Along the same lines, in the context of immigration, see BverwG 1 C 19.09, 26 October 2010, para. 23.

80 CRR, 26 May 2005, 459358, V.; CRR, 28 January 2005, 448119, C.; CRR, 4 April 2005, 487639, N.; and CNDA, 15 January 2009, 594649, R.

81 *SRBBBB and Minister for Immigration and Multicultural and Indigenous Affairs*, 2003; and *SRCCCC and Minister for Immigration and Multicultural and Indigenous Affairs*, 2004.

82 Awb 02/71646, 2 November 2004.

83 *SRBBBB and MIMIA*, 2003; and *SRCCCC and MIMIA*, 2004.
84 Adopted by the General Assembly of the United Nations on 15 December 1997.
85 Adopted by the General Assembly of the United Nations on 9 December 1999.
86 Adopted by the General Assembly of the United Nations on 15 November 2000.
87 Article 5.1.
88 *Jayasekara v. Canada*, 2009. In January 2004, Jayasekara was arrested in New York State on drug charges and pled guilty to the criminal sale of the controlled substance opium in the third degree and to criminal possession of marijuana. In March 2004, he was convicted and sentenced to twenty-nine days in jail and a five-year probation period.
89 Four cases did not provide a legal analysis of the principles involved but came to the factual conclusion that the Immigration and Refugee Board member had applied the principles in question correctly. See *Roberts v. Canada (Citizenship and Immigration)*, 2011 FC 632, dealing with drug offences committed in the US; *Durango v. Canada*, 2012 (use of a forged document in the U.S); *Tincul v. Canada (Citizenship and Immigration)*, 2013 FC 628 (homicide in Moldova); and Canada *(Citizenship and Immigration) v. Pulido Diaz*, 2011 FC 738 (property offences such as theft and robbery). In the latter case the exclusion by the Immigration and Refugee Board was overruled – one of the few cases in which this result was reached.
90 *Simkovic v. Canada (Citizenship and Immigration)*, 2014 FC 113 (CanLII) (tax evasion in Slovakia).
91 *Poggio Guerrero v. Canada (Citizenship and Immigration)*, 2012 FC 937 (CanLII) (drug trafficking in the US); *Valdespino Partida v. Canada (Citizenship and Immigration)*, 2013 FC 359 (CanLII) (theft in the US); *Vucaj v. Canada (Citizenship and Immigration)*, 2013 FC 381 (CanLII) (drug trafficking in the US); and Canada *(Citizenship and Immigration v. Nwobi*, 2014 FC 520 (CanLII) (drug trafficking in Germany and killing in Nigeria).
92 *Febles v. Canada*, 2014, para. 62.
93 *Jung v. Canada (Citizenship and Immigration)*, 2015 FC 464 (CanLII), para. 38.
94 *Jung v. Canada*, 2015, para. 48 (fraud in Korea); *Tabagua v. Canada (Citizenship and Immigration)*, 2015 FC 709 (CanLII) (forgery and identity fraud in Georgia); *Mohamed v. Canada (Citizenship and Immigration)*, 2015 FC 1006 (CanLII) (terrorism in Sri Lanka); Mustafa v. Canada (Citizenship and Immigration), 2016 FC 116 (CanLII) (forgery and identity fraud in the US); and *Omar v. Canada (Citizenship and Immigration)*, 2016 FC 602 (CanLII) (aggravated assault in the US); *Sajid v. Canada (Citizenship and Immigration)*,

2016 FC 981 (CanLII) (fraud and illegal arms exports in the US); and *A. B. v. Canada (Citizenship and Immigration)*, 2016 FC 1385 (CanLII) (child abduction in Hungary).

95 *Vucaj v. Canada*, 2013.

96 *Canada v. Nwobi*, 2014.

97 *Canada (Citizenship and Immigration) v. Lopez Velasco*, 2011 FC 627 (CanLII); and *Canada (Citizenship and Immigration) v. Ammar*, 2011 FC 1094 (CanLII). Both cases dealt with minor sexual offences in the US, resulting in the persons not being excluded in Canada, as these offences did not meet the threshold of serious criminality. In the same vein, see *Vucaj v. Canada*, 2013, and *Narkaj v. Canada (Citizenship and Immigration)*, 2015 FC 26 (CanLII) (breaking and entering in the US). For examples where exclusion was upheld, see *Hernandez Gomez v. Canada (Citizenship and Immigration)*, 2014 FC 271 (CanLII) (weapons offences in the US); and *Reyes v. Canada (Citizenship and Immigration)*, 2015 FC 1015 (CanLII) (assault in the US).

98 *Canada (Citizenship and Immigration) v. Raina*, 2012 FC 618 (CanLII).

99 *Guerra Diaz v. Canada (Citizenship and Immigration)*, 2013 FC 88 (CanLII) (providing money and untraceable phones to a drug cartel in Mexico, but not amounting to a serious offence); *Gamboa Micolta v. Canada (Citizenship and Immigration)*, 2013 FC 367 (CanLII); and *Notario v. Canada (Citizenship and Immigration)*, 2014 FC 1159 (CanLII) (fraud in the United Arab Emirates), although this last case is slightly more circumspect by saying that "there is no hard and fast rule that the conduct must be criminal in the potential country of refuge" and that "the gravity of a crime must be judged against international standards" – the exclusion ruling was overruled.

100 *Sanchez v. Canada (Citizenship and Immigration)*, 2013 FC 913 (CanLII), (drug trafficking in the US), upheld on appeal in *Sanchez v. Canada (Citizenship and Immigration)*, 2014 FCA 157 (CanLII).

101 *Poggio Guerrero v. Canada*, 2010 FC 384 (CanLII); *Canada v. Raina*, 2012 (sexual offences in New Zealand); *Gamboa Micolta v. Canada*, 2013 (burglary and evading arrest in the US); *Gudima v. Canada (Citizenship and Immigration)*, 2013 FC 382 (CanLII) (assault in the US); and *Canada (Citizenship and Immigration) v. Pierre*, 2013 FC 810 (CanLII) (burglary in the US).

102 *Gamboa Micolta v. Canada*, 2013; and *Unachukwu v. Canada (Citizenship and Immigration)*, 2014 FC 199 (CanLII) (spousal assault in the US).

103 *Narkaj v. Canada*, 2015.

104 *Gudima v. Canada*, 2013.

105 *Shire v. Canada (Citizenship and Immigration)*, 2012 FC 97 (CanLII); and *Narkaj v. Canada*, 2015.

106 Ibid.

107 *Vucaj v. Canada*, 2013.

108 *Rojas Camacho v. Canada (Citizenship and Immigration)*, 2011 FC 789 (Can-
LII) (drug trafficking in the US); *Hernandez Febles v. Canada (Citizenship
and Immigration)*, 2011 FC 1103 (CanLII) (assault with a deadly weapon in
the US); *Martinez Cuero v. Canada (Citizenship and Immigration)*, 2012 FC
191 (CanLII) (drug trafficking in the US); *Feimi v. Canada (Citizenship and
Immigration)*, 2012 FC 262 (CanLII) (murder in Greece); *Poggio Guerrero v.
Canada* 2012 (drug trafficking in the US); *Cho v. Canada (Citizenship and
Immigration)*, 2013 FC 45 (CanLII) (various serious crime in Korea as a
member of a gang); *Ospina Velasquez v. Canada (Citizenship and Immigration)*, 2013 FC 273 (CanLII) (armed robbery and drug offences in the US);
Valdespino Partida v. Canada, 2013; and *Sanchez v. Canada*, 2013 (this case
also makes it clear that a change in legislation in Canada making an offence
more or less serious later than at the time it was committed is not relevant
for this proposition; this position was conclusively confirmed in *Febles v.
Canada*, 2014, 60).

109 *Hernandez Febles v. Canada*, 2011; *Feimi v. Canada*, 2012, confirmed by *Febles
v. Canada*, 2014; and *Skoro v. Canada (Citizenship and Immigration)*, 2015 FC
139 (CanLII) (drug trafficking in the US).

110 *Rojas Camacho v. Canada*, 2011; *Abu Ganem v. Canada (Citizenship and Immi-
gration)*, 2011 FC 1147 (CanLII) (manslaughter in Israel); *Radi v. Canada
(Citizenship and Immigration)*, 2012 FC 16 (CanLII) (domestic assault in the
US); *Cho v. Canada*, 2013; and *Ospina Velasquez v. Canada* 2013.

111 *Chernikov v. Canada (Citizenship and Immigration)*, 2013 FC 649 (CanLII)
(drunk driving causing bodily harm in the US). However, see *Profitt v. Canada*, 2015, where it is said that "evidence of unflattering post-conviction non-
criminal behaviour (e.g. failure to accept full responsibility for one's past) is
also irrelevant."

112 *Guerra Diaz v. Canada*, 2013; and *Villalobos v. Canada (Citizenship and Immigration)*, 2015 FC 60 (CanLII) (drug trafficking in Mexico). In *Jimenez v.
Canada (Citizenship and Immigration)*, 2012 FC 1231 (CanLII), the claim
regarding duress was rejected because the applicant, who had the onus to
prove this claim, did not provide any evidence in support.

113 *Notario v. Canada*, 2014.

114 *Abu Ganem v. Canada*, 2011.

115 *Canada (Citizenship and Immigration) v. Toktok*, 2013 FC 1150 (CanLII) (writing a false cheque in Turkey). The non-exclusion finding was upheld.

116 *Arevalo Pineda v. Canada (Citizenship and Immigration)*, 2010 FC 454

(CanLII) (sexual assault in the US); *Naranjo v. Canada (Citizenship and Immigration)*, 2011 FC 1127 (CanLII) (money laundering in the US); and *Radi v. Canada*, 2012.

117 *Mohamad Jawad v. Canada (Citizenship and Immigration)*, 2012 FC 232 (CanLII) (drug possession), in which the exclusion finding was overruled; *Simkovic v. Canada*, 2014.

PART THREE

Crimmigration Responses
to "Migration Crises":
Historical and Comparative Perspectives

7

Attrition through Enforcement and the Deportations of Syrians from Jordan and Turkey

Petra Molnar

Tarek,[1] a twenty-five-year-old lanky Syrian refugee, smokes cigarette after cigarette on the banks of the Bosphorus Strait in Istanbul, his hands visibly shaking with each drag. He has been living in Istanbul for a few years now, since he crossed at an unofficial border crossing in southeastern Turkey and made his way to the bustling metropolis. These days, he does not sleep much, "maybe three hours a day"; he works long hours at a mechanics shop, without a work permit, to make ends meet. When asked why he does not register with the Turkish authorities or the United Nations High Commissioner for Refugees (UNHCR), he becomes visibly agitated: "Why would I register? To go to jail and back to Syria?"[2]

Stories like Tarek's highlight the precarity of unregistered refugees who fear the very real risk of detention and deportation back to Syria. The return of Syrian refugees from host countries into zones of active conflict has been documented in both Turkey and Jordan, in contravention of domestic policies and international law, including the principle of non-refoulement. While Turkey and Jordan should be commended for handling an incredibly large number of Syrian refugees over the last six years with relative stability, detention and deportation policies are ultimately an ineffective way to control the numbers of Syrian refugees and instead perpetuate a discretionary system that violates international law.

In times of "crisis,"[3] the need of the sovereign nation under perceived threat to strengthen and police its borders becomes apparent.[4] However, Turkey and Jordan's securitization of their physical borders with Syria also extends to their domestic policy to exercise broad discretion to detain and deport Syrian refugees for a host of reasons that the state sees fit. The criminalization of migration in times of ongoing protracted conflict highlights the numerous strategies through which receiving states seek to manage and control migrant populations. The lens of "attrition through enforcement," or encouraging self-deportation by making life less satisfying, is a useful analytical tool through which to highlight the mechanisms of population control that Turkey and Jordan employ to demarcate, dislocate, and eventually deport Syrian refugees for a host of reasons. The concept of "attrition through enforcement" often appears in debates on irregular migration in the United States, where conditions are to be made expressly unliveable for irregular migrants to spur mass self-deportations.[5] This concept highlights how the state in its quest to regulate migrant population employs both hard-line as well as discretionary policies to criminalize, exclude, marginalize, and otherwise disempower migrants. While heavily used in the European and North American contexts, the criminalization of migration and attrition through enforcement take on very different approaches in the context of the ongoing Syrian conflict.

The concept of attrition through enforcement has been adapted to policies of detention and deportation with regard to Syrian refugees in the neighbouring host countries of Turkey and Jordan, where thousands of Syrian refugees live a precarious existence without access to meaningful work, social services, or community. These practices also highlight the malleability of international law doctrines such as non-refoulement, when host countries actively deter and both implicitly and explicitly encourage the return of refugees to a site of active conflict. The principle of non-refoulement, or not returning refugees to countries where they will face persecution, is at the core of international refugee protection. It is enshrined in numerous international instruments[6] and is widely considered to be customary international law and/or a peremptory norm. This means that all states, regardless of whether they are party or not to the Refugee Convention or other human rights treaties incorporating the prohibition against refoulement, are bound to comply with a prohibition on refoulement.[7] Furthermore, there are also other international humanitarian instruments designed to protect "war refugees" fleeing zones of active conflict by preventing their return to zones of conflict.[8]

This chapter is based on fieldwork conducted on behalf of the International Human Rights Program (IHRP), based at the University of Toronto's Faculty of Law. In May and June 2015, the IHRP conducted forty-five interviews with fifty-one people in Turkey (Istanbul, Gaziantep, and Antakya) and Jordan (Amman and Irbid), including lawyers, doctors, frontline practitioners working with NGOs and INGOs, and Syrian refugees in both countries. The purpose of this project was to assess the impact of Canada's resettlement and refugee protection policies on Syrian refugees living with HIV. The population profiled for this project, those particularly at risk of HIV transmission, were marginalized by multiple intersecting sources, including, but not limited to, people who have experienced sexual and gender-based violence (SGBV), people who identify as lesbian, gay, bisexual, transgender, or intersex (LGBTI), former detainees, and sex workers.

All interviews adhered to strict confidentiality principles and were conducted using an open-ended questionnaire. Most interviews were conducted in private offices of NGOs and INGOs, while some were more informal. Many of the interviews with service providers and NGO and INGO workers were followed up with by email or Skype in 2016. The interviewees were fully informed about the nature and purpose of our report, as well as the manner in which their information would be used. They were also explicitly provided the option of not participating or remaining anonymous in the final report. All of the interviewees agreed to share their experiences and participate in the research; some chose anonymity and others changed or deleted their names for security reasons during the course of the interview or in subsequent communications with the authors. None of the interviewees received incentives in exchange for their participation. The interviews were conducted in-person, with the exception of approximately ten interviews, which were conducted either by phone or e-mail, including correspondence with an organization in Beirut, Lebanon. Additional contacts were gathered using the snowball sampling method, based on established contacts in the region though journalistic, legal, and not-for-profit networks.

The primary purpose of this research project was to ascertain Canada's refugee policies and their impacts on Syrian refugees and host populations living with HIV, and it resulted in an internal report being released to the Canadian government by the IHRP.[9] However, links also emerged between the criminalization and detainability of certain types of "undesirable" Syrian refugees and broader state practices, giving rise to this chapter. As other pieces in this collection illustrate, the criminalization of migration has been observed in multiple jurisdictions globally through various legislative and policy means. What is particularly striking in countries such as Turkey and Jordan that have absorbed the majority of Syrian refugees during the ongoing conflict is the level of discretion in state practices that criminalize certain categories of refugees over others, rendering them precarious and deportable. Criminalization, or the risk thereof, also creates a climate that encourages refugees to self-deport, or move to other neighbouring countries and further inland into Europe. This chapter will highlight particular measures that Turkey and Jordan use to render refugees deportable, mainly the criminalization of work permit infractions and communicable diseases. It will also examine how state practices make life unliveable, by attrition through enforcement, to encourage refugees to self-deport.

Critical examinations of discretionary state practices that criminalize migration and create multiple tiers in the ability to exercise one's right to seek protection are paramount at a time when the Western world continues to resettle only a fraction of the world's refugees. When populist leaders spread fear, misinformation, and distrust through their statements and policies, it is often the rights of the most marginalized refugee communities that are most adversely affected.

SYRIA'S CONFLICT:
"THE WORST HUMANITARIAN DISASTER OF OUR TIME"[10]

The former United Nations High Commissioner for Refugees, António Guterres, has characterized Syrian refugees as "the biggest refugee population from a single conflict in a generation. It is a population that needs the support of the world but is instead living in dire conditions and sinking deeper into poverty."[11] As of April 2018, the UNHCR estimated the total number of Syrian refugees at about 5.65 million.[12] In addition, there are at least 6.5 million internally displaced people (IDPs) within Syria.[13] Exact numbers of fatalities are difficult to verify due to the ongoing conflict. However, according to Human Rights Watch and the Syrian Center for Policy Research (SCPR), an independent Syrian research organization, by 2016, war fatalities had amounted to over 470,000[14] and the number of injured and killed since the start of the conflict in 2011 is approximately 11.5 per cent of the population.[15] Syrian civilians are actively targeted in urban centres by the Assad regime[16] and by armed militants, including members of the Islamic State, also known as ISIS or Daesh.[17] As a result of ongoing violence, huge numbers of Syrians have fled to neighbouring countries such as Turkey, Jordan, and Lebanon, estimated to host as high as 95 per cent of the total number of refugees. This has created a precarious situation for the refugees as well as for host country communities as the conflict continues.

Under international law, there is an obligation on all states that are signatories to the 1951 Refugee Convention to provide international protection, including the physical relocation of refugees. When protection cannot be guaranteed in the country where refugees first sought asylum, resettlement to a third country becomes an option. The UNHCR is mandated by its statute and by the UN General Assembly Resolutions to oversee resettlement as one of the three "durable solutions" to refugee crises around the world.[18] Resettlement is a small but vital piece of the international refugee response. However, the UNHCR estimates that only approximately 3 per cent of the overall Syrian refugee population has been offered viable resettlement.[19] Therefore, neighbouring countries continue to deal with large numbers of arriving Syrian refugees.[20] This creates a strain on resources and social services, and exacerbates the tension between host populations and Syrian refugees. It also, unfortunately, exacerbates problematic policies of interdiction, detention, and deportation of this population.

JORDANIAN RESPONSES TO THE SYRIAN CONFLICT

The Hashemite Kingdom of Jordan shares its northern border with Syria. Since the start of the Syrian conflict in 2011, Jordan has received approximately 1.4 million registered and unregistered refugees.[21] The UNHCR coordinates the overall refugee response in collaboration with the Government of Jordan. Jordan has two main refugee camps housing Syrian refugees: the Zaatari refugee camp complex and the Azraq refugee camp, both under the mandate of the Syrian Refugee Affairs Department (SRAD) of Jordan and managed by the UNHCR. There is also a privately operated Emirati Jordanian camp, access to which is incredibly difficult to obtain and which operates its own set of admission standards outside the mandate of the UNHCR.[22] There are also tent cities in the area around the areas of Ramtha, Cyber City, and King Abdullah Park, near the border with Syria's southern Dara'a province, as well as a large urban refugee population in cities such as Irbid, Mafraq, and Amman. According to a UNHCR report,[23] 84 per cent of Syrian refugees in Jordan were living outside of refugee camps in 2014. Unfortunately, the exact numbers of Syrians living outside Jordanian refugee camps are difficult to verify. Many Syrians were already living and working in Jordan before the start of the conflict, and families have blended for generations. Syrians are also involved in both formal and informal economies in Jordan without registering with the UN or with the Jordanian authorities.

Closed or partially closed borders between Syria and Jordan exacerbate the potential for unregulated detention of Syrian refugees. While informal border points remain open along the Jordan-Syria border, according to Human Rights Watch,[24] as of October 2017, all crossings have been officially sealed. This has created a precarious security and humanitarian situation in which thousands of Syrian refugees are trapped in border areas as they try to enter Jordan. For example, in June 2015, Human Rights Watch[25] obtained satellite imagery of approximately 175 tent structures in the border area between Syria and Jordan. By June 2016, the International Committee of the Red Cross (ICRC) estimated that "around 60,000 people are currently without food, water or healthcare."[26] These border regions operate outside the reach of the Jordanian authorities and are very dangerous. They are cut off from humanitarian assistance and Jordan has declared the area as outside of its reach. This area is also difficult to monitor for NGOs and INGOs, leaving large numbers of Syrian refugees in geographic as well as legal limbo.

Jordan's Refugee Policies

The principle of non-refoulement is the "cornerstone of asylum and of international refugee law."[27] Under the Refugee Convention, the principle of non-refoulement prohibits a state from removing a refugee to a country where their life or freedom would be threatened on account of their race, religion, nationality, membership of a particular social group, or political opinion. Article 33(1) of the Refugee Convention states: "No Contracting State shall expel or return ('refouler') a refugee in any manner whatsoever to the frontiers of territories where his life or freedom would be threatened on account of his race, religion, nationality, membership of a particular social group or political opinion." This principle ensures that all persons can fully enjoy their human rights, including the right to life, liberty, and security of the person, and freedom from torture or cruel, inhuman, or degrading treatment or punishment. Returning a refugee to persecution or danger threatens these rights.

However, Jordan has not signed or ratified the 1951 Refugee Convention or its 1967 Protocol. Nevertheless, it is a signatory to the 1984 *United Nations Convention against Torture* and is bound by Article 3, which enjoins states not to return or expel any person to states where they would be in danger of being tortured. Article 21 of the Jordanian Constitution prohibits the extradition of political refugees,[28] and according to the UNHCR,[29] the Jordanian government considers Syrians to be refugees. However, Jordanian law lacks clear domestic refugee legislation or policy to protect refugees.[30] For example, Law No. 24 of 1973 on Residence and Foreigners' Affairs requires those entering the country as political asylum seekers to present themselves and register at a police station within three days of arrival.[31] Article 31 grants the administrative body of the Ministry of the Interior (MOI) the power to determine whether persons who entered illegally will be detained and deported on a case-by-case basis.[32] However, the law does not identify conditions under which people will be eligible for asylum.[33]

Jordan issued its only domestic refugee-specific directive in 1998 in the form of a memorandum of understanding (MOU) with the UNHCR.[34] This MOU gives the UNHCR the right to determine the refugee status of asylum seekers in Jordan. Article 1 of the MOU removes any geographic and time limitations for asylum seekers, and Article 2(1) respects the concept of non-refoulement.[35] According to the UNHCR,[36] in the absence of any international or national legal refugee instruments in force in Jordan, the MOU "establishes the parameters for cooperation between UNHCR and the Government." This cooperation includes UNHCR interventions in the detention of refugees, as will be discussed below.

Foreigners, including refugees, cannot live in Jordan without a residency permit.[37] Refugees do not automatically acquire rights to residency, employment, public education, or healthcare.[38] Instead, they must register with the Jordanian MOI. As part of a new registration effort,[39] or the "urban verification exercise,"[40] every foreign national in Jordan must also undergo health screening.[41] This screening is required for each person over the age of twelve in order to obtain a registration identity card from the MOI. However, many Syrians do not have the documents necessary to obtain an MOI identity card legally, because their passports were confiscated when they crossed into Jordan. As of April 2014, close to 220,000 Syrian passports have been lost over the years spanning the conflict.[42] As a result, Syrian refugees who cannot register for the MOI identity card or access healthcare and services must resort to obtaining identification through forged documentation.[43] The Norwegian Refugee Council[44] estimates that at the beginning of 2016, almost one year after the beginning of the new "urban verification exercise," meant to supposedly improve tracking and registration procedures for Syrian refugees, approximately 250,000 Syrian refugees remained without updated government registration, without which they struggle to access local public health clinics, hospitals, and schools.

The ongoing conflict in Syria, discretionary policies by the Jordanian state, and the inability of Syrian refugees to work and fully participate in Jordanian society all exacerbate the precarity of the Syrian population in Jordan. Policies of exclusion and population control result in the criminalization of Syrian refugees, justifying their subsequent detention and deportation, and in some cases even spurring "voluntary" deportations when conditions become unliveable.

Deportations from Jordan

The following findings rely on field research from the summer of 2015 by the author. However, at time of publication, deportations of Syrian refugees continue to be routinely documented in Jordan. In October 2017, Human Rights Watch released an investigative report detailing multiple allegations of refoulement, or forced return, to zones of active conflict in Syria.[45]

Forcible detainment and deportations to Syria were documented by a number of interviewees in May and June 2015. The principal reasons why Syrian refugees have been detained and deported from Jordan are for work permit infractions (including for Syrian doctors and medical practitioners) and vague "security reasons," with the possibility of Syrian refugees also rendered deportable by virtue of living with a communicable disease such as tuberculosis or HIV/AIDS. While there do not appear to be any official reports by the Jordanian authorities of these deportations, and numbers are difficult to verify, the UNHCR[46] has publically acknowledged that they are aware of deportations of Syrian refugees from Jordan.

Moreover, there are a number of local reports on the deportation of Syrians from Jordan. For example, Hazm al-Mazouni, a Syrian journalist with Ammannet, a news agency based in Amman, Jordan, released a report in June 2015, for which he was the principal investigator, that documented a total of fifty-eight deportations since 2014.[47] During an interview in June 2015, al-Mazouni estimated that there were also approximately eleven cases of children under the age of eighteen who were deported from the Zaatari camp back to Syria with their families for a variety of undefined "security concerns." In al-Mazouni's experience, deportations occurred relatively quickly, often less than twenty-four hours after the person was apprehended.[48] Of the nineteen cases found by al-Mazouni and his colleague, sixteen were also deported on Thursdays, Fridays, and Saturdays, which are considered holidays in Jordan. Al-Mazouni thought this was to curtail access to legal representation and the UNHCR. According to al-Mazouni, out of the nineteen cases investigated, one person died in Syria in a bombardment, while five people were in detention, with at least some inside an al-Nusra prison in June 2015. Four people were volunteers with local organizations and were deported alongside wounded Syrian refugees, allegedly for not being allowed to work in Jordan.[49]

The UNHCR[50] is aware of these deportations, and given its close relationship with the Jordanian government, it serves as the primary advocacy mechanism for the release of those detained. The UNHCR's deportation unit liaises with the governorate, which has administrative oversight over enforcing deportations and intervenes on individual cases. The agency also has a twenty-four-hour hotline and liaison officers who attempt to find out where the person is detained and intervene as soon as possible to secure the person's release. The UNHCR also has some access into the administrative detention facilities where people are held in order to halt any deportations. It is also aware of children in detention and works to secure their release.[51]

Deportations for Work Permit Infractions

As mentioned, one of the main reasons why a Syrian refugee may be detained and deported is for work permit infractions. This includes documented cases of practicing Syrian physicians and medical personnel. The Justice Center for Legal Aid (JCLA) is a legal aid organization in Amman, Jordan, that regularly represents Syrian refugees living and working in Jordan. As was noted by one of the lawyers working for the JCLA, work permits for Syrians are very difficult to obtain in Jordan, and it is forbidden to work without one by law.[52] For example, in the JCLA's experience, only those with rare PhDs from Syria may be given work permits in Jordan. For the rest of the Syrian population, they must resort to working without a work permit, and if they are caught by Jordanian authorities, they may be sent into one of the refugee camps or deported back to Syria. This happened to Yaser,[53] a middle-aged Syrian lawyer, who sat in on the meeting with the author and the JCLA staff. He came with his family to Jordan from Syria but was caught working without a work permit, detained, and ultimately sent to the Azraq refugee camp. After a few weeks, he managed to escape from the camp, walked through the desert to catch a transport truck to Amman, and rejoined his family in Amman. He is now extra careful about his work and status as a Syrian urban refugee living in Jordan. Yaser now spends his time volunteering at the JCLA, lending his legal expertise from Syria, but continues to be unable to work without proper authorization.

The JCLA has documented a number of other cases of refugees being deported and has represented Syrian clients facing deportation from Jordan.[54] According to an assistant at the clinic, the idea is that if "you are a refugee, you shouldn't work, and UNHCR should be paying your food. You should not be influencing the Jordanian economy."[55] However, the inability to work and earn a sustainable income creates a host of problems, including a lack of access to healthcare and services. For example, while Yaser's family was covered for comprehensive healthcare by virtue of being present in Jordan before the start of the conflict, he only had access to coverage available to uninsured Jordanians and had to pay for any additional care he needed.[56]

The detention and deportations of Syrian doctors and medical personnel have also been observed. Rashid al-Malki is a physician from Syria who came to Irbid, a city in northern Jordan in October 2014.[57] He was working as a physiotherapist in Syria but had to escape to Jordan because he was wanted by the Syrian authorities. He now works in Irbid, Amman, and Ramtha as an intermediary referring physician in a network of fifty doctors, including approximately twenty Syrian physicians. Al-Malki sends Syrian patients who contact him to Jordanian doctors who are able to provide them with the required services. Doctors such as al-Malki are clearly in high demand: over the course of the two-hour interview in June 2015, his phone rang non-stop and he had received over 3,000 WhatsApp messages from his patients since that morning.

In June 2015, al-Malki was aware of at least ten Syrian physicians who had been deported from Ramtha hospital in early 2015. These physicians were working with wounded refugees and were providing referrals to specialists in Ramtha, a city in the northwest of Jordan. When they disappeared, Médecins Sans Frontières took on the mission in Ramtha. Al-Malki was also aware of the imprisonment and deportation of three other Syrian doctors with whom he worked regularly who were deported in March 2015 for working without a work permit. Two additional Syrian doctors were later caught for working in a hospital. According to al-Malki, they were initially detained but had since received bail and were fighting their deportations in court.[58]

Doctors like al-Malki cannot openly practice medicine in Jordan. Some practice under the name and licence of Jordanian doctors, with some having to pay up to 300 Jordanian dinars, or about C$550, to do so. This creates an unwelcome environment for Syrian physicians in an overburdened medical system. As al-Malki notes, "Unfortunately we are losing our own Syrian doctors. Many are leaving to Germany. For example, a rare specialist in bone diseases and three other neurosurgeons are gone. This is a huge loss for the Syrian situation, as they were a huge gain. We need these kinds of specialists ... For example, a specialist doctor, a cousin of mine, is the only doctor in vascular surgery in the north of Jordan. But because of the strictness of the Jordanian government, he chose to go back to work inside Syria in January 2015."[59] The threat of detention and deportation forces many Syrian physicians to either abandon their practice completely, or greatly limit the scope of their work.

The detention and deportation of Syrian doctors is a troubling phenomenon. As the once-robust Jordanian healthcare system becomes increasingly taxed from providing services to both Syrians and Jordanians, actively engaging Syrian medical experts and doctors would alleviate some of the strain. For example, there is currently only one hospital in the Middle East dedicated to providing free reconstructive surgery for people injured in war.[60] The Jordanian healthcare system is dealing with complex cases as a result of the ongoing active conflict in Syria. Many cases require ongoing medical care, such as physiotherapy, rehabilitation, and prosthetics support for adult and children amputees. According to Hazm al-Mazouni, a journalist with Amman-net, "[p]hysiotherapy treatment is very limited and only a few sessions are offered. NGOs try to fill in, but do not have the capacity, and others do it at random. People need time and care to adjust to their new life with lost limbs, and have to get used to wearing prosthetics. Some have lesions and allergies and it is very difficult."[61] As a number of physicians explained, cases involving trauma and complex medical needs as a result of war wounds, such as burn victims, amputees, and refugees requiring ongoing rehabilitation, were not widely present in the Jordanian medical system before the Syrian conflict. In addition, cases involving psychological trauma and vulnerable survivors of sexual and gender based violence (SGBV) and detention inside Syria also require ongoing care and access to treatment and services that are very difficult to obtain in Jordan.

Detention and Deportation for Communicable Diseases [62]

Another troubling reason why Syrian refugees may be detained and deported from Jordan is by virtue of having a communicable disease, such as tuberculosis or HIV/AIDS. According to the Joint United Nations Programme on HIV and AIDS (UNAIDS),[63]Jordan is among fifty-nine countries, territories, and areas that deny entry or residence to people because of their HIV status. Jordan is also one of twenty-six countries that currently deport people who are living with HIV.[64] The UNHCR[65] has explicitly stated that deportation of a refugee solely on the basis of their HIV status would breach the Refugee Convention and customary international law.[66]

A number of interviewees noted that a refugee might be refouled back to Syria if they have a communicable disease, such as HIV/AIDS or tuberculosis. According to Mohammed al-Nassir, a lawyer specializing in combating the stigma around LGBTI and HIV/AIDS issues in Jordan, it is Jordanian policy to deport anyone who tests HIV positive while undergoing registration in Jordan, including an HIV-positive Syrian refugee. However, it is not clear whether any HIV-positive Syrians have actually been removed from Jordan under this policy.

Nonetheless, for Adam Coogle of Human Rights Watch, there was "no question that people are being deported" back to Syria.[67] This was echoed by a number of Jordanian and international medical experts working in Amman, as well as on the northern border with Syria.[68] A number of medical experts in Jordan also noted the deportations of Syrian patients in the middle of the course of treatment for so-called "security reasons." It is unclear what types of security reasons warrant deportation in the middle of medical treatment, but a number of interviewees suspected that being diagnosed with a communicable disease would qualify as a ground for deportation. There have been two cases of HIV-positive Iraqi refugees who were referred to the Jordanian government for access to anti-retroviral treatment but have since disappeared. It is unclear whether they were deported by the Jordanian authorities or whether they are in detention. There have also been documented cases of Syrian sex workers being deported on the grounds of both work permit infractions and potential communicable diseases.

Communicable diseases such as HIV/AIDS are a very publically sensitive issue that the Jordanian government does not openly discuss, especially in pertaining to the Syrian refugee population. While it is clear that testing for HIV/AIDS does sometimes occur as part of the registration process, it is unclear whether these tests are accurate and how the medical information is handled, with the possible result of discrimination and breaches of confidentiality. In the experiences of the physicians interviewed, while large samples of blood may be collected from the Syrian refugee population, there simply is no capacity to test everyone. There were also a number of cases reported of Syrian refugees being able to register without ever having to provide a blood sample.

Jordanian policies of detention and deportation for work permit infractions, communicable diseases, and nebulous security concerns actively criminalize Syrian refugees, particularly those who are not registered and those who may be further marginalized by being unable to legally work or access healthcare. While there are no official government reports corroborating forced deportations from Jordan, the UNHCR has publically acknowledged that they are aware of deportations of Syrian refugees.[69] By casting these Syrian refugees as detainable and deportable, and by ensuring that conditions of life in Jordan preclude the full participation of Syrian refugees in society, the Jordanian state makes life extremely difficult for certain subsets of the

Syrian refugee populations, in some cases even spurring "voluntary" deportations when conditions become unliveable.

TURKISH RESPONSES TO THE SYRIAN CONFLICT

The Republic of Turkey has received the greatest number of Syrian refugees in the world. It has overtaken Lebanon, and as of June 2017 supports between 2.9 million and 3.5 million registered and unregistered Syrians,[70] in addition to over 300,000 refugees from other countries.[71] The number of refugees in Turkey causes considerable strain on Turkish infrastructure and security.[72] By October 2015, the Syrian refugee response cost Turkey approximately US$7.5 billion.[73]

On 23 November 2015, Human Rights Watch[74] reported that Turkey effectively closed all its borders to try to reduce the number of refugees coming into the country, forcing large numbers to remain in Syria near the border region. As of February 2018, borders continue to be officially closed, and fighting has intensified as Turkey has become more actively involved in the conflict.[75] Turkey's geographic proximity to Syria is keenly felt in Turkey. For example, on 21 August 2016, fifty-one people died in the Turkish city of Gaziantep as a result of a suicide bomber linked to the conflict in Syria.[76] Other border towns were also targeted in 2016.[77]

As of April 2018, the number of registered refugees in Turkey was 3,588,877.[78] The UNHCR estimates that as of 2017, only approximately 10 per cent of Syrian refugees in Turkey are living in camps, with 90 per cent of Syrian refugees living in urban centres such as Istanbul, Ankara, and smaller cities such as Gaziantep, Kilis, and Antakya along the Turkey-Syria border.[79] Smaller urban communities feel the presence of large numbers of Syrians acutely. For example, Gaziantep, which was home to approximately 300,000 urban refugees in 2014, is just sixty kilometres from Syria and has been nicknamed "Little Aleppo" or "Aleppo in Exile."[80]

Rising numbers of Syrian refugees in Turkey affect the country's ability to provide affordable legal, health, and social services. Since 2012, Turkey has experienced chronic unemployment, which politicians and the public link to the arrival of Syrian refugees into an already unstable economy.[81] The Turkish political landscape is also in flux. In November 2015, the Justice and Development Party (Adalet ve Kalkınma Partisi, or AKP), led by Recep Tayyip Erdoğan, the president of Turkey, regained its parliamentary majority in a snap re-election campaign.[82] It had lost the general election earlier in the year.[83] Opposition leaders have openly criticized Turkey's response to the Syrian conflict and supported closing the border and reducing services during tough economic times.[84] An attempted coup in July 2016, which led to extraordinary repressive measures by the Erdoğan government, further destabilized the country.[85] In April 2017, the Erdoğan government also held a referendum to consolidate power and transform the country from a parliamentary system to an executive presidency.[86] It is unclear how this uncertain political climate will affect services for Syrian refugees in the region.

Turkish Refugee Policies

Syrians in Turkey are not considered refugees under Turkish law. Turkey is a signatory to the 1951 Refugee Convention and the 1967 Additional Protocol on the Status of Refugees. Despite this, Turkey has maintained the geographic limitation enshrined in Article 1B(1) of the Refugee Convention, granting Convention refugee status only to refugees fleeing Europe.[87] As a result, non-European refugees in Turkey are only entitled to temporary protection,[88] and are expected to resettle in a third country. Turkey's legislation also directly promotes the permanent settlement of people with "Turkish descent and culture"[89] to regulate the background of the population in Turkey, and does not extend these same protections to migrants who cannot establish a direct link with Turkey, such as Syrian refugees seeking protection in Turkey.

A 2013 Law on Foreigners and International Protection maintained the geographic limitation, and coincided with an increased arrival of Syrians in the country.[90] A 2015 report by the Migration Policy Institute describes Turkey's attempt to harmonize its refugee and asylum policy with the European Union,[91] while maintaining the problematic geographic exclusion. Only refugees coming from Europe continue to be eligible for recognition as Convention refugees in Turkey; refugees from elsewhere are given only temporary protection, and expected to resettle in a third country. Alongside the Law on Foreigners and International Protection, Turkey also enacted a new Temporary Protection Regulation, which came into effect on 22 October 2014.[92] This new regulation governs the process of registering and documenting refugees until a safe return to Syria can be implemented. It also grants access to health and education services, as well as permission to work.[93] However, Turkey continues to refuse to recognize Syrians as Convention refugees. As a result, Syrian refugees have "guest" status and are provided with only temporary protection,[94] despite the now protracted nature of the conflict and no prospect of a timely resolution.[95]

This exclusionary legal framework, coupled with ongoing social marginalization and increasing vulnerability to labour and sexual exploitation, exacerbates the precarity of the Syrian refugee population in Turkey. It also highlights the state's policies of attrition through enforcement to actively make life as difficult as possible for Syrian refugees. Refugees who do not register with the state are at risk of being detained or deported if caught. However, the threat of detention and deportation also discouraged refugees from registering to access healthcare, legal, and social services. This phenomenon is very problematic, as Syrian refugees are unlikely to leave Turkey anytime soon. The Syrian conflict has become protracted and is intensifying, and Turkey has become an active participant in the fighting along its borders. The inability to participate fully in Turkish society disrupts community and social cohesion between the Turkish and refugee populations. Turkish policies of detention and deportation of Syrian refugees are also in direct contravention of international law.

Detention and Threat of Deportation
of Syrian Refugees in Turkey

Syrian refugees face the possibility of detention in Turkey. The principal law governing immigration detention, the Law on Foreigners and International Protection, stipulates that detention can be ordered for a variety of reasons: flight risk, violation of exit or entry rules, use of fraudulent documents, not leaving Turkey in the granted period without an acceptable excuse, and being found to constitute a threat to public order and security or public health.[96] The law specifies that the detention of persons seeking protection should be an exceptional measure.[97] Article 54 provides for deportation based on several immigration-related grounds, including overstaying a visa, cancellation of a residence permit, violating the provisions of an entry or stay, and rejection of an application for international protection.[98] To date, the Global Detention Project has not been able to verify the exact numbers of short-term or long-term "removal centres," formerly known as "foreigner guest houses."[99]

Total numbers of detained Syrian refugees in Turkey are difficult to verify; they range from 300 to a couple thousand.[100] However, there have been a number of publicized cases of Syrian refugees being detained in Turkey. For example, in May 2016, Amnesty International advocated for the release of seven out of twelve Syrian refugees detained in the Düziçi camp in Osmaniye Province, in southern Turkey. Amnesty also reported that the other five Syrian refugees – a woman and her four children – requested to be returned to Syria and were taken to the Syrian border by Turkish authorities.[101] Amnesty has also highlighted the troubling practice, since mid-January 2016, of a daily rounding up and expelling by Turkish authorities of groups of around one-hundred Syrian men, women, and children to Syria from Turkey's southern border provinces, with the total of deported Syrian refugees numbering in the thousands.[102] The unofficial practice of deporting Syrians from southern Turkey back into areas of active conflict has been characterized as an "open secret."[103] These forced returns are in direct contravention of the principle of non-refoulement and are illegal under Turkish and international law. For example, the Turkish policies of detention and deportation are at direct odds with the jurisprudence of the European Court of Human Rights (the "Strasbourg Court"). While this court has not explicitly addressed Turkish refugee policies pertaining to Syrian refugees, in its recent decision of *L.M. and Others v. Russia*,[104] the Court unanimously held that the forced return of asylum seekers to Syria would violate the European Convention on Human Rights (ECHR), both its Article 2, the right to life, and Article 3, the prohibition of torture and of inhuman or degrading treatment. The fear of detention and possible deportation to Syria also acts as a deterrent for refugees for registering with Turkish authorities and the UNHCR. As a result, large numbers of Syrians living in Turkey do not obtain registration.

This experience is illustrated by the case of Tarek, the twenty-five-year-old Syrian refugee whose perspective opened this chapter. In May 2015, Tarek spoke about his life in the bustling metropolis of Istanbul as an unregistered Syrian refugee. During a late night conversation on the banks of the Bosphorus in the Karaköy neighbourhood, he explained that at some point after the start of the Syrian conflict, he was a member of both the Syrian Army and the Free Syrian Resistance. As the fighting intensified, Tarek absconded from both and fled to Turkey, entering through an unofficial crossing without registration. He has been living in Istanbul ever since. Tarek's existence is precarious. He works illegally at a mechanics shop to make ends meet, and explains that it is very difficult for Syrian refugees to work in Istanbul. However, Tarek does not plan to register. He stated: "I don't need your money; I just need you to give me a chance. A job. I don't need you to give me $5 every day. Just one chance. One chance to make myself ... I just want to [be] alive. I want to marry ... maybe have children."[105] The young man's hands visibly shook as he recounted his experiences in Turkey: "I forget Syria. When I think about how I lived ... Yesterday, I worked from 6 a.m. to 1 a.m. That's only 5 hours of rest. In Syria, I would work for only 6 to 7 hours every day. Now there is no life. I just sleep, eat, go to work ... maybe forever."[106]

ATTRITION THROUGH ENFORCEMENT AND THE DEPORTABILITY OF SYRIAN REFUGEES FROM TURKEY AND JORDAN

The ongoing social and economic marginalization and the practice of detaining and deporting Syrian refugees do not only violate domestic and international law. These policies also highlight more subtle mechanisms of population control employed by the state, which mixes hard-line policies to make life unliveable for Syrian refugees, pressuring them to exercise their "choice" to return to Syria. While exact numbers of so-called voluntary returnees are difficult to verify, especially with official borders between Turkey, Syria, and Jordan officially closed, it is important to interrogate the elision between encouraged and coerced return to a site of active conflict.

Attrition through enforcement, sometimes called self-deportation, is usually associated with the comprehensive strategy in the United States of driving away the unauthorized migrant population by making life unliveable.[107] This policy has been in use since at least 2005, when the American restrictionist organization the Center for Immigration Studies (CIS) first delineated a strategy of attrition through enforcement to explicitly "bring about a steady reduction in the total number of illegal immigrants."[108] Over the years, these strategies have included laws that expand detention and the threat of deportation, the denial of benefits, national restrictions to obtaining identity documents and driver's licences, and increased border enforcement.[109] Notable examples where attrition through enforcement has been introduced into state legislation include Alabama and Arizona.[110] The impact of similar policies on migrant mothers in Texas has also been studied.[111] Internationally, there is some focus on attrition through enforcement-type policies in Israel's treatment of Sudanese and Eritrean refugees. For example, Human Rights Watch[112] has documented the links between Israel's explicit denial of meaningful asylum and registration processes, unlawful detention, unclear rights to work, lack of access to healthcare, and the explicit refoulement to Eritrea and third countries.

As all these policies highlight, the migrant population becomes construed as an amorphous threat to the nation, echoing fears of being engulfed by floods of uncontrollable masses of refugees.[113] The threat of disruption to state order by a mass "Other" leads to the creation of implicit and explicit policies of demarcation, dislocation, and expulsion of the suspect population.[114] By detaining Syrian refugees and threatening them with an imminent deportation that they cannot control, states such as Turkey and Jordan create an environment in which choosing to self-deport becomes a rational alternative to being at the mercy of the host state. Returning to Syria is an exercise in the mirage of agency and choice in a dislocated existence. While it is difficult to verify how many Syrians are self-deporting after being detained by Turkish and Jordanian authorities, a number of cases have been documented.[115] Creating a mechanism in which refugees self-police the space they occupy and subsequently "choose" to leave allows the state to abdicate responsibilities over its broader policies of refoulement, which violate international law. The ongoing and persistent social and economic exclusion of Syrian refugees in Turkey, including lack of access to healthcare for unregistered refugees, and the inability to exercise the right to work or education, increases the marginalization of the refugee population. However, the draconian policies of detention and deportation meant to spur self-deportations also trigger other grave consequences. Not only is attrition through enforcement ineffective and in contravention of domestic and international laws by pressuring refugees to return to a zone of active conflict, it also disrupts community and social cohesion between host countries and the refugee population.[116] Refugees at risk of being deported or those encouraged to leave by threat of detention are more reluctant to register and access healthcare, legal, and social services. As highlighted by the experiences of Tarik, the young Syrian man in Istanbul, many people explicitly do not register with the authorities or with the UNHCR for fear of deportation. They continue to work in the informal economy of the host country without the ability to seek resettlement in a third country and do not have access to the services available to registered refugees. This, paradoxically, renders the state's goals of controlling the migrant population moot, since by the implementation of hard-line policies of detention and deportation only create more unaccounted and unregistered refugees who are likely to remain in the host country indefinitely. The very policies that are meant to control and manage the refugee population instead perpetuate an ongoing cycle of precarity for millions of Syrians that is unlikely to change as the conflict in Syria continues.

However, while beyond the scope of this chapter, it should be pointed out that there is also an element of personal strategy in choosing not to register in countries such as Turkey and Jordan. Although such countries are traditionally construed as "transit countries," a distinction that itself is also being problematized,[117] it is possible that Syrian refugees are exercising their agency to not register. Instead, they live and work until they can raise enough funds to move to their ultimate destination countries in Europe or even North America. Furthermore, the threat of deportation back to Syria serves as a deterrent in attrition through enforcement policies, as returning to Syria involves the risk of violence and inhumane or degrading treatment. As a result, Syrian refugees may simultaneously seek to avoid detention and deportation back to Syria, while also "self-deporting" from Turkey and Jordan, and moving on to another country. Nevertheless, these strategies should not preclude Syrian refugees from accessing their basic rights in the countries that have currently received them, and their migration from zones of active conflict should not be criminalized through the use of detention and deportation.

CONCLUSION

This chapter has looked at how Turkey and Jordan's policies to control and manage the large refugee population have created a regime in which attrition through enforcement, or making life unliveable under the threat of detention and deportation, can render some Syrian refugees to self-deport. These policies of deterrence and the criminalization of migration also encourage Syrian refugees to seek a better life in more promising places such as Europe or North America. Unfortunately, for those who remain in the region, these policies act as a deterrent to registering with Turkish and Jordanian authorities and accessing healthcare and social services because of the fear of possible detention and deportation. The unregistered refugee population does not have the same access to social services, healthcare, and legal assistance, and is unable to participate in resettlement to third countries.

Not much attention has been paid to the deportations of Syrians back into the zone of active conflict. Concerted local advocacy efforts to stop and prevent detention and deportations of Syrian refugees should be bolstered by an international response directly condemning the practice. However, as is highlighted by the ongoing policy to detain and deport Syrian refugees in Jordan and Turkey, such policies are a result of ongoing social disruption, strained economies and health sectors, and an overall lack of resources for the neighbouring countries to deal with millions of Syrian refugees who will likely continue to live in the region for the foreseeable future. Any durable solutions and future directions for responses to the Syrian conflict must address the impact on host countries such as Jordan and Turkey, and must help alleviate the strain that manifests in draconian and discretionary policies of detention and deportation of Syrian refugees into zones of active conflict.

The intersection between instability in the region, strained infrastructure in states that have to respond to the majority of the Syrian refugee population, and malleable domestic laws on granting protection to refugees results in a regime in which the most marginalized refugee communities are at risk. This marginalization is heightened by the rendering of these refugees by these states as deportable, based on their medical conditions, HIV status, sexual orientation, or perceived association with opaque "security risks." Policies of deterrence also undermine social cohesion in Turkey and Jordan, when already limited resources should be devoted to finding long-term sustainable solutions to the large numbers of refugees who do not have a likely prospect of return to Syria. As the conflict continues, the unfortunate result of the increasing desperation of host states is policies of attrition through enforcement. These reactionary policies strengthen the discretionary criminalization of certain groups of Syrian refugees, make these refugees deportable, and, in extreme cases, cause life to be so unliveable that returning to a zone of active conflict is more bearable than remaining.

ACKNOWLEDGMENTS

The author would like to acknowledge the International Human Rights Program (IHRP) at the University of Toronto, Faculty of Law, for allowing her the use of the data that forms the basis of this article, in particular Samer Muscati, director of the IHRP; Kristin Marshall, staff lawyer, who also collected the data; and the Elton John AIDS Foundation, which funded the IHRP project. The author would also like to thank Mayss al-Zoubi, Syrian activist in southern Turkey, and Etaf Roudan, journalist with Ammannet in Amman, Jordan, without whom none of this work would have been possible, as well as all the interviewees who graciously shared their time for the purposes of this project.

NOTES

1 Names and identifying features have been changed to protect the refugee's anonymity.

2 International Human Rights Program (IHRP) in-person individual interview in Istanbul, Turkey (26 May 2015).

3 The term "crisis" is used in an illustrative way only, as this article does not want to perpetuate the damaging discourses of associating refugee movements with tropes of fear, such as a "flood," or an "influx." See Jan Blommaert, "Language, Asylum, and the National Order," *Current Anthropology* 50, no. 4 (2009): 415–41; Liisa Malkki, "Speechless Emissaries: Refugees, Humanitarianism, and Dehistoricization," *Cultural Anthropology* 11, no. 3 (1996): 377–404; Liisa Malkki, *Purity and Exile: Violence, Memory, and National Cosmology Among Hutu Refugees in Tanzania* (Chicago: Chicago University Press, 1995); Jared Goyette, "Wave Upon Wave of Journalists Are Describing the Arrival of Refugees in Apocalyptic Terms," *Public Radio International*, 29 January 2016; Roger Zetter, "Labeling Refugees: Forming and Transforming a Bureaucratic Identity," *Journal of Refugee Studies*, 4 no. 1 (1991) 39–62; and Roger Zetter, *Creating Identities, Diminishing Protection and the Securitisation of Asylum in Europe*, eds. Susan Kneebone, Dallal Stevens, and Loretta Baldassar (Abingdon: Routledge, 2015).

4 See Sara Ahmed, "Affective Economies," *Social Text* 22, no. 2 (2004): 117–39; and Susan Buck-Morss, "A Global Public Sphere?" *Situation Analysis* no. 1 (2002): 10–19.

5 Michele Waslin, "Discrediting 'Self Deportation' as Immigration Policy: Why an Attrition Through Enforcement Strategy Makes Life Difficult for Everyone," *Immigration Policy Center*, 2012, https://www.american immigrationcouncil.org/sites/default/files/research/Waslin_-_Attrition _Through_Enforcement_020612.pdf.

6 Article 33(1) of the 1951 *Convention Relating to the Status of Refugees* ("Refugee Convention") (and Article 1[1] of its 1967 Protocol) and Article 7 of the *International Covenant on Civil and Political Rights*. Although the European Convention on Human Rights does not explicitly provide a provision prohibiting refoulement, it has consistently found such a prohibition "inherent in the general terms of Article 3." See, for example, *Soering v. United Kingdom*, Application No. 14038/88; *Chahal v. United Kingdom*, Application No. 22414/93; and *Saadi v. Italy*, Application No. 37201/06.

7 Laura Létourneau-Tremblay, "Expulsion of Refugees from Russia to Syria Would Violate International Obligations," *RefLaw*, 2016, http://www.reflaw .org/expulsion-of-refugees-from-russia-to-syria-would-violate-international- obligations.

8 "Fourth Convention, Relative to the Protection of Civilian Person in Time of War," *Geneva Conventions of 12 August 1949* (Geneva: International Committee of the Red Cross, 1949): 153–221. See also the *Convention Against Torture and Other Cruel, Inhuman or Degrading Treatment or Punishment* ("Convention Against Torture"), 10 December 1984, 1465 UNTS 85 (entered into force 26 June 1987).

9 Petra Molnar and Kristin Marshall, "On Vulnerable Ground: Syrian Refugees at Risk of HIV in Turkey and Jordan: Recommendations For Canada's Response, International Human Rights Program," University of Toronto Faculty of Law (internal report released to the Ministry of Immigration, Refugees, and Citizenship and Ministry of Foreign Affairs, 21 July 2016).

10 "Total Number of Syrian Refugees Exceeds Four Million for First Time," UNHCR, 9 July 2015, http://www.unhcr.org/559d67d46.html; and António Guterres, "MENA Consultations for the World Humanitarian Summit, Remarks by António Guterres, UNHCR," UNHCR, 3 March 2015, http://www .unhcr.org/553a48919.html.

11 António Guterres, "MENA Consultations for the World Humanitarian Summit, Remarks by António Guterres, UNHCR," United Nations High Commissioner for Refugees (UNHCR), 3 March 2015, http://www.unhcr.org /553a48919.html.

12 "Syria Regional Refugee Response," United Nations High Commissioner for Refugees (UNHCR), Operational Portal, Refugee Situations, 2018, https://data2.unhcr.org/en/situations/syria.

13 "Syrian Arab Republic," United Nations Office for the Coordination of Humanitarian Affairs (OCHA), 2018, http://www.unocha.org/syria. Exact numbers of IDPs are difficult to verify. See, for example, "Syria Complex Emergency – Fact Sheet #8," United States Agency for International Development (USAID), 21 September 2015, https://www.usaid.gov/crisis/syria/fy15/fs08; and "Country Profiles: Syria," Internal Displacement Monitoring Centre (IDMC), 2017, http://www.internal-displacement.org/middle-east-and-north-africa/syria. See also "Internally Displaced People," United Nations High Commissioner for Refugees (UNHCR), 7 July 2016, http://www.unhcr.org/sy/29-internally-displaced-people.html.

14 "Syria: Events of 2016," Human Rights Watch, 2016, https://www.hrw.org/world-report/2017/country-chapters/syria.

15 Note that the figure of 470,000 fatalities reported by SCPR is twice the estimated figure of 250,000 reported by the UNHCR, which stopped counting Syria's dead in mid-2014, citing lack of access and diminishing confidence in data sources. See Ian Black, "Report on Syria Conflict Finds 11.5% of Population Killed or Injured," *Guardian*, 11 February 2016, http://www.theguardian.com/world/2016/feb/11/report-on-syria-conflict-finds-115-of-population-killed-or-injured.

16 "Un Envoy Voices Deep Concern over Syria Barrel Bombing," Al Jazeera, 23 July 2015, http://www.aljazeera.com/news/2015/07/envoy-voices-deep-concern-syria-barrel-bombing-150723074309340.html.

17 "Syria: Deliberate Killing of Civilians by ISIS," Human Rights Watch, 3 July 2015, https://www.hrw.org/news/2015/07/03/syria-deliberate-killing-civilians-isis.

18 "Solutions," UNHCR, 2018, http://www.unhcr.org/pages/49c3646cf8.html. The durable solutions of the UNHCR are voluntary repatriation (refugees returning home), local integration (supporting refugees integrating into host communities), or resettlement to a third country in situations where it is impossible for a person to go back home or remain in the host country.

19 "Syria Regional Refugee Response," United Nations High Commissioner for Refugees (UNHCR), Operational Portal, Refugee Situations, 19 April 2018 (19 October 2015), http://data.unhcr.org/syrianrefugees/regional.php.

20 As of 26 April 2018, the estimated population of registered Syrian refugees is 3,588,877 refugees in Turkey, 991,165 in Lebanon, and 661,859 in Jordan, with additional populations of 248,382 in Iraq, 128,507 in Egypt, and

33,545 in the North African Region. "Syria Regional Refugee Response," United Nations High Commissioner for Refugees (UNHCR), Operational Portal, Refugee Situations, 9 May 2018, http://data.unhcr.org/syrianrefugees /regional.php.

21 Note that there is a widely recognized discrepancy regarding the total number of Syrian refugees in Jordan. It is very difficult to obtain an exact figure, as the unregistered refugee population can also be comprised of split families, as well as Syrians who work in Jordan. Approximately 650,000 refugees have registered with the government, while upwards of 750,000 remain unregistered. "Global Focus: Jordan," United Nations High Commissioner for Refugees (UNHCR), http://reporting.unhcr.org/node/2549.

22 Ibid.

23 "Living in the Shadows: Jordan Home Visits Report 2014," United Nations High Commissioner for Refugees, 2014, http://unhcr.org/jordan2014urban report/home-visit-report.pdf.

24 See Human Rights Watch, "'I Have No Idea Why They Sent Us Back': Jordanian Deportations and Expulsions of Syrian Refugees," 2 October 2017, https://www.hrw.org/report/2017/10/02/i-have-no-idea-why-they-sent-us-back/jordanian-deportations-and-expulsions-syrian. See also "Jordan: Syrians Blocked, Stranded in Desert," Human Rights Watch, 3 June 2015, https://www .hrw.org/news/2015/06/03/jordan-syrians-blocked-stranded-desert.

25 Ibid.

26 Bethan Staton, "Syrian Refugees Stuck on Jordan Border 'Have Nothing,'" Al Jazeera, 23 June 2016, http://www.aljazeera.com/news/2016/06/syrian-refugees-stuck-jordan-border-160623062555653.html.

27 UNHCR Note on the Principle of Non-Refoulement," United Nations High Commissioner for Refugees, 1997, http://www.refworld.org/docid /438c6d972.html.

28 Constitution of the Hashemite Kingdom of Jordan, 1952, Art. 21, http://www.refworld.org/docid/3ae6b53310.html.

29 "Global Focus: Jordan," UNHCR.

30 "Access to Work for Syrian Refugees in Jordan: A Discussion Paper on Labour and Refugee Laws and Policies," International Labour Organization, Regional Office for Arab States, 2015, http://www.ilo.org/beirut/publications /WCMS_357950/lang—en/index.html.

31 Jordan: Law No. 24 of 1973 on Residence and Foreigners' Affairs, 1973, Art. 11 (unofficial English language translation), http://www.refworld.org/cgi-bin/texis/vtx/rwmain?docid=3ae6b4ed4c.

32 Ibid., Art. 31.

33 Ibid.
34 "Memorandum of Understanding Between the Government of Jordan and UNHCR," United Nations High Commissioner for Refugees, 5 April 1998 (unofficial English language translation), http://mawgeng.unblog .fr/files/2009/02/moujordan.doc.
35 Ibid.
36 "Global Focus: Jordan," UNHCR.
37 Law No. 24 of 1973 on Residence and Foreigners' Affairs, Art. 31.
38 "Legal Status of Individuals Fleeing Syria: Syria Needs Analysis Project – June 2013," ACAPS, 2013, http://www.reliefweb.int/sites/reliefweb.int/files /resources/legal_status_of_individuals_fleeing_syria.pdf.
39 "2015 Situation Report on International Migration: Migration, Displacement and Development in a Changing Arab Region," United Nations and the International Organization of Migration, 2015, http://publications .iom.int/system/files/pdf/sit_rep_en.pdf.
40 "Urban verification" refers in particular to the MOI exercise of re-registering Syrians residing outside of camps to provide them with a new MOI identity card. See "2015 Situation Report," United Nations and the International Organization of Migration.
41 "Jordan: Living on the Margins – Syrian Refugees in Jordan Struggle to Access Health Care," Amnesty International, 2016, https://www.amnesty .org/en/documents/mde16/3628/2016/en.
42 "Legal Status of Individuals Fleeing Syria," ACAPS.
43 Hazem al-Mazuni and Hanan Khandaji, "Confiscated Syrian ID Papers and the Emergence of a Black Market in Jordan," Ammannet, 9 September 2014, http://ar.ammannet.net/news/237023.
44 "Drivers of Despair: Refugee Protection Failures in Jordan and Lebanon," Norwegian Refugee Council, 2016, https://www.nrc.no/globalassets /pdf/reports/drivers-of-despair.pdf.
45 See Human Rights Watch, "'I Have No Idea Why They Sent Us Back.'"
46 Sara Elizabeth, "Jordan Rounds up Refugees," The Times, 16 May 2015, available at http://www.unhcr.org/cgi-bin/texis/vtx/refdaily?pass=52fc6fbd5 &id=54e18b055.
47 Hazim al-Hamwi and Musab Shawabkeh, "Jordan Puts the Lives of Syrian Refugees at Risk by Forcibly Returning Them to Their Country," Ammannet, 15 June 2015, http://ar.ammannet.net/news/251221. See also "Jordan: Vulnerable Refugees Forcibly Returned to Syria," Human Rights Watch, 12 November 2014, https://www.hrw.org/news/2014/11/23/jordan-vulnerable-refugees-forcibly-returned-syria.

48 Hazm al-Mazouni, in-person individual interview by the International Human Rights Program, Amman, Jordan, 5 June 2016.

49 Ibid.

50 Elizabeth, "Jordan Rounds Up Refugees."

51 Ibid.

52 In late June 2016, the Jordanian Ministry of Labour announced that it has issued 11,500 work permits to Syrian refugees. However, it is unclear which sectors these work permits are for and whether more will be able to be obtained. See also Laila Azzeh, "11,500 Syrians Issued Work Permits – Ministry," *Jordan Times*, 18 June 2016, http://www.jordantimes .com/news/local/11500-syrians-issued-work-permits-%E2%80%94-ministry.

53 Name has been changed to protect the identity of the interview subject. JCLA, in-person group interview by the International Human Rights Program with JCLA, Amman, Jordan, 2 June 2015.

54 For example, as noted by the lawyers at JCLA, in the last week of May 2014, a Syrian husband and wife were caught working as sex workers. The husband was taken to prison in Irbid and the Jordanian authorities wanted to deport him, his wife, and their four children. However, the JCLA succeeded in stopping their deportation. JCLA, in-person interview by the International Human Rights Program, Amman, Jordan, 2 June 2015.

55 Name has been changed to protect the identity of the interview subject. JCLA, in-person group interview by the International Human Rights Program, Amman, Jordan, 2 June 2015.

56 Ibid.

57 Ibid.

58 Ibid.

59 Ibid.

60 "Jordan's Rehabilitation Clinic for Victims of War," Al Jazeera, 19 July 2015, http://www.aljazeera.com/programmes/thecure/2015/07/jordans-rehabilitation-clinic-victims-war-150719111938377.html.

61 Hazm al-Mazouni, in-person individual interview by the International Human Rights Program, Amman, Jordan, 5 June 2016.

62 For a more detailed discussion on the intersections between health rights and deportations of Syrian refugees in Jordan, see Petra Molnar, "Discretion to Deport: Intersections between Health and Detention of Syrian Refugees in Jordan," *Refuge* 33, no. 2, 18–31.

63 "Denying Entry, Stay and Residence Due to HIV Status: Ten Things You Need to Know," Joint United Nations Programme on HIV/AIDS (UNAIDS),

2010, http://www.unaids.org/sites/default/files/media_asset/jc1738_entry _denied_en_0.pdf.

64 Ibid.

65 "Note on HIV/AIDS and the Protection of Refugees, IDPs and Other Persons of Concern." United Nations High Commissioner for Refugees, 2006, http://www.unhcr.org/444e20892.html.

66 The UNHCR argues that a person with HIV/AIDS does not fall within the national security exceptions provided within these provisions, as they are meant to apply as a last resort to persons representing "a very serious future danger to the security of the country of refuge." "Note on HIV/AIDS," UNHCR, para. 26 and footnotes 26 and 27.

67 Adam Coogle, Human Rights Watch, in-person individual interview by the International Human Rights Program, Amman, Jordan, 1 June 2015.

68 Note that these medical practitioners cannot be openly identified as a result of ongoing security concerns.

69 Elizabeth, "Jordan Rounds up Refugees."

70 "Syria Regional Refugee Response," United Nations High Commissioner for Refugees (UNHCR), Operational Portal, Refugee Situations, 2018, https://data2.unhcr.org/en/situations/syria; and "Turkey," European Civil Protection and Humanitarian Aid Operations, 6 April 2018, http://ec.europa .eu/echo/files/aid/countries/factsheets/turkey_syrian_crisis_en.pdf. See also Ahmet İçduygu, "Syrian Refugees in Turkey: The Long Road Ahead," Migration Policy Institute, 2015, http://www.migrationpolicy.org/research/syrian-refugees-turkey-long-road-ahead. Registered Syrians in Turkey are ones who have gone through a registration procedure with either the Turkish government at their point of arrival, or the UNHCR. Syrian refugees have access to certain healthcare services and medication free of charge if they register with the Turkish government under the Temporary Protection program, through which they receive an identity card. Unregistered refugees crossed into Turkey by irregular means and have not been registered. They have limited access to healthcare services and medication.

71 "Turkey," European Civil Protection and Humanitarian Aid Operations.

72 Mehmet Cetingulec, "Syrian Refugees Aggravate Turkey's Unemployment Problem," Al-Monitor, 4 July 2014, http://www.al-monitor.com/pulse/ru /originals/2014/07/cetingulec-syrian-refugees-turkey-unemployment-illegal-work.html.

73 Mehmet Cetingulec, "At a Cost of $500 Million Each Month, Turkey Staggers Under Growing Refugee Burden," Al-Monitor, 20 October 2015, http://www.al-monitor.com/pulse/originals/2015/10/turkey-syria-refugees-spent-billion-in-three-months.html.

74 "Turkey: Syrians Pushed Back at the Border," Human Rights Watch, 23
    November 2015, https://www.hrw.org/news/2015/11/23/turkey-syrians-
    pushed-back-border.

75 "Turkey/Syria: Border Guards Shoot, Block Fleeing Syrians," Human Rights
    Watch, 3 February 2018, https://www.hrw.org/news/2018/02/03/turkey/syria-
    border-guards-shoot-block-fleeing-syrians; Gerry Simpson, "Dispatches: ISIS
    Advance Traps 165,000 Syrians at Closed Turkish Border," Human Rights
    Watch, 27 May 2016, https://www.hrw.org/news/2016/05/27/dispatches-isis-
    advance-traps-165000-syrians-closed-turkish-border; Louisa Loveluck and
    Zakaria Zakaria, "Syria's Bloodiest Battle Is yet to Come – and 1 Million
    Civilians Are at Risk," *Washington Post*, 30 May 2017, https://www.washington
    post.com/world/middle_east/syrias-bloodiest-battle-is-yet-to-come—and-
    1-million-civilians-are-at-risk/2017/05/29/279a5c8c-3596-11e7-ab03-
    aa29f656f13e_story.html; "Q&A: The EU-Turkey Deal on Migration and
    Refugees," Human Rights Watch, 3 March 2016, https://www.hrw.org/news
    /2016/03/03/qa-eu-turkey-deal-migration-and-refugees; and Louisa Loveluck
    and Hiba Dlewati, "Up to 70,000 Syrian Refugees Flee to Turkey's Closed
    Border," *Telegraph*, 6 February 2016, http://www.telegraph.co.uk/news/world
    news/middleeast/syria/12144248/Up-to-70000-Syrian-refugees-flee-to-
    Turkeys-closed-border.html.

76 "Mourning in Gaziantep," Al Jazeera, 22 August 2016, http://www.al
    jazeera.com/indepth/inpictures/2016/08/mourning-gaziantep-
    160822102951102.html.

77 "Rockets Strike Turkish School Near Syria Border," Al Jazeera, 18 January
    2016, www.aljazeera.com/news/2016/01/turkish-school-hit-rockets-syrian-
    border-160118130650000.html.

78 "Syria Regional Refugee Response," UNHCR.

79 "UNHCR Turkey Factsheet – October 2017," UN High Commissioner for
    Refugees (UNHCR), 11 October 2017, https://reliefweb.int/report/turkey
    /unhcr-turkey-factsheet-october-2017.

80 Christina Maza, "In Turkey, Syria's Urban Refugees Struggle to Make Ends
    Meet," *Muftah*, 3 October 2014, http://muftah.org/turkey-syria-urban-
    refugees/#.VdPZ2_lVikp.

81 Cetingulec, "Syrian Refugees Aggravate."

82 "Turkey Election: Ruling AKP Regains Majority," BBC News, 2 November
    2015, http://www.bbc.com/news/world-europe-34694420.

83 "Erdogan Says Turkey to Hold Snap Election on November 1," Al Jazeera, 21
    August 2015, http://www.aljazeera.com/news/2015/08/turkey-election-body-
    proposes-november-1-snap-polls-150820080553216.html.

84 Joe Dyke and Noah Blaser, "What Do Turkish Elections Mean for Syrian

Refugees?" IRIN, 9 June 2015, http://www.irinnews.org/report/101607
/what-do-turkish-elections-mean-for-syrian-refugees. See also the public criticism by the leader of Turkey's main opposition party (the Republican People's Party, or CHP), Kemal Kılıçdaroğlu, who openly criticized the issuance
of work permits to Syrian refugees when there continues to be work shortages for Turkish nationals and a high unemployment rate. Ajans Haber,
"Kemal Kılıçdaroğlu 'Suriyelilere değil Türklere iş bulun,'" 16 November
2014, http://m.ajanshaber.com/killicdaroglu-suryelidere-degil-turklere-is-
bulun-haberi/140016.

85　Gul Tuysuz and Eliott C. McLaughlin, "Failed Coup in Turkey: What You
Need to Know," CNN, 18 July 2016, http://www.cnn.com/2016/07/18
/middleeast/turkey-failed-coup-explainer/index.html.

86　Umut Uras, "Polls Close in Turkey's Constitutional Referendum," Al Jazeera,
16 April 2017, http://www.aljazeera.com/news/2017/04/polls-close-turkey-
constitutional-referendum-170416142150842.html.

87　Turkey has retained a geographic limitation to its ratification of the 1951
Refugee Convention, and it only recognizes those fleeing as a consequence
of "events occurring in Europe" as Convention Refugees. However, regardless of this geographical limitation, Turkey must still abide by the principle
of non-refoulement, to which no reservations can be made (see Refugee
Convention, Arts. 1B[1] and 42). Furthermore, Turkey is party to other
human rights instruments that also prohibit refoulement of persons to
countries where they are at risk of torture or cruel, inhuman, or degrading
treatment, such as the UN Convention against Torture, which Turkey ratified
on 2 August 1988. *The Convention against Torture and Other Cruel, Inhuman
or Degrading Treatment or Punishment*, 10 December 1984, 1465 UNTS 85
(entered into force 26 June 1987).

88　Article 1B(1) of the 1951 Refugee Convention provides: "For the purposes
of this Convention, the words 'events occurring before 1 January 1951' in
article 1, Section A, shall be understood to mean either: (a) 'events occurring in Europe before 1 January 1951'; or (b) 'events occurring in Europe or
elsewhere before 1 January 1951', and each Contracting State shall make a
declaration at the time of signature, ratification or accession, specifying
which of these meanings it applies for the purposes of its obligations under
this Convention." Congo, Madagascar, Monaco, and Turkey adopted alternative (a), the geographical limitation. Turkey expressly maintained its declaration of geographical limitation upon acceding to the 1967 Protocol. See
"State Parties to the 1951 Convention Relating to the Status of Refugees
and the 1967 Protocol," United Nations High Commissioner for Refugees,
5, http://www.unhcr.org/3b73b0d63.pdf.

89 İçduygu, "Syrian Refugees in Turkey."

90 In the 1990s, Turkey enacted domestic legislation to address the influx of economic and forced migrants into its territory. As a result of the arrival of Iraqi refugees in the early 1990s, Turkey introduced the first detailed regulation regarding asylum seekers and refugees in 1994. It clarified conditions for submitting a temporary asylum claim in Turkey, and maintained the geographic limitation of the 1951 Geneva Convention. "Turkey: Regulation No. 1994/6169 on the Procedures and Principles Related to Possible Population Movements and Aliens Arriving in Turkey Either as Individuals or in Groups Wishing to Seek Asylum Either from Turkey or Requesting Residence Permission in Order to Seek Asylum from Another Country," National Legislative Bodies/National Authorities, 1994, http://www.refworld.org/docid/49746cc62.html. See also İçduygu, "Syrian Refugees in Turkey," 5; Kemal Kirişçi, "UNHCR and Turkey: Cooperating Toward an Improved Implementation of the 1951 Convention" *International Journal of Refugee Law* 13, no. 1–2 (2001): 38–55; and Kemal Kirşçi, "Border Management and EU-Turkish Relations: Convergence or Deadlock," Robert Schuman Centre for Advanced Studies, European University Institute, Cadmus, 2007, http://cadmus.eui.eu/handle/1814/7988. In 2013, the Law on Foreigners and International Protection replaced the 1994 regulation and again maintained the geographic limitation. Turkey: Law No. 6458 on 2013 of Foreigners and International Protection, 2013, http://www.refworld.org/docid/5167fbb20.html.

91 İçduygu, "Syrian Refugees in Turkey."

92 Ibid.

93 Ibid.

94 "Population Influx from Syria to Turkey: Life in Turkey as a Syrian Guest," Prime Ministry Disaster and Emergency Management Authority (AFAD), 2014.

95 Osman Bahadır Dinçer, Vittoria Federici, Elizabeth Ferris, Sema Karaca, Kemal Kirişci, and Elif Özmenek Çarmıklı, "Turkey and Syrian Refugees: The Limits of Hospitality," Brookings Institute, 2013, http://www.brookings.edu/~/media/research/files/reports/2013/11/18-syria-turkey-refugees/turkey-and-syrian-refugees_the-limits-of-hospitality-(2014).pdf.

96 Turkey: Law No. 6458 of 2013 on Foreigners and International Protection, National Legislative Bodies/National Authorities, 2013, http://www.refworld.org/docid/5167fbb20.html.

97 Ibid.

98 Ibid.

99 Ibid.

100 Louisa Loveluck, "Syrian Refugees in Turkey 'Denied Access to Lawyers and Specialised Medical Care,'" *Telegraph*, 17 May 2016, http://www.telegraph.co.uk/news/2016/05/17/syrian-refugees-in-turkey-denied-access-to-lawyers-and-specialis.

101 "Turkey: Syrian Refugees Released from Detention," Amnesty International, 26 May 2016, https://www.amnesty.org/en/documents/eur44/4124/2016/en.

102 "Turkey: Illegal Mass Returns of Syrian Refugees Expose Fatal Flaws in EU-Turkey Deal," Amnesty International, 1 April 2016, https://www.amnesty.org/en/press-releases/2016/04/turkey-illegal-mass-returns-of-syrian-refugees-expose-fatal-flaws-in-eu-turkey-deal.

103 .Ibid.

104 *Case of L. M. and Others v. Russia* (40081/14 40088/14 40127/14).

105 In-person individual interview by the International Human Rights Program, Istanbul, Turkey, 26 May 2015.

106 Ibid.

107 Waslin, "Discrediting 'Self Deportation.'"

108 Mark Krikorian, "Downsizing Illegal Immigration: A Strategy of Attrition Through Enforcement," Center for Immigration Studies, 2005, https://cis.org/Downsizing-Illegal-Immigration.

109 Waslin, "Discrediting 'Self Deportation.'"

110 For a more thorough discussion of the history and development of attrition through enforcement, see Angela S. García, "Return to Sender? A Comparative Analysis of Immigrant Communities in 'Attrition Through Enforcement' Destinations," *Ethnic and Racial Studies* 36, no. 11 (2013): 1,849–70.

111 Stephanie J. Silverman, "Mothers Versus Texas: Ethical Problems with Local 'Attrition Through Enforcement' Ordinances in the United States," *The Critique*, January/February 2016 (special issue: "And Who Is My Neighbor? Immigration, Human Rights and Sovereignty"), http://www.thecritique.com/articles/mothers-versus-texas-ethical-problems-with-local-attrition-through-enforcement-ordinances-in-the-united-states-2.

112 "'Make Their Lives Miserable': Israel's Coercion of Eritrean and Sudanese Asylum Seekers to Leave Israel," Human Rights Watch, 2014, https://www.hrw.org/report/2014/09/09/make-their-lives-miserable/israels-coercion-eritrean-and-sudanese-asylum-seekers.

113 Ahmed, "Affective Economies."

114 Nik Theodore, "Policing Borders: Unauthorized Immigration and The Pernicious Politics of Attrition," *Social Justice* 38, no. 1–2 (2011).

115 "Turkey: Syrian Refugees Released," Amnesty International.

116 For a discussion on the impacts of attrition through enforcement on immigrant mothers and children in the United States, see Jorge R. Fragoso, "The Human Cost of Self-Deportation: How Attrition Through Enforcement Affects Immigrant Women and Children," *Wisconsin Journal of Law, Gender and Society* 28, no. 1 (2013): 69.

117 See, for example, Petra Molnar, "Discretion to Deport: Intersections Between Health and Detention of Syrian Refugees in Jordan," *Refuge*, 2017, https://refuge.journals.yorku.ca/index.php/refuge/article/view/40401. For further discussion of the inadequacy of the term "transit migration" in ongoing refugee situations, see also Robyn C. Sampson, Sandra M. Gifford, and Savitri Taylor, "The Myth of Transit: The Making of a Life by Asylum Seekers and Refugees in Indonesia," *Journal of Ethnic and Migration Studies* 42, no. 7 (2016): 1135–52.

8

Is the US Gaming Refugee Status for Central Americans? A Study of the Refugee Status Determination Process for Central American Women and Their Children

Galya Ben-Arieh

In mid-2014 there was a surge in Custom and Border Patrol apprehensions of families in the southwest border of the United States. Whereas 14,855 families were apprehended in the 2013 fiscal year, in 2014 that number had jumped to 68,445, with most of the apprehensions (52,326) occurring in the Rio Grande Valley. Indeed, there was an over 500 per cent increase in apprehensions in the Rio Grande Valley from the previous year. Most of that jump occurred in May and June, with 29,102 families apprehended in those two months alone.[1] Most of the migrants crossing in the Rio Grande Valley were from Central America.[2] In the first weeks of the surge, the Obama administration reacted to the situation by issuing a statement that these migrants would be quickly deported. As then-Secretary of Homeland Security Jeh Johnson said, "This is a challenge to our border security, and, especially because of kids, it clearly has an humanitarian dimension. But, in the final analysis we know that our borders are not open to illegal migration, and our message to people in Central America is if you come here illegally, we will send you back, consistent with our laws and our values."[3] That plan was circumvented through the effort of volunteers coordinated by the Pro Bono Project, of the American Immigration Lawyers Association and the American Immigration Council, at the Federal Law Enforcement Training Center's detention facility in Artesia, New Mexico (Artesia Pro Bono Project). The detention centre in Artesia opened on 27 June 2014 and was where mothers and their accompanying children were placed pending deportation. In cases where families had crossed together, husbands were separated and sent to a different detention centre. With access to pro bono counsel, the women were able to submit motions to reopen their cases, and once their stories were heard, most were found to have a credible fear of returning home. This means that they had passed the threshold-screening standard to quickly identify potentially meritorious claims to protection, and as a result the US was obligated to submit their case for further examination by an immigration judge in the context of removal proceedings and adjudicate their claims to refugee status through a refugee status determination (RSD) process.[4]

Over the course of the next two years, as the pro bono project expanded and the lawyering grew more successful, the administration shifted from a policy of deportation to the creation of massive detention facilities and family raids. Although the Obama administration eventually acknowledged that some of the migrants had legitimate refugee claims, the administration continued to develop its four-prong policy to deter spontaneous border crossings. The first prong was a program to process the admission of unaccompanied Central American children in their country of origin (in-country processing), which in July 2016 was expanded to allow their entire families to qualify, including siblings older than twenty-one, parents, and other relatives who acted as caregivers. This unaccompanied minor program remained small, with only 600 people entering from Central America as refugees since the influx began and 2,880 minors approved to enter but awaiting final processing. The second was an agreement with Costa Rica to serve as a temporary host for Central Americans waiting to be processed for refugee status. The third was $750 million in foreign aid to Central America to address the root causes of the migration.[5] The fourth prong was the detention of those who arrived spontaneously across the border into the United States. Refugees who arrive at the border are detained, and the administration has accelerated deportation before they have the chance to pursue asylum claims, and without assistance from lawyers.[6] The Trump administration has continued the four-prong policy, also known as the "Alliance for Prosperity," under the direction of Department of Homeland Security (DHS) Secretary John Kelly, who helped the Obama administration design the policy when he was the commander of the United States Southern Command, the United States Department of Defense unit responsible for American military operations in Central America, South America, and the Caribbean.

Although media and public attention has focused on the European refugee flows, the Central American situation has come to be known as "the other refugee crisis," with Democrats critical of the administration's classification of the Central American flow as part of immigration enforcement rather than an ongoing humanitarian crisis[7] and Republicans calling for tougher enforcement. Although the number of apprehensions along the southwest border dropped in the 2015 fiscal year to 39,838, that number spiked again in the 2016 fiscal year, reaching the figures witnessed in 2014, with 58,720 apprehensions by the end of July. Once again, the highest numbers of family unit apprehensions are in the Rio Grande Valley (39,326), although other sectors along the southwest border have seen a more sizable increase in family unit apprehensions.[8] Data of border crossings for the past four decades, however, reveals that there is no "crisis" of undocumented arrivals in terms of numbers that are fairly regular.[9] Instead, the crisis is the institutional breakdown resulting from border enforcement practices that require unprecedented detention and administrative processes. The Central American refugee crisis in the United States has undermined humanitarian policy at the border, with detention reaching record numbers[10] and the almost complete breakdown of the immigration court system and asylum process, with "rocket docket" expedited hearings for Central Americans and severe backlogs of up to four years for other cases.

Through a qualitative case study of the Artesia Pro Bono Project that draws upon interpretive and observational analysis of the contestation between official policies, government managerial and discretionary practices and rules, judicial rulings, and the lawyering process, this chapter examines the institutional crisis in the border enforcement practices and RSD process for Central American women and children as an *interactional* legal process between government agents, decision makers, lawyers, claimants, and advocates. Goodwin-Gill discusses the "grass-roots dynamic"[11] – an integrated civil society component that is supposed to be rights informing and protecting. Lon L. Fuller's theory of law as an interactional process provides insight into the shortcomings of grassroots civil society efforts, in which governmental actors in the legal institution serve their own individual ver-

sion of the shared purpose. Fuller theorizes that a contradictory purpose in the law contributes to the proliferation of legal principles –
"creeping legalism" – that enable the pursuit of these individual versions undermining due process and rule of law. My analysis of lawyering on behalf of the detained Central American women and children
shows that while the purpose of the law of refugee protection in the
United States Refugee Act of 1980 (1980 Refugee Act),[12] which is
grounded in the 1951 *Convention Relating to the Status of Refugees* (the
Refugee Convention),[13] is the humanitarian protection of refugees,
executive policies and legislative managerial directions focused on
deterrence and border security present government agents and adjudicators with a conflicting purpose that undermines the role of law
and legal process in the protection of refugees. Drawing on Fuller's
analytic framework, the study finds that, given the conflict in purpose, effective lawyering on behalf of the humanitarian protection of
refugees leads to an increase on the part of government agents in the
use of discretion and informal rulemaking, resulting in a "creeping
legalism" that serves to maintain an overall restrictive RSD process as
part of the deterrence policy objectives. The study contributes a street-
level bureaucratic analysis of the RSD process in questioning "who
really provides protection, who acts as gatekeeper, and what the
impact of extant power relations and bureaucratic rationality are on
the production and regulation of asylum space."[14] The study offers
insight into the way in which the interactions of lawmakers, adjudicators, and official agents in rule making, the exercise of discretion,
managerial direction, and informal administration in the RSD process
for detained Central American women and children transform the
adjudication of refugee status, from a process intended to protect refugees into a deterrence system in violation of our own commitment to
asylum, human rights, and the dignity of these women and children
fleeing persecution. The study contributes to discussions about the
changing nature of asylum systems in Western countries that have
shifted to a *crimmigration* strategy for those who seek asylum status
pursuant to irregular entry across a national border.

REFUGEE STATUS DETERMINATION
AS AN INTERACTIONAL LEGAL PROCESS

Fuller, one of the most important American legal theorists of the
twentieth century, offers crucial insights into the questions we ought

to be asking about the situation of RSD for Central Americans in the United States. Fuller's conception of law was based in "eunomics" – "the science, theory, or study of good order and workable social arrangements."[15] Fuller's particular contribution was his concept of law as an interactional process. In Fuller's account, legal institutions are intended to accomplish three things: solve social problems, embody moral aspirations and define moral relationships, and have legal competence – to reflect the distinctiveness of different legal institutions in purpose, structure, and capacity to resolve substantive problems.[16] This entails a subsidiary concern with regard to the limits of the effectiveness of different institutions and the pathological forms they are liable to generate.[17] After placing the problem of refugee protection within Fuller's conception of law, the next two sections will introduce RSD as an interactional legal process and discuss the nature of the purposeful enterprise of RSD, as well as of the contradictory purpose of "deterrence," which undermines the capacity and effectiveness of RSD as the shared commitment to afford refugees humanitarian protection.

Under the Refugee Convention, a refugee is someone who "owing to a well-founded fear of being persecuted for reasons of race, religion, nationality, membership of a particular social group or political opinion, is outside the country of his nationality and is unable or, owing to such fear, is unwilling to avail himself of the protection of that country."[18] While persecution is not defined in international law, over the past decade the United Nations High Commissioner for Refugees (UNHCR) has issued guidelines and national courts have issued decisions expanding what constitutes persecution to include LGBTI and gender-based persecution, and in limited cases, gang-related claims.[19] Given the expansion of the refugee category and an increase in people seeking asylum, one would expect to see an increase in the granting of refugee status. Instead, the overall rates of asylum have remained constant or have decreased over the past decade.[20] What should we make of the seeming anomaly that the expansion of the jurisprudence of what constitutes "persecution" under refugee law has not produced any effect on the protection of refugees who undergo an RSD process? While some scholars have studied judicial decisions empirically to demonstrate the inconsistencies of the asylum process[21] and the contentious politics of immigration to explain the restrictive asylum system in the US,[22] Fuller's interactional concept of law leads us to instead examine the legal institution itself – the informal practices, rulemaking, managerial direction, and discretion in administrative processes that serve to maintain a restrictive national asylum system.

Research on international and US refugee law has focused mainly on the development of refugee law and jurisprudence. Scholars have analyzed the substantive legal principles of persecution[23] and the need for authoritative interpretation across international jurisdictions.[24] While analyses of formal refugee law are important, they tell us little about the relationship between the institutional design and refugee protection, or RSD as a legal process. More recently, empirical research on the US asylum process has provided us with an understanding of the random factors that produce variance in decision outcomes in asylum adjudication,[25] factors other than the merits of a case that have an effect on grant rates,[26] and the effect of particular immigration judges on outcomes. Empirical studies suggest that institutional analysis of the legal process is more relevant to understanding whether refugee law has purpose, shape, and force. For example, recent studies have found that immigration courts are prone to inaccurate fact-finding in asylum cases due to internal structural problems, such as circumscribed appellate reviews and a shortage of resources and time for immigration judges to adequately consider each case, casting doubt on the capacity of the asylum adjudicatory process. Unlike in civil law statutory systems, in common law systems the legal process is central to the question of the nature of the law. Common law systems, such as they exist in the United States, are by nature interactional, in that the legal process is embedded in what Fuller distinguishes as the legal institution, which is, essentially, the law. In order to understand the nature of the legal institution as a purposive and problem-solving enterprise, one must examine the interactional relationships within the legal institution. In the United States the legal institution of refugee law is comprised of a range of adjudicators, including border agents, asylum officers, immigration judges, bureaucrats such as detention staff and officials, police, lawyers, and advocates. Therefore, it is the on-the-ground contestation and interaction of these officials with lawyers and asylum applicants, in the legal process over legal interpretation and the rules of due process, that form refugee law as a rights-based protection system – a social and humanitarian enterprise to address the problem of refugee protection.

Fuller sees the legal process as providing legal mechanisms that structure relationships. Legality requires bonds that link people to some common purpose or social enterprise. The danger, for Fuller, is that in an effort to maintain the seeming neutrality of the judicial process, the process becomes dominated by the legal principle of organization, and the shared commitment gets lost. He calls this "creeping legalism." While we tend to think "that the state, and the multitude of activities necessary to sustain it, are morally neutral except as the human actions involved may be judged by moral standards applicable to all forms of human behaviour, governmental and nongovernmental alike," this view ignores "the concept of institutional role – the role of the citizen, the judge, the lawgiver, the cop on the corner" and erects "a strong taboo against any recognition that each of these roles requires for its proper discharge a distinctive kind of personal commitment."27 In other words, there must be a shared commitment, and the agents making decisions must have a personal commitment towards the shared purpose of the legal institution in order for law to function properly. When these agents lose sight of the shared purpose, and legal rules and principles come to dominate, you have "creeping legalism."

If we take Fuller's view, then the RSD process in the United States can be considered a purposeful enterprise with a collective commitment to protect refugees, as defined in the 1980 Refugee Act,28 dependent on the interaction of lawmakers, adjudicators, lawyers, and claimants who contribute collectively to refugee law. Fuller's interactional theory suggests an analytic framework for the case study of the RSD process for Central American women and their children. The framework begins by identifying the purposeful enterprise of RSD and then seeks to analyze whether the legal institution responsible for RSD – comprised of all the agents in the institution – is competent in its purpose, structure, and capacity to resolve substantive problems of RSD, and if not, seeks to determine the limits to the legal institution's effectiveness, and the pathological forms it is liable to generate. These pathological forms are understood as "creeping legalism," defined as (1) a greater reliance on rules to define members' duties and entitlements; (2) a concordant shift in accountability based on tangible harms or benefits that flow from specific acts, rather than on more judgemental assessments of character and motive; and (3) the articulation of strict procedural requirements for distributing benefits and burdens.29 Through this analysis we can question whether the process succeeds, or whether it so fails to protect human life that it violates the minimum requirement, as H.L.A. Hart theorized, of a legal system to comport with basic features of human life that, given the minimal aim of survival, provide completing reasons for the rules in question.[30]

REFUGEE LAW AND THE RSD PROCESS
AS A PURPOSEFUL ENTERPRISE

This section sets out the purpose of refugee law and the RSD process as defined in the 1980 Refugee Act and in the Refugee Convention that is its basis. I argue that refugee law suffers from an internal contradiction of purpose that limits the effectiveness of the RSD process for Central Americans and contributes to a pathological "culture of disbelief" – that is, a denial of legitimate refugee claims. The following section offers an interactional analysis of the Artesia Pro Bono Project to discuss the pathological condition of "creeping legalism" in the RSD process, which has transformed the humanitarian purpose into a deterrence system in violation of human rights.

The right to seek and enjoy asylum and be granted protection from persecution is a core human right protected under the Refugee Convention and inscribed in the United States through the 1980 Refugee Act. Under the Act, a refugee is someone who is outside his or her country of nationality and is unable or unwilling to return to and receive protection in that country because of persecution or a well-founded fear of future persecution on account of race, religion, nationality, political opinion, or membership in a particular social group. According to the UNHCR's *Handbook and Guidelines on Procedures and Criteria for Determining Refugee Status under the 1951 Convention and the 1967 Protocol Relating to the Status of Refugees* (UNHCR *Handbook*), recognition of refugee status does not make a person a refugee, but rather declares a person to be one.[31] In other words, a person is a refugee as soon as he or she meets the legal criteria in the refugee definition. RSD is not a constitutive process, but a declarative one, meaning that the purpose of the legal process is to confirm that the person meets the criteria of the legal definition, with the onus on the state to contest the claim for refugee status.[32] The combination of the declaratory process of refugee recognition and Article 31 of the Refugee Convention, which provides for nonpenalization on account of illegal entry,[33] recognizes an imbalance of power in that refugees cannot force a hearing.[34] The drafters placed the onus on the state to contest that the person is a refugee, preventing a state from simply circumventing its obligation to protect refugees by never asking the question "are you a refugee," thereby avoiding having to declare a person a refugee.[35]

Hamlin's analysis of the history of the 1980 Refugee Act reveals that it has never achieved the purpose it was designed for, which was to limit executive control by creating a system of RSD for asylum seekers that was based on individualized assessment. As well, this system was to exist in addition to the system of executive parole, which is based on national origin, thus bringing the American asylum system in line with the Refugee Convention.[36] The purpose, in other words, was to depoliticize the recognition of refugee status and create a more humanitarian system. As Hamlin states, while "on paper, 1980 represented a major transition from the previous ad hoc, executive driven, group-based system to an administrative process based on the non-ideological UN definition of a refugee," executive policies have continued to focus on ways to avoid individual processing for "asylum seekers with no strategic political value" through interdiction, detention, and expedited removal.[37] The potential turning towards a less politicized, humanitarian RSD process occurred in the early 1990s, when the Immigration and Naturalization Service (INS) initiated a number of reforms in response to growing criticism and the mobilization of advocates who highlighted the tensions and hypocrisy in the existing system.[38] At this time, the INS established a specialized Asylum Corps who continue to assess eligibility for refugee status as an "affirmative" administrative process in which a person who arrives in the United States may submit an application for asylum within one year of entry. Since this is an administrative and not a legal process, legal counsel is not permitted at this stage, although a lawyer may accompany the person to the asylum interview. Applicants whose claims are denied are referred to immigration court if they do not possess a valid visa. While this is a positive development, as annual asylum applications increased "tenfold, from 16,622 new applicants in 1985, to 182,769 applicants in 1995," the Asylum Office backlog grew to insurmountable levels[39] and the "huge institutional strain on the American RSD system ... only exacerbated the already apparent ideological friction."[40] As Hamlin notes: "By 1994, the modern era of asylum policy-making was born, one that focused on reducing administrative burdens, and is characterised by high levels of inter-branch conflict, as both the courts and Congress became far more active players in asylum policy than ever before."[41] In summary, the purpose of the RSD process suffers in its competency in terms of its purpose and capacity to resolve RSD problems. When the system is politicized it limits access to the process to deserving refugees, and when it *has* sought to become less politicized, it suffered from the lack of institutional capacity to process the rise in refugee claims.

The passing of the Illegal Immigration Reform and Immigrant Responsibility Act (IIRAIRA)[42] in 1996 ushered in a new era of asylum policy in the US, shifting the focus of asylum policy to deterrence through stricter border control, a one-year time limit on applying for asylum, narrower grounds for which asylum could be granted, removal of the right to work for people whose asylum applications are pending, and a policy of mandatory detention and expedited removal. These reforms represent a contradictory purpose in the RSD process of "deterrence," undermining the shared commitment to humanitarian protection for refugees who cross the border irregularly. Whereas US refugee law acknowledges and protects refugees who enter without a valid visa,[43] the reforms criminalize asylum seekers who come across the border, putting into question the ability of the 1980 Refugee Act and the RSD process to properly function as law, given the contradiction.

There are a number of pathological forms that flow from this contradiction of purpose between deterrence and humanitarian relief that limits the effectiveness of the RSD process in the case of Central Americans. As examples, this section considers the "culture of disbelief" and the government's "no-bond" policy for the women and their accompanying children detained in the Artesia detention centre. The response of the United States government to the surge of people – mostly women and children – arriving at the southern border from Central America, beginning at the end of 2014, was based on the assumption that migrants from Central America are not refugees, and therefore they can be successfully deterred from entering the US with the threat of detention. The argument, as stated by former US Attorney for the Southern District of California Peter Nunez, was that previously deported migrants seeking to reunite with their families in the United States were "gaming the system" by "learning specific phrases they can say at a border facility, such as 'I have a legitimate fear,' that automatically qualified them for consideration of asylum."[44] The argument, according to government affidavits opposing bonds for the detained women in Artesia who were represented by the Artesia Pro Bono Project, was that "[a]ccording to debriefings of Guatemalan, Honduran, and Salvadoran detainees, the high probability of a prompt release, coupled with the likelihood of low or no bond, is among the reasons they are coming to the United States." This led the government to conclude that "implementation of a 'no bond' or 'high bond' policy would significantly reduce the unlawful mass migration of Guatemalans, Hondurans, and Salvadoran(s)."[45] The government's logic was that a surge in the number of migrants who claimed fear of persecution or torture after they entered the United States (i.e., entered and did not present themselves to a border agent, but were apprehended, and therefore detained and placed in removal proceedings), meant that the claims must not be genuine. This logic was proven false by the fact that, after motions to reopen were submitted by counsel, most of the women in Artesia passed their interviews before an asylum officer establishing a credible fear. The final report of the Artesia Pro Bono Project documents that, "[a]lthough *all* 1200 immigrants detained at Artesia were supposed to have been deported, in fact, almost 70% were released."[46] The government's argument that a no-bond policy was needed to ensure that the migrants appeared in court does not hold true either, based on empirical findings. Ingrid Eagly and Steven Shafer analyzed over 1.2 million immigration cases, finding that when respondents in removal proceedings were given counsel, 93 per cent attended all of their future court hearings. The same was true for those seeking asylum in removal.[47] In other words, the presence of counsel is the strongest indicator of court appearance, yet the logic of deterrence places significant obstacles to obtaining legal counsel.

Moreover, according to Hamlin: "this association between unsuccessful asylum claims and actively fraudulent or undeserving claims requires much more elaboration. It not only assumes that there is a particular percentage of asylum-seekers who possess the qualities of a true refugee, it assumes that they can be discovered through a process of regularised inquiry, and that they will not be prevented by policies of deterrence from lodging a claim in the first place. The realities of asylum seeking and administrative decision-making cast serious doubt on these assumptions."[48] The women detained in Artesia from June to December 2014 were subject to numerous policies that were part of the overall executive policy of "detain and deport" that prevented them from lodging a claim, and where they did lodge a claim with legal counsel, presented obstacles to a regularized inquiry. The detention centre itself was isolated, located hours from the nearest major metropolitan area. Detention centre policies restricted access to phones, limiting all calls to three minutes. Detainees were given no notice of upcoming interviews for establishing a credible fear or asylum proceedings in their case, meaning they had no time to prepare. Since the detention centre did not have a childcare facility, the women were forced to answer traumatic questions, including detailing instances of rape, while their children were present. As a result, the client I represented chose not to speak about her rape in her interview with the asylum officer.[49]

The assumption of the US government in its executive policy of detention for Central Americans apprehended at the border, that these migrants have gamed the asylum system by falsely claiming "credible fear," needs to be examined more fully as a question of institutional design and legal process. Even if we assume or can verify that some migrants are in fact attempting to "game the system," questions still remain with regards to how this compares to the gaming being done by the United States through its control and authority over the RSD process. The concerns over "bogus" asylum seekers have reached global proportions, drastically shrinking asylum space in Western countries, where the assumption is that all irregular border crossers are economic migrants, "queue jumpers" or "bad refugees."[50] Scholars have documented the "culture of disbelief" and "culture of denial" in the asylum hearings[51] and have shown how it plays out in the "performance of law" in immigration courts.[52] There have also been studies on the particular way in which the culture of disbelief affects women's claims to sexual and gender-based violence.[53] The case of Central Americans brings out the pathological condition of disbelief and denial as it plays out for refugees apprehended and detained upon entry at the border.

In the absence of sufficient transparency regarding the RSD process taking place during US border apprehensions and detention, it can be difficult to assess how decisions made by government agents correspond with US refugee policy. The IIRAIRA created the expedited removal process that was expanded in 2006. Through expedited removal, the US Customs and Border Protection (CBP) was granted authority to screen asylum seekers at the point of entry and make an initial assessment of whether an asylum seeker has a "credible fear" of persecution if returned to his or her home country. The CBP agent is responsible for flagging persons apprehended without authorization who may have a "credible fear" during the legal procedure of apprehension that requires the agent to complete a "record of sworn statement in proceedings." The form contains template questions, includ-

ing "Why did you leave your home country or country of last residence," "Do you have any fear or concern about being returned to
your home country or being removed from the United States," and
"Would you be harmed if you are returned to your home country or
country of last residence."[54] Once flagged, the person meets with an
asylum officer from the United States Citizenship and Immigration
Services (USCIS) who determines whether their fear of return is "credible" or "reasonable," at which point they are subject to a reinstatement of removal. The purpose of the "credible fear" interview is to
determine whether there is a significant possibility (a 10 per cent
chance) that they will prevail in an asylum hearing before an immigration judge.

An asylum process that, more often than not, rejects and/or deports
a bona fide refugee who is detained upon apprehension at the border
would be difficult to justify as a matter of public policy. Hamlin's
analysis of the expedited removal program reveals that it "prevents
many would-be asylum applicants from accessing the RSD system at
all, by processing claims at the border."[55] As Hamlin notes, "[p]art of
what makes expedited removal so effective at reducing asylum applications is that it is up to the discretion of the individual immigration
officer to decide how to pose questions about fear in the interview. If
no fear is explicitly expressed and their documents are otherwise
invalid for entry, the asylum seeker is summarily removed."[56] While
the US government initially only applied expedited removal provisions to noncitizens arriving at official entry points along the border
or at airports, known as "ports of entry," Human Rights Watch (HRW)
has found that, over the last decade, "the [DHS], which was established
in 2002 after the September 11, 2001 attacks on the United States, has
applied expedited removal procedures to people apprehended along
the entire US border. Under DHS regulations this includes people
apprehended within 100 miles of the border."[57] Hamlin found that
"data from Immigrations and Customs Enforcement (ICE) shows that
the programme has continued to grow each year since its inception,
and in 2009 (the last year for which data is available) expedited
removal accounts for 27 per cent of the removals that ICE conducts
annually."[58] Advocates maintain that the fact that people are making
the costly and difficult journey multiple times is sufficient evidence
that they have an urgent need to flee. Instead of being placed under
"reinstatement of removal," their consistent return should be trigger-
ing heightened concerns of protection needs.[59]

Given this data, we need to question how effective the American asylum system is in terms of identifying refugees apprehended at the border and detained through the credible fear process, prior to removal – in addition to it being a costly system with a very low accuracy rate. Furthermore, how is this ineffectiveness related to the overall purpose of refugee law and justice? In the absence of sufficient transparency regarding how determinations about credible fear are made, it is often difficult to assess the accuracy of the decisions made by border control agents and adjudicators in detention facilities. What we do know is that data from the DHS shows that approximately 70 per cent of the Central American women and children in the family detention centres were able to demonstrate a credible fear of returning to their country of origin, once they were able to access counsel through the Artesia Pro Bono Project, and that the vast majority of families were granted asylum or related humanitarian relief by an immigration judge.[60]

HRW conducted interviews with people who were deported to Honduras and issued a report concerning the situation of Central American migrants in the process to establish credible fear. Data from 2011 and 2012, which HRW obtained from the United States CBP under the Freedom of Information Act, shows a culture of denial. They found that:

few Central American migrants are identified by CBP as people who fear return to their country in the first stage of the expedited removal process. The data show that the vast majority of Hondurans, at least 80 percent, are placed in fast-track expedited removal and reinstatement of removal proceedings but only a minuscule minority, 1.9 percent, got flagged for credible fear assessments by CBP. The percentages for Mexico, Honduras, El Salvador, and Guatemala are similar, ranging from 0.1 to 5.5 percent. By comparison, 21 percent of migrants from other countries who underwent the same proceedings in the same years were flagged for credible fear interviews by CBP.[61]

The HRW report continues:

Virtually all of those we interviewed who had been apprehended at or near the border were deported summarily, via expedited removal or reinstatement of removal. Many said they had expressed their fears to US Border Patrol officials charged with screening for fear of return before being deported, but fewer than half of these were referred by US Border Patrol for a further assessment of whether they had a "credible" or "reasonable" fear of returning to Honduras. US law requires that when a migrant in expedited or reinstatement of removal expresses a fear of return to their country of origin, they be referred to a US Citizenship and Immigration Services (USCIS) asylum officer for an interview to determine whether their fear might qualify them for asylum or other protection.

Human Rights Watch was unable to corroborate claims about the specific dangers interviewees said they faced in Honduras. However, the experiences they described and the fears they expressed should have led US immigration authorities to give their cases sufficient scrutiny before they were returned to their home country. The principle of nonrefoulement, the right not to be returned to a place where one would likely face threats to life or freedom or other serious harm, recognized under both US and international law, demands as much.[62]

Whereas CBP is required to screen for credible fear, as HRW found for 2011 and 2012, it was usually not until after a person was transferred over to ICE for detention that referrals for credible fear determinations were made to USCIS by both immigration agencies and ICE, even though ICE is not required to do so. According to HRW, referrals of Hondurans increased from 1,108 people in 2006 to 8,539 in 2013.[63] As HRW reports, "In 2012, for example, CBP referred only 615 of the 2,405 Hondurans who eventually were flagged for credible fear interviews by USCIS. Approximately three-quarters of the credible fear referrals USCIS conducted in 2012 came from agencies other than the CBP, even though that year CBP was responsible for approximately 57 percent of all noncitizen apprehensions."[64]

In addition, the CBP screening process is itself fraught with procedural problems outlined by HRW and others who point to the shorter timeframe of CBP "credible fear" screenings under the expedited removal procedures than is required by the regular "credible fear" process. They also highlight that the interview is performed by a uniformed, and often armed, CBP officer in a crowded setting that limits privacy from young children, family, and strangers. Indeed, arrivals from Central America began to refer to the CBP detention as "le hieleras" (the ice box), for the frigid room in which they were screened and processed.[65]

To summarize, the RSD process contains an internal contradiction in purpose: it seeks to both fulfill the humanitarian purpose of refugee protection (to solve the problem of someone's loss of rights when they cross an international border in order to flee persecution) and deter migrants from crossing irregularly into the United States (to solve the problem of unauthorized immigration).[66] These conflicting purposes have resulted in an overall ineffectiveness of the refugee law as an institutional process. The following section builds on this analysis by examining the pathological condition of "creeping legalism" in the RSD process through the case of the Artesia Pro Bono Project.

CREEPING LEGALISM IN THE RSD PROCESS

An analysis of the Artesia Pro Bono Project, based on the aforementioned definition of "creeping legalism" and drawing on Fuller's framework of "creeping legalism," reveals that, as the lawyering became more successful, new and shifting governmental rules, discretionary acts, and procedural requirements created new layers that obstructed the legal process. Below I discuss these findings by presenting the breakthrough regarding bond determinations. Given these findings, I argue that if we understand law as an interactional concept, then deterrence introduces a conflicting purpose into the institution of refugee law such that lawyering on behalf of the humanitarian protection of refugees is not ultimately that effective in terms of the overall institution. This is because government agents, operating through an individual commitment to deterrence, use managerial discretion and informal practices and rulemaking to create an overly restrictive legal institution of refugee law. In other words, even as effective lawyering leads to policy changes or favourable legal rulings that further humanitarian protection for refugees, the deterrence logic ultimately prevails, as the government agents and bureaucrats at the various layers of the RSD process exercise their individual commitment to deterrence. The study suggests the need for further empirical work to test this hypothesis.[67]

After the Obama administration ended family detention at the T. Don Hutto detention centre in 2009, the policy in the US was to allow migrants arriving with children to be placed in removal proceedings before immigration judges. This policy underwent a shift during the summer of 2014 when, in June 2014, the DHS established two detention facilities in Artesia, New Mexico, and Karnes, Texas, with between 500 and 700 beds each to hold arriving families.[68] In September 2014, DHS announced plans to contract a private prison company, the Corrections Corporation of America, to build a 2,400-bed family detention facility in Dilley, Texas.[69]

Between 27 June 2014 and 29 December 2014, about 1,200 women and children were detained at the Federal Law Enforcement Training Center in Artesia, New Mexico. The Artesia Pro Bono Project began on 24 July 2014 and finished on 29 December 2014, at which point the organizations that had formed the project (the American Immigration Lawyers Association and the American Immigration Council) merged with the Catholic Legal Immigration Network and the Refugee and Immigrant Center for Education and Legal Services to form CARA, which has since been operating in Dilley and Karnes, Texas. During the time of this analysis, the Artesia Pro Bono project grew to include 300 lawyers working with 700 clients in detention. The project operated through a shared case management system and documentation database. The project's activities included "on the ground" volunteers at the detention centre doing intakes, preparing cases and representing the women and their children before asylum officers and in hearings before immigration judges, which took place through video conferencing. Remote teams of lawyers developed protocols and templates, and prepared bond motions and litigation strategies. I participated as a pro bono legal volunteer in the project, serving on the ground for a week in August 2014. The study is based on observation of the email correspondence among the volunteer lawyers, testimony of the lawyers in their video postcards and blogs, asylum and immigration judge case decisions, advocacy reports, media coverage, government memos, and executive policy. Through this database, I created a detailed timeline of the Artesia Pro Bono Project, charting executive orders, DHS policies, Executive Office of Immigration Review policies, immigration judge decisions and informal rule making, litigation strategies, media reports, Board of Immigration Appeals (BIA) decisions, Federal Court decisions, advocacy efforts and reports, and on-the-ground issues and concerns regarding due process and lawyering. Given the limited scope of this chapter, I will only focus on the contestation over bond policies. Through an analysis of bond policies, rules, and practices, I was able to identify three phases in the RSD legal process. The first phase began when the detention centre opened on June 24, at which time the government policy was one of deportation. This phase ended when the lawyers began their work at the detention centre and was replaced by a second phase in which the government policy was one of "no release" through the rejection of bond. The second phase ended when the lawyers were issued a favourable decision by the BIA ending the government's no-bond policy. I then charted the experience of the lawyers working on the ground across these phases, documenting shifts in informal rules and discretionary practices as they surfaced. I will discuss each of these phases and the findings below.

When the women, accompanied by their children, started to arrive in June 2014, the government implemented a plan to detain them at the Federal Law Enforcement Training Center in Artesia, New Mexico, as arrangements were made for their deportation. This deportation policy was challenged when a few of the women gained access to legal counsel in July. On July 24 the Artesia Pro Bono Project took up shop in the makeshift trailers at the detention centre, referring to themselves as the "fire brigade," and were able to stop the deportations. However, government lawyers from ICE opposed all bond requests on behalf of mothers and their children for release from the detention facilities. The government relied on *Matter of D-J*, a case from the post-9/11 era, arguing that the women posed a national security risk. The *D-J* decision was issued in the wake of the 9/11 terrorist attacks amidst concerns that Pakistanis and Palestinians were transiting through Haiti to gain access to the United States, entering with the Haitian boat arrivals.[70] The case set out the requirement for detention without the possibility of a bond in the situation of a declared national emergency where a mass migration, such as the Haitian crisis, would strain the ability of the DHS to process migrants. Relying on President Obama's reference to the Central American situation at the southern border as a "humanitarian crisis," the DHS submitted expert opinions that the "crisis" posed a national security risk, in justification of its no-bond policy.[71] In a letter to the DHS seeking support for legal counsel, the Association of Pro Bono Counsel asked the DHS to stop the no-bond policy, stating, "These practices by DHS trial counsel have amounted to an effective 'no bond' policy that does not comport with the facts of the detainees' circumstances. Continuing to detain women and children under these circumstances is a policy that undermines the government's credibility and impedes basic notions of due process."[72] The immigration judges situated at that time in Arlington, Texas, and hearing the cases through teleconferencing, mainly ruled in favour of the no-bond policy by rejecting bond or issuing very high bond amounts that the women could not pay. There was only one judge who rejected the policy and, using her discretion, awarded a low bond.[73] For the judges who did issue a bond, the government insisted on appealing all of the bond decisions, preventing the release of the women pending an appeal, which would take an additional six months before the women could file a habeas petition. As one of the Artesia team lawyers wrote in an email, "Who knew DHS would stoop so low actually to appeal sizable bonds for moms and children who have been found to have a credible fear of persecution and substantial ties to the United States."[74] Another attorney noted that the government's appeals were targeting the one "rogue" immigration judge who was exercising her discretion to go against the government's no-bond policy.[75] As the government instituted the new practice of appealing the bond determinations, the administration announced the opening of a new detention centre in Dilley, Texas.[76]

The litigation team developed its own bond template, made available on 23 September 2014, drawing upon experts to refute the government's analysis and conclusions that the women posed a national security risk in that they would fail to show up at immigration hearings. The strategy worked, bond amounts were reduced to an average of $3,000, and the BIA issued unpublished decisions overturning immigration judge decisions to deny bond.[77]

Just as the pro bono group started winning and thought all the women would be released, on 20 November 2014, the same evening that President Obama announced his executive order of Deferred Action for Parents of Americans (DAPA),[78] the government began to secretly transfer the women out of Artesia and into the new, larger facility at Karnes, and announced that Artesia would be closed. As Stephen Manning, one of the team leaders, wrote in an email sent the next day:

Team Artesia,

Last night, in the middle of the President's dramatic speech about preserving family unity, his delegates in Artesia decided that they would immediately begin transferring our clients to Karnes. Without notice. Without warning. It didn't matter if there were bond hearings scheduled, merits hearings scheduled. Nothing mattered – other than there was a plane available for transport.

Christina raised the red alarm, the AILA [American Immigration Lawyers Association] HQ team with our AIC [American Immigration Council] partners – right after the President's speech conferred & developed a plan. The disconnect from what the compassionate-ish words of the President and his crushing policies towards these refugees was shocking.

Two prong plan: we sue them & we negotiate with them. Our position: the transfer will take place in an orderly fashion respectful of the right to counsel and in no way should prejudice access to counsel or the presentation of our client's claims. Midnight transfers, just like midnight deportations are unacceptable. Pretty reasonable, right?

Reasonableness is such an irrelevant after thought for Obama & his deportation-crew. After an evening of negotiations, a morning of stonewalling, we implemented the "sue them" prong: the OTG [on the ground] team drafted litigation pleadings, we connected with our AIC & IRP [Immigrant Rights Project] allies to file and then, lo and behold, a small breakthrough in the stonewall: we have a tentative understanding that the original transfers scheduled for this morning will not take place until after Thanksgiving, Nov. 25. Our negotiations continue. What part of the 5th Amendment is so hard for the Obama Administration to understand?[79]

The executive determination to open the facility at Dilley and transfer the women guaranteed that the detention of Central Americans would be ongoing.

On 16 December 2014 the American Civil Liberties Union (ACLU) filed a nationwide class action lawsuit challenging the government's no-bond policy,[80] and the United States District Court issued a preliminary injunction on 20 February 2015,[81] prompting the government to shift its approach of arguing every bond case. This made it much more difficult for the pro bono team, which operated on volunteers who had to prepare each and every case. The government was therefore able to use this high-bond strategy to prevent the release of the women from detention. As one volunteer said, "Before it was draining for the limited legal services to litigate every bond, but now it's no better because we have to litigate to reduce the bond, since ICE is not complying with the injunction."

The findings above show that as the lawyering became more effective, government agents added multiple procedural tiers to the RSD legal process that undermined what the lawyers had achieved. Although migrants and legal advocates have agency in how they present their claims to refugee status, it is the government that sets the rules and can change them. Most often, it is legal advocates who contest the rules as being in violation of due process, whereas government advocates tend to argue on grounds of public policy. Adjudicators are usually called upon to balance these competing demands. In this way, agency and power serve to undermine refugee law. The analysis concerning bonds shows the way in which formal and informal rules and decisions of officials during the RSD process contribute to overall social control by regulating the terms and place of detention, access to legal counsel, access to bond, the forum where claims and appeals will be heard, family unity, the issuance of nonprecedential decisions, the promulgation of nonprecedential memorandum, and guidance notes. Whereas the laws governing asylum in the US as enacted in the Immigration and Nationality Act[82] provide statutory rules regarding asylum status, all the factors mentioned above fall within the boundaries of administrative policy and discretion that can be changed without legislative oversight.

CONCLUSION

In Fuller's institutional account of law, the proper functioning of refugee law requires a shared commitment to achieve its humanitarian purpose. This shared commitment has the tendency to get lost in the legal principles of the process (which he refers to as "creeping legalism"). The problem of losing sight of this shared commitment is not just one for judges and lawgivers; rather, the institutional role includes that of the citizen, the cop on the corner, the guard at the detention centre, and the filing clerk at the court, all of whom are required for the law's proper discharge to conduct their duties with a distinctive kind of personal commitment. The proliferation of formal and informal rules – "creeping legalism" – has enabled policy to tip in favour of deterrence, with official agents operating as a kind of private association serving their own version of the shared commitment to refugee law, undermining the humanitarian purpose of the legal institution.

The analysis in this study of the Artesia Pro Bono Project's representation of Central American women and their accompanying children, therefore, calls into question the effectiveness of the US institution of asylum protection under the 1980 Refugee Act. The key finding of the study is that a policy of deterrence has introduced a conflicting purpose into the institution of refugee law such that lawyering on behalf of the humanitarian protection of refugees is not ultimately that effective in terms of the overall institution. This is because government agents, preferencing deterrence and operating through their own individual understanding of the institution, use managerial discretion and informal practices and rulemaking to create an overall restrictive legal institution of refugee law. These findings call into question whether the legal institution of refugee law succeeds in fulfilling its purpose or whether it so fails to protect human life that it violates the minimum requirement of a legal system to comport with basic features of human life that, given the minimal aim of survival, provide completing reasons for the rules in question. Although the study raises the importance of legal assistance in maintaining the shared purpose of refugee law, it also offers insight into the ways in which legal assistance will fail to have an overall effect on refugee protection unless measures are introduced to address the individual commitments of government agents to further deterrence.

Michel Agier has written about the ways in which humanitarianism and policing go hand in hand to enable Western states to keep refugees in "spaces of exception" – that is, removed from the reach of legal jurisdiction.[83] Although asylum has rarely been a purely humanitarian act, driven instead by political considerations, new developments call into question the extent to which the humanitarian policy of asylum has been transformed into a system of deterrence. Even for those advocating for asylum policy to be political, there are concerns for legal process and justice that need to be considered. Just as we would not want an administrative process in place that regularly denies social benefits to those who deserve them or a criminal process that regularly puts innocent people behind bars, as a society committed to the rule of law, we want to know that our asylum process produces, on the whole, accurate results, and that people can access the benefits of the asylum process as provided by law.

In assessing the effectiveness of an asylum system, we also need to consider the question of access to the process. Consider a situation in medicine in which new knowledge shows that many more people than previously though suffer from a disease and would benefit from a particular treatment. Now suppose that, having knowledge of the costs of this new treatment and studies showing that many people will now be diagnosed with this disease, the government comes up with a scheme to limit the number of people who will receive the diagnosis. In other words, once they have the diagnosis, the law says they have to be treated – but if they never receive the diagnosis, there is no obligation to treat. In this scenario, limiting access to a diagnosis would raise concerns about the effectiveness of the process in achieving its purpose. Similarly, if the government's deterrence policies so limit bona fide refugees from accessing the asylum process, this should raise serious concerns about RSD as a legal institution.

Beyond the United States, future work is needed to assess the effect and unintended consequences of current American RSD policy and practices on the nascent asylum systems in Mexico, Brazil, Costa Rica, and other Central and South American countries that are seeing higher flows of refugees than in the past. Mexico, a signatory to the Refugee Convention with its own asylum system, received funding of $86 million from the US State Department to modernize its southern border following the 2014 Central American surge across the US border. According to reports, "[t]he funding is being used to improve 'inspection technologies and things like new border checkpoints, roadblocks, even naval bases along the coast of Mexico's southern border.'"[84] As a result, "[b]etween October and April 2015, Mexico apprehended more than 92,000 Central American immigrants, compared to 49,893 detained in the same period last year. In contrast, the US apprehended approximately 70,000 Central American migrants, far less than the 159,103 the year before."[85]

In April 2016, the UNHCR called for urgent action to help Central Americans fleeing violence, detailing that "last year alone 3,423 people, most of them from El Salvador and Honduras, sought asylum in Mexico. This was a 164 per cent increase over 2013 and a 65 per cent increase since 2014. Asylum claims by Salvadorans were up almost four times over this period," and that "[t]he number of asylum claims in other parts of the region from people fleeing violence in El Salvador, Honduras and Guatemala – the 'Northern Triangle of Central America' – has also risen dramatically."[86]

In February 2017, DHS Secretary John Kelly signed two memos to implement the Trump administration executive order on "Border Security and Immigration Enforcement Improvements."[87] The Border Memo expanded expedited removal to cover the interior of the country, increased the evidentiary standards in the credible fear screening process and committed to take all necessary action and "allocate all available resources to expand detention capabilities and capacities at

or near the border with Mexico to the greatest extent practicable."[88]
Practical consequences of the Border Memo are that more women
and children in detention have been deported and that US officials
have been impeding access to asylum at the ports of entry along the
US–Mexico border.[89] The expanded US commitment to detention
and deportation means that countries in the region, primarily Mexico, are being affected by new flows that need to be examined. For
example, since Trump was elected in November 2016, asylum applications in Mexico have doubled and detentions along the southwestern US border have fallen.[90] What is the nature of protection that
these emerging asylum systems are providing to Central American
refugees? Are these countries adopting the deterrence practices of the
US, or are they respecting human rights?

ACKNOWLEDGMENTS

I would like to thank David FitzGerald and the Center for Comparative Immigration Studies for inviting me to present an earlier version of this work at their Seeking Asylum in North America joint
speaker series, cosponsored by University of California, San Diego
and California Western School of Law. Thanks also to the editors of
this volume, to Bruce Spencer for his guidance, and to Jodie Chan
for her research assistance with this project. My deepest gratitude
goes to the women who had the courage to flee their countries in
search of a haven in the United States and the legal service providers
who assist them.

NOTES

1 "United States Border Patrol Southwest Family Unit Subject and Unaccompanied Alien Children Apprehensions Fiscal Year 2016: Statement by Secretary Johnson on Southwest Border Security," US Customs and Border Protection (CBP), last published 18 October 2016, https://www.cbp.gov/news
room/stats/southwest-border-unaccompanied-children/fy-2016.

2 Ibid. US Customs and Border Protection statistics show that apprehensions of migrants "other than Mexicans" in the Rio Grande Valley in
Fiscal Year 2014 accounted for 76 per cent (192,925 out of a total of
252,600). While 2014 was the height of border crossing, in 2016 the numbers were still high with 64.4 per cent (140,496 out of 218,110) in Fiscal
Year 2016.

3 "Remarks by Secretary of Homeland Security Jeh Johnson at the American
   Bar Association Annual Convention – As Prepared for Delivery," Homeland
   Security, 9 August 2014, https://www.dhs.gov/news/2014/08/09/remarks-
   secretary-homeland-security-jeh-johnson-american-bar-association-annual.

4 See, "Credible Fear Guidelines" (Refugee, Asylum, and International Operations Directorate Officer Training Asylum Division Officer Training Course,
   US Citizenship and Immigration Services – RAIO, 28 February 2014), 11.

5 Julie Hirschfeld Davis, "U.S. to Admit More Central American Refugees,"
   New York Times, 26 July 2016, http://www.nytimes.com/2016/07/27/us
   /politics/obama-refugees-central-america.html.

6 See "Immigration Policy Update – 'Catch and Release,'" American Immigration Lawyers Association (AILA), 8 September 2016, AILA Doc. No. 16090803,
   http://www.aila.org/infonet/immigration-policy-update-catch-and-release.

7 See "Durbin Meets with DHS Secretary & White House Chief of Staff to
   Discuss Central American Refugee Crisis" (press release, Dick Durbin United States Senator Illinois," 3 July 2016), http://www.durbin.senate.gov
   /newsroom/press-releases/durbin-meets-with-dhs-secretary-and-white-house-
   chief-of-staff-to-discuss-central-american-refugee-crisis.

8 "United States Border Patrol Southwest Family Unit," CBP.

9 See Robert Warren, "Surge in Immigration in 2014 and 2015? The Evidence
   Remains Illusory," Center for Migration Studies, 31 August 2016,
   http://cmsny.org/publications/warren-immigration-surge-illusory.

10 In 2006 the DHS under the Bush administration detained on average 21,450
   people on a daily basis. The daily number of detainees grew under the Obama
   administration. In July 2016 the average number of people detained for immigration purposes reach a high of 37,350. See "Catch and Release," AILA.

11 Guy Goodwin-Gill, "Editorial: The Dynamic of International Refugee Law,"
   International Journal of Refugee Law 25, no. 4 (2014): 656.

12 United States Refugee Act of 1980 (Public Law 96-212).

13 *Convention Relating to the Status of Refugees* (Refugee Convention), 189 UNTS
   137/[1954] ATS 5. The US did not ratify the 1951 Refugee Convention, but
   did ratify the 1967 Protocol Relating to the Status of Refugees, 606 UNTS
   267/[1973] ATS 37.

14 Adam Saltsman, "Beyond the Law: Power, Discretion, and Bureaucracy in
   the Management of Asylum Space in Thailand, *Journal of Refugee Studies* 27,
   no. 3 (2014): 458.

15 Lon L. Fuller, *The Principles of Social Order*, ed. Kenneth I. Winston (Port-
   land: Hart Publishing, 2002), 14.

16 Ibid., 14–15.

17 Ibid.

18 Refugee Convention, Art. 1.

19 Susan F. Martin, "Gender and the Evolving Refugee Regime," *Refugee Survey Quarterly* 29, no. 2 (2010): 104–21; and Riikka E. Morrill, "The Plight of the Persecuted: The European Union and United States Asylum Law," *Suffolk Transnational Law Review* 33, no. 1 (2010).

20 Rebecca Hamlin, *Let Me Be a Refugee: Administrative Justice and the Politics of Asylum in the United States, Canada, and Australia* (New York: Oxford University Press, 2014).

21 Jaya Ramji-Nogales, Andrew I. Schoenholtz, and Philip G. Schrag, *Refugee Roulette: Disparities in Asylum Adjudication and Proposals for Reform* (New York: New York University Press, 2011).

22 Rebecca Hamlin, "Illegal Refugees: Competing Policy Ideas and the Rise of the Regime of Deterrence in American Asylum Politics," *Refugee Survey Quarterly* 31, no. 2 (2012): 33–53; Idean Salehyan and Marc R. Rosenblum, "International Relations, Domestic Politics, and Asylum Admissions in the United States," *Political Research Quarterly* 6, no. 1 (2008): 104–21; and Philip G. Schrag, *A Well-Founded Fear: The Congressional Battle to Save Political Asylum in America* (New York: Routledge, 2000).

23 James C. Hathaway and Michelle Foster, *The Law of Refugee Status*, 2nd ed. (Cambridge: Cambridge University Press, 2014); Deborah E. Anker, *Law of Asylum in the United States* (Minnesota: Thomson West, 2013).

24 James C. Hathaway, "A Global Solution to a Global Refugee Crisis," Open Global Rights, 29 Feburary 2016, https://www.openglobalrights.org/global-solution-to-global-refugee-crisis; Hamlin, *Let Me Be a Refugee*; and James C. Simeon, *The UNHCR and the Supervision of International Refugee Law* (Cambridge: Cambridge University Press, 2013).

25 Ramji-Nogales, Schoenholtz, and Schrag, *Refugee Roulette*.

26 Philip G. Schrag, Andrew I. Schoenholtz, and Jaya Ramji-Nogales, *Lives in the Balance: Asylum Adjudication by the Department of Homeland Security* (New York: NYU Press, 2014).

27 Fuller, *Principles of Social Order*, 75.

28 United States Refugee Act of 1980 (Public Law 96-212).

29 Fuller, *Principles of Social Order*, 68.

30 H. L. A. Hart, *The Concept of Law* (Oxford: Oxford University Press 2012), 3rd ed., 48–9.

31 United Nations High Commissioner for Human Rights (UNHCR), *Handbook and Guidelines on Procedures and Criteria for Determining Refugee Status Under the 1951 Convention and the 1967 Protocol Relating to the Status of Refugees* ("UNHCR Handbook"), reissued, Geneva, December 2011, HCR/1P/4/Eng /Rev.3, para. 28.

32 Hathaway and Foster, *Law of Refugee Status*, 25–6.

33 Article 31(1) provides: "The Contracting States shall not impose penalties, on account of their illegal entry or presence, on refugees who, coming directly from a territory where their life or freedom was threatened in the sense of Article 1, enter or are present in their territory without authorization, provided they present themselves without delay to the authorities and show good cause for their illegal entry or presence," and Article 31(2) that "The Contracting States shall not apply to the movements of such refugees restrictions other than those which are necessary and such restrictions shall only be applied until their status in the country is regularized or they obtain admission into another country." Refugee Convention, Art. 31 and 32.

34 Hathaway and Foster, *Law of Refugee Status*, 28–30.

35 Ibid., 26.

36 Hamlin, "Illegal Refugees," 43.

37 Ibid., 43–4.

38 Ibid, 46.

39 Ibid., 46. By the end of the 1994 fiscal year, the backlog at the Asylum Office was 425,000 cases.

40 Ibid., 46.

41 Ibid., 47.

42 Illegal Immigration Reform and Immigrant Responsibility Act (IIRAIRA), H.R. 3610, Public Law 104-208, 110 Stat. 3009-546., 104th Congress, 30 September 1996.

43 This right is enshrined in the Refugee Convention, Art. 31, and inscribed in the 8 US Code, section 1158(a)(1).

44 Christian De La Rosa, "Deportees Accused of Gaming System by Requesting Asylum," Fox 5, 13 March 2014, http://fox5sandiego.com/2014/03/13 /deportees-seeking-asylum-accused-of-gaming-the-system.

45 Phillip T. Miller, assistant director of Enforcement and Removal Operations (ERO) field operations for DHS, in an affidavit.

46 Stephen Manning, "Ending Artesia: The Artesia Report," Innovation Law Lab, 20 January 2014, https://innovationlawlab.org/the-artesia-report.

47 Ingrid V. Eagly and Steven Shafer, "A National Study of Access to Counsel in Immigration Court," *University of Pennsylvania Law Review* 16, no. 1 (2015): 1–91.

48 Hamlin, "Illegal Refugees," 37.

49 These issues were raised in an American Civil Liberties Union (ACLU) lawsuit, *MSPC v. Johnson* (1:14-cv-01437 [DDC]), filed on 22 August 2014 on behalf of the women. See "Groups Sue U.S. Government Over Life-Threatening

Deportation Process Against Mothers and Children Escaping Extreme Violence in Central America," American Civil Liberties Union, 22 August 2014, https://www.aclu.org/news/groups-sue-us-government-over-life-threatening-deportation-process-against-mothers-and-children (accessed 12 September 2016). When I arrived at the Artesia detention centre in late August 2014, the ACLU was preparing this lawsuit documenting these obstructive practices. I represented one of the plaintiffs mentioned in the lawsuit after a motion was filed so that she could have a new credible fear interview.

50 Alex Neve, "The Bogus Rhetoric About Bogus Refugees," *Slaw: Canada's Online Legal Magazine*, 21 March 2014, http://www.slaw.ca/2014/03/21/the-bogus-rhetoric-about-bogus-refugees; Petra Molnar Diop, "The "Bogus" Refugee: Roma Asylum Claimants and Discourses of Fraud in Canada's Bill C-31," *Refuge* 30, no 1 (2014); Eric Neumayer, "Bogus Refugees? The Determinants of Asylum Migration to Western Europe," *International Studies Quarterly* 49, no. 3 (2005): 389–409; and Vicki Squire, *The Exclusionary Politics of Asylum* (Basingstoke: Palgrave Macmillan, 2009).

51 James Souter, "A Culture of Disbelief or Denial? Critiquing Refugee Status Determination in the United Kingdom," *Oxford Monitor of Forced Migration* 1, no. 1 (2011): 48–59.

52 Jessica Anderson, "The Culture of Disbelief: An Ethnographic Approach to Understanding an Under-Theorized Concept in the UK Asylum System" (working paper series, no. 102, Refugee Studies Centre, University of Oxford, 2014).

53 Deborah Singer, "Failing at Each Hurdle: Assessing the Crediblity of Women's Asylum Claims in Europe," in *Gender in Refugee Law: From the Margins to the Centre*, eds. Efrat Arbel, Catherine Dauvergne, Jenni Millbank (New York: Routledge, 2014): 46–72.

54 Form I-867AB Record of Sworn Statement in Proceedings under Section 235(b)(1) of the Immigration and Nationality Act.

55 Hamlin, "Illegal Refugees," 49.

56 Ibid., 49–50.

57 "'You Don't Have Rights Here': US Border Screening and Returns of Central Americans to Risk of Serious Harm," Human Rights Watch, 16 October 2014, https://www.hrw.org/report/2014/10/16/you-dont-have-rights-here/us-border-screening-and-returns-central-americans-risk.

58 Hamlin, "Illegal Refugees," 50.

59 "Department of Homeland Security Streamlines Removal Process Along U.S. Border," *Government Technology*, 31 January 2006, http://www.govtech.com/policy-management/Department-of-Homeland-Security-Streamlines-Removal.html.

60 See the letter to President Barack Obama by organizations to enforce the Flores Settlement, 17 March 2015 (AILA Doc. No. 15031860, posted 18 March 2015).

61 "Human Rights Watch Daily Brief, 27 October 2014," Human Rights Watch, 27 October 2014, https://www.hrw.org/news/2014/10/27/human-rights-watch-daily-brief-27-october-2014.

62 Ibid.

63 Ibid.

64 Ibid.

65 Ibid. Human Rights Watch observed the interview location for detainees at the McAllen Border Patrol station in Texas in July 2014. CBP officers showed Human Rights Watch a large public space in which they process migrants at a horseshoe-shaped table designed to accommodate multiple officer-migrant pairs in close proximity.

66 Hamlin, "Illegal Refugees," 35. Rebecca Hamlin documents "the relationships between competing policy approaches, illustrating how the sudden demise of the dominant approach to policy-making made room temporarily for another approach, only to be trumped by a third," and shows how "[t]his new regime of deterrence has had a major impact on asylum-seeker admissions because it has resulted in a significant decline in the number of asylum claims that are made annually."

67 The author was granted access to the American Immigration Lawyers Association (AILA) database to perform the study, but when the project grew, her access was denied by AILA based on confidentiality issues.

68 "Human Rights Watch Daily Brief, 27 October 2014," 2014.

69 Ibid.

70 See *Matter of D-J-*, 23 I&N Dec. 572 (A.G. 2003).

71 Julia Edwards, "In Shift, U.S. Officials Fight Release on Bond of Migrants: Lawyers," Reuters, 19 September 2014, http://www.reuters.com/article/us-usa-immigration-bond-idUSKBN0HE0DE20140919.

72 David A. Lash and Steven H. Schulman, Association of Pro Bono Counsel, Letter to Alejandro Mayorkas, Deputy Secretary, Department of Homeland Security, 13 October 2014, https://www.apbco.org/wp-content/uploads/2014/10/APBCo-letter-to-A-Mayorkas-12-Oct-2014.pdf.

73 Data on file with the author of all bonds for the period from 14 August to 21 October show that until 2 October, bonds ranged between $30,000 to $3,000, with an average of $10,128, whereas after 2 October, bonds dropped to a range between $8,000 and $1,500, with an average of $3,000.

74 Artesia Team email, dated 23 September 2014 (on file with the author).

75 Artesia Team email, dated 24 September 2014 (on file with the author).

76 "ICE to Open Additional Facility in South Texas to House Adults and Children," US Immigration and Customs Enforcement, 21 September 2014, https://www.ice.gov/news/releases/ice-open-additional-facility-south-texas-house-adults-children.

77 See Daniel M. Kowalski, "Unpub. BIA Bond Victory; El Salvador; Asylum; El Paso; Virginia," LexisNexis Legal Newsroom Immigration Law, 5 October 2014, accessed 12 September 2016, https://www.lexisnexis.com/legalnewsroom/immigration/b/insidenews/archive/2014/10/05/unpub-bia-bond-victory-el-salvador-asylum-el-paso-virginia.aspx.

78 "Remarks by the President in Address to the Nation on Immigration," White House: President Barack Obama, 20 November 2014, https://www.whitehouse.gov/the-press-office/2014/11/20/remarks-president-address-nation-immigration.

79 Stephen Manning, "Update on Transfers from Artesia," email to the pro bono team of lawyers representing clients in the makeshift detention centre set up at the Federal Law Enforcement Training Center in Artesia, New Mexico, 21 November 2014. Published with the author's permission.

80 "ACLU Sues Obama Administration for Detaining Asylum Seekers as Intimidation Tactic" (press release, American Civil Liberties Union, 16 December 2014), https://www.aclu.org/news/aclu-sues-obama-administration-detaining-asylum-seekers-intimidation-tactic.

81 *RILR v. Johnson*, 80 F. Supp. 3d 164 (DDC 2015).

82 Immigration and Nationality Act, section 208, 8 US Code, section 1158.

83 Michel Agier, *Managing the Undesirables: Refugee Camps and Humanitarian Government* (Cambridge: Polity Press, 2011).

84 May Pascaud, "Is Mexico Doing the US's Dirty Work on Central American Migrants?" PRI's The World, 23 June 2015, http://www.pri.org/stories/2015-06-23/mexico-doing-us-s-dirty-work-deporting-central-american-migrants.

85 Ibid.

86 Nora Sturm, "UNHCR Calls for Urgent Action as Central America Asylum Claims Soar," United Nations High Commissioner for Refugees, 5 April 2016, http://www.unhcr.org/news/latest/2016/4/5703ab396%20/unhcr-calls-urgent-action-central-america-asylum-claims-soar.html.

87 Executive Order 13768, 25 January 2017.

88 "Implementing the President's Border Security and Immigration Enforcement Improvements Policies," Department of Homeland Security, 20 February 2017, https://www.dhs.gov/sites/default/files/publications/17_0220_S1_Implementing-the-Presidents-Border-Security-Immigration-Enforcement-Improvement-Policies.pdf.

89 Former immigration enforcement chiefs questioned the legality of the

expanded deportation program. See Alan Gomez, "Trump's Quick Deportation Plan May Be Illegal, Past Immigration Chiefs Say," *USA Today*, 24 February 2017, https://www.usatoday.com/story/news/nation/2017/02/24/president-trumps-expedited-removal-plan-may-be-illegal/98276078; and "Violations at the Border: The El Paso Sector," Human Rights First, 2017, http://www.humanrightsfirst.org/sites/default/files/hrf-violations-at-el-paso-border-rep.pdf.

90 See "Facing Walls: USA and Mexico's Violation of the Rights of Asylum Seekers, Amnesty International, 15 June 2017, https://www.amnestyusa.org/reports/facing-walls-usa-mexicos-violation-rights-asylum-seekers.

9

A Population Takes Flight: The Irish Famine Migration in Boston, Montreal, and Liverpool, and the Politics of Marginalization and Criminalization

Dan Horner

The decade between 1845 and 1855 was a transformative moment in the history of human migration across the North Atlantic world. Over one million Irish people fled a crushing famine and social upheaval in their native land.[1] The ensuing wave of migration unfolded on an unprecedented scale. The impact on port cities across the North Atlantic world – particularly in Britain, the Province of Canada, and the United States – where the vast majority of these migrants fled through and to, was enormous. Local officials were forced to respond rapidly to an influx of migrants on their shores. That a significant portion of these migrants were in a state of material destitution and in many cases were suffering from diseases contracted aboard the ships that they travelled on added to the challenge. As is the case in the twenty-first century, these events made a lasting impact on the political culture of the regions that they affected. The famine migration occurred at a moment in history when the political approach to issues surrounding migration was being shaped by a staunch liberalism.[2] As a result, public officials confronted this mounting crisis motivated by a reluctance to authorize state intervention into migration. Instead, they were determined to allow private interests, like the firms that operated shipping companies and the landlords who had owned the land that migrants had been displaced from, to continue overseeing the migration process with little in the way of governmental oversight. As the famine migration crisis accelerated, however, the public's calls for a more vigorous state intervention forced public officials to shift their approach to governance.

This chapter will examine how this human tragedy and political crisis unfolded in Liverpool, Boston, and Montreal: three port cities that were particularly affected by these events. It examines how the public and the authorities in these jurisdictions responded to the challenges that came with mass migration in the modern era. By outlining the varied responses to the Irish famine migration and the crises that it produced, we can begin to rethink both the role that the state played in the process of migration and the political ramifications of changing social and cultural attitudes towards migrants. On both sides of the Atlantic, Irish migrant communities were marginalized. They occupied the lowest rungs of an industrializing economy, and their attempts to make ends meet in unforgiving environments led to disproportionately frequent encounters with the criminal justice system.[3] This fuelled prejudices against the Irish communities in these three cities for decades.

It is worth reflecting on how the shifts that occurred in public attitudes and political policy relating to immigration during the 1840s created precedents that we continue to grapple with in the second decade of the twenty-first century. The parallels between the Irish famine migration crisis and the current refugee crisis gripping Europe are striking. In the Irish migration crisis, as in the current refugee crisis, hundreds of thousands of men, women, and children risked precarious conditions to flee famine and social upheaval in their native lands in search of a new home – one bearing the promise of a more stable future for themselves and their children. While some were welcomed with open arms, other migrants encountered a backlash that grew increasingly heated in their host cities, and which was closely linked to the process of criminalization. As is the case today, populist political leaders played to the anxieties of the voting public, promising restrictive measures on immigration. They did so through processes that amounted to the gradual criminalization of migration – adopting harsher quarantine measures and easing the path to deportation. As is the case in the twenty-first century, many of these policies were adopted in a rushed and ad hoc manner.[4] That there are important continuities linking these two crises is evidence, however, of a deeper stability in governing mass migration. The response to the Irish famine migration crisis in three different host jurisdictions demon-strates, to varying degrees, a willingness to marginalize migrants and strip them of their rights in order to placate an anxious and political-ly engaged public. In many ways, this response bears a close resem-blance to that which is being adopted in countries across Europe and North America today.

THE IRISH FAMINE AND MIGRATION CRISIS

The crisis in Ireland was complicated and was rooted in several layers of social change, some of which were decades in the making, others of which took hold very quickly. At its core, it was the product of the transition to capitalism.[5] Since the second half of the eighteenth cen-tury, philosophers and economic theorists like Adam Smith had been publishing treatises on how a sharper focus on maximizing efficiency in farming and manufacturing would elevate the quality of life not only for those who owned property and invested their capital in spec-ulative ways, but also for the masses.[6] Inspired by this, reformers be-gan to critique the way that agriculture was organized across much of the North Atlantic world. Large tracts of land were owned by a single wealthy landlord and parcelled into numerous small farms, each rent-ed out to small-scale tenants who produced little more than what their families needed for subsistence. It was a practice that had shaped rural life in Ireland for centuries, and was inextricably bound up with how authority was wielded in feudal societies.[7]

To a new generation of agricultural reformers motivated by the ethos of capitalism, however, this arrangement was striking in its inef-ficiencies. They encouraged landlords to evict their tenants and engage in more large-scale and intensive agricultural practices.[8] By growing large quantities of single crops, they would produce greater profits. As these reforms were implemented at an accelerating pace across Ireland in the 1830s and 1840s, it quickly became apparent that their human cost would be staggering. Displaced tenant farming fam-ilies made their way across the country in search of new means of eco-nomic survival. Meanwhile, the potato crop, which had been a staple of the Irish diet for centuries, failed for several consecutive years, adding to the social upheaval of the period. Estimates of how many of Irish men, women, and children were displaced vary, but there is a consensus that well over one million left the country during the cri-sis, with numbers reaching their peak in the second half of the 1840s.[9]

All the ingredients necessary for tragedy on a staggering scale were in place. This migration was a harrowing experience, marked by hunger, upheaval, and outbreaks of collective violence along routes out of the country.

A crucial element of this story is that this was an economically diverse group of migrants, and they pursued migratory strategies that were geared towards their own circumstances. Some were able to migrate to other parts of Ireland, where they had kinship connections that allowed them to re-establish themselves. The vast majority, however, left their country of origin on ships bound for the west coast of England and Scotland. London and bustling port cities like Southampton, Bristol, Liverpool, and Glasgow grew rapidly during this period. These cities were either in the midst of or perched on the precipice of industrialization. Workshops, factories, and docks provided a source of paid employment to these migrants, though the work was often precarious and dangerous.[10] This process was not seamless. The Irish migrants, especially at the peak of the famine migration, were frequently in a state of destitution when they arrived at British ports, having sold their possessions and given any savings to the highly exploitative firms that were transporting them out of the country. The private institutions and local parishes that assisted the poor and the displaced were, as the famine migration accelerated, overwhelmed by the demands being placed on them. They lacked the resources to provide care for the migrants, which led to a notable increase in the number of destitute men, women, and children in these port cities, especially in the streets and neighbourhoods surrounding the docks where ships landed. Competition for jobs and accommodations was fierce, and the few resources these migrants had often went to paying highly inflated prices to savvy local providers looking to make a profit on this social upheaval. Faced with these challenging circumstances, many famine migrants remained in or nearby these bustling British port cities, where the sudden expansion of the labour pool became a crucial component of the Industrial Revolution. The majority of these migrants, however, did have the resources to continue their migration onwards to North America. It was the possibility of establishing themselves as independent farmers on the North American frontier that drew many to pursue the final and most perilous interval of their migration.[11] They boarded cramped and insalubrious cargo ships in ports along the west coast of Britain and made their way to North America, with numbers peaking in the second half of the 1840s and the first years of the 1850s. The dream of establishing themselves as independent farmers, however, proved elusive to the vast majority of migrants, who were not able to produce the necessary capital. Many ended up remaining in cities, where they, too, became an essential component of an emerging industrial working class.[12]

The famine migration was marred, and ultimately defined, by an extensive outbreak of typhus. Typhus was a deadly disease that flourished in the sorts of conditions that were rife during the famine migration crisis. It preyed on people gathered in large numbers in crowded and unsanitary conditions, where fleas that fed off rats would be in close proximity to human beings. Barracks and other military installations had long been the epicentres of typhus outbreaks.[13] During their flight from famine, Irish migrants huddled together in barns, warehouses, ships, and cellars – similar spaces that made them prone to these outbreaks. The lack of scientific consensus on the disease deepened the contentious reaction that Irish migrants received. A faction of the public in the three cities in question here argued vehemently that typhus threatened to spread through the air and infect the broader community – what is known as the miasmatic theory of disease transmission. Their knowledge of epidemics had developed in the shadow of cholera, which seemed to spread in this manner. They therefore insisted that local governments greet the migrants with stepped-up quarantine procedures. Others, including famed Liverpool public health physician William Duncan, argued – correctly, in hindsight – that the only danger typhus posed was to those who came in direct, close contact with people who had contracted the disease.

These migrants arrived in communities that had a pre-existing infrastructure designed to assist newcomers in the process of settlement. This came in many forms. There was a shared network of public and private philanthropy that existed on both sides of the Atlantic, and which spoke to a shared ideological and political approach to poverty. Institutions like workhouses were constructed to provide social assistance to the poor in exchange for their labour. Local parishes and civic governments provided limited charity to the neediest residents, and this was often supplemented by religious institutions. All of this reflected the commonly held notion during this period that, ultimately, the poor were to blame for their own state of misfortune. With regard to the migration process itself, each of these cities had limited quarantine institutions that were equipped to deal with migrants carrying diseases from other parts of the globe – the 1832 global cholera epidemic being the most dramatic example in living memory, at that time, of the potential deadly impact of disease.[14]

Despite this past experience with the dangers of destitute migrants carrying communicable diseases into densely populated urban centres, as the flow of migrants continued to grow exponentially with each passing year in the mid-1840s, public officials discovered that the institutions and processes designed to deal with disease were quickly overwhelmed by the scale of the famine migration. Ships carrying migrants backed up in the harbours of Liverpool, Boston, and Montreal. Quarantine stations soon did not have adequate space or personnel to monitor the condition of the migrants flowing through them. The funds at the disposal of local parishes, civic governments, and philanthropic organizations became rapidly depleted, raising concerns that the migrants would become entrenched in urban poverty. That these conditions were the product of the unwillingness of various levels of government to sufficiently fund this infrastructure was rarely debated in public circles. Concerns were also expressed that the migrant crisis would have an adverse effect on the poor communities that had already settled in the cities and relied on periodic assistance from these sources.[15] It was in the midst of discussions such as these that the notion that the migration crisis posed a threat to the social fabric became increasingly prominent.

THE IRISH MIGRANTS IN LIVERPOOL

No community outside Ireland felt the impact of the famine migration to the same degree that Liverpool did. By the 1840s, Liverpool had been a major hub of migration and the most important port city on the west coast of Britain for the better part of two centuries. In the eighteenth century, the city's fortunes had risen with the transatlantic trade in African slaves, many of whom were circulated through the city's port before being sent to destinations across the Atlantic world.[16] When displaced tenant farming families began to flee Ireland in the face of famine and social upheaval, Liverpool became the destination of choice for the vast majority, as it was already an important shipping centre. The city offered opportunities for employment. As an important commercial city, Irish migrants who arrived in good enough physical condition to work were able to find precarious employment as day labourers on the docks.[17]

The quantitative impact of the famine migration on this bustling port city was staggering, particularly in 1847, when the flow of migrants peaked. By the end of April, 150,000 migrants had landed in Liverpool – a city with a population of roughly 350,000 at the time. Although approximately 40,000 of those migrants quickly departed Liverpool for other points in Britain or North America, it was estimated at the time that well over 100,000 migrants remained in the city. By the end of that summer, the number of migrants who had passed through Liverpool had climbed to nearly 300,000, though we do not know precisely how many subsequently departed the city.[18] A significant proportion of those migrants had no choice but to rely upon public assistance, and questions of material support for the migrants thus became the defining issue of debates about the famine migration. Much of this centred around the provisions made available through amendments in 1834 to Britain's Poor Law, the legislation that dictated the obligations that jurisdictions across the country had towards people in need of financial assistance.[19] Under these amendments, adults who did not have the means to support themselves could obtain assistance from their local parish. In exchange, however, adults would have to labour in a workhouse, a provision introduced to discourage people from relying on assistance rather than seeking employment. The element of this New Poor Law, as it was known, that came under attack from the Liverpool public during the famine migration crisis was that this system was funded by local ratepayers. In other words, Irish migrants fleeing the upheaval in their native land and settling in Liverpool were being supported by taxes collected from the local authorities in that city. The landlords who had essentially pushed them into this migration were not being held financially accountable for their strategies. In the eyes of many Liverpool commentators, their city was shouldering a remarkable financial and social burden.[20] Irish landlords and others with a financial stake in the sorts of liberal agricultural reforms they were carrying out were amassing enormous profits, while it was left to the ratepayers of Liverpool and a handful of other port cities to finance the massive displacement of impoverished tenant farmers. Civic elites and the broader public in Liverpool identified this inability of the New Poor Law to make provisions for the increasing transiency of the working classes as a major structural problem, and they began to lobby for an increase in financial assistance to the city.[21] While some identified the imperial authorities in London as a major part of the problem, due to their unwillingness to reinforce the institutions designed to care for the needy, frustrations were frequently taken out on the migrants themselves. Despite numerous reports being printed in the press describing how desperate the situation was in Ireland, many remained convinced that Irish migrants were, in essence, playing the system – that they had migrated to British cities like Liverpool because they were aware that they would receive financial assistance from the local authorities.[22] This only deepened the notion circulating in the Liverpool public sphere at the time that the city was shouldering far too great a burden with regards to the famine migration crisis. This notion certainly coloured the public's reaction to this uptick in migration. In the face of an imperial government that remained committed to its laissez-faire approach in managing the situation, local officials in the city began to strategize ways to respond to the public's calls for more decisive action. While they did not have the authority to ban ships carrying migrants from landing in Liverpool's harbour, they could use public funds to more rigidly enforce the existing quarantine measures.[23] As the migration crisis accelerated in the spring of 1847, public health officials began venturing out into the harbour to inspect ships before they had the opportunity to dock. When they discovered migrants on board who appeared to be ill, the migrants were removed to the lazaretto – a quarantine facility on board a ship anchored on the River Mersey.

The most decisive measure taken by the parish authorities in Liverpool, however, would be adopted in June 1847. After parliament passed the Poor Law Removal Act to streamline the process, the authorities in Liverpool began to force Irish migrants who were relying on public relief to return to their country of origin. This is a stark and early example of the criminalization of migration. By the end of 1847 roughly 15,000 migrants had been forced to board ships returning them to the port nearest their original point of departure from their native land.[24] Despite the difficulties faced by the most economically disadvantaged migrants in Liverpool, there is evidence to suggest that most wished to avoid this fate. Migrants in the most desperate of circumstances, therefore, would have been forced to choose between drawing on public relief and risking the very real possibility of being forced to return to the famine and social upheaval of their native land, or attempting to survive in the inhospitable environment of industrializing Liverpool without social assistance. Meanwhile, the

Liverpool encountered by migrants fleeing the famine crisis in Ireland was inhospitable on both a material and cultural level.[25] Because the Irish migrant community was amongst the city's poorest, they had frequent encounters with Liverpool's modernizing police force, which focused much of their attention on the city's working-class community.[26] Meanwhile, with migrants pouring into the city by the thousands on a daily basis, finding shelter became a pressing challenge. Unscrupulous landlords embraced this as an opportunity, renting out the cellars of buildings they owned in the neighbourhoods surrounding the harbour. Economically disadvantaged migrants did not have the luxury of turning these offers down, and families crowded into these small, cold, and poorly ventilated spaces.[27] These conditions tended to exacerbate the symptoms of the illnesses that many migrants had contracted during their flight from Ireland – most notably, typhus. While some were able to land precarious employment, others struggled to do so. These economic struggles were inextricably linked to the poor social status of the Irish community in Britain, where newspaper editorials and popular tracts dismissed the Irish as superstitious drunkards who, because of their lack of initiative towards self-improvement and industry, were, at the very least, partially responsible for their own misfortunes.[28] In this hostile climate, it is hardly surprising that many migrants were eager to continue their journeys.

THE IRISH MIGRANTS IN BOSTON

Most migrants set their sights on the bustling cities of the Atlantic seaboard – Boston, Baltimore, and New York were three of the most sought after destinations. The hopes of many who were determined to land on American soil were dashed by a series of local provisions that made this a challenging process. Irish and German immigration to the United States had been increasing at a steady rate since the end of the Napoleonic Wars in 1815. This trend had divided the American public.[29] The states on what was then the western frontier of the United States supported this influx of European migrants, who they hoped would play an integral role in the creation of an agricultural society on lands seized – in many cases violently – from Indigenous Peoples. In the bustling cities that lined the Atlantic seaboard, however, public opinion was not as accommodating.[30] As was the case in Liverpool, there were concerns that European countries were exporting their least desirable citizens to America – those who would never succeed in becoming productive labourers or independent farmers, but would become mired in the crime-ridden urban working class.[31] Cities like Baltimore, Boston, and New York were undergoing rapid growth during this period and dealing with all the social tensions that came with it – most notably a spike in poverty and requests for social assistance. Thus, while the federal government maintained a relatively open stance towards immigration, state and municipal governments on the east coast used their powers to implement restrictive policies that effectively prevented Irish migrants who were fleeing the famine from landing on American soil.

In 1819 the federal government of the United States attempted to create a compromise on these issues by adopting the Passenger Act, which placed restrictions on immigration into the country by dictating how many passengers each ship could carry into the country based on the amount of cargo the ship was carrying.[32] It also laid out a minimum amount of space in steerage that each passenger had to have access to. These policies were, effectively, a form of immigration control, as they drove up the cost of immigrating to American cities.[33] However, as nearly each passing year in the 1820s and 1830s set new records for immigration into the United States, the public demanded tighter restrictions, and political leaders who had built their careers on the exploitation of anti-immigrant sentiment and, more specifically, anti-Catholic sentiment were pleased to craft legislation that responded to these concerns. Massachusetts, along with a number of other states, began to pass ordinances that necessitated increasingly close supervision of who was entering the country on board ships docking in its ports. Taxes were levied on ships based on how many immigrants were on board, and captains had to provide local officials with detailed manifests outlining the identities of each passenger. Extra fines were levied if public health officials discovered evidence of typhus or other communicable diseases on board.[34] Failure to provide this information would result in ships being turned away from Boston's port.[35] The costs associated with such measures explains why many migrants fleeing the famine and social upheaval in Ireland chose to migrate instead to British North America, though many did slip over the American border by land shortly after arriving in Quebec City or Montreal. In this context, the criminalization of migration can clearly be seen to be rooted in the practices of law, regulation, and the policing of public health.

These measures did succeed in keeping the numbers of Irish migrants entering the United States at Boston low during the second half of the 1840s, but only by inflating the numbers entering through ports throughout British North America. Still, there was a significant growth in migration in Boston during this period, with upwards of 30,000 migrants arriving in 1847 alone, a number exponentially greater than that recorded in previous years.[36] Coverage of the crisis in the American press likely did much to reinforce the public's attitude towards migration and the threat posed by supposedly "undesirable" migrants. Words like "overflowing" and "overrun" were used in describing the effect that Irish migrants were having on the city.[37] As was the case in Liverpool, local charities and the workhouses reported that they were unable to cope with the rising numbers of migrants demanding assistance in some form. Boston's strategy for dealing with the famine migration centred around a hastily constructed hospital and quarantine facility on Deer Island, located in Boston Harbor.[38] This was where attempts were made to isolate the sick from the healthy, and to make sure that, within the legal framework outlined above, only those migrants who were categorized as "desirable" were able to make their way to the mainland. Local officials were under strict orders to turn away any migrant who they deemed too old, infirm, and incompetent, or either physically or mentally disabled – in the nomenclature of the time, an "idiot."[39] As was the case in Liverpool, the primary public policy response to the famine migration crisis was to extend the amount of time ships were obligated to spend in quarantine before their entrance into the harbour was permitted. This quarantine period was extended in Boston to twenty days in June in an effort to assuage public concerns about the spread of typhus, cases of which had already been reported in predominately Irish neighbourhoods in the city's south end.[40] Officials were determined, in other words, to employ their limited powers in an effort to ensure that only the right kinds of immigrants were settling in Boston.

Despite the legislation that was in place to prevent what was occurring in Liverpool from unfolding in Boston, there was still a palpable sense amongst the public that events were spiralling out of control. Even before the wave of Irish migration brought on by the famine, politics in the state of Massachusetts featured a strong sectarian undercurrent. The Know Nothing movement was beginning to attract strong support from the city's Protestant community. They considered the growing demographic of the Catholic community, the result of immigration from Ireland and Catholic regions of Germany, as a very real threat to American democracy.[41] Catholics, these nativist commentators insisted, did not possess the same commitment to democratic institutions and American values as did Protestants. This perspective was reinforced by the upheaval surrounding the famine migration. As was the case in Liverpool, Boston's elite and the broader public perceived the Irish migrants fleeing the famine to be immoral and lacking in the sorts of industrious habits that would make them productive citizens of the United States. This provided moral and political legitimacy for the sorts of harsh restrictions discussed earlier. When reports were published in the local press noting that legislation had prevented a ship loaded with Irish migrants from landing at Boston, they were written in language that was clearly meant to be celebratory in tone. One such ship, carrying 188 passengers from Cork, Ireland, was turned away because the captain was unable to provide bonds for each of the passengers. These bonds would have provided evidence that the passengers had the means of supporting themselves upon landing. Without such evidence, the authorities could claim they had reason to believe that the passengers would become dependent on social assistance in Boston. Many of the passengers, the report continued, were clearly stricken with typhus, and many more were in a state of insubordination. They were provided with some provisions and sent away to Saint John, New Brunswick, where, presumably, local authorities were less stringent in their monitoring of immigration.[42] Despite reports that the quarantine facility on Deer Island was struggling to assist over 2,000 patients, and that hospitals across the city were overburdened with similar cases, reports of ships being turned away from Boston were common in the American press throughout the summer of 1847.

Boston's strategy of using its local authority to turn away as many famine migrants as possible proved to be surprisingly short lived. A series of Supreme Court decisions at the end of the 1840s, known as the Passenger Cases, ruled that the taxes and tests that the state of Massachusetts had been imposing on prospective migrants were unconstitutional, as immigration was under federal jurisdiction.[43] These practices were thus overturned, suddenly making migration to the United States much more affordable to transatlantic migrants. This led to a significant restructuring of transatlantic migration, with the flow of Irish migrants choosing, by the early 1850s, to land in Boston and other American port cities rather than in British North America.[44]

This did not, however, change the contentious attitudes towards Irish migrants that were nurtured in Boston's public sphere, most notably amongst many of the city's old Protestant elite. In 1854, just as the famine migration was beginning to ebb, the Know Nothing movement swept the Massachusetts state elections with a platform promising limits on immigration, a twenty-year waiting period for migrants aspiring to obtain American citizenship, and proposals to limit alcohol sales that clearly had Boston's Irish community in its crosshairs.[45] The city's Irish population, the majority of whom could trace their roots in Boston back to the famine migration, were relegated to the bottom rungs of the economic ladder and the margins of public life well into the twentieth century and became targets of the criminal justice system.[46]

THE IRISH MIGRANTS IN MONTREAL

Montreal had undergone a rapid and substantial growth in immigration from Ireland in 1845 and 1846, but nothing on a scale that would prepare them for the social upheaval of 1847. News began appearing in the local press before the commencement of the shipping season on the St. Lawrence River that the crisis in Ireland had only deepened during the winter months, and that any hope that the flow of migrants across the Atlantic might subside was increasingly appearing to be based in false optimism.[47] A colonial plan for managing migration had been in place since the cholera outbreak of 1832. Ships would be inspected at Grosse Isle, a hospital and quarantine station located in the middle of the St. Lawrence River just up from Quebec City.[48] Once migrants had been cleared by medical officials to continue their journey, those seeking to travel to Montreal or beyond would board steamboats that would deliver them to Montreal. As a final precaution, the colonial government had built temporary sheds to house migrants suspected of carrying communicable diseases along the banks of the Lachine Canal on the city's western periphery. As the start of the 1847 migration season neared, colonial officials employed by the government of the Province of Canada, working in consultation with representatives of the imperial government in London, addressed the first stirrings of public anxiety by pledging to reinforce the existing quarantine station at Grosse Isle and to improve the facilities along the canal.[49] These measures, they insisted, would be sufficient to manage the flow of migrants, who, the colonial government reminded the public, were destined primarily for settlement on British North America's western frontier.

As was the case in Liverpool, however, in 1847 these reinforced measures and institutions designed to manage migration were quickly swamped by the unprecedented scale of migration across the Atlantic. At the height of the shipping season, upwards of 2,000 men, women, and children were disembarking at Montreal's port on a daily basis.[50] With public concerns about the overwhelming presence of destitute migrants on the city's streets and the looming threat of a typhus epidemic, a feeling of crisis settled over the city. Editorial pages in the local press and overflowing public meetings bristled with accusations that colonial officials in Montreal and the imperial government in London were not taking sufficient steps to ensure that the public was being protected.[51] The public rallied around calls for more restrictive quarantine procedures.[52] In a commercial city like Montreal, however, such proposals faced resistance from the merchant community, who were concerned that extending the quarantine process would slow the movement of commodities across the Atlantic and thereby negatively affect their bottom lines. As was the case in Liverpool and Boston, it was officials at the civic level who proved most responsive to the public's demands for action. They responded by passing an emergency bylaw that created a Board of Health with sweeping powers.[53] Composed of physicians, politicians, and representatives of each of the city's wards, the board of health focused their attention on two areas. The first was to assuage public fears that the typhus outbreak among the Irish migrants was rooted in the poor sanitary conditions found in the disadvantaged neighbourhoods where many migrants were settling upon their arrival in the city. For this, the board was given broad powers to order residents to clean their properties under threat of arrest. Second, and to much public fanfare, they began to explore alternatives to the system put in place by the colonial government to manage migration.

Public concern in Montreal over the Irish famine migration during the summer of 1847 centred around the presence of destitute migrants on the city's streets and the proximity of the immigrant sheds to the broader community. Within weeks of its creation, the board of health unveiled a solution that, they argued, would do much to address both of these problems. They proposed the construction of a quarantine station on the Iles de Boucherville, a cluster of islands just down the St Lawrence River from Montreal.[54] This facility would have the benefit of protecting Montrealers from the diseases carried by the migrants, thereby addressing concerns that such illnesses could be carried through the air from the sheds on the banks of the canal into the city's densely populated neighbourhoods. Under this plan, Irish migrants would face a double layer of detention upon their arrival in Montreal – a decisive step towards the criminalization of migration.

The proposal was met with widespread support from the public, across the city's sectarian and linguistic divides.[55] It was seen as the most reasonable means available to restore order to the migration process and ensure that Montreal would be shielded from the manifestations of the crisis unfolding in Ireland. The new facility, however, would not come to pass. The committee formed by the colonial government to investigate the crisis and respond to the demands of the board of health rejected it out of hand.[56] Their argument was, first and foremost, a financial one. Building a second quarantine facility from scratch would simply place too great a burden on the public purse. The colonial government defended the efficacy of the so-called fever sheds on the outskirts of Montreal, noting that for the fraction of the cost of building the facility proposed by the Board of Health, they could continue with improvements to the existing facilities. They also criticized the board of health for not taking into account the experience of the migrants. They reminded the public that under the plan proposed by the Board of Health, migrants who had passed through quarantine at Grosse Isle would be forced to undergo a second round of quarantine on the Iles de Boucherville. This, the colonial authorities argued, simply represented too great an intrusion. This was not a question, first and foremost, of their rights as individuals, though it is clear that the liberalism of the colonial authorities played a role in shaping this response. Their response was also shaped by concerns about dependency.[57] Spending weeks in quarantine at two different facilities, they argued, would have the unintended consequence of habituating these migrants to a life of dependence on the state. Despite the feeling of crisis and the anxiety of the public during 1847, colonial officials remained committed to their vision for managing migration: that the most effective policy was to keep government intervention to an absolute minimum. Although they were committed to protecting the general public from the spread of epidemic disease, they insisted that most migrants were looking to become subsistent as quickly as possible and that public policy ought not to do anything to impede that goal. Their conflict with the Board of Health also reveals how contested the science around the transmission of typhus was during this period. The Board of Health was playing to the widely held belief that the disease could spread through miasmas – that is, that it could be carried on the breeze from the immigrant sheds on the outskirts of Montreal into the city.[58] The colonial government, meanwhile, would prove to be correct in arguing that typhus could only be transmitted through close contact with the infected.

Montreal remained on the razor's edge for the remainder of the 1847 shipping season. Of the hundreds of thousands of migrants who passed through the city that summer, 6,000 would die of typhus in the immigrant sheds. Many more took up residence in Montreal – a demographic bubble that would make Montreal a predominately English-speaking city for the better part of the next two decades.[59] As was the case in Liverpool and Boston, the Irish migration reinforced a pivotal role that the city would play in the broader history of the colony – as a hub for migration, and a site where the migration process would create the labour pool necessary for the transition from commercial to industrial capitalism. As was also the case in Boston and Liverpool, Irish migrants would become the frequent targets of the city's nascent police force, and compared with other ethnic communities in the city were disproportionately represented in the ranks of those arrested on charges related to interpersonal violence and sex trade work.[60]

COMPARING THE LIVERPOOL, BOSTON, AND MONTREAL IRISH MIGRANT EXPERIENCES

Local authorities in Liverpool, Boston, and Montreal, in conjunction with officials at the national, state, colonial, and imperial levels of government, debated and adopted different strategies for addressing the crisis in migration that occurred during the second half of the 1840s, and in 1847 in particular. While these policies differed significantly, they demonstrate the flexibility of liberal governance during this period, as public officials sought to address the public's apprehensions about mass migration. In Liverpool and Boston, officials succumbed to the public's demands for more restrictive policies, while the colonial government in the Province of Canada defended its policy of allowing thousands of migrants to arrive in the colony with only a minimal effort devoted to crafting and implementing a comprehensive policy on the issue. Either way, the migration crisis provoked by the upheaval of the Irish famine was a pivotal moment in shifting the way that the public and the state conceptualized migration. It would no longer be sufficient to leave this process to the whims of private interests. In the second half of the nineteenth century, governments across the North Atlantic world began to pay much closer attention to the patterns of human mobility. They carried out initiatives to collect more information on who was crossing their borders and settling in their towns and cities.[61] The bungling of the quarantine process that occurred to differing degrees in Liverpool, Boston, and Montreal during the crisis would, the public was assured, not be repeated, as the medical inspection of migrants became increasingly thorough in the decades that followed.

As the summer of 1847 drew to a close, commentators expressed hopes that they had successfully weathered the famine migration crisis. The numbers of migrants fleeing Ireland for the bustling port cities of the North Atlantic world would remain high, but gradually diminish in the first years of the 1850s. Solutions to the social problems that came with these massive waves of migration were not resolved during this time. The public remained agitated by the presence of destitute migrants on the streets of their cities. The growing working classes of these three cities had a significant Irish component to them, and their marginalization is made clear in their disproportionately frequent encounters with the criminal justice system in the second half of the nineteenth century. The number of reported cases of typhus declined, but 1849 saw a global outbreak of cholera, which posed a much greater risk both to the migrants and to the broader communities that they were settling into.

CONCLUSION

How do these shared histories of the Irish famine migration help us think through the migration crises of the twenty-first century? By examining this historical moment we can begin to piece together how the modern infrastructure for governing the process of migration was legitimized as it emerged. Although different procedures were implemented in Liverpool, Boston, and Montreal, in each instance we see local officials and the national authorities grappling with the widely held conviction that mass migration threatened to disrupt the social and political order in their respective jurisdictions. While procedures such as quarantining migrants, onboard ship inspections, and bonds for each passenger had been practiced for centuries, the accelerating scale of migration in the middle decades of the nineteenth century, resulting from the social crisis unfolding in Ireland, coupled with the transition to industrial capitalism, brought about demands to increase the regulation, and in many cases the intensification, of these practices.[62] Concerns that the rapid influx of migrants into these three bustling port cities would lead to social unrest pushed local authorities to attempt to contain these migrant communities at quarantine stations and famine sheds, and later to assign municipal police forces to carefully patrol immigrant neighbourhoods, where they could monitor everything from drunkenness to poor sanitary practices. When we place these actions in the context of industrialization, it becomes clear that what public officials were grappling with here was how to, on short notice, manage the unexpected emergence and rapid growth of an urban industrial working class in these three cities. This shift in demographics and social relations brought about the increasing circulation of migrants across the North Atlantic world that today might appear inevitable in hindsight but was clearly a contentious issue at the time.

The famine migration provides insight into the ways that mass migration would come to reshape societies and politics in the modern world. The issues that continue to prompt debate in the twenty-first century – around jurisdictional issues, about the degree to which individual rights can be infringed upon in the name of public health, and about how the political debate around migration and the experience of migrants serve to marginalize vulnerable communities – were all in play during the Irish famine migration crisis.[63] Both in the nineteenth century and today, periods of social upheaval and political unrest in one region get transported around the globe by the resulting jump in migration. Studying the historical precedents established in the nineteenth century can shed light on how, although public policy is often implemented and enforced in a climate of crisis, there is a significant degree of stability in how public officials and the broader community negotiate the challenges that come with mass migration.

Finally, what we see in public reactions to the famine migration in these three cities, whether with regard to popular sentiment or debates over legislative responses to the situation, is an increasing distance between migrant communities and the general public. Immigration had long been a contentious issue, but the unprecedented scale of the migration and the shifting role of the state – to varying degrees – in these three jurisdictions did much to enshrine the outsider status of these migrants. Even those who greeted the famine migrants with sympathy, including some who risked their lives to care for those struck by typhus, often employed rhetoric that cast these migrants as outsiders, not as prospective citizens or members of a community. With their lives already marred by crisis and displacement, these migrants saw themselves cast as social problems, as the anonymous products of upheaval and crisis. Unbeknownst to those caught up in these events, precedents were being set for how migrants would be conceptualized as part of a larger urban community for centuries to come.

We can see ways in which the crises of the contemporary world have been foreshadowed by these earlier events. Take, for example, the way that migrants were frequently conceptualized first and foremost as a threat to the stability of the regions to which they were fleeing, and how this was used to justify proposals to use the law to regulate and curtail their mobility. A migrant fleeing famine in mid-nineteenth-century Ireland aboard a so-called "coffin ship" bound for North America and a migrant fleeing social upheaval and armed conflict in Libya aboard a small fishing vessel bound for the islands of Italy are likely to face a very similar reception: a public deeply divided on the desirability of their presence, and a legal framework crafted in part to assuage those demanding the shutting of borders. They are also likely to be marginalized socially, in part through disproportionate and frequent encounters with the criminal justice system. Human displacement and precarious migration would come to be cornerstones of a modern world in which the mobility of people continues to accelerate. In the three cases examined here, we see how public anxieties over the impact of immigration pushed the state towards innovative practices in surveillance and regulation – a trend that is familiar to observers in the twenty-first century. Similarly, we can note the reluctance expressed in these three cities at the time to provide material support to the migrants – a reaction that was fundamentally about barring these vulnerable migrants from full membership in the community. These reactions suggest that when it comes to affluent societies grappling with how to manage crises in migration, there is much to be gained from turning an eye to historical parallels to recent events. Doing so reminds us that such crises are a persistent and defining feature of our societies. Furthermore, they draw our attention to how the gradual criminalization of migration is shaped by intermittent crisis, in ways that lay the groundwork for an extended process of marginalization.

NOTES

1 For effective overviews of the Irish Famine and its accompanying wave of migration, see Kerby Miller, *Emigrants and Exiles: Ireland and the Irish Exodus to North America* (Oxford: Oxford University Press, 1988); and Christine Kinealy, *A Death-Dealing Famine: The Great Hunger in Ireland* (London: Pluto Press, 1997).

2 My understanding of nineteenth-century liberalism, particularly with regards to the way that its advocates created sharp divisions between public and private, and how this was used to defend a deep reluctance towards state intervention, has been shaped by Patrick Joyce's *The Rule of Freedom: Liberalism and the Modern City* (London: Verso, 2003).

3 For a diverse and nuanced overview of the Irish experience with the nineteenth-century criminal justice system, see the essays in Kyle Hughes and Donald MacRaild, eds., *Crime, Violence, and the Irish in the Nineteenth Century* (Liverpool: Liverpool University Press, 2017).

4 This argument is made by Julien Jeandesboz and Polly Pallister-Wilkins in "Crisis, Routine, Consolidation: The Politics of the Mediterranean Migration Crisis," *Mediterranean Politics* 21, no. 2 (2016): 316–20.

5 For the period between the capitalist reforms and the famine, see Christine Kinealy, *This Great Calamity: The Irish Famine, 1845–1852* (Dublin: Gill and Macmillan, 1994).

6 See Murray Milgate and Shannon Stimson, *After Adam Smith: A Century of Transformation in Politics and Political Economy* (Princeton: Princeton University Press, 2011).

7 For more on changing patterns and practices of Irish agriculture, see Gearóid Ó Tuathaigh, *Ireland Before the Famine, 1798–1848* (Dublin: Gill and Macmillan, 2007).

8 For a case study of an Irish community on the brink during the famine that puts a human face on these broader social changes, see Robert Scally, *The End of Hidden Ireland: Rebellion, Famine, and Emigration* (Oxford: Oxford University Press, 1995).

9 Miller, *Emigrants and Exiles*, 290–5.

10 For an overview of Irish migration to industrializing Britain, see Roger Swift and Sheridan Gilley, *The Irish in the Victorian City* (London: Croom Helm, 1985).

11 For an overview of Irish migration to British North America, see Donald
   Akenson, *The Irish in Ontario: A Rural History* (Montreal: McGill-Queen's
   University Press, 1984).

12 There is an extensive literature on the place of the Irish in the twentieth-
   century North American urban working class. Three particularly important
   titles are Noel Ignatiev, *How The Irish Became White* (New York: Routledge,
   1995); David Roediger, *The Wages of Whiteness: Race and the Making of the
   American Working Class* (London: Verso, 1991); and James Barrett, *The Irish
   Way: Becoming American in the Multiethnic City* (New York: Penguin, 2012).

13 Margaret Humphreys, "A Stranger in Our Camps: Typhus in American History," *Bulletin of Historical Medicine* 80 (2006): 269–90; and Ann Hardy,
   "Urban Famine or Urban Crisis? Typhus in the Victorian City," *Medical History* 32 (1988): 401–25.

14 For more on the politics around quarantine, see Krista Maglen, *The English
   System: Quarantine, Immigration and the Making of a Port Sanitary Zone*
   (Oxford: Oxford University Press, 2016). On the global cholera epidemic of
   1832, see Charles Rosenberg, *The Cholera Years: The United States in 1832,
   1849, and 1866* (Chicago: University of Chicago Press, 1987); and David
   Arnold, *Colonizing the Body: State Medicine and Epidemic Disease in Nineteenth-Century India* (Berkeley: University of California Press, 1993), ch. 4.

15 For an example of this sort of rhetoric, see the editorial printed in Montreal's
   La Minerve, 14 October 1847.

16 For an overview of Liverpool's extensive role in the slave trade, see the
   essays in *Liverpool and Transatlantic Slavery*, eds. David Richardson, Anthony
   Tibbles, and Suzanne Schwarz (Liverpool: Liverpool University Press, 2007).

17 For more on the precarious condition of the Liverpool Irish and violence in
   nineteenth-century Liverpool, see Frank Neal, *Sectarian Violence: The Liverpool Experience, 1819–1914: An Aspect of Anglo-Irish History* (Manchester:
   Manchester University Press, 1988).

18 For an overview of the typhus outbreak in Liverpool, see Frank Neal, *Black
   '47: Britain and the Famine Irish* (London: Macmillan, 1998), ch. 5.

19 For an overview of the British Poor Law during this period, see David Eng-
   lander, *Poverty and Poor Law Reform in 19th Century Britain, 1834–1914* (New
   York: Routledge, 2013).

20 For expressions of this in the local press, see the *Liverpool Mercury*, 29 January 1847; 5 March 1847; 30 April 1847; 18 June 1847.

21 For examples of Liverpool's civic elites complaining of their city's burden
   and tabling calls for more assistance from London, see Liverpool Records
   Office, Health Committee, General Purposes Sub-Committee, Minute
   Book, June–October 1847.

22 *Liverpool Mercury*, 29 January 1847.

23 Measures to do so were often contentious as a result of public uncertainty about the nature of typhus. Many of these new quarantine stations were built in close proximity to the city, and the public feared that put them at risk if the disease did spread in the air. See the *Liverpool Albion*, 7 June 1847.

24 For more on the Poor Law Removal Act of 1847, see the *Liverpool Mercury*, 22 June 1847; 29 June 1847; and 2 July 1847; and Matthew Gallman, *Receiving Erin's Children: Philadelphia, Liverpool and the Irish Famine Migration, 1845–1855* (Chapel Hill: University of North Carolina Press, 2000), 30.

25 Neal, *Black '47*, ch 4.

26 See, for example, John Belchem, *Irish, Catholic, and Scouse: The History of the Liverpool Irish, 1800–1939* (Oxford: Oxford University Press, 2007), ch. 7.

27 The renting out of these cellars to destitute migrants became the target of public health reformers in Liverpool during this period. See William Frazer, *Duncan of Liverpool* (London: Hamish Hamilton, 1947), 23–44.

28 Neal, *Sectarian Violence*, ch. 2.

29 Aristide Zolberg, *A Nation by Design: Immigration Policy in the Fashioning of America* (Cambridge: Harvard University Press, 2006), 100–2.

30 Ibid., 135.

31 For more on the social experience of the Boston Irish, see Dennis Ryan, *Beyond the Ballot Box: A Social History of the Boston Irish, 1845–1917* (Amherst: University of Massachusetts Press, 1989).

32 Ibid., 111.

33 Hidetaka Hirota, "'The Great Entrepot for Mendicants': Foreign Poverty and Immigration Control in New York State to 1882," *Journal of American Ethnic History* 33, no. 2 (Winter 2014): 6.

34 For more on Massachusetts' legislation on immigration during this period, see Kunal Parker, "State, Citizenship, and Territory: The Legal Construction of Immigrants in Antebellum Massachusetts," *Law and History Review* 19, no. 3 (2001): 583–643.

35 For a report on a ship being redirected to Halifax from Boston as a result of these regulations, see the *Baltimore Sun*, 29 June 1847.

36 David Kales, *The Boston Harbor Islands: A History of an Urban Wilderness* (Charleston: The History Press, 2007), 65.

37 For a report on the state of Boston during the summer of 1847 containing this sort of language, see the *Baltimore Sun*, 3 June 1847.

38 See Kales, *Boston Harbor Islands*.

39 See, for example, the language in the Commonwealth of Massachusetts' law regulating immigration: *An Act to Prevent the Introduction of Paupers, from Foreign Ports or Places*, 1819, http://archives.lib.state.ma.us/handle/2452/110236.

40 Kales, *Boston Harbor Islands*, 66.

41 For more on nativism and the Know Nothing movement, see Tyler Anbinder, *Nativism and Slavery: The Northern Know Nothings and the Politics of the 1850s* (Oxford: Oxford University Press, 1993); and John Mulkern, *The Know-Nothing Party in Massachusetts: The Rise and Fall of a People's Movement* (Boston: Northeastern University Press, 1990).

42 See *Baltimore Sun*, 1 July 1847.

43 For a discussion of the United States Supreme Court rulings on the Passenger Cases, see Gerald Neuman, *Strangers to the Constitution: Immigrants, Borders, and Fundamental Law* (Princeton: Princeton University Press, 1996), 28.

44 For details of the Passenger Acts of 1855 and its impact on migration across the British Empire, see David Northrup, *Indentured Labour in the Age of Imperialism, 1834–1922* (Cambridge: Cambridge University Press, 1995).

45 See Anbinder, *Nativism and Slavery*, and Mulkern, *The Know-Nothing Party in Massachusetts*.

46 For a discussion of class and identity with regards to the Irish in the United States in the long nineteenth century, see Roediger, *The Wages of Whiteness*.

47 See, for example, *La Minerve*, 14 February 1847.

48 For more on Grosse Isle, see Marianna O'Gallagher, *Grosse Île: Gateway to Canada, 1832–1937* (Dublin: Carraig Books, 1984). On the 1832 cholera epidemic in Canada, see Geoffrey Bilson, *A Darkened House: Cholera in Nineteenth-Century Canada* (Toronto: University of Toronto Press, 1980).

49 *La Minerve*, 1 July 1847.

50 Ibid.

51 See, for example, *Montreal Gazette*, 15 July 1847.

52 *La Minerve*, 19 August 1847.

53 *Montreal Gazette*, 9 June 1847; *La Minerve*, 4 June 1847.

54 *La Minerve*, 1 July 1847.

55 *La Minerve*, 15 July 1847.

56 Journals of the Legislative Assembly of the Province of Canada, Session 1847, vol. 7, Appendix N, Report from the Commissioner of Public Works.

57 Journals of the Legislative Assembly of the Province of Canada, Session 1847, vol. 6, 197–9.

58 For an overview from this period on debates over miasmatic theories of disease transmission, see William Duncan, "The Public Hygiene of Great Britain" in *British and Foreign Medical Review*, vol. 18 (July–October 1844), 492–512.

59 For more on the Irish experience in Montreal, see Sherry Olson and Patricia Thornton, *Peopling the North American City: Montreal, 1840–1900* (Montreal: McGill-Queen's University Press, 2011).

60 Mary Anne Poutanen has noted that the majority of women arrested on charges related to sex trade work in early nineteenth-century Montreal were Irish migrants. See Poutanen, *Beyond Brutal Passions: Prostitution in Early-Nineteenth-Century Montreal* (Montreal: McGill-Queen's University Press, 2015), 138. For how the Irish were relegated to the lowest rungs of the city's occupational ladder during these years, see Olson and Thornton, *Peopling the North American City*, ch. 7.

61 For an overview of this process, see Lisa Chilton, "Managing Migrants: Toronto, 1820–1880," *Canadian Historical Review* 92, no. 2 (2011), 231–62.

62 For a legal history of quarantine, see Lawrence Gostin, *Public Health Law: Power, Duty, Restraint* (Berkeley: University of California Press, 2008).

63 For an effective overview of the current migration crisis around the Mediterranean Sea that raises similar questions about popular anxiety and public policy, see Kelly Greenhill, "Open Arms Behind Barred Doors: Fear, Hypocrisy and Policy Schizophrenia in the European Migration Crisis," *European Law Journal* 22, no.3 (2016): 317–32.

PART FOUR

Criminalizing Refugees
and Other Forced Migrants:
Current Dynamics, Future Challenges,
and Prospects

10

Back to the Future:
Shifts in Canadian Refugee Policy
Over Four Decades

Peter Goodspeed

The world changed the morning of 2 September 2015, when Alan Kurdi's small, lifeless body was photographed, lying face down, in the surf of Golden Beach, near the Turkish resort of Bodrum. With the click of a shutter, the capturing of a single death would transform public perceptions of the worst humanitarian crisis the world had seen in seven decades. Shock, guilt, and outrage fought with sorrow over an innocent child's passing. For one jarring moment, public policy and public opinion confronted the stark realities of a refugee crisis that has inflicted permanent scars on the twenty-first century. In the process, Canadians rediscovered a national tradition of compassion and abandoned what had become a decade of casual indifference towards refugee policy.

This chapter will look at what changed the morning Alan Kurdi died, and why. It will compare Canada's response to the current Syrian refugee crisis with our actions in other crises that preceded it – most notably the Indochinese (or Southeast Asian) refugee crisis of 1979 to 1980. It will examine discrepancies between those two events and outline the broad transitional forces that have shaped Canada's reactions to refugees over four decades. In doing this, the chapter will examine the lessons that can be learned from the two different crises and their implications for the future.

The morning that Turkish journalist Nilüfer Demir photographed Alan Kurdi's corpse, she had been roaming the beach near Bodrum to report on the latest catastrophe to strike the thousands of Syrian refugees who were trying to flee to Greece aboard small, overcrowded rubber dinghies.[1] With 3,771 confirmed deaths, 2015 was the deadliest year on record for migrants and refugees crossing the Mediterranean. The International Organization for Migration reported that 214,266 Syrians fled to Europe that year. At one point, Greece, the initial European destination for most Syrian refugees, was recording an average of 3,400 arrivals each day.[2] But in the pre-dawn darkness of September 2, a pair of dinghies sailing from Bodrum overturned on the way to the nearby Greek island of Kos, drowning a dozen people. Alan Kurdi, his five-year-old brother Galip, and his mother Rihan, 35, were among the dead.

Alan's father, Abdullah Kurdi, a refugee from the war-torn Syrian town of Kobanî, on the border with Turkey, had paid Turkish smugglers €4,000 (about C$5,860) for four spaces in an inflatable rubber dinghy to make the thirty-minute trip to Greece.[3] He survived the tragic sinking and later described his desperate but unsuccessful attempts to rescue his family. "My children slipped through my hands," he said. "It was dark and everyone was screaming. I tried to catch my wife and children but there was no hope. One by one, they died."[4]

Abdullah Kurdi and his family had lived in Turkey for two years after fleeing Syria's civil war in Damascus and then Aleppo, only to be forced to flee again from Kobanî by the brutality of the Islamic State. Unable to work legally, Kurdi, a barber by trade, held a series of poorly paid jobs in Turkey's underground economy and was dependent on remittances from relatives simply to feed his family. "I couldn't provide anything to my children, and my parents were helping us with the essentials, even though I had a small salary," he said later in a radio interview.[5]

His sister, Tima, who lives in Port Coquitlam, British Columbia, had hoped to resettle Kurdi's family in Canada under the country's private refugee sponsorship program. She temporarily abandoned the idea in June 2015, after her attempts to sponsor another brother, Mohammad, and his four children, who were in Germany, had been rejected by the Canadian government.[6] Relatives said that this rejection led Abdullah Kurdi to decide to attempt to flee to Kos with his family.[7]

Citizenship and Immigration Canada officials said Mohammad Kurdi's sponsorship application was sidelined for being "incomplete."[8] As a result of refugee reforms introduced in 2012, refugees seeking sponsorship from a "Group of Five" or a "Community Sponsor" in Canada needed to have their status certified by the United Nations High Commissioner for Refugees (UNHCR) or recognized by a third country to qualify for resettlement. But it is almost impossible for refugees fleeing the Syrian crisis to receive such certifications, as the UNHCR is too overwhelmed caring for the 4.5 million Syrians who have fled their country to conduct individual investigations.

Still, months before Alan Kurdi died, the Canadian government was being severely criticized for not doing enough to help Syrian refugees.[9] In July 2013, Canada had promised to resettle 200 government-sponsored and 1,100 privately sponsored Syrian refugees by the end of 2014.[10] But a year later, as Syria's civil war entered its fourth, blood-soaked year, Canada had resettled fewer than 150 Syrians.[11] In the same time period, Sweden, which has only about a quarter of Canada's population, had opened its doors to more than 30,000 Syrians,[12] and Germany was bracing to receive another 800,000 refugees.[13]

Alan Kurdi's death highlighted in a brutal way the desperation faced by Syrian refugees. But it also rapidly became a catalyst that transformed the Syrian refugee crisis into a major issue in Canada's forty-second general election. The tragedy marked a sudden and fundamental shift in Canadian attitudes toward the Syrian crisis and sparked demands to do something to help Syrian refugees. In the heat of a hard-fought campaign, the Kurdi tragedy inevitably became politicized, as Canada's major parties immediately sought to distinguish themselves by promising reforms and vowing to dramatically increase the number of Syrian refugees Canada was prepared to help. Immigration Minister Chris Alexander, who eventually lost his seat in the election, immediately suspended campaigning to return to Ottawa to deal with the fallout from the Kurdi case, while the Liberal and New Democratic parties tried to outbid each other in promising to provide increased relief to refugees who could be resettled in Canada.

The political ramifications of Alan Kurdi's death, however, were peripheral to a more fundamental resurgence in the Canadian public's interest in private refugee sponsorship. In a matter of hours after the toddler's death was publicized – on the news and around the world on the Internet – thousands upon thousands of Canadians were clamouring to find out what they could do to help sponsor a Syrian refugee family. The public's desire to help refugees was reflected in November when the new Liberal government took office and, in one of its first administrative acts, changed the name of Citizenship and Immigration Canada to Immigration, Refugees and Citizenship Canada.

This broad, public interest in refugees had been absent in Canada for a number of years, as I discovered when I was awarded the Atkinson Foundation's annual journalism fellowship in 2014 and devoted a year to studying Canadian refugee policy.[14] I submitted my research proposal to the Atkinson Foundation's selection committee in January 2013, intending to study the refugee experience in Canada in the context of the country's new asylum determination procedures and a massive increase in international migration. The topic seemed ripe for reporting. Refugee policy was one of the most contentious issues in Canadian political life and Canada had just created a new asylum system with passage of the Balanced Refugee Reform Act in 2010 and the Protecting Canada's Immigration System Act in June 2012.[15] The war in Syria was just ramping up and the xenophobic rhetoric of Europe's far-right political parties was creeping into immigration discussions worldwide. It seemed a good time to look at the ideas, the interests, the institutions, and the rhetoric surrounding Canada's refugee system.

REFORM AND RHETORIC

A quick survey of Canada's refugee record exposed a harsh new reality – there was a growing gap between Canada's rhetoric and how it actually treated refugees. There had been a dramatic shift in national attitudes and policies, and as a result it was harder for refugees and asylum seekers to come to Canada. A year after the reforms of 2012, Canada sheltered and resettled its lowest number of refugees in two decades.[16] In 1990 Canada brought in 15,485 government-assisted refugees.[17] In 2013, the figure was 5,781.[18] At the same time, reforms to Canada's asylum system had slashed the number of potential refugees seeking shelter in Canada. In 2008 there were 35,000 asylum claims in Canada.[19] In 2013 there were only 10,000.[20]

Even more damning was the fact Canada's dramatic refugee declines came when the rest of the world was struggling to cope with the worst international refugee crisis since the Second World War. According to the UNHCR the number of refugees, asylum seekers, and displaced people worldwide reached an unprecedented 65.3 million people in 2016.[21] Yet while asylum applications in the world's top forty-four industrial countries increased by 28 per cent in 2013 – surging by 25 per cent in the United States – they were cut in half in Canada.[22]

Those plummeting Canadian statistics were directly related to immigration reforms that reduced refugee rights in Canada – attempts to slash government spending and an increased emphasis on security and economic development over humanitarian concerns.[23]

A general tightening of Canada's immigration procedures under Canada's Conservative-led governments between 2006 and 2015 slashed refugee claims, in particular through the application of the 2004 Safe Third Country Agreement with the United States.[24] The implementation of a more restrictive and expedited hearing process for refugee claimants from forty-two "Designated Countries of Origin" that were regarded generally as being respectful of human rights also resulted in further reductions.[25] In addition, Canada imposed visa restrictions on selected "refugee producing countries," such as Mexico and the Czech Republic, and imposed new penalties on airlines and shipping companies that transported improperly documented passengers to Canada.[26]

Conservative government spokesmen repeatedly defended the 2012 refugee reforms, saying they would ultimately save the government $1.6 billion over five years by reducing what they regarded as "bogus" refugee claims.[27] The reforms were also accompanied by a marked shift in rhetoric. Refugees were depicted as "economic freeloaders" and refugee resettlement was portrayed as an optional work of charity rather than a moral obligation or a vital national interest.[28]

Canada's old refugee determination system also invited criticism for being slow, costly, inefficient, and a boon to human traffickers. With a backlog of 45,000 unresolved asylum claims and waiting periods of up to three years for hearings, critics claimed the old system actually encouraged people to play the system in the hopes of getting into Canada.[29] As a result, arguments raged over how to differentiate between persecuted refugees and opportunistic economic migrants. In the process, border control became a focus of "law and order politics," with the stress on security over human rights.

The shadow of fear cast by the terrorist attacks of 11 September 2001 also caused Canadians to react differently to refugees. The resentment, uncertainty, and fear engendered by terrorism has translated into a new focus on security issues, with demands to patrol borders, intercept migrants, and seek safeguards from foreign threats.

Combined with "law and order politics," the result has been a demo-
nization of immigrants and refugees, and a focus on "fraud" and
"abuse." Canadians bolstered their security, restricted migration, and
expanded surveillance, all while trying to deter, deflect, and block
potential asylum claimants from ever coming to Canada to make
refugee claims.[30]

In general, by the time the Syrian refugee crisis blossomed, it was
harder for refugees and asylum seekers to come to Canada than at any
time in the past. Canada's immigration policies were more demanding, more selective, and more self-serving than in the past.

It wasn't always this way.

THE SUMMER OF 1979

In the summer of 1979, Canadians confronted a pressing international refugee crisis with a uniquely Canadian combination of policies, compassion, and personalities. In a matter of months, Canadians surprised themselves and the world by opening their doors and
their hearts to 60,000 refugees from all over Southeast Asia. In just
eighteen months, tens of thousands of individuals, families, churches, and neighbourhood groups rallied to rescue and resettle refugees
from Vietnam, Laos, and Cambodia, as those countries unravelled
under the horrific combination of new wars, Cambodia's Killing
Fields, and the vindictive policies of Vietnam's conquering commu-
nist ideologues.

The Indochinese refugee or "boat people" crisis was rooted in the
tragedy of the Vietnam War, and, like the war itself, it had initially
been watched by Canadians, from a safe distance, with casual indifference. The United States' withdrawal from Vietnam in 1975 was
accompanied by an initial flood of refugees fleeing defeat and fearing retribution. But, for the most part, those first refugees were safely resettled in the United States. Over the course of the next four
years, however, nearly a million other people fled Vietnam in ram-
shackle boats, up to half of whom are believed to have died escaping,
either by drowning, starving, being eaten by sharks, or getting mur-
dered by pirates in the Gulf of Thailand. The growing exodus went
virtually unnoticed by the world's news media until late 1978, when
the world suddenly focused on the plight of 2,504 Vietnamese
refugees who fled their homeland aboard a small, rusting cargo ship,
the *Hai Hong*.[31]

Denied permission to land in surrounding countries, the decrepit freighter lay at anchor off the coast of Malaysia for weeks as the world's statesmen discussed what to do with the ship and its desperate human cargo. Suddenly, the world's media brought the "boat people" tragedy into Western living rooms through stories and photographs of the *Hai Hong's* cramped quarters, the suffocating heat, people too sick or weak to stand, and refugee children with open sores.

As Canadians fretted over the world's failure to help the refugees, their government moved to break the international stalemate by agreeing to resettle 604 of the *Hai Hong's* passengers. In the final months of 1978, as those refugees were airlifted to Canada, welcoming committees sprang up across the country to receive them. Churches, community groups, and individuals donated clothing or offered housing and promised the refugees jobs.[32]

Still, Southeast Asia's refugee crisis continued unabated, as tens of thousands of people risked everything they had to escape. Thousands continued to die, and those who did land safely in nearby countries were rejected, shunned, and caged. The world's news media eagerly latched onto their stories of hardship and betrayal, of courage and cowardice, of despair and hope. And Canadians responded.

A federal election was held during April and May 1979, and just as the new Progressive Conservative government of Joe Clark was taking power, the exodus from Indochina soared to more than 50,000 people a month.[33] The drama on Asia's high seas drew the attention of Canadians away from their more mundane problems. They watched intently as a new, unknown, and untested government faced its first major international crisis.

Emotions ran high and comparisons were made constantly between the plight of the Indochinese refugees and the victims of the Holocaust. News of Pol Pot's death camps and Vietnam's "re-education camps" conjured nightmares of Nazi concentration camps, and the sight of rusty freighters crammed with frightened refugees triggered guilty memories of the MS *St Louis* and Canada's shameful failure to give nearly a thousand Jewish people sanctuary in 1939, when they so desperately needed it.[34]

It was late June 1979 when Howard Adelman, a philosophy professor at York University, finished a six-week stay at his family cottage on an island in Ontario's Georgian Bay. He had been working in isolation on a book on the German idealist philosopher Georg Wilhem Friedrich Hegel and had also just finished writing an article for a scholarly journal on research being done into the reception that German Jewish refugees had received in Canada, the United States, and Britain in the late 1930s. Upon his return to Toronto, he sifted through six weeks of old newspapers to catch up on what had happened while he had been away and was stunned by the Vietnamese "boat people" crisis that had exploded across the news media.[35]

Adelman felt he had to do something. Motivated by the same activism with which he had been engaged in the 1960s, when he had cofounded Rochdale College, Toronto's controversial experiment in alternative education, Adelman called a meeting. He invited the local Catholic priest, two rabbis, an alderman, and ministers from the Anglican and United Churches to his home to discuss the Indochinese exodus.

Fifteen people gathered in Adelman's living room on June 24 with the intention of drafting a petition urging the month-old government of Prime Minister Joe Clark to do something. Ron Atkey, the new immigration minister in Clark's cabinet, was Adelman's local MP.

"We knew nothing and just wanted to write a letter to tell Ron, 'Come on, get off your ass and do something,'" says Adelman. "That was the purpose of this meeting. He was our MP so we thought we might have some influence over him."[36]

Just as the meeting was about to start, two civil servants, André Pilon and Bob Parkes, from the Department of Immigration's Ontario Settlement Office, arrived at the door and asked if they could sit in on the gathering. As the group discussed the need to protest, Pilon asked if he could say a few words.

"He told us about the provision in the new 1976 immigration legislation that allowed an organization or group of five Canadians to sponsor a refugee and suggested we might wish to engage in a demonstrable act of witnessing and not just write a letter," Adelman says.

"Wouldn't it be better if you actually *did something*?" is the way Adelman recalls Pilon's suggestion.

"To the Christians in the room, the idea of 'witnessing' appealed very strongly and we all thought it was a good idea," says Adelman. "We forgot about the letter and we decided we'd sponsor fifty people over the summer."

"We'd do our good deed and then go home. I planned to hang

around Toronto an extra day to organize a street sponsorship group and then return north to continue my writing," he recalls.

Adelman wouldn't see his cottage again for two years and his book on Hegel was never finished. Unknown to Adelman, a graduate student who had sat in on his Sunday meeting worked as a freelancer for the *Globe and Mail*, and when the meeting was over he had contacted the newspaper's flamboyant columnist Dick Beddoes and told him what had happened.

"Beddoes wrote a very imaginative column that described how a philosopher hero abandoned his book on 'Haykel' [sic], rode south on his white steed from his island in the north and founded Operation Lifeline to rescue the Indochinese boat people," Adelman says. "Essentially, it was a totally mythological story. Beddoes even named our group Operation Lifeline. We didn't name it anything. But he named it and he put my phone number at the bottom of the column."[37]

At 6 a.m. the morning after Beddoes' column appeared in the *Globe and Mail*, Adelman was sitting at his desk working when a woman telephoned from Marystown, Newfoundland.

"I want to help Operation Lifeline," she told him.

"I had no idea what she was talking about," Adelman recalls. "'Why are you calling me?' I asked her. So she read me the column. I said, 'OK, you are now the chairwoman of the Marystown chapter of Operation Lifeline.'"

When Adelman hung up the phone, it immediately rang again.

"It never stopped ringing for two weeks," he says. "Literally, every time you put the phone down, it rang. Within ten days, we had sixty-eight chapters of Operation Lifeline across the country."

"Volunteers showed up at the door and I assigned them tasks like manning the phone and keeping records of new chapters, and people who couldn't reach us by phone arrived at the door. Some of them were carrying bundles of cash in their hands."

Within two weeks, the group that met in Adelman's living room had already sponsored its fifty refugees. "It was a kind of spontaneous outpouring of various skills," Adelman says.

Around the time Adelman was rummaging through his six weeks' worth of newspapers, Ron Atkey was spending a weekend at his cottage preparing for his new job as immigration minister. Among the government documents and reports he brought with him was an advance copy of a chapter from a forthcoming book by Canadian historians Irving Abella and Harold Troper, *None Is Too Many*, which detailed Canada's refusal to offer aid or sanctuary to German Jews fleeing the Nazi Third Reich in the 1930s. The manuscript was given to Atkey by his deputy minister, Jack Manion, who had already made it required reading for senior officials in his department. The chapter Atkey read dealt with the tragedy of the MS *St Louis*, a ship carrying 937 Jews that was refused permission to land in Canada, Cuba, and the United States in 1939. The refugees were eventually forced back to Europe and most of the passengers died in the Holocaust.

When Atkey returned to Ottawa and turned his attention to the problem of the Vietnamese "boat people," he used the manuscript to influence his cabinet colleagues, asking them: "Do we want to be known as the government that said no?"[38]

As the Vietnamese crisis unfolded, Canada gradually increased the number of people it planned to help. An initial decision to accept 5,000 Vietnamese refugees was more a token of solidarity with the United States than a commitment to the refugees. But as the crisis worsened, the new Conservative government decided to increase the number of government-sponsored refugees to 8,000. Provisions for private sponsorship had been in place since the spring of 1978 but few Canadians understood or were interested in the scheme. By the spring of 1979, fewer than 100 private sponsorships had been concluded.[39] By the end of the year, however, 7,000 new Canadian sponsoring groups would privately sponsor 29,269 refugees.[40]

The same weekend that Adelman and Atkey were struggling to comprehend the problem of the "boat people," Ottawa Mayor Marion Dewar, a former public health nurse, decided to spend a weekend away with her husband at a resort in the Gatineau Hills. It rained and she ended up spending most of her time playing bridge and watching television, which was filled with reports on the crisis in Asia. By the time she returned home, she was determined to do something and organized a meeting with local church leaders and Canadian immigration officials, who told her Canada's quota to help 8,000 refugees had already been half filled.[41]

"I said, you've only got 4,000 left? We'll take them," she recalled later to the *Ottawa Citizen*. "It was very slap-happy. It stuck in my mind: 4,000. We've got almost 400,000 [people] in Ottawa. Surely we can handle that."[42]

Within a month, "Project 4000" was underway and residents of Canada's capital piled onto the refugee sponsorship bandwagon, signing up to support and welcome destitute families from halfway around the world. By the end of July, two days before attending a crucial international conference on the "boat people" in Geneva, Switzerland, Flora MacDonald, Canada's secretary of state for external affairs, challenged Canadians, and the rest of the world, by announcing that the Canadian government would match whatever commitments the Canadian public would make to resettle up to 50,000 Indochinese refugees.

The public response was so immediate and so overwhelming that the target of 21,000 sponsored refugees, matched with 21,000 government-supported refugees, was met by November. Small church congregations of 100 people or fewer lined up to sponsor as many as six families, employers promised sponsors jobs for refugees, and small grocery stores offered free fruit and vegetables to families for a year.[43] In the end, Canada resettled 60,000 Indochinese refugees between 1979 and 1980, approximately 26,000 of whom were government assisted and 34,000 privately sponsored.[44]

"When the music began with the Vietnamese boat people, Canada already had its dancing shoes on," says Mike Molloy, a retired diplomat and former ambassador to Jordan, who was the chief coordinator of Canada's "boat people" rescue operation in 1979.[45] Programs were in place, politicians and senior civil servants were on side, and the public was primed and willing to help. But it was the political decision to go ahead that galvanized Canadians and energized the rescue effort, Molloy says.

"It took a lot of guts to come up with a program to bring in 50,000 people," he says. "We were only about a decade and a half into the idea of open immigration. To go before the people and say we are going to bring in 50,000 from a place far, far away, that was only heard of in a war context, took a heck of a lot of political courage."[46]

The way MacDonald explained it, Canada really had no choice but to act as it did. "Countries like Canada have to provide a relief valve if we want to prevent hundreds of thousands more people from dying," she told a meeting of the Canadian Club in September 1979. "There was absolutely no choice about Canada having to accept refugees for resettlement. At least there was no choice if we are going to be able to live with our consciences – and to me that means no choice."

"But there was a choice as to how we were to do this," she said. "One way would have been for the government to just arbitrarily pick a figure and say we will bring in this number and look after them. But we knew that the distress of these refugees had touched the hearts of Canadians. We knew that thousands of people from coast to coast had already been looking for a way in which they, as private citizens, could help."

"Not only does this give an opportunity for Canadians to satisfy their need to help directly in a tragic situation," MacDonald said, "but it also allows the Canadian people to determine the total number of refugees who will come here."[47]

Canada's outpouring of kindness in 1979 was a defining moment for the country, one recognized internationally in 1986 when the people of Canada became the first and only nation ever to be awarded the UNHCR Nansen Refugee Award in recognition of "their essential and constant contribution to the cause of refugees."[48]

Over time, however, Canada's generosity would wane. Refugee policies and processes strained under the weight of constant crisis, and public attitudes shifted. When, in the summer of 1999, twenty years after the miracle of the "boat people," 599 desperate Chinese migrants put to sea in four decrepit boats and arrived off the coast of British Columbia, their reception was quite different. They, too, dominated the news for eighteen months, but, unlike the Indochinese refugees of 1979, they were imprisoned and paraded before television cameras in handcuffs and leg shackles. Their arrival was greeted with political hysteria, demands for a tighter refugee determination process, and complaints about "illegal migrants" and "queue jumpers" who relied on criminals to gain entry to Canada. At one point, the *Victoria Times Colonist* ran a front-page story headlined "Go Home" about a poll showing that 97 per cent of the newspaper's readers felt the Chinese "boat people" should be sent back to China immediately.[49] Editorials in the *National Post* claimed that if the Chinese migrants were allowed to stay in Canada, the country's sovereignty would be at risk.[50] Amidst widespread speculation of more "migrant ships" sailing to Canada, critics seriously questioned the government's ability to safeguard Canada's borders. Diane Francis, a columnist with the *National Post*, claimed the integrity of the immigration and refugee systems was at risk, along with the health and welfare of Canadians. "Through sheer incompetence, Ottawa is ruining lives, exposing Canadians to grave risks and financing the creation of a criminal class that will hurt this country for years to come," she claimed. "If these boatloads are not deported … the government of Canada should be sued by the provinces, municipalities, taxpayer organizations and other victims of refugee crimes."[51]

Within twenty years, Canada, Canadians, and the Canadian media had moved far beyond the spectacular generosity of the initial "boat people" crisis.

What changed, and why?

COMPASSION OVERWHELMED

The answer might be found by examining Canada and the world's reaction to a second, intense wave of refugees that swept over Southeast Asia in the late 1980s and early 1990s. After the initial mass exodus from Southeast Asia ended in 1980, refugees continued to slip out of Vietnam and surrounding countries. For a short while, between 1980 and 1986, the numbers being resettled overseas outpaced the incoming refugees. But by late 1986 that had changed and another wave of asylum seekers swept over Thailand and Hong Kong. By 1989 as many as 300 refugees a day were arriving in Hong Kong, and by the end of June 1990 there were 54,341 Vietnamese refugees being held in closed detention camps in the then-British colony.[52]

At their overpopulated worst, the Hong Kong camps earned a reputation for squalid hopelessness and sporadic violence. For many who lived there, the camps were teeming cesspools of brutality. People were held in appalling conditions. The refugees slept and lived in cage-like compounds, furnished with three-tier bunks. Robbery and physical and sexual abuse were rampant. There was constant tension, and the threat of riots and hunger strikes. Gangs, controlled by Vietnamese thugs known as *dai gohs* (big brothers), terrorized entire sections of the camps. Children grew up never knowing a natural family life and witnessed frequent acts of self-mutilation and daily despair.

This second exodus from Vietnam in the mid-1980s was marked by a dramatic shift in the type of asylum seeker arriving in Hong Kong. The later waves came mainly from northern Vietnam and consisted of economic migrants seeking a better life, as opposed to the political refugees from the south fleeing persecution. Tension between the two groups was rife. On several occasions, gangs from northern and southern Vietnam squared off and fought pitched battles using knives fashioned from sharpened pail handles and spears made from bed frames. Fights, which frequently ended in stabbings, were nightly occurrences in some camps. Entire families would cower under their beds, and prison guards were reluctant to intervene. Social workers who worked in the camps said it was not uncommon to find children there who suffered from post-traumatic stress disorder, complete with feelings of terror, recurrent nightmares, flashbacks, and persistent fears. Lawyer Pam Baker, chairperson of Refugee Concern, a volunteer group that provided legal services to Hong Kong's asylum seekers, insisted that children born in the camps, who had never known freedom, might never have a chance at a normal life.

"For the little ones, who know no other life, it is terrible," she said at the time. "They think all animals are rats, because they have never seen any other sort of animal."[53]

To Hong Kong's credit, it never turned back a boat. Over the years the Hong Kong government spent more than $1 billion caring for the refugees, and at the peak of the exodus in 1979 was housing 68,695 "boat people" in crowded, makeshift camps. By October 1991, however, the figure still stood at 64,300, and most of those people never had a chance of being resettled overseas.[54] Nearly 90 per cent of the Vietnamese asylum seekers who arrived in Hong Kong in the late 1980s and early 1990s were declared "illegal migrants" who were ineligible for resettlement.[55] They were condemned to spend years living in despair and deprivation in overcrowded detention centres, former army barracks, abandoned factories, and floating barges and out-of-service ferries.

From 1975 to 1988, Indochinese refugees in Asia were almost automatically resettled. But after 1988 they had to undergo a screening process, based on the 1951 *Convention Relating to the Status of Refugees*,[56] which is the basis of Canada's own refugee determination process. After 1988, Vietnamese asylum seekers could only qualify as refugees if they could prove they had fled their country because of political or religious persecution. If they left simply because they did not like communism or because they wanted to improve their standard of living, they were categorized as illegal immigrants and kept indefinitely in detention camps until they could be convinced to go back home.[57]

Whenever reporters were allowed into Hong Kong's migrant camps in the 1990s they would be surrounded by frustrated and frightened crowds of people who pushed tattered letters and photographs into the journalists' hands. The letters contained the aspirations of the "boat people" – accounts from relatives or former neighbours who had been resettled in the West a decade earlier, who now enjoyed new lives, in new countries, and who had posed for family photographs in front of a new house or car or Christmas tree. The detained asylum seekers believed their present torment was just a gateway to that paradise – if only they could be resettled overseas. But the overwhelming majority were unable to prove they were refugees with a "well-founded fear of persecution" if they returned to Vietnam. As a result, they were designated "economic migrants" and condemned to live for months and in some cases years in enforced idleness and growing despair.

The drama and pathos of the refugees in Hong Kong's camps from 1989 to 1995 was not all that different from the exodus of 1975 to 1979. Yet the outcomes were incredibly different. That difference was likely rooted in a drastic shift in public attitudes towards asylum seekers and a growing acceptance of the verdict of the Vietnam War. A decade after the initial Indochinese exodus, it seemed the world had no room or patience for refugees. It was as if compassion had been overwhelmed by sheer numbers.

While indifference thrives on ignorance, it is also fed by mind-numbing repetition. The repetitive tragedies that dominated the end of the last century and the beginning of the twenty-first have left a legacy of callous disregard. In an era of twenty-four-hour, all-news television, the public has had a surfeit of tragedy to deal with. The Soviet invasion of Afghanistan turned central Asia into a running sore for thirty-six years; the Middle East was wracked by wars in Lebanon, Iraq, Iran, Israel, and Kuwait; the Soviet Union itself collapsed; Africa was tormented by a deadly AIDS epidemic, famines in Ethiopia and Somalia, and genocide in Rwanda; and the former Yugoslavia collapsed into eight years of ethnic cleansing and crimes against humanity. The people who were stranded in Asia's refugee camps in the 1990s were actually the last victims of the Vietnam War. They were simply shunted aside by history as it moved on.

Now, in a media age driven by the Internet, the public's attention span is considerably shorter and news goes "viral" for shorter periods of time. As a result, chronic emergencies, such as civil wars and famines, or complex crises that are difficult to understand, are too frequently regarded by readers, viewers, and editors alike as being neither immediate enough nor spectacular enough to deserve extensive coverage. Millions may have died in a complicated conflict such as the civil war in the Democratic Republic of Congo – the deadliest struggle the world has seen since the Second World War[58] – but the Indian Ocean tsunami of 2004,[59] which killed 230,000 people in fourteen countries, received far more media attention in just six weeks than the Congo did in a blood-soaked decade. The discourse of disaster, of "a wave of death" that tore children from their parents' arms and left devastation in its wake, held universal appeal. It struck a powerful chord with the public and stimulated unparalleled charitable donations. Yet other, more complicated events in some of the world's poorest countries have fallen off the West's public "radar" entirely. It is a sad fact of modern life that the public is less likely to donate money or energy to long-term, sustainable, humanitarian causes than they are to respond to acute emergencies.[60]

The technologies driving new media are also changing the ways in which news influences people. Nearly a fifth of the world's population – 1.4 billion people – logs on to Facebook each day, and the social media platform is now responsible for driving up to 18.16 per cent of all traffic to individual news sites.[61] According to the Pew Research Center, about 30 per cent of adults in the United States get their news on Facebook.[62] This trend means that something as serious as Syria's pain and destruction and the plight of millions of desperate refugees is now being reduced to a 140-character tweet or placed on equal footing with pet photos or videos of a friend's "ice bucket challenge." When Howard Adelman sifted through his six weeks of accumulated newspapers in the summer of 1979, he read about the "boat people" and concluded "something had to be done." Today, people may be just as likely to scroll through an equivalent disaster on their cell phones with a mere flick of a finger.

The photo of Alan Kurdi, dead on the beach, was an exception. One stark, shattering image seemed to suddenly change everything. As Jonathon Gatehouse, writing in *Maclean's* at the time, put it: "Indifference has a price, along with a name and a face."[63]

LIFELINE SYRIA

Five months before Alan Kurdi died in Turkey, a concerned group of people in Toronto came together to discuss ways to help Syrian refugees. The group, which consisted of retired civil servants, former politicians, social workers, academics, resettlement workers, and former activists from the Indochinese refugee crisis, had concluded that the Canadian government, which had resettled only 360 government-assisted refugees from Syria in almost five years, was not doing enough.[64] Their answer was to create Lifeline Syria, a Toronto-based initiative that drew its inspiration from Adelman's 1979 Operation Lifeline.

Launched on 17 June 2015, Lifeline Syria aimed to recruit, train, and assist private sponsors to welcome and support 1,000 Syrian refugees to be resettled as permanent immigrants in the Greater Toronto Area (GTA) over two years.[65] Working closely with existing sponsorship organizations and community organizations, as well as members of the local Syrian-Canadian community, Lifeline Syria intended to publicize the plight of Syrian refugees while teaching Canadians how they could participate in the private-sponsorship process.

"If our vision is realized, GTA residents will come out of the woodwork either to be sponsors, or to assist sponsors and our Syrian newcomers," Lifeline Syria's chair, Senator Ratna Omidvar, and Joseph Yu Kai Wong, the original vice-chair of Operation Lifeline in 1979, wrote in the *Toronto Star*.[66]

"Picture the libraries hosting extra classes and special events. Schools offering scholarships for Syrian students. Parks hosting concerts and potlucks. Companies headhunting Syrians and coaching them in their new positions. And we know some smart students will create an app so a mother in Leslieville can find a family in Roncesvalles in need of a stroller, and a teacher in Vaughn can find a student in Scarborough who needs a tutor."

"With the GTA setting the course, others may follow, and Winnipeg, Vancouver, and Halifax could launch their own citizen-led chapters to do the same," they said.

Within two weeks of its launch, Lifeline Syria was hosting "sold out" public information meetings at Toronto City Hall's council chambers for 200 to 300 people who were interested in learning how to sponsor a Syrian refugee family. During June and July it held two or three such meetings every week at locations across the city. Lifeline Syria's website began to receive an average of 300 views a day, and the group started sharing information online with a host of other communities outside Toronto that were interested in establishing similar organizations.

Criticism of the government's refugee policies grew increasingly shrill as Canada entered a historically long general election in the summer of 2015. In August 2015, Conservative Party leader Stephen Harper opened his re-election campaign promising to bring in an additional 10,000 Syrian and Iraqi refugees to Canada over the next four years.[67] But the opposition parties immediately rejected that proposal, arguing it was not enough. The New Democratic Party promised to bring 46,000 Syrian refugees to Canada over four years, while the Liberals repeated an earlier promise to bring 25,000 Syrian refuges to Canada by the end of 2015.[68]

The political debate remained largely impersonal and focused on numbers and targets – until Alan Kurdi died. Then, with the violent suddenness of a summer thunderstorm, everything changed. The Canadian public moved far ahead of their political leaders and parties in demanding more help for Syrian refugees. Alan's death refocused the debate and abruptly ended a decade of indifference.

For weeks after Alan died, the top Google search term in Canada was, "How to Sponsor a Syrian?"[69] At Lifeline Syria the phone and computer systems repeatedly crashed as the group was overwhelmed with offers of help. In the first twenty-four hours after Alan's death, Lifeline Syria's website views jumped from 300 to 1,600 visits a day and stayed that way for weeks. Settlement agencies across the country also scrambled to meet incessant public demands for information on refugee sponsorship. Churches, mosques, and synagogues joined together to bring in refugees; businesses stepped forward with offers of food, furniture, accommodation, and jobs; community groups and street committees launched fundraising campaigns to sponsor Syrian families; landlords and property companies reserved hundreds of apartments for refugees; and school children and their parents launched a "1,000 School Challenge," urging communities to compete by each sponsoring a refugee family.[70] Within ten months of its launch, Lifeline Syria had 422 sponsorship groups at various stages of the sponsorship process and had submitted applications to resettle over 900 Syrian refugees.[71]

"I can't provide refugees fast enough for all the Canadians who want to sponsor them," complained Canada's immigration minister, John McCallum.[72]

Canada's new Liberal government rushed to try and meet its election promise of resettling 25,000 government-assisted Syrian refugees by the end of 2015, but found it impossible to process that many cases in just two months. Still, 40,081 Syrian refugees arrived in Canada between 4 November 2015 and 29 January 2017, including 21,876 government-assisted refugees, 14,274 privately sponsored refugees, and 3,931 blended visa office-referred refugees.[73]

Canadians took great pride in their sudden display of humanitarianism and the domestic news media relished stories cataloguing commendable public responses to the Syrian crisis. It was as if readers and viewers could not get enough stories about refugees enduring their first Canadian winter or experiencing warm fuzzy feelings of acceptance in a strange land after years of uncertainty and fear. Some refugee advocates felt the feel-good news coverage amounted to a massive Internet "selfie" in which Canada's admiration for its own response to the Syrian crisis threatened to overshadow the narratives of the Syrians themselves.[74]

Canadian support for the new Liberal government's response to the refugee crisis remained strong more than a year after Alan Kurdi's death called the nation to action. A Nanos Research survey, conducted between 28 April and 3 May 2016, found that 68 per cent of Canadians supported the government's overall response to the Syrian crisis, while 30 per cent were opposed or somewhat opposed to it.[75] A year later, Canadians remained similarly split on the issue of Syrian refugee resettlement. An Angus Reid Institute poll in February 2017 determined that 25 per cent of Canadians thought their government should have followed the example of US President Donald Trump, when he signed an executive order indefinitely banning the resettlement of Syrian refugees in the United States, as part of a move to also bar people from seven Muslim-majority countries in the Middle East from entering the country.[76] While some Canadians expressed concern over both the speed and number of Syrian refugees being resettled, nearly 58 per cent of Canadians continued to endorse the Syrian project.[77]

Overall, Canadians have worked tirelessly to assist Syrian refugees and their sponsors. In the process they breathed new energy and life into what had previously been a waning private refugee sponsorship system. So far, Canadian support for private sponsorships has outpaced the government's own resettlement efforts, and extra resources have had to be deployed to meet the growing public demand to process and resettle privately sponsored refugees.[78] Canadians have forced their own government to open Canada's doors wider.

It is an example that has not gone unnoticed internationally. As the volunteer communications director with Lifeline Syria during its first year of existence, I was inundated with interview requests from foreign news media who were genuinely enthralled by Canada's eagerness to help. Officials from countries as different as Norway, Ireland, the United States, and the United Kingdom also regularly contacted Canadian refugee advocates to see if the Canadian experience might be replicated in their countries.[79] During a visit to Ottawa, Filippo Grandi, the United Nations High Commissioner for Refugees, publicly urged wealthy Western countries to consider replicating Canada's public and private refugee sponsorship programs. "We think it is an important model that can be exported with some help and some advising and could be very productive," he said.[80] In December 2016, Canada and the UNHCR cosponsored a meeting in Ottawa to showcase Canada's private refugee sponsorship program as a potential model for other countries.[81] The conference had ninety participants, including representatives from Argentina, Australia, Brazil, Chile, Germany, New Zealand, the United Kingdom, and the United States.

CONCLUSION

Canada has a national ethic of welcoming refugees, even when our friends and allies may be reluctant to act. It was symbolic, therefore, that newly elected Prime Minister Justin Trudeau greeted the first planeload of Syrian refugees to reach Canada, in December 2015, with hugs and handshakes, while a year later, one of President Trump's first acts as president was to ban the resettlement of Syrian refugees in the United States indefinitely.

As a result of the Syrian refugee crisis, Canadians have rediscovered their compassion and the usefulness of private refugee sponsorship. The death of Alan Kurdi became a politicized tragedy that played a significant role in the 2015 federal general election, and it drew attention to the previous Conservative government's restrictive refugee policies. Those policies limited the resettlement of refugees and subjected sponsors to prolonged delays, annual quotas, and uncertainty. This, combined with the Conservative government's meagre attempt to resettle fewer than 300 government-assisted refugees, infuriated Syrian Canadians, who felt shut out and unable to help relatives and friends who were in urgent need of it. But it also angered other Canadians, who felt their government should be doing more.

The election debate over Canada's reaction to the Syrian crisis and the new federal government's decision to resettle significant numbers of refugees in a relatively short period of time gained Canada significant international attention. But more importantly, it allowed Canadians to rediscover and re-experience the success of the 1978 to 1980

Indochinese refugee movement. A new generation of Canadians were introduced to the potential and propriety of private refugee sponsorship. At a time when governments are reluctant to assume new responsibilities for refugees, Canada's private sponsorship program offers civil society a template for taking the lead.

Many of the lessons of the Indochinese refugee crisis of 1979 can be applied to the Syrian crisis.[82] Public support for private sponsorship still has the potential to outstrip the government's resettlement efforts, despite an approval process that is long, complex, tedious, and frustratingly uncertain. One significant difference during the first four years of the Syrian crisis, however, was the Conservative government's deliberate attempt to shift the burden of Syrian refugee resettlement onto private sponsors without prior consultation or subsequent assistance. In 2013, when it set its first target for helping Syrian refugees, the Conservative government assigned 85 per cent of the load to private sponsorship groups that were already labouring under a huge backlog of cases, annual caps, and long government processing delays. Under the new Liberal government, the emphasis has been on rapidly resettling 25,000 government-assisted refugees and temporarily lifting limits on privately sponsored refugees. It is still too early to know what final role private sponsorships will play in the Syrian crisis, since processing delays and staff shortages have continued to push many private sponsorship resettlements a year or two into the future.[83]

Since Alan Kurdi's death, governments have struggled to cope with public demands for increased private sponsorships. When the Liberal government met its initial target of 25,000 refugee resettlements in February 2016, private sponsors became worried that the government's commitment to process their applications was waning. Some were outraged when told they would have to wait until 2017 for their sponsored refugees to be cleared to come to Canada.[84] Those frustrations stand in stark contrast to the rapid, flexible, and highly successful resettlement process that took place in 1979 to 1980, when Canada resettled 60,000 Indochinese refugees in just under eighteen months. During the "boat people" crisis, private sponsorship was a new and evolving project. During the Syrian crisis, Canada's private sponsorship system has suffered from a lack of consultation, staff shortages, and a bureaucratic rigidity that may, perhaps, be predictable in a program that is thirty-eight years old. Still, governments will need to find ways to respond to the Canadian public's increased willingness to privately sponsor refugees. If it does not, the viability of the entire process may be threatened. Restrictions on who can be spon- sored, how many, and from where, combined with burdensome bureaucracy and delays, threaten to undermine one of the most suc- cessful refugee resettlement programs in history.

Mark Twain is reputed to have quipped: "History doesn't repeat itself but it often rhymes." Canada's response to the Syrian refugee cri- sis appears to support that observation. Canadians have turned to their past to cope with a crisis in the present, and the result will cer- tainly shape the country's future.

The Canadian response to the Syrian refugee crisis has gone through a cycle that ranged from casual indifference to intense con- cern. But, as in 1978, it finally settled on private refugee sponsorship as a solution that addressed both immediate humanitarian needs and our national ambitions.

Since 1978, Canada's privately sponsored refugee program has reset- tled more than 200,000 refugees, and these refugees, according to a government study released in 2007, tend to become self-supporting far more quickly than government-assisted refugees.[85] Canadians have repeatedly taken in large numbers of refugees, and rather than being a burden on the country, they have consistently become enthusiastic contributors to Canada. At its core, private refugee sponsorship is an exercise in nation building. In addition to rescuing refugees, Canadi- ans reap the benefits of cross-cultural exchanges and opening a win- dow onto a future filled with promise.

James Nguyen, a Toronto logistics expert, was five years old when his family fled Vietnam aboard a small boat in the fall of 1980. After spending six months in a squalid refugee camp in Malaysia, he and his family were resettled in Canada as part of the privately sponsored refugee program. Now a university graduate and successful business- man, he was among the first volunteers to help Lifeline Syria sponsor Syrian refugees. Along with several other former Vietnamese refugees- turned-Canadians, he launched Vietnamese Canadians for Lifeline Syria and raised funds to sponsor three Syrian families.

"We know what it is like to be refugees," he said.[86]

That's another Canadian tradition: paying it forward – going back to the future.

NOTES

1 Craig Silverman, "How the Photos of Alan Kurdi Changed the Conversation from 'Migrants' to 'Refugees,'" BuzzFeed News, 14 December 2015, https://www.buzzfeed.com/craigsilverman/how-the-photos-of-alan-kurdi-spread-online.

2 "IOM Counts 3,771 Migrant Fatalities in Mediterranean in 2015," International Organization for Migration, 5 January 2016, http://www.iom.int/news/iom-counts-3771-migrant-fatalities-mediterranean-2015.

3 Adam Withnall, "Aylan Kurdi's Story: How a Small Syrian Child Came to Be Washed up on a Beach in Turkey," Independent, 3 September 2015, http://www.independent.co.uk/news/world/europe/aylan-kurdi-s-story-how-a-small-syrian-child-came-to-be-washed-up-on-a-beach-in-turkey-10484588.html.

4 Adnan R. Khan, "Alan Kurdi's Father on His Family Tragedy: 'I Should Have Died with Them,'" Guardian, 22 December 2015, https://www.theguardian.com/world/2015/dec/22/abdullah-kurdi-father-boy-on-beach-alan-refugee-tragedy.

5 Mark MacKinnon, "'I Was Only Hoping to Provide a Better Life for My Children,' Father of Drowned Migrant Boy Says," Globe and Mail, 3 September 2015, http://www.theglobeandmail.com/news/world/they-died-in-my-arms-father-of-drowned-migrant-boy-speaks-out/article26207543.

6 Patrick Kingsley and Safak Timur, "Stories of 2015: How Alan Kurdi's Death Changed the World," Guardian, 31 December 2015, https://www.theguardian.com/world/2015/dec/31/alan-kurdi-death-canada-refugee-policy-syria-boy-beach-turkey-photo.

7 Canadian Press, "Father of Drowned Syrian Boy Alan Kurdi Blames Canada for Death of Wife and Son," CBC, 11 September 2015, http://www.cbc.ca/news/world/father-of-drowned-syrian-boy-alan-kurdi-blames-canada-for-death-of-wife-and-son-1.3223846.

8 "Canada Says It Never Denied a Refugee Application for Alan Kurdi and His Family," National Post, 3 September 2015, http://news.nationalpost.com/news/canada/canadian-politics/chris-alexander-suspends-campaign-after-news-that-canada-rejected-drowned-boys-refugee-application.

9 Peter Goodspeed, "Canada Slow to Respond to Syrian Refugee Crisis," Toronto Star, 19 September 2014, https://www.thestar.com/news/atkinsonseries/2014/09/22/canada_slow_to_respond_to_syrian_refugee_crisis.html. See also Yamina Tsalamlal, "Amnesty Accuses Ottawa of Dragging Its Heels on Syrian Refugee Crisis," iPolitics, 5 December 2014, http://ipolitics.ca/2014/12/05/amnesty-accuses-ottawa-of-dragging-its-heels-on-syrian-refugee-crisis; and

Lee Berthiaume, "Government Faces Questions About Anti-Muslim Bias over Syrian Refugees," *Ottawa Citizen*, 12 December 2014, http://ottawacitizen.com/news/politics/government-faces-questions-about-anti-muslim-bias-over-syrian-refugees.

10 Goodspeed, "Canada Slow to Respond."

11 Peter Goodspeed, "Why Has Canada Only Taken in 200 Syrian Refugees?" *Toronto Star*, 19 September 2014, https://www.thestar.com/news/atkinsonseries/2014/09/22/delay_delay_delay.html.

12 "Syrian Refugees Meet Sweden's Open Arms," United Nations Regional Information Centre for Western Europe, 24 February 2014, https://www.unric.org/en/un-newsletter/29064-swedens-open-arms.

13 Agence France-Presse (AFP), "Germany on Course to Accept One Million Refugees in 2015," *Guardian*, 8 December 2015, https://www.theguardian.com/world/2015/dec/08/germany-on-course-to-accept-one-million-refugees-in-2015.

14 Karissa Donkin, "Veteran Journalist Peter Goodspeed Wins Atkinson Fellowship," *Toronto Star*, 13 June 2013, https://www.thestar.com/news/gta/2013/06/13/veteran_journalist_peter_goodspeed_wins_atkinson_fellowship.html.

15 Balanced Refugee Reform Act, SC 2010, ch. 8; Protecting Canada's Immigration System Act, SC 2012, ch. 17.

16 "CCR Decries Dramatic Drop in Refugees Resettled to Canada," Canadian Council for Refugees, 7 March 2013, http://ccrweb.ca/en/bulletin/13/03/07.

17 "A Statistical Profile of Government-Assisted Refugees," Social Research and Demonstration Corporation, 1 May 2002, www.srdc.org/uploads/statistical_profile.pdf.

18 Parliament of Canada, "Assistance for Government-Sponsored Refugees, Chosen Abroad," Library of Parliament Research Publications, 29 August 2014, http://www.lop.parl.gc.ca/content/lop/ResearchPublications/2011-94-e.htm.

19 "2008 Global Trends: Refugees, Asylum-Seekers, Returnees, Internally Displaced and Stateless Persons," United Nations High Commissioner for Refugees, 2009, 16, http://www.unhcr.org/statistics/country/4a375c426/2008-global-trends-refugees-asylum-seekers-returnees-internally-displaced.html.

20 Josh Wingrove, "Refugee Claims Hit 'Historic Low' as Ottawa's Policy Faces Fresh Criticism," *Globe and Mail*, 22 January 2014, http://www.theglobeandmail.com/news/politics/refugee-claims-hit-historic-low-as-ottawas-policy-faces-fresh-criticism/article16461486.

21 Adrian Edwards, "Global Forced Displacement Hits Record High," United Nations High Commission for Refugees, 20 June 2016, http://www.unhcr

.org/news/latest/2016/6/5763b65a4/global-forced-displacement-hits-record-high.html.

22 "Asylum Trends 2013: Levels and Trends in Industrialized Countries," United Nations High Commissioner for Refugees, 3, www.refworld.org/docid /532c325c4.html.

23 Audrey Macklin, "Disappearing Refugees: Reflections on the Canada–US Safe Third Country Agreement," *Columbia Human Rights Law Review* 36 (2005): 365-426. See also James Bissett, "Abusing Canada's Generosity and Ignoring Genuine Refugees: An Analysis of Current and Still-needed Reforms to Canada's Refugee and Immigration System," Frontier Centre for Public Policy, 28 October 2010, https://fcpp.org/2010/10/28/media-release-abusing-canadas-generosity-and-ignoring-genuine-refugees-an-analysis-of-current-and-still-needed-reforms-to-canadas-refugee-and-immigration-system; and Martin Collacott, "Canada's Immigration Policy: The Need for Major Reform," Public Policy Sources, No. 64, Fraser Institute, 2003, https://www.fraserinstitute.org/sites/default/files/CanadasImmigration Policy.pdf.

24 "Monitoring Report: Canada–United States 'Safe Third Country' Agreement," United Nations High Commissioner for Refugees," 2006, www.unhcr.org/home/PROTECTION/455b2cca4.pdf. See also Efrat Arbel and Alletta Brenner, "Bordering on Failure: Canada-U.S. Border Policy and the Politics of refugee Exclusion," Harvard Immigration and Refugee Law Clinical Program, Harvard Law School, 2013, http://harvardimmigration clinic.files.wordpress.com/2013/11/bordering-on-failure-harvard-immigration-and-refugee-law-clinical-program1.pdf.

25 "Designated Country of Origin Scheme Is Arbitrary, Unfair, and Unconstitutional," Canadian Association of Refugee Lawyers, 14 December 2012, http://www.carl-acaadr.ca/our-work/issues/DCO.

26 "An Interview with Gloria Nafziger and Alex Neve of Amnesty International," Canadian Civil Liberties Association, 19 May 2015, https://ccla.org/an-interview-with-gloria-nafziger-and-alex-neve-of-amnesty-international.

27 Government of Canada, Citizenship and Immigration Canada, "Annual Report to Parliament on Immigration, 2014," 31 October 2014, http://www.cic.gc.ca/english/resources/publications/annual-report-2014.

28 Shauna Labman, "Queue the Rhetoric: Refugees, Resettlement and Reform," *University of New Brunswick Law Journal* 62 (2011): 55–64. See also Alex Neve and Tiisetso Russell, "Hysteria and Discrimination: Canada's Harsh Response to Refugees and Migrants Who Arrive by Sea," *University of New Brunswick Law Journal* 62 (2011): 37–45.

29 Martin Collacott, "Canada's Inadequate Response to Terrorism: The Need for Policy Reform," Fraser Institute Digital Publication, 2006, https://www .fraserinstitute.org/sites/default/files/InadequateResponsetoTerrorism.pdf.

30 Pia Oberoi and Eleanor Taylor-Nicholson, "The Enemy at the Gates: International Borders, Migration and Human Rights," *Laws* 2 (2013): 169–186.

31 Michael Enright, "The Vietnam War: Canada's Role, Part Two – The Boat People," *Rewind*, CBC Radio, 30 April 2012, http://www.cbc.ca/radio/rewind /the-vietnam-war-canada-s-role-part-two-the-boat-people-1.3048026. See also Dara Marcus, "Saving Lives: Canada and the *Hai Hong*," *Bout de Papier* 28, no. 1 (2014): 24–7, available at http://cihs-shic.ca/wp-content/uploads/2014 /07/Saving_Lives_by_Dara_Marcus_bout_de_papier_28_1.pdf.

32 Peter Goodspeed, "GTA Man Once a Vietnamese Refugee Trapped on Boat," *Toronto Star*, 19 September 2014, https://www.thestar.com/news /atkinsonseries/2014/09/22/gta_man_once_a_vietnamese_refugee_trapped _on_boat.html.

33 "The State of the World's Refugees 2000 – Chapter 4: Flight from Indochina," United Nations High Commissioner for Refugees, 2000, 82–83, www.unhcr.org/3ebf9bad0.pdf.

34 Peter Goodspeed, "Can Canada Duplicate Its Boat People Rescue with Syrian Refugees?" *Toronto Star*, 26 September 2014, https://www.thestar.com /news/atkinsonseries/2014/09/26/can_canada_duplicate_its_boat_people _rescue_with_syrian_refugees.html.

35 Goodspeed, "Can Canada Duplicate."

36 Howard Adelman, in an interview with the author, November 2013.

37 Dick Beddoes, "A Rush of Aid," *Globe and Mail*, 27 June 1979, 8.

38 Ron Atkey, "The Indochinese Refugee Movement 1975–80 and the Launch of Canada's Private Refugee Sponsorship Program," (presentation at Channeling Canadian Concerns, a Canadian Immigration Historical Society conference, York University, Toronto, Ontario, 22 November 2013), https://www .youtube.com/watch?v=OYWzIqhg2fs.

39 Government of Canada, Employment and Immigration Canada, "Indochinese Refugees: The Canadian Response, 1979 and 1980," 1982.

40 Ibid.

41 Brian Buckley, *Gift of Freedom: How Ottawa Welcomed the Vietnamese, Cambodian, and Laotian Refugees* (Renfrew, Ontario: General Store Publishing, 2008), 31.

42 Bruce Ward, "We'll Take Them: New Book Tells How a Rookie Ottawa Mayor Rallied the City Behind Project 4000," *Ottawa Citizen*, 30 April 2008.

43 Margaret Daly, "Vietnamese Being Brought to Canada: Boat People Campaign Running Full Steam," *Globe and Mail*, 4 July 1979, 5.

44 Government of Canada, "Indochinese Refugees."

45 Mike Molloy, interview with the author, November 2013 and June 2014.

46 Mike Molloy, interview with the author, June 2014.

47 Flora MacDonald, "Canada's Foreign Policy and Relations" (speech by the secretary of state for external affairs to the Canadian Club of Canada, Montreal, 17 September 1979).

48 Jean-Pierre Hocké, "UNHCR Nansen Refugee Award to the People of Canada" (presentation by the United Nations High Commissioner for Refugees at the National Arts Centre, Ottawa, 1986), https://www.youtube.com/watch?v=U8TF3pt3xK4.

49 Joshua Greenberg, "Opinion Discourse and Canadian Newspapers: The Case of the Chinese 'Boat People." *Canadian Journal of Communication* 25, no. 4 (2000): 517–37, http://www.cjc-online.ca/index.php/journal/article/view/1178/1100.

50 Greenberg, "Opinion Discourse and Canadian Newspapers."

51 Diane Francis, "Refugee Process in This Country Needs Makeover: Boat Incidents an Example of Ottawa's Mismanagement," *National Post*, 13 August 1999, A8.

52 Peter Goodspeed, "Boat People Today May Not Find a Welcome," *Toronto Star*, 27 June 1989, A12; and Peter Goodspeed, "The Last of the Boat People to Be Sent on Their Way," *National Post*, 2 May 2000, A13.

53 Pam Baker, interview ith the author, Hong Kong, April 1994.

54 Susan Schwartz, "Weighing the Cost of Boat People Against World's Woes," *South China Morning Post*, 9 September 2001, http://www.scmp.com/article/357169/weighing-cost-boat-people-against-worlds-woes.

55 Kathleen Marie Whitney, "There Is No Future for Refugees in Chinese Hong Kong," *Boston College Third World Law Journal* 18, no. 1 (1998), 5, http://lawdigitalcommons.bc.edu/twlj/vol18/iss1/2.

56 *Convention Relating to the Status of Refugees*, 189 UNTS 150, entered into force 22 April 1954.

57 "Indefinite Detention and Mandatory Repatriation: The Incarceration of Vietnamese in Hong Kong," Human Rights Watch, 3 December 1991, https://www.hrw.org/reports/pdfs/h/hongkong/hongkong91d.pdf.

58 "Democratic Republic of Congo," Enough Project, 2017, accessed 25 December 2017, https://enoughproject.org/conflicts/congo.

59 "Tsunami of 2004 Fast Facts," CNN, 12 December 2017, http://www.cnn.com/2013/08/23/world/tsunami-of-2004-fast-facts/index.html.

60 Harriet Grant, "UN Agencies 'Broke and Failing' in Face of Ever-Growing Refugee Crisis," *Guardian*, 6 September 2015, https://www.theguardian.com/world/2015/sep/06/refugee-crisis-un-agencies-broke-failing.

61 "Number of Daily Active Facebook Users Worldwide as of 1st Quarter 2018 (In Millions)," Statista: The Statistics Portal, 2018, https://www.statista.com/statistics/346167/facebook-global-dau; and Craig Zevin, "Pinterest, Google, & Instagram Big Winners as Facebook Share of Visits Falls 8% in 2017," Shareholic, https://blog.shareaholic.com/search-engine-social-media-traffic-trends-report-2017.

62 Drew DeSilver, "Facebook Is a News Source for Many, but Only Incidentally," Pew Research Center, Fact Tank: News in the Numbers, 4 February 2014, http://www.pewresearch.org/fact-tank/2014/02/04/facebook-is-a-news-source-for-many-but-only-incidentally.

63 Jonathan Gatehouse, "His Name Was Alan Kurdi," *Maclean's*, 3 September 2015, http://www.macleans.ca/news/world/his-name-was-alan-kurdi.

64 Howard Adelman, "Canada a Peaceable Kingdom in a World of Dramatic Change: Refugees 1979 – Part 1V on The Indo-Chinese Refugee Private Sponsorship Program," Howard Adelman (personal blog), 14 May 2015, https://howardadelman.com/tag/private-refugee-sponsorship.

65 "Launch of Syrian Refugee Settlement Initiative in Toronto," press release, Lifeline Syria, 17 June 2015, http://lifelinesyria.ca/press-release-june-17th-2015.

66 Ratna Omidvar, and Joseph Yu Kai Wong, "Let's Bring 1,000 Syrian Refugees to the GTA," *Toronto Star*, 17 June 2015, https://www.thestar.com/opinion/commentary/2015/06/17/lets-bring-1000-syrian-refugees-to-the-gta.html.

67 Jordan Press, "Conservative Campaign Promise Would Bring in 10,000 Iraqi and Syrian Refugees," *Globe and Mail*, 10 August 2015, http://www.theglobeandmail.com/news/politics/conservative-campaign-promise-would-bring-in-10000-iraqi-and-syrian-refugees/article25902909.

68 Sonja Puzic, "NDP, Liberals Say Harper 'Failed' to Live up to Refugee Promises," CTV News, 2 September 2015, http://www.ctvnews.ca/politics/election/ndp-liberals-say-harper-failed-to-live-up-to-refugee-promises-1.2544948.

69 Mike MacDonald, "'How to Sponsor a Syrian?' Is Canada's Top Google Query on Refugees," CBC News, 4 September 2015, http://www.cbc.ca/news/trending/how-to-sponsor-a-refugee-syria-canada-1.3215814.

70 Antonia Zerbisias, "Sponsor Syrian Refugee – Canada's Top Google Search: Sponsoring a Syrian Refugee Is All the Rage in Canada," Al Jazeera, 19 January 2016, http://www.aljazeera.com/indepth/opinion/2016/01/sponsor-syrian-refugee-canada-top-google-search-160118071153769.html.

71 "Updates on Lifeline Syria Processes," Lifeline Syria, 29 July 2016, http://lifelinesyria.ca/updates-on-lifeline-syria-processes.

72 Jodi Kantor and Catrin Einhorn, "Refugees Encounter a Foreign Word: Wel-

come," *New York Times*, 1 July 2016, http://www.nytimes.com/2016/07/01/
world/americas/canada-syrian-refugees.html.

73 Government of Canada, Immigration, Refugees and Citizenship Canada,
"#WelcomeRefugees: Key Figures," 2017, http://www.cic.gc.ca/english
/refugees/welcome/milestones.asp.

74 Afifa Hashimi, "A Critical Look at Canadian Perspectives on the Global
Refugee Crisis," 22 March 2016, Check Your Head, http://checkyourhead
.org/blog/a-critical-look-at-canadian-perspectives-on-the-global-refugee-crisis.

75 Michelle Zilio, "Not Enough Resources for Syrian Refugees in Canada:
Poll," *Globe and Mail*, 9 May 2016, http://www.theglobeandmail.com/news
/politics/not-enough-resources-for-syrian-refugees-in-canada-poll/article
29935148.

76 Shawn McCarthy, "Sizable Minority Says Canada Is Accepting Too Many
Refugees: Poll," *Globe and Mail*, 20 February 2017, http://www.theglobe
andmail.com/news/politics/sizable-minority-says-canada-is-accepting-too-
many-refugees-poll/article34087415.

77 Emma Paling, "Refugees in Canada: 1 Quarter Want Trump-Style Ban on
Syrian Refugees," Huffington Post Canada, 20 February 2017, http://www
.huffingtonpost.ca/2017/02/20/canada-syrian-refugees_n_14887314.html.

78 Michelle Zilio, "Sponsors Frustrated by Slowing Pace of Resettling Syrian
Refugees," *Globe and Mail*, 24 March 2016, http://www.theglobeandmail
.com/news/politics/sponsors-frustrated-by-slowing-pace-of-resettling-syrian-
refugees/article29390093.

79 Amber Nasrulla, "Forget Maple Syrup, Hockey & Justin Bieber: Canada's
Best-Known Export Should Be Refugee Policy," Yahoo News, Daily Brew, 31
August 2016, https://ca.news.yahoo.com/forget-maple-syrup-hockey-justin-
bieber-124041306.html.

80 Stephanie Levitz, "Canada's Refugee Effort Hailed as Model for World by
Head of UN Agency," CBC News, 21 March 2016, http://www.cbc.ca/news
/politics/un-refugee-private-government-sponsor-1.3501400.

81 "Global Refugee Sponsorship Initiative Promotes Canada's Private Refugee
Sponsorship Model," United Nations High Commissioner for Refugees,
16 December 2016, http://www.unhcr.org/news/press/2016/12/58539e524
/global-refugee-sponsorship-initiative-promotes-canadas-private-refugee
.html.

82 Naomi Alboim, "Lessons Learned from the Indochinese and Syrian Refugee
Movements," Policy Options, 18 May 2016, http://policyoptions.irpp.org
/magazines/may-2016/lessons-learned-from-the-indochinese-and-syrian-
refugee-movements.

83 As of 29 January 2017, 40,081 Syrian refugees have been resettled in Canada

since 4 November 2015. Of those, 21,876 were government-assisted refugees, 3,931 were blended visa office referrals, and 14,274 – or just 36 per cent – were privately sponsored refugees. Government of Canada, "#Welcome Refugees: Key Figures," https://www.canada.ca/en/immigration-refugees-citizenship/services/refugees/welcome-syrian-refugees/key-figures.html.

84 Zilio, "Sponsors Frustrated by Slowing Pace."
85 Government of Canada, Citizenship and Immigration Canada, "Summative Evaluation of the Private Sponsorship of Refugees Program, Final Report," 2007, http://www.cic.gc.ca/english/resources/evaluation/psrp/psrp-summary .asp.
86 Debra Black, "Vietnamese Refugees Prepare to Sponsor Syrian Families," *Toronto Star*, 16 December 2015, https://www.thestar.com/news /immigration/2015/12/16/vietnamese-refugees-prepare-to-sponsor-syrian-families.html.

11

Scoping the Range of Initiatives for Protecting the Employment and Labour Rights of Illegalized Migrants in Canada and Abroad

Charity-Ann Hannan and Harald Bauder

In an era of the increasing criminalization of migration in Canada and abroad, key civic and political actors are looking for alternative ways to regulate migration. They are developing concrete counter measures to grant safety to people fleeing war and oppression, and to offer security to migrants who are denied rights and belonging.[1] One concrete measure is the "sanctuary city," a designation in which cities provide illegalized migrants with access to city services – including, but not limited to, libraries, health clinics, schools, emergency shelters, recreation programs, and food banks – without fear of being reported to immigration enforcement authorities.[2] In these cities, municipal councils and administrations have rejected national policies and practices of exclusion and seek to provide city services to all residents, including those without federal immigration status. These cities, however, do not provide illegalized migrants with access to services and programs that protect workers' employment and labour rights – which fall under federal, provincial, and territorial jurisdictions in Canada, and federal and state jurisdictions in the United States. Despite the implementation of sanctuary cities, many illegalized migrants may therefore continue to be exploited by their employers.[3]

In the US, for example, illegalized migrant workers are tied to local employers, forced into accepting inequitable remuneration for their

Charity-Ann Hannan and Harald Bauder

work, and kept in low-paying positions that citizens would not accept.[4] Similarly, illegalized migrant workers in Canada are paid less than their "legal" counterparts and are disproportionately hired into precarious, nonunionized, part-time, and seasonal jobs that lack benefits.[5] Unequal access to employment insurance, health care, social services, and driver's licenses further aggravates their vulnerable position in Canadian labour markets. To provide protection to this vulnerable group of workers, policy changes are required at the provincial scale. Activists and researchers are therefore advocating for a "sanctuary province."[6] How to achieve a sanctuary province while respecting federal policies, however, remains unclear. To gain an understanding of how to move towards a policy that extends employment and labour rights to illegalized migrant workers, this chapter examines the illegalization process and illegalized migrants' employment and labour experiences, and explores the policies, services, and programs being implemented in cities and regions in Canada, the US, and the UK that aim to provide illegalized migrant workers with equitable access to employment and labour rights.

Several terms are currently in use to identify migrants who do not have the state's permission to reside within its boundaries, including illegal, undocumented, precarious, non-status, irregular, and unauthorized migrants.[7] We use the term "illegalized migrant" because this term "shifts the emphasis away from the individual and towards the recognition of a societal process that situates immigrants in positions of precarity and illegality."[8] The illegalization of migrants has a long history in Canada. The Immigration Act of 1869 identified specific criteria that migrants had to meet in order to obtain documentation entitling them to legally reside in Canada.[9] More recently, Canada's 1973 Non-Immigrant Employment Authorization Program (NIEAP) and subsequent temporary foreign worker program (TFWP) established a new class of temporary residents with limited pathways to permanent residency. Many TFWs thus become illegalized if their contracts get lost in bureaucratic red tape or if they overstay their temporary permits.[10] Given the increase in the number of temporary foreign workers (TFWs) in Canada, greater restrictions to refugee admission, and other policy changes at the federal level,[11] the number of illegalized migrants is also likely on the rise.[12] Recent estimates suggest that as many as 200,000 illegalized migrants live in Toronto alone, with another 200,000 living with "precarious" status.[13]

As the problem of illegalization grows, activist and civic organizations are raising awareness about employment and labour violations that illegalized migrants are facing.[14] While populist voices blame illegalized migrants for stealing jobs from citizens, driving down wages, and draining welfare systems,[15] research findings indicate that it is employers' exploitation and abuse of illegalized migrant workers that is driving down wages. They further indicate that the illegalizing of migrants by federal states provides employers with a readily exploitable workforce.[16]

The next section of this chapter provides important background information on the illegalization of migrants in Canada, illegalized migrant workers' employment and labour experiences, and how employers benefit from exploiting and abusing illegalized migrant workers. Thereafter, we outline our guiding questions and methods. In the subsequent section, we discuss potential policies, programs, and practices available to provinces and territories that aim to provide illegalized migrant workers with equitable access to employment and labour rights.

ILLEGALIZED MIGRANTS: THE MAKING OF AN EASILY EXPLOITABLE AND DISPOSABLE WORKFORCE

While employers in Canada and other Western countries have a long history of exploiting immigrants during periods of heightened economic competition, employers have most recently turned towards exploiting illegalized migrant workers. After examining the low-wage labour market in the US, for example, Morales found that employers prefer undocumented workers to TFWs during phases of rapid industrial transformation because their lack of legal protection prevents them from unionizing and/or protesting wage erosion.[17] De Genova argued that "the category 'illegal alien' is a profoundly useful and profitable one that effectively serves to create and sustain a legally vulnerable – and hence, relatively tractable and thus 'cheap' – reserve of labor."[18] Bauder similarly concluded that "the distinction that nation-states create where otherwise no differences between people exist denies many migrants citizenship, status and/or rights and subsequently exposes them disproportionately to economic exploitation."[19] Although employing illegalized migrants can be of value to profit-motivated employers,[20] the illegalization of migrants creates barriers for the economic security of these migrants. Schierup et al., for example, argue that:

[e]xclusivist migration policies, together with the "irregularization" of citizenship have forged a globally fragmented and disposable labour force in industry, entertainment, hospitality, care-work, cleaning, and domestic services subject to long hours of dangerous, demanding, demeaning, and dirty work in permanent fear of dismissal and, potentially deportation. These workers are exceedingly vulnerable and many basic labour, citizenship, and human rights simply do not apply to them. It is a precarious workforce present globally; segmented and discriminated against through ascription of race and ethnicity and also gender through insertion into specific sections of the local and national labour markets.[21]

Support for this argument can be found in the federal immigration laws implemented in Canada, the United States, and the United Kingdom (in 1976, 1986, and 1996, respectively) that criminalize the employment of illegalized migrants through employer sanctions. One of the main purposes of these laws was to deter employers from hiring illegalized migrants in order to encourage migrants to return to their countries of citizenship. Canada's Immigration Act of 1976 stated:

Every person who knowingly engages in any employment [of] any person, other than a Canadian citizen or permanent resident, who is not authorized under this Act to engage in that employment is guilty of an offence and liable (a) on conviction on indictment, to a fine not exceeding five thousand dollars or to imprisonment for a term not exceeding two years or to both; or (b) on summary conviction, to a fine not exceeding one thousand dollars or to imprisonment for a term not exceeding six months or to both.[22]

Employer sanctions were also included in Canada's 2001 Immigration and Refugee Protection Act (IRPA), which states "every person commits an offence who ... employs a foreign national in a capacity in which the foreign national is not authorized under this Act to be employed."[23] Penalties for violating this law were increased: "(a) on conviction to indictment, to a fine of not more than $50,000 or to imprisonment for a term of not more than two years, or to both; or

(b) on summary conviction, to a fine of not more than $10,000 or to imprisonment for a term of not more than six months, or to both."[24]

The 1986 United States Immigration Reform and Control Act (IRCA) and the United Kingdom's 1993 Asylum and Immigration Appeals Act (AIAA) include similar employer sanctions.[25] Instead of being deterred from hiring illegalized migrant workers, however, employers continued to employ and exploit them. After 9/11, employers began responding to illegalized migrant workers who tried to unionize, fight for wages owed to them, or fight for decent pay, by reporting them to enforcement agencies that would later arrest and/or deport them.

This practice began after 9/11 as countries strengthened their enforcement agencies. Prior to 9/11, for example, the Royal Canadian Mounted Police (RCMP) was responsible for the enforcement of immigration entry and exit policies in Canada. By 2003, a separate body, called the Canada Border Services Agency (CBSA) was created to ensure "the security and prosperity of Canada by managing the access of people and goods to and from Canada."[26] CBSA's responsibilities include administering federal immigration legislation, detaining people who may pose a threat to Canada, and removing people who are inadmissible to Canada.[27] In the United States, the Immigration and Naturalization Service (INS) was responsible for enforcing employer sanctions between 1986 and 2003. In 2003, the Department of Homeland Security (DHS) assumed this responsibility, and Immigration and Customs Enforcement (ICE) was created to enforce employer sanctions through worksite raids.[28]

In the United Kingdom, the United States, and Canada, employer sanctions have led to an increase in the number of workplace raids since the late 2000s.[29] In the UK, these raids have targeted, in particular, ethnic minority-owned businesses.[30] Between 2006 and 2008, the DHS in the United States also increased enforcement actions at workplaces, resulting in the detainment and/or deportation of hundreds of illegalized migrant workers.[31] In Canada, the CBSA conducted the largest workplace raid in the country's history in April 2009.[32]

Workplace raids and the criminalization of migrant workers infringe on illegalized migrants' ability to organize and are associated with declining wages and labour standards.[33] The recent legislative changes are especially at odds with long-standing international efforts to address the illegalization of migrants. The International Labour

Organization (ILO) and the United Nations adopted conventions in
1975 and 1990, respectively, to extend labour and employment rights
to illegalized migrant workers. The ILO's 1975 Convention concerning Migrations in Abusive Conditions and the Promotion of Equality
of Opportunity and Treatment of Migrant Workers advocates for the
equality of treatment for undocumented migrant workers and their
families with respect to rights arising out of past employment, in
regards to remuneration, social security, and other benefits.[34] Similarly, the UN's 1990 International Convention on the Protection of
the Rights of All Migrant Workers and Members of Their Families
declares that states are to provide illegalized migrants with a range of
civil, social, and labour rights, including "rights to enforce employment contracts against employers, to participate in trade unions, and
to enjoy protection of wage, hour and health regulations in the workplace."[35] The Convention further states that "employers shall not be
relieved of any legal or contractual obligations, nor shall their obligations be limited in any manner by reason of any ... irregularity"[36] in
the migrant workers' stay or employment. Unfortunately, Canada,
Britain, and the United States have not ratified either convention,
which demonstrates these countries' unwillingness to formally extend
labour and employment rights to illegalized migrants.[37]

In addition, the criminalization of employing illegalized migrants
through employer sanctions, in conjunction with stricter enforcement policies and practices, has unintentionally created an environment that enables employers to exploit illegalized migrants based on
their lack of legal status. In the United States, the enforcement of
employer sanctions has made illegalized migrant workers "vulnerable to employer abuse by creating a perverse set of incentives for
employers to exploit them and by deterring undocumented workers
from speaking out against this abuse."[38] In this case, the prioritization
of immigration laws over employment laws has created "a perverse
economic incentive for employers to employ undocumented workers, because employers can deny them the most basic workplace protections and escape responsibility by simply calling for an immigration inspection."[39]

To address the exploitation of illegalized migrant workers, activists
and researchers have advocated for comprehensive regularization and
legalization programs.[40] Canada, the United States, and European
countries have a long history of regularization and legalization programs.[41] Canada's regularization programs include the Chinese

Adjustment Statement Program (1960 to 1972), section 34 of the 1967 immigration laws that allowed visitors to apply to be permanent residents from within Canada, the Immigration Appeal Board Act (1967 to 1973), the Adjustment of Status Program (1973), the Minister's Review Committee (1983 to 1985), the Deferred Removal Orders Class (DROC) (1994 to 1998), and Humanitarian and Compassionate (H&C) Applications (2004).[42]

Regularization and legalization programs, however, can also have unintended negative consequences for the very people they aim to help. While these programs may improve the labour market experiences and outcomes of the workers who become regularized, they often worsen the labour market outcomes and experiences of migrants who remain illegalized. For example, after the implementation of the IRCA in the United States in 1986,[43] employers began to pay illegalized migrants less than legal migrants and citizens for the same work.[44] Employers also began to threaten illegalized migrant workers, saying that they would contact migration authorities if the workers reported labour violations or made efforts to unionize.[45] Instead of discouraging migrants to live and work in the United States, "the net effect of US immigration and border policies enacted during the period from 1985 to 2010 was to increase the vulnerability and undercut bargaining power at the low end of the US labor force, most notably dominated by immigrant workers."[46] In their more recent forms, regularization and legalization programs are therefore seen as failing to provide the solution to exploitative practices by employers towards illegalized migrant workers.

In Canada, provincial and territorial employment and labour laws seek to protect all workers.[47] In Ontario, for example, the Employment Standards Act (ESA), Occupational Health and Safety Act (OHSA), Labour Relations Act (LRA), and the Ontario Human Rights Code (OHRC) should therefore apply to all workers, independent of migration status. Similar legislations protect workers in the US and Britain, but increasingly restrictive federal immigration laws and strengthened federal enforcement agencies are preventing and/or deterring illegalized migrants – who risk being arrested, detained, and deported – from accessing these rights. To address this shortcoming at the federal level, some municipalities and states in the US have passed their own laws or initiated their own policies and practices.[48] In Europe and Australia, too, sub-state levels of government are challenging national policies and practices that illegalize migrants.[49] Canadian municipalities are following suit, with Toronto and Hamilton becoming sanctuary cities in 2013 and 2014, respectively, followed more recently by Vancouver, London (Ontario), and Montreal.

GUIDING QUESTIONS AND SCOPE OF THE STUDY

Federal immigration laws in Canada, the US, and the UK are ultimately responsible for illegalizing migrants, but many government policies, programs, and services fall under provincial or territorial jurisdiction. This gives provinces, territories, and regions the capacity to enact policies and implement programs to protect illegalized migrant workers from exploitation, support their equitable employment, and provide them with other important government services (including heath care, housing services, and post-secondary education). Below, we take a look beyond Canada to examine the policies, programs, and services that municipalities, regions, and states have implemented to prevent employers from exploiting illegalized migrant workers and to provide these workers with equitable access to employment and labour rights. The following questions guide this investigation:

1 What programs, policies, and services have been created (or are being considered) by municipalities, regions, and states to prevent employers from exploiting and abusing illegalized migrant workers and to provide illegalized migrant workers with equitable access to employment and labour rights?
2 How successful have these programs, policies, and services been?
3 Which programs, policies, and services would be feasible for Canadian provinces and territories to adopt?

To answer these questions, we conducted a scoping review of the English-language literature.[50] We included peer-reviewed academic literature, non-peer-reviewed grey literature (e.g., community-based research reports, discussion papers or reviews, government documents, theses, information guides, and unpublished manuscripts), and labour market and immigration policies and legislation in the analysis. Due to 1978 marking the beginning of the public and academic discourse on "illegalized" migrants,[51] we limited the analysis to literature published after 1977. To identify items to be included in the analysis, we used the following keywords and combinations: undocumented, irregular status, precarious status, alien(s), illegal(s), unauthorized, informal labour, and non-status. These keywords were crossed with the keywords immigrant(s), migrant(s), and newcomer(s). Additionally, we used the third-level keywords work(ers), employees, and employers. These keywords were also crossed with "labour market policy" and "immigration policy." Publications that contained two or more keywords from each of the four groups were included in the sample for analysis. We also consulted reference lists from articles and public media sources (e.g., newspaper articles) to identify additional and supplementary literature. We then conducted a narrative review of our dataset, which included the identification of common themes among the findings, and the categorizing of information according to themes.

FINDINGS

Our analysis revealed that municipal, regional, and/or state governments in Canada, the US, and the UK have implemented a variety of programs, policies, and services to prevent employers from exploiting and abusing illegalized migrant workers and to provide these workers with equitable access to employment and labour rights. These can be grouped into seven categories: (1) memorandums of understanding (MOUs), (2) identification cards and driver's licenses, (3) noncooperation, (4) collaboration with civic organizations, (5) anti-retaliation policies, (6) building public support, and (7) systemic inclusion.

MOUs and Formalized Collaboration Agreements

While examining a series of incidents that occurred in the United States between 2005 and 2008, immigration lawyers found that immigration enforcement had trumped labour rights. These incidents involved illegalized migrants being fired, arrested, detained, and deported through the actions of ICE, which (1) provided enforcement on behalf of employers, their surrogates, and other police agencies; (2) conducted immigration-focused surveillance in the midst of labour disputes; (3) provided enforcement despite having full knowledge of an ongoing labour dispute; (4) engaged in subterfuge to carry out enforcement; and (5) interfered with the administration of justice by arresting workers on courthouse steps.[52] One study, for example, found that an employer told two employees who were trying to recover wages owed to them that he "will call immigration if they continue with their case." The employees continued with their case, and shortly after receiving the threat, one was detained by immigration officials and deported.[53]

In response to such labour rights violations, the DHS and the Department of Labor (DOL) updated their interagency MOU, which enumerates how the agencies balance their distinct and sometimes contradictory immigration- and employment-enforcement efforts.[54] Specifically, the MOU prohibits ICE from conducting immigration-related investigations while DOL is performing worksite investigations over labour disputes. The MOU also isolates information about potentially unauthorized workers from ICE, protects the agencies from manipulative outside parties such as employers, and limits enforcement activities so that the actions of agencies do not conflict with each other's goals. The MOU further protects employers from simultaneous worksite and immigration investigations.[55]

To effectively protect illegalized migrants from abusive employers, any MOU between municipal, federal, and provincial or territorial governments requires strong enforcement mechanisms. The MOU between DHS and DOL, for example, protects against immigration enforcement during a DOL investigation, but it does not similarly preclude enforcement while workers are asserting their rights in other ways, such as pursuing federal litigation. Braker therefore suggests further modifying the MOU to limit immigration enforcement during employment litigation and other agency investigations.[56]

In contrast to the United States, MOUs in Canada have been met with outright public opposition. In February 2015, for example, the "Transportation not Deportation" campaign led to the termination of an MOU between the Vancouver Transit Police and the Pacific Region Enforcement Centre of CBSA, which had increased immigration enforcement. Under this MOU, the Transit Police reported 328 people to CBSA between 2007 and 2013. After the termination of the MOU was announced, activist-scholar Harsha Walia declared that "transit police will not be enforcing immigration policy."[57] Yet this does not necessarily mean that all MOUs are ineffective. Rather, as seen within the United States, MOUs between municipalities, provinces, territories, and states have the potential to be effective if they are created and implemented to protect illegalized migrants from federal immigration authorities.

Non-Cooperation Statements

In addition to conducting workplace raids, federal immigration en-forcement agencies have cooperated with other federal, regional, and municipal departments to conduct public raids. For example, on 14 August 2014, Ontario's Ministry of Transportation cooperated with CBSA to conduct a roadside commercial vehicle inspection, which resulted in the apprehension of twenty-one illegalized migrants who were on their way to work.[58] These raids have made illegalized mi-grants fearful of participating in their communities and accessing ser-vices that require them to leave their homes, such as medical services, city services, police services, and public transportation for commuting to work. Some municipalities, including sanctuary cities, have there-fore stopped partnering with federal immigration agencies that sup-port such raids.

Provinces and territories can end cooperation with federal authori-ties in a similar way. Ontario's transportation minister, for example, announced that his ministry had ended its partnership with CBSA shortly after an investigation into the August 2014 raids, stating that immigration-related raids do not align with the Ministry's mandate.[59] Such non-cooperation policies reduce the possibility of illegalized migrants being arrested while commuting to and from work.

Driver's Authorizations and Identification Cards

The Ontario Ministry of Transportation's announcement in 2014 that it would end its collaboration with CBSA, in which they would iden-tify and hand over illegalized migrants to CBSA during commercial vehicle traffic stops,[60] marked a positive step towards improving the safety of illegalized migrants while they travelled to and from work and/or other destinations. Nevertheless, illegalized migrants in Ontario can remain vulnerable if they are unable to legally obtain per-mission to drive a vehicle. Driver's licenses, in particular, serve as offi-cial identification, which is needed in many situations beyond driving a vehicle.

The lack of access to a driver's license adversely affects the ability of illegalized migrants to negotiate their working conditions, which are "circumscribed by the risks of driving to get to and from work."[61] Being caught driving without a license can result in substantial fines, arrest, detainment, and/or deportation. Illegalized migrants tend to therefore tolerate poor working conditions at a job that is easy to commute to rather than risk a longer commute to a better job.[62] Lacking a driver's license can also prevent illegalized migrants from obtaining jobs that require driving a vehicle.

In the United States, several states have therefore allowed illegalized migrants to obtain driver's authorization cards. These cards "establish that the bearer has passed the necessary test and is allowed to drive,"[63] and must be visibly distinct from a formal driver's license, which can also be used for identification purposes. While the criteria that illegalized migrants must meet to obtain a driver's authorization varies between states, proof of local residency, a taxpayer ID, and/or consular identification is usually required.[64] Many of the driver's authorizations issued to illegalized migrants include a descriptor that states the license is valid for driving only, and "not valid for federal identification, voting, or public benefits purposes," or that it may not be used "to consider an individual's citizenship or immigration status, or as a basis for a criminal investigation, arrest, or detention."[65] Nevertheless, many illegalized migrants choose to obtain a driver's authorization to improve their employment and labour opportunities, and to increase their safety while commuting to work.[66] As of April 2014, illegalized migrants were allowed to have driver's authorizations in ten American states.

In addition to offering a driver's license, provinces and territories can also issue identification cards to illegalized migrants. Municipal ID cards, which are currently available in six US municipalities, make it safer for illegalized migrants to interact with frontline city workers, move around in the city, participate in local commerce, and access municipal facilities, which in turn facilitates their integration into labour markets.[67] To protect the identities and addresses of illegalized migrants who apply for ID cards, Solidarity City Network suggests that there should be clear parameters on the sharing of ID information with federal immigration authorities.[68]

Capacity-Building with Civic Organizations

NGOs, unions, and activist organizations have been raising awareness about the employment and labour rights of illegalized migrant workers and providing support systems for enforcing these rights.[69] In the United States, both the National Employment Law Project (NELP), a nonprofit legal organization, and the Workers Defense Project have played significant roles in conducting and disseminating research that raises awareness of employers' exploitation of illegalized migrant workers and the need for support systems to help these workers enjoy their rights – especially in the construction, food, and meat and poultry industries.[70] In Canada, Justicia for Migrant Workers (J4MW), Caregivers Action Centre, No One Is Illegal, Migrante, and the Migrant Workers Alliance For Change (MWAC) have advocated for migrants' rights as workers' rights. Unions across Canada are also supporting such efforts in addition to raising awareness about the labour market consequences of allowing employers to exploit illegalized migrants.[71]

The Southern Ontario Sanctuary Coalition similarly advocates on behalf of illegalized migrants. The coalition came together in the early 1990s after a number of Eritreans were arguably wrongfully deported. Although the coalition does not advocate for illegalized migrant workers' rights specifically, in 2012 the organization met with over a dozen churches to seek sanctuary for failed refugees fearing deportation. In 2012 alone, there were four cases of sanctuary in the Toronto area.[72]

In addition, NGOs, unions, and activist organizations have recently made considerable gains in raising awareness about the rights of illegalized migrants – reducing their fear of reporting abusive employers to authorities – and providing support systems to help them access these rights. To ensure that this information and these services reach all illegalized migrants, partnerships with government organizations and more funding are required,[73] but it is unclear how to make these partnerships most effective. Further research with NGOs, unions, and activist organizations should be conducted to determine how provinces and territories could help them achieve their goals.

Anti-Retaliation Policies

In addition to exploiting illegalized migrant workers, employers have retaliated against illegalized migrant workers who report labour and employment rights violations to the authorities, or who attempt to unionize, by firing them or reporting them to immigration enforcement authorities.[74] Even though illegalized migrants are more likely than legal residents and citizens to face labour and employment rights violations (e.g., injuries), they are less likely to report these violations to the authorities due to employer retaliation.[75] To protect illegalized migrant workers from employer retaliation, municipalities and regions have implemented anti-retaliation policies.[76]

For example, California has passed several bills to broaden anti-retaliation policies.[77] These laws prohibit employers from retaliating, discriminating, or taking adverse action against an employee or a prospective employee for exercising any right under the state's Labor Code, filing or participating in a complaint with the California Division of Labor Standards Enforcement (DLSE), whistleblowing, or participating in political activity or a civil suit against an employer.[78] Penalties have also been increased for retaliation, including fines up to US$10,000 per employee for each instance to be awarded to the employee(s) who suffered the violation. The new laws also broaden protections for illegalized migrants by including penalties for employers who report, or threaten to report, their employees' migrant status after they have exercised a labour right. It further prohibits unfair immigration-related practices, including improper requests for documents to prove work authorization, threatening to file a false police report, or contacting immigration authorities. Furthermore, the laws make it easier for workers to update their personal information if and when they acquire legal status, without fear of retaliation for doing so. However, because litigation has not yet been brought forth, the reach of these new laws is difficult to predict.[79]

Build Public Support

Researchers have argued that the myths about the alleged effects that illegalized migrants have on the labour market and social welfare system need to be dispelled, as do the public's fears and anxieties about non-citizens.[80] Such myths and unfounded fears and anxieties have influenced municipal and regional governments to implement anti-immigrant legislation. Between May 2006 and September 2007, for example, 131 cities and counties in thirty American states passed or proposed laws that included rental restrictions towards illegalized migrants, employer sanctions, English-language rules, labour prohibitions, and enforcement of immigration law.[81]

Compared to the US, where the employment and labour experiences of 11 million illegalized migrants are well documented, and where many policies that support the advancement of their employment and labour rights are emerging, very little information exists about the experiences of illegalized migrant workers in Canada. Detailed information about illegalized migrants is key to the implementation of measures at the provincial and territorial level to protect these migrants in the labour market. In Canada, illegalized migrants are "undocumented," which is an inherent barrier to obtaining accurate data on their numbers, location, skills, occupation, employment situation, and other characteristics.

Systemic Inclusion

Although a large number of municipal institutions and service providers use their discretionary powers to provide equitable access for illegalized migrants, few use their discretionary powers to keep information about their status confidential from federal immigration authorities.[82] Most administrative staff and service providers may, in fact, be unaware that they are allowed to provide access to illegalized migrants, that they do not need to ask for their clients' status documents, or that they are not required to pass information on to federal immigration authorities.[83] A recent evaluation of Toronto's sanctuary policies and practices, for example, found that a majority of staff at city-funded agencies were not providing services to illegalized migrants due to inadequate training and confusion about the needs of illegalized migrant communities.[84] In contrast, evaluations of service delivery procedures and training of administrative staff in the US have led to improved services to illegalized migrants in such places as New Haven, San Francisco, Chicago, and Dayton.[85]

Conducting similar evaluations of service procedures and training of administrative staff at provincial and territorial levels could similarly improve services to illegalized migrant workers. For example, training staff to protect the employment rights of illegalized migrant workers, rather than report these workers to authorities, could potentially encourage illegalized migrants to report employer abuse and/or exploitation to the proper authorities (e.g., an employment standards officer). In turn, reports of workplace violations could eventually discourage employers from exploiting illegalized migrants.

CONCLUSION

As a result of an increasing reliance on TFWs, greater restrictions to refugee admission, and other policy changes at the federal level, it is expected that the number of migrant workers who become illegalized in Canada will continue to grow. In addition, changes to federal immigration law and an increase in enforcement capacities have made these workers more vulnerable, and thus more open to exploitation by unscrupulous employers. All of this is characteristic of an era in which migrants are increasingly criminalized.

In the absence of federal immigration reform, a range of options are available to provincial and territorial governments to counter these developments – to prevent employers from exploiting and abusing illegalized migrant workers and to provide illegalized migrant workers with equitable access to employment and labour rights. Some of these policies, programs, and services have been applied in the US to varying degrees of success. Given the different legal and administrative national context, however, not all such initiatives may translate easily from a US to a Canadian context, or from municipal to provincial and territorial contexts. Due to the limited scope of this chapter, we were only able to provide a rough overview of the possible areas in which provinces and territories could act. Further analysis is necessary to explore in greater detail the degree to which and the ways in which particular policies, programs, and services can be applied in particular Canadian provinces and territories.

In addition, our review focused on access to equitable employment and labour opportunities for illegalized migrant workers. We did not directly address other important areas, such as access to education, housing, or health services. While additional research is needed to understand how illegalized migrants can gain fair access to these services, we believe that initiatives for access to equitable employment for illegalized migrants would be a significant step towards establishing a sanctuary province or territory.

Any such steps towards establishing a sanctuary province or territory must be taken with the utmost care. Illegalized migrants are an extremely vulnerable population. Sanctuary city policies have been critiqued for creating a false sense of security among illegalized migrants, through creating an inaccurate impression that they provide protection against federal immigration enforcement.[86] Provincial and territorial governments should work very closely with NGOs, activist organizations, and unions to avoid oppositional political backlash and to manage any negative reaction that may result from extending such rights to vulnerable populations. In addition, the provision of identification documents or driver's authorizations to illegalized migrants must be administered in a way that prevents the leakage of status information to federal immigration authorities. Furthermore, any provincial or territorial initiative must be careful not to break federal law. Ideally, however, the federal government would begin to reform federal immigration policy to include measures that ensure access to equitable employment for *all* residents in Canada.

ACKNOWLEDGMENTS

This research draws on work by the Solidarity City Network and No One Is Illegal – Toronto. Neither the Solidarity City Network nor No One Is Illegal are necessarily endorsing or agreeing with the contents of this paper. We would like to thank Susan Barrass at the Ryerson Centre for Immigration and Settlement (RCIS) for her insightful comments. An earlier version of this chapter was published as an RCIS Working Paper available at www.ryerson.ca/rcis.

NOTES

1 Harald Bauder, *Migration Borders Freedom* (London: Routledge, 2016).
2 Harald Bauder, "Sanctuary Cities: Policies and Practices in International Perspective," *International Migration* 55, no. 2 (2017): 174–87; and Jennifer Ridgley, "The City as a Sanctuary in the United States," in *Sanctuary Practices in International Perspectives: Migration, Citizenship and Social Movements*, eds. Randy Lippert and Sean Rehaag (Abingdon, UK: Routledge, 2013): 219–31.
3 Graham Hudson, Idil Atak, Michele Manocchi and Charity-Ann Hannan, "(No) Access T.O.: A Pilot Study on Sanctuary City Policy in Toronto, Canada," (RCIS Working Paper No. 2017/1, Ryerson Centre for Immigration and Settlement, 2017), https://www.ryerson.ca/content/dam/rcis/documents/RCIS%20Working%20Paper%202017_1GHudsonFinal%20.pdf.
4 Ruth Gomberg-Munoz and Laura Nussbaum-Barberena, "Is Immigration Policy Labor Policy? Immigration Enforcement, Undocumented Workers, and the State," *Human Organization* 70, no. 4 (2011): 366–75.
5 Luin Goldring and Patricia Landolt, "The Impact of Precarious Legal Status on Immigrants' Economic Outcomes," Institute for Research on Public Policy (IRPP), IRPP study no. 35, 2012.
6 Harald Bauder, "Sanctuary City: Toronto's Signal to Ottawa and Queen's Park," *Toronto Star*, 27 February 2013, https://www.thestar.com/opinion/editorialopinion/2013/02/27/sanctuary_city_torontos_signal_to_ottawa_and

_queens_park.html. See also No One is Illegal – Toronto, http://toronto
.nooneisillegal.org.

7 Luin Goldring, Carolina Berinstein, and Judith K. Bernhard, "Institutionaliz-
ing Precarious Migratory Status in Canada." *Citizenship Studies* 13, no. 3
(2009): 239–65; and Beth Lyon, "When More Security Equals Less Workplace Safety: Reconsidering US Laws That Disadvantage Unauthorized
Workers," *University of Pennsylvania Journal of Labor and Employment Law* 6
(2003): 571–611.

8 Harald Bauder, "Why We Should Use the Term Illegalized Immigrant" (RCIS
Research Brief No. 2013/1, Ryerson Centre for Immigration and Settlement,
2013–18 http://www.ryerson.ca/content/dam/rcis/documents/RCIS_RB
_Bauder_No_2013_1.pdf.

9 Charity-Ann Hannan, "Illegalized Migrants," in *Immigrant Experiences in
North America*, eds. Harald Bauder and John Shields (Canada: CSPI, 2015),
144–63.

10 City of Toronto, Social Development, Finance and Administration, "Undocumented Workers in Toronto," 22 October 2012, http://www.toronto.ca
/legdocs/mmis/2013/cd/bgrd/backgroundfile-55291.pdf; Goldring and Landolt, "The Impact of Precarious Legal Status"; and Lilian Magalhaes, Christine Carrasco, and Denise Gastaldo, "Undocumented Migrants in Canada: A
Scope Literature Review on Health, Access to Services, and Working Conditions," *Journal of Immigrant and Minority Health* 12, no. 1 (2010): 132–51.

11 Lotf Ali Jan Ali, "Welcome to Canada? A Critical Review and Assessment of
Canada's Fast-Changing Immigration Policies" (RCIS Working Paper No.
2014/6, Ryerson Centre for Immigration and Settlement, 2014), http://www
.ryerson.ca/content/dam/rcis/documents/RCIS_WP_Ali_Final.pdf.

12 Fay Faraday, "Made in Canada: How the Law Constructs Migrant Workers'
Insecurity," Metcalf Foundation, 2012, http://metcalffoundation.com/wp-con-
tent/uploads/2012/09/Made-in-Canada-Summary-Report.pdf; Peter H. Saw-
chuk and Arlo Kempf, "Guest Worker Programs and Canada: Towards a
Foundation for Understanding the Complex Pedagogies of Transnational
Labour," *Journal of Workplace Learning* 20, no. 7–8 (2008): 492–502; Magal-
haes, Carrasco, and Gastaldo, "Undocumented Migrants in Canada"; and
"Making Ontario Home 2012: A Study of Settlement and Integration Ser-
vices for Immigrants and Refugees," Ontario Council of Agencies Serving
Immigrants (OCASI), 2012, http://www.ocasi.org/downloads/OCASI_MOH
_ENGLISH.pdf.

13 "Towards a Sanctuary City: Assessment and Recommendations on Municipal Service Provisions to Undocumented Residents in Toronto," Solidarity

City Network, 2013, accessed 17 November 2014, http://solidarity
city.net/learn/report-towards-a-sanctuary-city.

14 No One Is Illegal – Toronto, http://toronto.nooneisillegal.org; Navjeet
    Sidhu, "Accessing Community Programs and Services for Non-Status Immi-
    grants in Toronto: Organizational Challenges and Responses," Social Plan-
    ning Toronto, 2013, http://www.socialplanningtoronto.org/wp-content
    /uploads/2013/08/Accessing-Community-Programs-and-Services-for-Non-
    status-Immigrants-in-Toronto-Organizational-Challenges-and-Responses.pdf;
    "Towards a Sanctuary City," Solidarity City Network; "Undocumented? No
    Status? No Work Permit? Know Your Rights!," Workers' Action Centre, 2014,
    accessed 1 November 2017, http://www.workersactioncentre.org/wp-content
    /uploads/dlm_uploads/2014/09/fs-undocumented-eng.pdf; and "Your Rights
    at Work: Action Guide for Fair Employment," Workers' Action Centre, 2011,
    accessed 4 October 2015, http://www.workersactioncentre.org/wp-content
    /uploads/dlm_uploads/2011/12/YourRightsAtWork-Feb2015.pdf.

15 Natalie Alcoba, "'Their First Stop Is the Welfare Office': Bid to Improve Ser-
    vice Access for Illegal Workers Sparks Furious Toronto Council Debate,"
    National Post, 22 February 2013, http://news.nationalpost.com/2013/02/22
    /sanctuary-city-council-takes-steps-to-help-undocumented-workers-feel-more-
    comfortable-accessing-city-services; and Jack Aubry, "Canadians Want Illegal
    Immigrants Deported: Poll," CanWest News Service, 20 October 2007,
    http://www.immigrationwatchcanada.org/2007/10/20/canadians-want-illegal-
    immigrants-deported-poll.

16 "Giving the Facts a Fighting Chance: Addressing Common Questions on
    Immigration," American Immigration Council, 14 December 2015,
    http://www.immigrationpolicy.org/research/addressing-common-questions-
    immigration; James J. Kielkopf, "The Economic Impact of Undocumented
    Workers in Minnesota," Hispanic Access to College Education Resources
    (HACER), 2000, http://www.macalester.edu/courses/econ108/hacer.pdf;
    Chirag Mehta, Nikolas Theodore, Iliana Mora, and Jennifer Wade,
    "Chicago's Undocumented Immigrants: An Analysis of Wages, Working
    Conditions, and Economic Contributions," University of Illinois at
    Chicago, Center for Urban Economic Development, 2002; and Ramanujan
    Nadadur, "Illegal Immigration: A Positive Economic Contribution to the
    United States," *Journal of Ethnic and Migration Studies* 35, no. 6 (2009):
    1,037–52.

17 Rebecca Morales, "Transitional Labor: Undocumented Workers in the Los
    Angeles Automobile Industry," *International Migration Review* (1983):
    570–96.

18 Nicholas P. De Genova, "Migrant 'Illegality' and Deportability in Everyday Life," *Annual Review of Anthropology* 31, no. 1 (2002): 419–47.

19 Harald Bauder, "Nation, 'Migration' and Critical Practice," *Area* 45, no. 1 (2012): 56–62, https://www.academia.edu/12770083/Nation_migration_and_critical_practice.

20 Harald Bauder, *Labor Movement: How Migration Regulates Labor Markets* (New York: Oxford University Press, 2006); and J. David Brown, Julie L. Hotchkiss, and Myriam Quispe-Agnoli, "Does Employing Undocumented Workers Give Firms a Competitive Advantage?," *Journal of Regional Science* 53, no. 1 (2013): 158–70.

21 Carl-Ulrik Schierup, Ronaldo Munck, Branka Likić-Brborić, and Anders Neergaard, "Introduction," in *Migration, Precarity and Global Governance: Challenges and Opportunities for Labour*, eds. Carl-Ulrik Schierup, Ronaldo Munck, Branka Likić-Brborić, and Anders Neergaard (UK: Oxford University Press, 2015), 2.

22 Immigration Act, 1976-77, ch. 52, s. 1, http://www.refworld.org/docid/3ae6b5c60.html.

23 Immigration and Refugee Protection Act (IRPA), SC 2001, ch. 27, http://laws.justice.gc.ca/eng/acts/i-2.5.

24 IRPA, 2001.

25 Renée Suarez Congdon, "Comparing Employer Sanctions Provisions and Employment Eligibility Verification Procedures in the United States and the United Kingdom," *Indiana International and Comparative Law Review* 18 (2008): 391–435; Shannon Gleeson, *Conflicting Commitments: The Politics of Enforcing Immigrant Worker Rights in San Jose and Houston* (Ithaca: Cornell University Press, 2012), http://digitalcommons.ilr.cornell.edu/cgi/viewcontent.cgi?article=1076&context=books; and Beth Lyon, "22 New International Human Rights Standards in Unauthorized Immigrant Worker Rights: Seizing an Opportunity to Pull Governments Out of the Shadows," in *Human Rights and Refugees, Internally Displaced Persons and Migrant Workers*, ed. Anne F. Bayefsky (Brill Online Books and Journals, 2005): 551–82, http://booksandjournals.brillonline.com/content/books/10.1163/ej.9789004144835.i-599.187.

26 "Our Charter," Canada Border Services Agency (CBSA), 2010, accessed 1 November 2017, http://www.cbsa-asfc.gc.ca/agency-agence/charter-charte-eng.html.

27 "Citizenship Pathways and Border Protection: Canada," 2015, Library of Congress, accessed 1 November 2017, http://www.loc.gov/law/help/citizenship-pathways/canada.php.

28 Congdon, "Comparing Employer Sanctions Provisions"; and Beth Lyon, "When More 'Security' Equals Less Workplace Safety: Reconsidering US Laws that Disadvantage Unauthorized Workers," *University of Pennsylvania Journal of Labor and Employment Law* 6, no. 3 (2004): 571–611.

29 Alice Bloch, Leena Kumarappan, and Sonia McKay, "Employer Sanctions: The Impact of Workplace Raids and Fines on Undocumented Migrants and Ethnic Enclave Employers," *Critical Social Policy* 35, no. 1 (2015): 132–51. Rebecca Smith, Ana Ana Avendaño, and Julie Martínez Ortega, "Iced Out: How Immigration Enforcement has Interfered with Workers' Rights," Cornell University, ILR School, 2009, http://digitalcommons.ilr.cornell.edu/cgi/viewcontent.cgi?article=1020&context=laborunions; and Ben Wood, "Workplace Raids: Canada's New Immigration Policy?," *Canadian Dimension* 43, no. 5 (2009): 24–5, http://connection.ebscohost.com/c/articles/45442115/workplace-raids-canadas-new-immigration-policy.

30 Bloch, Kumarappan, and McKay, "Employer Sanctions."

31 Smith, Avendaño, and Ortega, "Iced Out."

32 Wood, "Workplace Raids."

33 American Federation of Labor and Congress of Industrial Organizations (AFL-CIO), "Seven Immigration Myths and Facts," Cornell University, ILR School, 2011, http://digitalcommons.ilr.cornell.edu/laborunions/75; Julie Braker, "Navigating the Relationship Between the DHS and the DOL: The Need for Federal Legislation to Protect Immigrant Workers' Rights," *Columbia Journal of Law and Social Problems* 46 (2012): 329–59; Josiah McC Heyman, "State Effects on Labor Exploitation: The INS and Undocumented Immigrants at the Mexico-United States Border," *Critique of Anthropology* 18, no. 2 (1998): 157–80; and Smith, Avendaño, and Ortega, "Iced Out."

34 Luiz Arthur Bihari, "Clashing Laws: Exploring the Employment Rights of Undocumented Migrants," *University of Toronto Faculty of Law Review* 69 (2011): 9–30; and Linda S. Bosniak, "Human Rights, State Sovereignty and the Protection of Undocumented Migrants Under the International Migrant Workers Convention," *International Migration Review* 25, no. 4 (1991): 737–70.

35 Bosniak, "Human Rights, State Sovereignty," 741.

36 *International Convention on the Protection and the Rights of All Migrant Workers and Members of Their Families*, 1990, pt. 3, Art. 25, http://www.ohchr.org/EN/ProfessionalInterest/Pages/CMW.aspx.

37 Bihari, "Clashing Laws."

38 Gleeson, *Conflicting Commitments*, 8.

39 Smith, Avendaño, and Ortega, "Iced Out," 10–11.

40 Michele LeVoy and Nele Verbruggen, "Ten Ways to Protect Undocumented Migrant Workers," Platform for International Cooperation on Undocumented Migrants (PICUM), 2005, http://www.undocumentary.org/assets/work/publications/Reports/WorkPubl%20-%20Ten%20Ways%20to%20Protect%20Workers_EN.pdf; Parliament of Canada, Standing Committee on Citizenship and Immigration, "Temporary Foreign Workers and Non-Status Workers," 2009, http://ufcw.ca/Theme/UFCW/files/PDF%202009/TEMPFO~1.PDF; and Carola Suárez-Orozco, Hirokazu Yoshikawa, Robert Teranishi, and Marcelo Suárez-Orozco, "Growing up in the Shadows: The Developmental Implications of Unauthorized Status," *Harvard Educational Review* 81, no. 3 (2011): 438–73.

41 Kate Brick, "Regularizations in the European Union: The Contentious Policy Tool," Migration Policy Institute, 2011, http://www.migrationpolicy.org/research/regularizations-european-union; Erika Khandor, Jean McDonald, Peter Nyers, and Cynthia Wright, "The Regularization of Non-Status Immigrants in Canada 1960–2004," Centre of Excellence for Research on Immigration and Settlement (CERIS), 2004, http://accessalliance.ca/wp-content/uploads/2015/03/Regularization-Report.pdf; and Amanda Levinson, "The Regularisation of Undocumented Migrants: Literature Survey and Country Case Studies," University of Oxford, Centre on Migration, Policy and Society (COMPAS), 2005, https://www.compas.ox.ac.uk/media/ER-2005-Regularisation_Unauthorized_Literature.pdf.

42 Khandor, McDonald, Nyers, and Wright, "Regularization of Non-Status Immigrants."

43 Immigration Reform and Control Act (IRCA), 1986, http://library.uwb.edu/static/usimmigration/100%20stat%203359.pdf.

44 Alberto Dávila and José A. Pagán, "The Effect of Selective INS Monitoring Strategies on the Industrial Employment Choice and Earnings of Recent Immigrants," *Economic Inquiry* 35, no. 1 (1997): 138–50; Gomberg-Munoz and Nussbaum-Barberena, "Is Immigration Policy Labor Policy?"; Douglas S. Massey and Kerstin Gentsch, "Undocumented Migration to the United States and the Wages of Mexican Immigrants," *International Migration Review* 48, no. 2 (2014): 482–99; and "Undocumented Workers in the US Garment Sector: An Assessment and Guide for Brands," Verité, 2014, accessed 1 November 2017, http://verite.org/sites/default/files/images/Undocumented_US_Garment_Workers.pdf.

45 Faraday, "Made in Canada"; Gleeson, *Conflicting Commitments*; "Recovery of Unpaid Wages for Undocumented Workers: Immigrant and Nonstandard Worker Project – Fact Sheet for Advocates," National Employment Law Pro-

ject (NELP), 1005, accessed 1 November 2017, http://www.nelp.org/content
/uploads/tax-reporting-options.pdf; "Issue Brief: Workplace Rights of
Undocumented Workers after the Supreme Court's Hoffman Plastic
Ruling," National Employment Law Project (NELP), 2006, accessed 4
October 2016, http://www.workplacefairness.org/guide?attribute%5B
%5D=349; Smith, Avendaño, and Ortega, "Iced Out"; and VERITE, "
Undocumented Workers in the US Garment Sector: An Assessment and
Guide for Brands."
46 Massey and Gentsch, "Undocumented Migration to the United States."
47 "Guide to Using Labour Market Information in Ontario," Ministry of Training, Colleges and Universities (MTCU), 2005, accessed 1 November 2017,
http://www.chs.ca/sites/default/files/uploads/guide_to_using_labour_market
_information_in_ontario.pdf.
48 Alexandra Alonso, "From Congress to the Suburbs: Local Initiatives to Regulate Immigration in the United States," *Migración y Desarrollo* 2 (2007):
65–82, http://meme.phpwebhosting.com/~migracion/rimd/revistas/rev9
/e4.pdf; Irene Bloemraad and Els de Graauw, "Patchwork Policies: Immigrant Integration in the United States," *Canadian Issues/Thèmes Canadiens*
(2013): 67–72; Maria Lorena Cook, "The Advocate's Dilemma: Framing
Migrant Rights in National Settings," *Studies in Social Justice* 4, no. 2 (2010):
145–64, http://digitalcommons.ilr.cornell.edu/cgi/viewcontent.cgi?article
=1775&context=articles; Liette Gilbert, "Immigration as Local Politics: Re-
Bordering Immigration and Multiculturalism Through Deterrence and
Incapacitation," *International Journal of Urban and Regional Research* 33, no. 1
(2009): 26–42; Doris Marie Provine, "Justice as Told by Judges: The Case of
Litigation over Local Anti-Immigrant Legislation," *Studies in Social Justice* 3,
no. 2 (2009): 231–45; S. Karthick Ramakrishnan and Tom Wong, "Immigration Policies Go Local: The Varying Responses of Local Governments to
Undocumented Immigration," *University of California, Riverside* (2007):
73–93, https://www.law.berkeley.edu/files/RamakrishnanWongpaperfinal
.pdf; and Miriam J. Wells, "The Grassroots Reconfiguration of US Immigration Policy," *International Migration Review* 38, no. 4 (2004): 1,308–47.
49 Susanne Schech, "Rescaling Sovereignty? Sub-state Responses to Irregular
Migrants," *Griffith Law Review* 22, no. 3 (2013): 785–803.
50 Hilary Arksey and Lisa O'Malley, "Scoping Studies: Towards a Methodologi-
cal Framework," *International Journal of Social Research Methodology* 8, no. 1
(2005): 19–32.
51 Charity-Ann Hannan, "Employment Equity and Access to Social Welfare for
Illegalized Immigrants: An Inclusive Approach that also Makes Economic
Sense" (RCIS Working Paper No. 2013/1, Ryerson Centre for Immigration

and Settlement, 2013), http://www.ryerson.ca/content/dam/rcis/documents
/RCIS_WP_Hannan_No_2013_1.pdf.

52 Smith, Avendaño, and Ortega, "Iced Out."

53 "Build a Better Nation: A Case for Comprehensive Immigration Reform,"
Workers Defense Project, 2013, accessed 2 November 2017, http://workers
defense.org/IMMIGRATION%20wdp%20color%20FINAL.pdf.

54 Braker, "Navigating the Relationship"; Smith, Avendaño, and Ortega, "Iced
Out."

55 Braker, "Navigating the Relationship"; Michael J. Wishnie, "Immigrants and
the Right to Petition," New York University Law Review, 78 (2003): 667–748,
http://digitalcommons.law.yale.edu/cgi/viewcontent.cgi?article=1944&contex
t=fss_papers.

56 Braker, "Navigating the Relationship."

57 H.G. Hamilton, "Vancouver Transit Police End Agreement with CBSA," rab-
ble.ca, 23 February 2015, http://rabble.ca/news/2015/02/vancouver-transit-
police-end-agreement-cbsa.

58 Richard Brennan, "Transport Ministry Permanently Cuts Ties with Canada
Border Agency," Toronto Star, 10 October 2014, https://www.thestar.com
/news/queenspark/2014/10/10/transport_ministry_permanently_cuts_ties_wi
th_canada_border_agency.html.

59 Brennan, "Transport Ministry Permanently Cuts Ties."

60 Nicholas Keung, "Advocates Condemn Traffic Stops of Migrants," Toronto
Star, 23 September 2014, http://torontostar.newspaperdirect.com/epaper
/viewer.aspx; and Brennan, "Transport Ministry Permanently Cuts Ties."

61 Gomberg-Munoz and Nussbaum-Barberena, "Is Immigration Policy Labor
Policy?"

62 Christopher Cruise, "Illegal Immigrants Can Now Get a Driver's License,"
VOA News, 18 January 2015, http://learningenglish.voanews.com/content
/illegal-immigrants-can-now-get-a-drivers-license/2598128.html; and
Gomberg-Munoz and Nussbaum-Barberena. "Is Immigration Policy
Labor Policy?"

63 Mary McThomas, Performing Citizenship: Undocumented Migrants in the United States (New York: Routledge, 2016).

64 Steven J. Escobar, "Allowing Undocumented Immigrants to Obtain Driver's
Licenses in New Mexico: Revising, Not Abandoning, the System," Washington University Journal of Law and Policy, 43 (2013): 285.

65 "12 States (and DC) That Allow Driver's Licenses for People in the Country
Illegally," ProCon.org, 3 February 2016,
http://immigration.procon.org/view.resource.php?resourceID=005535.

66 Christopher Cadelago and Jeremy White, "California Lawmakers Approve
     Measure to Allow Driver's Licenses for Illegal Immigrants," *Sacramento Bee*,
     13 September 2013, http://www.sacbee.com/news/politics-government
     /article2578787.html; and Cruise, "Illegal Immigrants Can Now Get a Dri-
     ver's License." Escobar, "Allowing Undocumented Immigrants."
67 Els de Graauw, "Municipal ID Cards for Undocumented Immigrants: Local
     Bureaucratic Membership in a Federal System," *Politics and Society* 42, no. 3
     (2014): 309–30.
68 "Towards a Sanctuary City," Solidarity City Network.
69 "Labor Leaders Announce National Mobilization Campaign for Immigra-
     tion Reform," American Federation of Labor and Congress of Industrial
     Organizations (AFL-CIO), 7 February 2013; Frank Bardacke, "The UFW and
     the Undocumented," *International Labor and Working Class History* 83 (2013):
     162–9; Tanya Basok, "The Intersections of the Economic and Cultural in US
     Labor's Pro-Migrant Politics," *Social Justice* 35, no. 4 (2008): 12–32; de
     Graauw, "Municipal ID Cards for Undocumented Immigrants"; Syed Hus-
     san, Mary-Elizabeth Dill, and Abeer Majeed, "May Day: Immigrant Rights
     Are Workers' Rights," *rabble.ca*, 30 April 2012, http://rabble.ca/news/2012/04
     /may-day-immigrant-rights-are-workers-rights; Joann Lo and Ariel Jacobson,
     "Human Rights from Field to Fork: Improving Labor Conditions for Food-
     Sector Workers by Organizing Across Boundaries," *Race/Ethnicity: Multidisci-
     plinary Global Contexts* 5, no. 1 (2011): 61–82; "Labour Without Borders:
     Towards a Migrant Workers' Bill of Rights," Ontario Federation of Labour
     (OFL), 2013, accessed 1 November 2017, http://ofl.ca/wp-content/uploads
     /2013.08-MigrantWorkers-Report.pdf; Maria Linda Ontiveros, "Out of the
     Shadows and into the Spotlight: Immigrants and Organized Labor," *Journal
     of Labor and Society* 11, no. 1 (2008): 157–64; "PICUM Submission: UN Com-
     mittee on the Protection of the Rights of All Migrant Workers and Mem-
     bers of their Families (CMW)," Platform for International Cooperation on
     Undocumented Migrants (PICUM), 2014, accessed 1 November 2017,
     http://www.ohchr.org/Documents/HRBodies/CMW/Discussions/2014/PICU
     M_CMW_DGD2014.pdf; and "Build a Better Nation," Workers Defense
     Project.
70 "Recovery of Unpaid Wages for Undocumented Workers," NELP; "Issue
     Brief: Workplace Rights of Undocumented Workers," NELP; "No Free Pass to
     Harass: Protecting the Rights of Undocumented Immigrant Women Work-
     ers in Sexual Harassment Cases," American Civil Liberties Union (ACLU)
     and National Employment Law Project (NELP), 2007, accessed 1 November
     2017, https://www.aclu.org/sites/default/files/pdfs/womensrights

/no_free_pass_20071119.pdf; Rebecca Smith and Eunice Hyunhye Cho, "Worker's Rights on ICE: How Immigration Reform Can Stop Retaliation and Advance Labor Rights," National Employment Law Project (NELP), 2013, http://www.nelp.org/page/-/Justice/2013/Workers-Rights-on-ICE-Retaliation-Report.pdf; "Build a Better Nation," Workers Defense Project; and Haeyoung Yoon, Tsedeye Gebreselassie, and Rebecca Smith, "Workplace Rights and Remedies for Undocumented Workers: A Legal Treatise," National Employment Law Project (NELP), 2013.

71 Alan Benjamin, "Labor and the Struggle for a Just Immigration Policy," Resistance phl, 16 February 2013, http://resistancephl.com/2013/02/16/labor-and-the-struggle-for-a-just-immigration-policy; and Hussan, Dill, and Majeed, "May Day."

72 Rick Westhead, "Failed Refugee Claimants Find Sanctuary in Toronto Churches," Toronto Star, 14 October 2012, https://www.thestar.com/news/world/2012/10/14/failed_refugee_claimants_find_sanctuary_in_toronto_churches.html; and Sean Rehaag, "No One Is Above the Law on Refugees: Churches Keep Canada from Violating International Law," Toronto Star, 30 July 2004, A19.

73 "Towards a Sanctuary City," Solidarity City Network.

74 Paul Harris, "Undocumented Workers' Grim Reality: Speak out on Abuse and Risk Deportation," Guardian, 28 March 2013, http://www.theguardian.com/world/2013/mar/28/undocumented-migrants-worker-abuse-deportation; and Smith, Avendaño, and Ortega, "Iced Out."

75 Roxana Mondragón, "Injured Undocumented Workers and Their Workplace Rights: Advocating for a Retaliation Per Se Rule," Columbia Journal of Law and Social Problems 44 (2010): 447–81.

76 "Retaliation Complaint Investigation Unit (RCI)," State of California, Department of Industrial Relations, 2016, accessed 1 November 2017, http://www.dir.ca.gov/dlse/dlsediscrimination.html; "No Free Pass to Harass" NELP and ACLU; and Mondragon, "Injured Undocumented Workers"; and Smith and Cho, "Worker's Rights on ICE."

77 Scott Hochberg, "The Impact of California's New Anti-Retaliation Protections for Immigrant Workers," On Labor, 15 October 2014, http://onlabor.org/2014/10/15/the-impact-of-californias-new-anti-retaliation-protections-for-immigrant-workers; and Sean-Patrick Wilson and Adam Y. Siegel, "California Broadens Immigration-Related Retaliation Protections," California Workplace Law Blog, 5 September 2014, accessed 1 November 2017, https://www.californiaworkplacelawblog.com/2014/09/articles/general/california-broadens-immigration-related-retaliation-protections.

78 "Recovery of Unpaid Wages for Undocumented Workers," NELP.

79 Hochberg, "Impact of California's New Anti-Retaliation Protections."

80 Cook, "The Advocate's Dilemma"; Hilary Parsons Dick, "Making Immigrants Illegal in Small-Town USA," *Journal of Linguistic Anthropology* 21, no. s1 (2011): E35–E55; Anita Alves Pena, "Undocumented Immigrants and the Welfare State: The Case of Regional Migration and U.S. Agricultural Labor," *Journal of Regional Science* 54, no. 1 (2014): 96–113; and LeVoy and Verbruggen, "Ten Ways to Protect Undocumented Migrant Workers."

81 Jill Esbenshade and Barbara Obzurt, "Local Immigration Regulation: A Problematic Trend in Public Policy," *Harvard Journal of Hispanic Policy* 20 (2008): 33–47; and Gilbert, "Immigration as Local Politics."

82 de Graauw, "Municipal ID Cards for Undocumented Immigrants"; and Kenny H. Nienhusser, "Role of Community Colleges in the Implementation of Postsecondary Education Enrollment Policies for Undocumented Students," *Community College Review* 42, no. 1 (2014): 3–22.

83 Nienhusser, "Role of Community Colleges"; Sidhu, "Accessing Community Programs and Services"; and "Towards a Sanctuary City," Solidarity City Network.

84 "Towards a Sanctuary City," Solidarity City Network.

85 de Graauw, "Municipal ID Cards for Undocumented Immigrants."

86 "Understanding Trust Acts, Community Policing, and 'Sanctuary Cities,'" American Immigration Council, 10 October 2015, accessed 1 November 2017, https://www.americanimmigrationcouncil.org/research/sanctuary-cities-trust-acts-and-community-policing-explained.

12

Progress towards
a Common European Asylum System?
The Migration Crisis in Europe

Judith Gleeson

Speaking on 9 May 1950, five years after the end of the Second World War, the French foreign minister, Robert Schuman, declared as his aim to "make war not only unthinkable but materially impossible." The Schuman Declaration, as it came to be called, is now recognized as the decisive beginning to seventy years of European integration and peace in Europe. The Schuman Declaration states:

> World peace cannot be safeguarded without the making of creative efforts proportionate to the dangers which threaten it.
>
> The contribution which an organized and living Europe can bring to civilization is indispensable to the maintenance of peaceful relations ...
>
> Europe will not be made all at once, or according to a single plan. It will be built through concrete achievements which first create a de facto solidarity.[1]

The drive to unite Europe came from what was then the largest migration within Europe that the continent had ever seen, the aftermath of two world wars, and a determination by the founding nations to ensure peace. The European family of nations had behind it centuries of internal wars and empires: England and France were once at war for 100 years. However, the Second World War had an enormous effect on civilian life, and the need to move from an informal system of sanctuary to a formal system of international protection for those at risk in their country of origin led to the drafting of the two great postwar instruments of protection: the 1950 European Convention on Human Rights and the 1951 Refugee Convention. Europe continued to put into effect Robert Schuman's plan for economic, and later political, integration; to put conflict beyond reach and generate prosperity for those who live in Europe.

The European Union, which sought to realize Schuman's vision, evolved out of the European Coal and Steel Community, via the European Free Trade Association and the European Economic Community (EEC). The European Union is founded on the twin principles of free movement of people, goods, and services, and free trade. From 1995, with the introduction of the Euro currency, there was a partial currency union within Europe, designed to facilitate free trade and freedom of movement – seen in many countries as a step toward a federal Europe. A total of eighteen European Union countries have adopted the Euro, with the United Kingdom among a group of ten that decided not to participate.[2]

In 2004, the European Union introduced a package of four interlocking instruments that together created the Common European Asylum System (CEAS), with the stated aim of establishing and maintaining a common European border, with free movement within that area. I consider the structure of that system later in this chapter.

The CEAS represented a period of European optimism that was short-lived. Following the world financial crisis in 2008, and the European crisis in 2011, the European project came under strain and Greece's membership of the Euro was thrown into doubt by huge debts. The fragile narrative of political and economic unanimity began to unravel. In a prophetic article published in the *Economist* in November 2011, Edward Carr analyzed the financial crisis and the political risks it posed:

> Some Europeans would like to put up carefully designed fences around the EU's still vast and wealthy market. Others, including a growing number of populist politicians, want to turn their nations inward and shut out not just the world but also the elites' project of European integration ... This is not some abstract philosophical choice. It is a fierce struggle for Europe's future ... While the world waits for Europe to make up its mind, catastrophe is in the air. It could take many forms. A country might storm out of

the euro – which the treaty forbids, but who could stop a determined government? ... Some people speculate that Germany
might lead a breakaway core of euro-zone countries ... Or perhaps
austerity might eventually lead to populists that turn away from
the euro – to hell with the consequences ... Economic and Monetary Union ... promised to bind a unified Germany into the EU
and pave the way for some sort of political union in Europe.
Today that dream has not vanished altogether, but the single market is under threat once more ... Can Europe turn back from the
abyss? Only if the core countries will support the rest as they submit themselves to radical political, social and economic reform.
Nobody should be under any illusions about how difficult that
will be.[3]

Alongside these economic issues, Europe had other emerging problems in the second decade of the twentieth century. A massive migration into Europe, in particular from North Africa, strained the ability
of individual countries to cope, and stressed the relatively new CEAS.
The rise of Islamic extremism brought large and small terrorist incidents in many European countries. By June 2014, ISIS controlled an
area in Iraq and Syria the size of Britain, where the destruction and
human rights abuses instigated by the group fuelled the migratory
pressure to Europe and elsewhere.[4]

The previous warmth of Europe's welcome for refugees cooled. The
asylum regimes of most countries became stricter, with new and
stronger criminal sanctions for immigrants, but also for those in the
wider society. The United Kingdom already had a significant number
of immigration offences on the statute book. Under the Immigration
Act 1971 (as amended over the years), it is a criminal offence to enter
the United Kingdom without leave, to obtain leave by deception, to
possess a document containing false immigration stamps, to fail to
depart at the end of any leave, or to fail to observe a condition of leave
to enter or remain. The document offences are the most prosecuted,
removal being preferred for the other circumstances: a conviction
under one of those offences is among the general grounds for refusal
of future applications, either within or outside the United Kingdom,
under the Immigration Rules HC 395 (as amended).[5]

The United Kingdom's criminal regime extends beyond the individual migrant. Facilitating unlawful entry to the United Kingdom is
an offence under the 1971 Act, including assisting entry in breach of

a deportation order. The Asylum and Immigration Act 1996 made it a criminal offence to employ illegal immigrants.

Now, following the Immigration Act 2014, the criminal offences regime extends to landlords, banks, doctors and hospitals, and marriage registrars. When introducing the bill for its third reading in the House of Commons on 30 January 2014, then-Home Secretary (now Prime Minister) Theresa May, said the following:

> The Bill will make it more difficult for illegal migrants to live in the United Kingdom by denying access to the tools of everyday life ... The changes that we propose will strengthen our ability to deal with those who are here illegally. We are, for example, strengthening our ability to enforce penalties for those who employ illegal workers. The system enabling employers to determine whether the workers whom they employ are here legally or not is in place, is well known and is running properly, and the same will apply in the other areas that we are discussing ... The Bill substantially reforms the removals system, and ensures that illegal migrants who have no right to be in the UK can be returned to their own countries more quickly.[6]

ASYLUM AND SANCTUARY
BEFORE THE TWENTIETH CENTURY

The concept of flight and refuge in another country did not begin in 1945. It has very old roots, going back to the concept of sanctuary in a church in the Middle Ages. Passports were not centrally issued and recorded in the United Kingdom until 1794,[7] five years after the beginning of the French Revolution, during which almost 3 per cent of the population of France sought sanctuary or asylum elsewhere in Europe, mainly in the United Kingdom.[8] The twentieth century before the Second World War saw a number of mass movements of migrants and refugees:

> Refugee groups have been coming to London for centuries. When England became a Protestant country, it attracted Protestant refugees fleeing persecution in Catholic Europe, notably French Huguenots, large numbers of whom arrived in London in the late 17th century. During the 19th century, the largest groups of refugees to arrive in London were Russian and Polish Russian

Jews, fleeing persecution from the Tsarist regime in Russia. Concern about overcrowding led to the Aliens Act of 1905, which tried to control the numbers of destitute arrivals but kept the door open to those fleeing religious persecution.[9]

In 1951, following the end of the Second World War, the United Nations adopted the Refugee Convention. In 1952, Denmark was the first country to become a state party to the Convention, followed by Belgium, Germany, Luxembourg, and Norway in 1953, and in 1954, the United Kingdom, Sweden, Australia, Austria, France, Israel, Italy, and Monaco. International support for the Convention continued, with a steady stream of new state parties during the twentieth century and the early years of the twenty-first century, reflecting the creation of new states across the world from political conflicts and the collapse of larger states. The Convention now has 144 signatory countries worldwide:[10] the last state party to join was Nauru, in June 2011.

The text of the Refugee Convention and the broad principles for international protection that it established have adapted surprisingly well to world changes in the last sixty-seven years. International protection is supplemented by a number of local refugee protection instruments, building on the Convention but providing protection adapted to a particular geographical region, such as the Organisation of African Unity Convention (1969), the Cartagena Declaration in Latin America (1984), and the CEAS (2004).[11]

EUROPEAN INTEGRATION IN THE TWENTIETH CENTURY

The EEC developed out of the European Coal and Steel Community. It began in 1957 with only six member states: Belgium, France, Germany, Italy, Luxembourg, and the Netherlands. Denmark, Ireland, and the UK joined in 1973; Greece, Spain, and Portugal in the 1980s; and Austria, Finland, and Sweden in 1995. Today there are a total of twenty-eight member states in the evolved European Union.

In 1986 at Schengen, Luxembourg, the six original EEC states created a free movement zone. The Schengen Treaty came into force in 1995 and removed internal borders for a group of European states (the Schengen Area), returning countries in the Schengen Area to something like the freedom of movement prior to the eighteenth century. Membership in the Schengen Area is not identical with that of the European Union: six of the twenty-eight EU member states remain outside it (Bulgaria, Croatia, Cyprus, Ireland, Romania, and the United Kingdom), and it includes four non-EU countries (Iceland, Norway, Switzerland, and Liechtenstein).[12] Any citizen or migrant with a Schengen visa, including a successful asylum claimant, may move freely in any of the twenty-six Schengen states. Asylum in any Schengen country gives access to the whole Schengen Area, which is a significant pull factor for asylum claims.

The Charter of Fundamental Rights of the European Union (CFEU), drafted in 2000, may represent the high point of the European integration project. In its preamble, it records the intention of all member states to move towards "ever closer union":

> The peoples of Europe, in creating an ever closer union among them, are resolved to share a peaceful future based on common values.
>
> Conscious of its spiritual and moral heritage, the Union is founded on the indivisible, universal values of human dignity, freedom, equality and solidarity; it is based on the principles of democracy and the rule of law. It places the individual at the heart of its activities, by establishing the citizenship of the Union and by creating an area of freedom, security and justice ...
>
> To this end, it is necessary to strengthen the protection of fundamental rights in the light of changes in society, social progress and scientific and technological developments by making those rights more visible in a Charter.[13]

All member states (except Poland and the United Kingdom) adopted Article 18 of the Charter: "The right to asylum shall be guaranteed with due respect for the rules of the Geneva Convention of 28 July 1951 and the Protocol of 31 January 1967 relating to the status of refugees and in accordance with the Treaty on European Union and the Treaty on the Functioning of the European Union."[14]

Member states thus accepted a shared responsibility to welcome asylum seekers in a dignified manner, ensuring they would be treated fairly and that their cases would be examined to uniform standards so that no matter where in the European Union an applicant applies for asylum, the outcome will be similar.

THE COMMON EUROPEAN ASYLUM SYSTEM

When the CEAS was created, the European Union consisted of just nine member states: Denmark, Ireland, the United Kingdom, Greece, Spain, Portugal, Austria, Finland, and Sweden. It was created just before the expansion of the European Union in 2004 and thereafter. The European Union now has twenty-eight states, extending south and east to create a powerful union of 500 million people. It was always intended that the CEAS would be revised regularly, to reflect the changing requirements of its operation. The four principal interlocking CEAS instruments were recast in 2013 and now comprise the following:

- the Refugee Qualification Directive 2011/95/EU on standards for the qualification of non-EU nationals and stateless persons as beneficiaries of international protection, for a uniform status for refugees or for persons eligible for subsidiary protection;[15]
- the Refugee Procedures Directive 2013/32/EU on common procedures for granting and withdrawing international protection;[16]
- the Reception Conditions Directive 2013/33/EU laying down standards for the reception of applicants for international protection;[17] and
- the Dublin Regulation (EU) 604/2013 establishing the criteria and mechanisms for determining the Member State responsible for examining an application for international protection lodged in one of the Member States by a third-country national (national of a non-member country) or stateless person.[18]

The 2003 directive on family reunification,[19] which has not been recast, provides for the reunification of refugee families. The 2001 directive on temporary protection[20] specifies procedures in the event of a mass influx of asylum seekers, but that directive has never been activated. The CEAS is likely to be recast again in the near future. Proposals for a further revision were published in May 2016.

CURRENT PROBLEMS
IN THE EUROPEAN UNION AND EUROPE

Progress towards a European super-state has ground to a halt under the joint strains of austerity, migration, and the United Kingdom's vote to leave the European Union (Brexit). There is a growing north–south divide within the European family, resulting from the pressures that migration has placed on the southern member states under the Dublin Regulation.

Europe is surrounded by water, and protecting its sea borders has been a preoccupation for centuries. Irregular entry into the EU, particularly by sea, began to increase sharply with the Arab Spring in 2010, and the uprisings in North Africa over the following three years, culminating in a vicious civil war in Syria, the rise of Islamic State, and its mass marketing of terrorism. In practice, whether they are fleeing instability in their countries of origin or seeking economic betterment, migrants arrive in the European Union's border states, which are the least well resourced, administratively and financially, to cope with a huge influx of new migrants. The pressures have been particularly acute in Greece, Italy, Bulgaria, and Hungary.

The Europe that was sympathetic, receptive, and protective in its response to Kosovans in the 1990s feels quite differently about present-day migrants from Syria, Iraq, and Africa. The advance of far-right parties across Europe in 2015 and 2016 reflected the public concern about levels of migration and the difficulty of integrating large numbers of new migrants into economies still recovering from the economic shocks and strains of recent years. Migrant numbers remain high and there is a fear that they bring negative social change (particularly in relation to the status of women), that some of the migrants are terrorists, and that they will need social benefits and take up work from the citizens of the host states.

Among the public, there is a fear of domestic terrorist attacks and the sense of an ever-present threat. The terrorist attacks in France, Germany, and Belgium in 2015 and 2016, and in the United Kingdom in 2017, have brought the risk uncomfortably close to home, with attacks in 2017 in London on Westminster Bridge, Parliament, London Bridge, and the Finsbury Park Mosque, and in Manchester at the Ariana Grande concert.

London was warned: on 31 July 2016, the Metropolitan Police commissioner, Sir Bernard Hogan-Howe, said that the British security services and police could not provide absolute protection from terrorism:

> I know that with each new outrage, and especially those on our doorstep on the Continent, there is a greater sense of fear ... I

know you want me to reassure you. I am afraid I cannot do that entirely. Our threat level has been at "Severe" for two years. It remains there. It means an attack is highly likely – you could say it is a case of when, not if … The threat we all face is very real … But defeating terrorism is as much about refusing to be afraid as anything else.[21]

The scale of refugee movement that Europe is now dealing with is enormous: according to European Council on Refugees and Exiles (ECRE) figures, in 2014, 662,000 asylum claimants were living in the twenty-eight member states of the European Union, including, for this purpose, Norway and Switzerland.[22] In 2017, the United Nations High Commissioner for Refugees (UNHCR) estimated that there were 65.6 million displaced people around the world; 22.5 million refugees recognized under the UNHCR mandate or protected by UNRWA (United Nations Relief and Works Agency for Palestine Refugees) in Palestine, over half of them under eighteen years old; and 10 million stateless people, the highest numbers of displacements on record.[23]

An average of 28,300 people left their homes every day in 2016 because of conflict and persecution.[24] Over half of all refugees in the world in 2017 came from South Sudan (1.4 million), Afghanistan (2.5 million), and Syria (5.5 million).[25] Despite attempts to end the conflict, the war in Syria continues to generate forced migration and refugees.

For a year from 2013 to 2014, the seas between North Africa and Southern Europe were patrolled – deep into the dangerous waters off Libya – by the Operation Italian Mare Nostrum rescue project, which ended in October 2014. That operation was considered financially unsustainable for Italy at a cost of €9 million per month. Frontex (the European Agency for the Management of Operational Cooperation at the External Borders of the Member States of the European Union) provided a cheaper option: it limited the area patrolled to 30 miles off the Italian coast and was expected to cost less than €4 million a month, a significant reduction. In its risk analysis for January to March 2016,[26] Frontex recorded that almost 285,000 people had arrived in Europe by sea in just three months, fewer than in the last quarter of 2015, but almost five times the number – 60,500 – who arrived in the same quarter in 2015. The real levels of migration may be much higher.

On 19 April 2015, a boat containing about 900 migrants capsized in Libyan waters on its way to the EU and 800 migrants drowned. That was not the last boat to sink: the International Organization for Migration's Missing Migrants Project estimated that there were 314,000 arrivals by sea in Southern Europe in 2015, with 3,600 deaths at sea, and in 2016 there were 508,347 arrivals and just under 3,000 drowned in the first ten months alone.[27]

Following the terrorist attacks across Europe, the political wind has changed. There is fear of the stranger and hostility, just as there was at the beginning of the twentieth century. There has been a competition between the European states to look the toughest, the meanest, the least generous – to persuade the traffickers to take the migrants next door and leave their country alone.

Fences and boundaries are being erected in Europe in an endeavour to stem and manage the flow of migrants on a country-by-country basis. There have been fences in Ceuta and Melilla (Spanish enclaves in Morocco in North Africa) since 1993, and in the Western Sahara generally since the late 1980s. According to Jaume Castan Pinos of the School of Politics, International Studies and Philosophy at Queen's University Belfast, "the successful integration of the EU has led to an intensification of frontier problems with non-EU states. In fact, the process of European integration which has led to the abolition of internal borders and the reinforcement of external ones (Schengen), has deepened the Mediterranean divide between the North and the South and has encouraged Southern mistrust."[28]

In June 2015, Hungary in Eastern Europe built a border barrier to reinforce the natural river boundary between it and the former Yugoslavian state of Serbia.[29] Two new camps to hold migrants were built, and the fence was topped with razor wire. Migrants were deflected to Croatia, which simply led them to Croatia's border with Hungary. Construction of a second fence between Hungary and Croatia led to riots and the use of water cannon and tear gas on migrants who were trying to breach it.[30] By mid-September, Hungary was considering building a fence between it and Romania as well.[31]

Border barriers have been erected by Austria (on its borders with Slovenia[32] and Italy), Bulgaria (on its Turkish border),[33] Greece (on its Turkish border),[34] Macedonia (on its Greek border),[35] Slovenia (on its Croatian border),[36] Norway (on its Russian border),[37] and now in

Calais, France[38] to prevent access to the United Kingdom from the huge illegal migrant camp known as "The Jungle"[39] on the French side of the Channel Tunnel.

ASYLUM LAW IN EUROPE

Mirroring the building of physical fences came the tightening of national asylum procedures across Europe, including the introduction in many countries of stricter laws, fast-tracked or accelerated processing, and speedier returns. The following are just a few examples of tighter procedures in European countries.

The United Kingdom no longer gives indefinite leave to remain to recognized refugees: the period is usually now just five years, reviewable at the end of that time. Access to benefits is reduced and there is very little legal aid available for the protection of claimants. Those who are excluded from the Refugee Convention under Article 1F and the Qualification Directive under Article 12 are now subject to a regime of very short, rolling grants of permission, with no route to settlement.

The United Kingdom is not in the Schengen zone and has not adopted the recast Common European Asylum System directives, except for the Dublin III Regulation, which is to its advantage, as the United Kingdom is entitled to seek the return of far more migrants to other European Union countries than to itself, due to its position in the north of the Eurozone.

In Hungary, asylum laws began to change in 2015. In 2016, the Hungarian Helsinki Committee published a document entitled "Hungary: Recent Legal Amendments Further Destroy Access to Protection, April–June 2016," decrying a government decree passed in April 2016 that terminated cash payments of €24 to asylum seekers and a school-enrolment benefit previously available for child asylum seekers; terminated integration support for refugees and beneficiaries of subsidiary protection; and reduced protection for both refugees and subsidiary protection beneficiaries to three years, from a period without limit for refugees (though status could be withdrawn at any time) and five years for subsidiary protection beneficiaries. The decree also reduced the period of housing available for refugees in refugee protection centres from sixty days to thirty, and basic health care from one year to six months. According to the Committee:

As a consequence, refugees and beneficiaries of a subsidiary protection status are now obliged to move out from the reception centre where they are accommodated, already a month after the [granting] of their status, and will not receive any targeted support for their integration (financial benefits, housing allowance, language course, etc.). These provisions may immediately force the few who actually get international protection in Hungary to homelessness and destitution, thus fundamentally questioning the effectiveness of the protection status granted.[40]

For those at the Hungarian border, the situation was also made more difficult. As of 13 June 2016:

Irregular migrants (regardless of whether or not they claim asylum) who are arrested within 8 km (5 miles) of either the Serbian-Hungarian or the Croatian-Hungarian border will be "escorted" by the police to the external side of the border fence, without assessing their protection needs or even registering them. Thus Hungary has authorised the automatic push-back of persons potentially in need of international protection from the territory of Hungary to the border area of weeks in order to be admitted to one of the few "transit zones" established as part of the border fence. During this period, asylum-seekers have no access to support or basic services (not even to toilet facilities or shelter from rain and sun).

In 2015 through to January 2016, the Danish police estimated that 92,000 migrants had travelled to or through Denmark, many moving on to Sweden and Norway. In 2016, 25,000 migrants were expected to seek asylum in Denmark. In January 2016, Denmark's government and coalition parties presented a list of thirty-four proposed measures to stem the movement of protection-seeking migrants to, or through, Denmark.[41] The measures brought into force so far include shorter residence permits and restrictions on family reunion, and, controversially, the seizure of valuables in the possession of asylum seekers entering Denmark, or of refugees already in Denmark, if they exceed DKK 10,000 (with exclusions for some items of sentimental value), on the basis that the Danish welfare state is reserved for those who cannot help themselves, not those who can, and that this includes protection-seeking migrants.

On 4 January 2016, Sweden began requiring identity checks on all public transport coming in to Sweden, and Denmark initiated temporary border controls along its German border, expected to remain in place until the Swedish controls ended.

In June 2016, Sweden, a nation previously very welcoming to migrants and asylum seekers, reduced the protection it granted to asylum seekers, initially limiting it to a three-year period.[42] New laws were adopted, removing the right to a permanent residence permit for asylum seekers found to be entitled to protection, and restricting family reunification. Refugee protection in Sweden will entail a three-year temporary protection visa, and for subsidiary protection, only thirteen months. Family reunion will now normally only be granted to minor children and partners, restricted to adult partners over twenty-one who can show that they lived together before coming to Sweden. Sweden also increased maintenance and accommodation requirements for family reunification. There are transitional provisions and some exceptions, but the regime is notably more restrictive than it was previously.

Due to Switzerland's small population, the 39,500 asylum seekers it received in 2015 amounted to nearly 0.5 per cent of its total population. After a reduction in early 2016, Switzerland eventually received over 85 per cent more asylum seekers in 2016 than in 2015. Switzerland began to change its asylum system in 2014, to speed up processing and make returns easier by centralizing the majority of asylum claims in federal reception centres. Following a legal challenge by the conservative right Swiss People's Party, the new system was approved by 68 per cent of Swiss voters in a June 2016 referendum and is now in force until 2019, when it will be reviewed. Sixty per cent of all asylum seekers are held in federal reception centres for up to 140 days. Free legal advice is available at these centres. Twenty per cent of asylum claims are processed in an accelerated procedure, and a further 40 per cent of claimants are processed under the Dublin Regulation. This allows for speedier and more consistent forcible returns. The remaining 40 per cent of claims are allocated to individual cantons under the extended procedure, which allows a maximum of twelve months for the asylum proceedings.[43]

THE 2015 EU MIGRATION AGENDA:
REFUGEE QUOTAS FOR MEMBER STATES

On 13 May 2015, the European Union published its Agenda on Migration, outlining immediate measures to respond to the Mediterranean crisis and a plan for better management of migration in the future, placing a country quota at the heart of its objectives. Of the Agenda, First Vice-President Frans Timmermans of the European Commission said: "The tragic loss of life in the Mediterranean has shocked all Europeans ... we need to find European solutions, based on internal solidarity and the realisation that we have a common responsibility to create an effective migration policy."[44] According to the Commission, it had "become clear that no member state can or should be left alone to address huge migratory pressures" and that the European response would combine "internal and external policies, make best use of EU agencies and tools, and [involve] all actors: Member States, EU institutions, International Organisations, civil society, local authorities and third countries."[45] As High Representative and Vice-President Federica Mogherini said:

> Migration is a shared responsibility of all Member States and all Member States are called now to contribute to tackling this historical challenge. And this is not only a European but a global challenge ... we all know that a real, long term response will come only from fixing the root causes; from poverty to instability caused by wars, to the crises in Libya and Syria. As the European Union, we are engaged and determined to cooperate with the international community on this.[46]

The Commission identified four pillars for the new Agenda on Migration:

1 *Reducing incentives for irregular migration:* sending European migration liaison officers to EU delegations in key third countries; strengthening the legal position of Frontex in relation to returns; enacting measures to make people smuggling a high-risk, low-return criminal activity; and addressing root causes through development cooperation and humanitarian assistance.
2 *Border management:* strengthening the role and capacity of Frontex to secure external maritime borders; helping third countries

improve their border management; and further pooling of coast guard functions at the EU level.

3 *A strong common asylum policy*: ensuring a full and coherent implementation of the CEAS by promoting systematic identification and fingerprinting, and by strengthening the Safe Country of Origin provisions of the Asylum Procedures Directive; and evaluating and possibly revising the Dublin Regulation.

4 *A new policy on legal migration*: focussing on maintaining Europe, a place in demographic decline, as an attractive destination for migrants, by modernizing and overhauling the Blue Card scheme, reprioritizing integration policies, and maximizing the benefits of migration policy to individuals and countries of origin, including facilitating cheaper, faster, and safer remittance transfers.[47]

The Commission also identified immediate actions that needed to be taken, including:

1 Tripling the capacities of and assets for the Frontex joint operations Triton and Poseidon (in 2015 and 2016).

2 Activating the emergency mechanism in Article 78(3) of the Treaty on the Functioning of the European Union (TFEU)[48] to help member states confronted with a sudden influx of migrants, through the redistribution of migrants within the EU.

3 Proposing an EU-wide resettlement scheme to offer 20,000 places across the EU for migrants in clear need of international protection, supported by €50 million in dedicated funding (in 2015 and 2016).

4 Working on a possible Common Security and Defence Policy (CSDP) operation in the Mediterranean to dismantle trafficking networks and fight people smuggling.[49]

The suggestions of redistribution and migrant quotas did not meet with universal approval. The United Kingdom's Home Office told British media that it "will oppose any EU commission proposals to introduce a non-voluntary quota."[50] In the end, only small numbers of refugees were redistributed under the Agenda on Migration, with the exception of those who fell under the terms of the EU-Turkey deal.

THE EU-TURKEY DEAL

The majority of those arriving in Greece in 2015 entered through Turkey, which is neither a member state nor an accession state of the European Union. The arrival figures in Greece from Turkey were 7,000 a day in October 2015 and 3,600 a day in December 2015. On 29 November 2016, Turkey and the European Union agreed on a joint action plan, the result of which was a drop in daily arrivals to below 2,200 by February 2016.[51]

On 20 March 2016, the EU-Turkey deal for processing asylum seekers outside the European Union came into effect. Migrants who arrived in Greece but did not claim asylum, or whose asylum claims failed, would be sent back to Turkey. Each arrival was to be individually assessed by Greek authorities. For each Syrian national returned to Turkey, up to a maximum of 72,000, one Syrian migrant would be resettled in the European Union, with priority given to those who had not tried to enter the European Union illegally.

The European Union agreed to speed up access to up to €3 billion in aid to Turkey to support migrants in that country, and in addition, it was agreed that Turkish citizens would have access to the Schengen zone by June 2016. Both sides agreed to re-energize Turkey's application to enter the European Union, with talks to begin in July 2016. Three asylum seekers lodged a legal challenge to the EU-Turkey deal in the Court of Justice of the European Union in June 2016.

On 15 July 2016, before the European Union membership talks had begun, there was a military coup attempt in Turkey, followed by widespread arrests of military personnel, academics, and judges.[52] The failed coup and the repressive measures taken thereafter by the Turkish government (including the arrest and detention of thousands of judges) damaged Turkey's prospects of European Union admission.

Initially, the EU-Turkey deal had the desired effect of nearly halting arrivals in Greece from Turkey, but the European Union has not paid the full €3 billion it promised, nor has it delivered on the Schengen visa relaxation for Turkish citizens. The numbers of migrants travelling into Greece from Turkey has since risen again, with the Syrian conflict continuing. Turkey has threatened to withdraw from the arrangement if the aid and the free movement for Turkish nationals within the European Union are not forthcoming.

CHANGES TO CEAS AND SCHENGEN
PROPOSED IN 2016

Further proposals for reform and recasting have been made for both the CEAS and the Schengen zone. The Schengen zone reform proposals, adopted by the European Council in May 2016, seek to bring down the border fences and return to a freedom of movement within the Schengen zone by November 2016.[53]

The European Union commissioner for migration, home affairs and citizenship, Dimitris Avramopoulos, has said:

> Schengen is one of the greatest achievements of European integration, and the Commission is committed to safeguarding it … The Commission will continue to provide comprehensive support to the Greek authorities. Significant progress has already been made and the EU-Turkey agreement has led to a sharp decrease of the arrivals in Greece. Today's decision paves the way for a return to the normal functioning of the Schengen area and the lifting of all internal border controls by the end of 2016.[54]

The Commission's proposals on reforming the CEAS, published in July 2016, intend to simplify and shorten the asylum procedures and decision making, discourage secondary movements of asylum seekers, and increase the integration prospects of migrants entitled to international protection. First Vice-President Timmermans has said, "The EU needs an asylum system which is both effective and protective, based on common rules, solidarity and a fair sharing of responsibilities. The proposed reforms will make sure that persons in genuine need of international protection get it quickly, but also that those who do not have the right to receive protection in the EU can be returned swiftly."[55] The Commission's proposals are as follows:

- *Simplify, clarify, and shorten asylum procedures*: shortening and streamlining the overall procedure, with decisions to be taken within six months or less. Provisions would be made for an accelerated procedure.
- *Ensure common guarantees for asylum seekers*: guaranteeing asylum seekers the right to a personal interview and to free legal assistance and representation during the administrative procedure.

Safeguards would be provided for asylum seekers with special needs and for unaccompanied minors.

- *Ensure stricter rules to combat abuse*: introducing new obligations to cooperate with the authorities, as well as strict consequences if these obligations are not met. Sanctions for abuse of the process, lack of cooperation, and secondary movements would include treating the application as being implicitly withdrawn or manifestly unfounded, or the application of the accelerated procedure.
- *Harmonize rules on safe countries*: making the safe country concepts mandatory, and completely replacing the designations of safe countries of origin and safe third countries with European lists within five years.[56]

The proposals reinforce the concept of identical protection in every member state for as long as it is needed. The reform package has been criticized by the Jesuit Refugee Service in Brussels as a "harmonisation down rather than up of protection standards ... [and a] race to the bottom."[57]

The Commission proposes to replace the Qualification Directive with a regulation, taking central control of the type of protection given and the duration of residence permits under a new European Agency for Asylum (EAA) (currently the European Asylum Support Office [EASO]).[58] The EAA would also require member states to take into account guidance prepared by the EAA on the situation in an asylum seeker's country of origin, as well as internal relocation options, while respecting the principle of non-refoulement.[59] Every time an international protection beneficiary is found in a member state where he or she is not entitled to stay or reside, the five-year period for eligibility for long-term residence would begin again.[60] There is to be a compulsory status review to take into account changes in circumstances in the country of origin that could effect the need for protection.[61] If asylum seekers do not "[participate] in integration measures" they may not have access to social security and certain types of social assistance.[62]

Reception conditions are to be harmonized, allowing for the provision of material support rather than money, and access to the labour market, at the latest, six months after the lodging of an asylum application.[63]

These proposals do not meet the fears that have impelled the erection of national physical and legal barriers, nor the demand across

Europe, and particularly in the United Kingdom, for border control
and national self-determination. Rather, they support the perception
that Brussels is taking central control of the protection system, over-
riding national sovereignty.

Where the Refugee Convention is permissive, allowing protection
to be provided by host countries in a number of ways, as long as the
relevant obligation is discharged, the second, recast CEAS will be highly prescriptive, removing any real control from within the host countries on the management of migration where international protection
is claimed.

These proposals seem unlikely to solve the inherent problems within CEAS. The proposals for Dublin IV were given a lukewarm reception from the EU Migration Law Blog[64] and, among others, from Klen
Jäärats, director for EU affairs in Estonia:

> Furthermore, including all asylum-seekers into the burden-shar-
> ing algorithm, instead of only people needing protection, means
> spreading failures of national migration policies across the EU ...
> The proposed solution – being algorithmic and without partici-
> pation by destination countries – also fails to build trust. Without
> the participation of all member states, it may become inefficient,
> ineffective and hugely expensive to administer by those states that
> cooperated. The Commission could have offered a change of
> course, but has instead proposed to make this controversial
> system permanent.[65]

BREXIT: THE UNITED KINGDOM'S VOTE TO LEAVE THE EUROPEAN UNION

On 23 May 2016, 52 per cent of United Kingdom voters in the Brexit referendum voted to leave the European Union, following a campaign in
which the negative effects of migration such as pressures on local
schools and hospitals, and competition for jobs, featured prominently.[66]

On 29 March 2017, Prime Minister May activated Article 50 of the
Lisbon Treaty, which provides an exit mechanism from the European
Union.[67] Article 50 states the following:

1 Any Member State may decide to withdraw from the Union in
  accordance with its own constitutional requirements.

2 A Member State which decides to withdraw shall notify the European Council of its intention. In the light of the guidelines provided by the European Council, the Union shall negotiate and conclude an agreement with that State, setting out the arrangements for its withdrawal, taking account of the framework for its future relationship with the Union. That agreement shall be negotiated in accordance with Article 218(3) of the Treaty on the Functioning of the European Union. It shall be concluded on behalf of the Union by the Council, acting by a qualified majority, after obtaining the consent of the European Parliament.

3 The Treaties shall cease to apply to the State in question from the date of entry into force of the withdrawal agreement or, failing that, two years after the notification referred to in paragraph 2, unless the European Council, in agreement with the Member State concerned, unanimously decides to extend this period.

4 For the purposes of paragraphs 2 and 3, the member of the European Council or of the Council representing the withdrawing Member State shall not participate in the discussions of the European Council or Council or in decisions concerning it.

5 A qualified majority shall be defined in accordance with Article 238(3)(b) of the Treaty on the Functioning of the European Union.

6 If a State which has withdrawn from the Union asks to rejoin, its request shall be subject to the procedure referred to in Article 49.[68]

In 2017, Prime Minister May laid before Parliament the European Union (Withdrawal) Bill (HL Bill 79).[69] Section 1 of the Bill, if enacted, will repeal the European Communities Act 1972, while Sections 2 to 6 provide for the saving of European Union-derived domestic legislation, the incorporation of direct European Union legislation into national law, and for the future interpretation of retained European Union law in the United Kingdom's national courts and tribunals.

Section 6 provides for the future divergence of United Kingdom law from that of the European Union. Under Section 6 of the bill as proposed, no national court will be bound by any principles laid down or decisions made on or after Exit Day by the Court of Justice of the European Union, nor can any reference to that Court be made on or after Exit Day, that courts and tribunals need not have regard to anything done on or after Exit Day by the Court of Justice, another European Union entity or the European Union itself. Any United Kingdom court or tribunal will take into account European Union jurisprudence "if it considers it appropriate to do so," but would not be bound to do so. The Supreme Court, and in most cases the Court of Appeal, would also not be bound by any retained European Union case law and must apply the national test when deciding whether to depart from retained European Union case law. The draft bill remains controversial and subject to change by lawmakers. It continues to progress through the United Kingdom Parliament at the time of writing.

The cost to the United Kingdom of leaving the European Union was negotiated in 2017, but there remain issues of free trade and free movement, as well as the effect of leaving on the Irish Good Friday agreement. The principal difficulty in the Brexit negotiations concerns the cost of leaving (the "divorce bill") and free movement of persons. The United Kingdom wants to be able to control its borders, but retain access to the free market in goods and services within the European Union. The position of the European Union is that free movement and the free market are indivisible. The negotiations have begun but will be difficult and contentious.

CONCLUSION: THE FUTURE OF THE CEAS

Europe is evolving under the migration pressures of the last few years. There are fences, both physical and legal; migrant camps on borders; and faster asylum processes, including new, fast-track processes in many countries, and speedier and more numerous forced removals and deportations. There is less public tolerance of difference; across Central and Southern Europe, and even in Scandinavia, the discourse is changing.

The future for the UK within – or outside – the CEAS, and indeed as a member of the European family, remains unclear. The European Union has arrived, very suddenly, at a point of sharp crisis on federalism, on its responsibilities with regard to asylum, and on free trade and free movement. The postwar dream of free trade in Europe, leading to a common interest in maintaining political links, and the freedom to work and live across the European continent, leading to political union and a lasting peace on the European continent, may be too much, too fast. Europe may have to change its aims and slow down its expansion if it is to survive.

In particular, the Dublin Regulation, with the pressure placed on frontier countries in the south and east of the continent, may have to be reformed or abandoned. The same is true of the Schengen free movement zone: when many countries erect "temporary" border fences and legal barriers, free movement becomes increasingly illusory.

Whether or not the CEAS, or the European Union itself, does survive, it seems likely that migrants from troubled countries around the world will continue to arrive in Europe in large numbers, and there will have to be a strategy in place to manage such migration, with or without the support of the CEAS or the legal analysis that the Court of Justice can provide.

NOTES

1 "Declaration of 9 May," Fondation Robert Schuman, 2018, https://www.robert-schuman.eu/en/declaration-of-9-may-1950.

2 "Use of the Euro: Euro Area 1999–2005," European Central Bank, Eurosystem, https://www.ecb.europa.eu/euro/intro/html/map.en.html.

3 "Staring into the Abyss," *Economist*, 12 November 2011, https://www.economist.com/node/21536872.

4 Adam Withnall, "Iraq Crisis: Isis Declares Its Territories a New Islamic State with 'Restoration of Caliphate' in the Middle East," *Independent*, 30 June 2014, http://www.independent.co.uk/news/world/middle-east/isis-declares-new-islamic-state-in-middle-east-with-abu-bakr-al-baghdadi-as-emir-removing-iraq-and-9571374.html.

5 "Immigration Rules Part 9: Grounds for Refusal," para. A320 to 324, https://www.gov.uk/guidance/immigration-rules/immigration-rules-part-9-grounds-for-refusal.

6 Parliament of the United Kingdom, third reading of the Immigration Bill 2014, Hansard 30 January 2014, http://www.publications.parliament.uk/pa/cm201314/cmhansrd/cm140130/debtext/140130-0004.htm#14013062003170.

7 Leo Benedictus, "A Brief History of the Passport: From a Royal Letter to a Microchip," *Guardian*, 17 November 2006, https://www.theguardian.com/travel/2006/nov/17/travelnews.

8 Alec Tritton, "Escaping the Guillotine: French Émigrés from Revolutionary France," Exodus: Movement of the People, 2013, http://www.exodus2013.co.uk/escaping-the-guillotine-french-emigres-from-revolutionary-franc.

9 "Refugees 1900–1950," Exploring 20th Century London, accessed 13 October 2016, http://www.20thcenturylondon.org.uk/refugees-1900-1950.

10 "States Parties to the 1951 Convention Relating to the Status of Refugees and the 1967 Protocol," United Nations High Commissioner for Refugees, accessed 13 October 2016, http://www.unhcr.org/protect/PROTECTION /3b73b0d63.pdf.

11 "Council Directive 2004/38/EC of 29 April 2004 on minimum standards for the qualification and status of third country nationals or stateless persons as refugees or as persons who otherwise need international protection and the content of the protection granted," EUR-Lex, Official Journal of the European Union, L 304/12, 30 September 2004, http://eur-lex.europa.eu/LexUri Serv/LexUriServ.do?uri=CELEX:32004L0083:en:HTML.

12 "Schengen: Controversial EU Free Movement Deal Explained," BBC News, 24 April 2016, http://www.bbc.com/news/world-europe-13194723.

13 "Preamble: Charter of Fundamental Rights of the European Union," EUR-Lex, Official Journal of the European Union, C 326/391, 26 October 2012, http://eur-lex.europa.eu/legal-content/EN/TXT/?uri=CELEX:12012P/TXT.

14 Ibid.

15 "EN – Recast Qualification Directive 2011/95/EU of 13 December 2011," European Database of Asylum Law (EDAL), http://www.asylumlawdatabase .eu/en/content/en-recast-qualification-directive-directive-201195eu-13-december-2011.

16 "Directive 2013/32/EU of the European Parliament and of the Council of 26 June 2013 on common procedures for granting and withdrawing international protection (recast)," EUR-Lex, Official Journal of the European Union, L 180/60, 29 June 2013, http://eur-lex.europa.eu/legal-content/EN/ALL/?uri =CELEX:32013L0032.

17 "Directive 2013/33/EU laying down standards for the reception of applicants for international protection (recast)," EUR-Lex, Official Journal of the European Union, L 180/96, 29 June 2013, http://eur-lex.europa.eu/legal-content /EN/ALL/?uri=CELEX:32013L0033.

18 "Regulation (EU) No 604/2013 of the European Parliament and of the Council of 26 June 2013 establishing the criteria and mechanisms for determining the Member State responsible for examining an application for international protection lodged in one of the Member States by a third-country national or a stateless person (recast)," EUR-Lex, Official Journal of the European Union, L 180/31, 29 June 2013, http://eur-lex.europa.eu/legal-content/EN/TXT/HTML/?uri=CELEX:32013R0604&from=EN.

19 EUR-Lex Access to European Law: "Council Directive 2003/86/EC of 22 September 2003 on the right to family reunification," EUR-Lex, Official Journal of the European Union, L 251/12, 3 October 2003, http://eur-lex.europa.eu /LexUriServ/LexUriServ.do?uri=OJ:L:2003:251:0012:0018:en:PDF.

20 "Council Directive 2001/55/EC of 20 July 2001 on minimum standards for giving temporary protection in the event of a mass influx of displaced persons and on measures promoting a balance of efforts between Member States in receiving such a person and bearing the consequences thereof," EUR-Lex, Official Journal of the European Union, L 212/12, 7 August 2001, http://eur-lex.europa.eu/LexUriServ/LexUriServ.do?uri=OJ:L:2001:212:0012:0023:EN:PDF.

21 Sir Bernard Hogan-Howe, "Met Chief Warns New UK Terror Atrocity 'Is a Case of When Not If': Britain's Top Cop Warns 600 Extra Armed Police Are 'Not Enough to Stop Attack," Daily Mail, Mail on Sunday, 30 July 2016, updated 1 August 2016, http://www.dailymail.co.uk/news/article-3716523/Met-chief-warns-new-UK-terror-atrocity-case-not-Britain-s-cop-warns-600-extra-armed-police-not-stop-attack.html.

22 "Common Asylum System at a Turning Point: Refugees Caught in Europe's Solidarity Crisis," Annual Report 2014/2015, Asylum Information Database (AIDA), http://www.asylumineurope.org/sites/default/files/shadow-reports/aida_annualreport_2014-2015_0.pdf.

23 "Figures at a Glance," United Nations High Commissioner for Refugees, 2017, accessed 20 July 2017, http://www.unhcr.org/figures-at-a-glance.html.

24 "Global Trends: Forced Displacement in 2016," United Nations High Commissioner for Refugees, 2017, http://www.unhcr.org/globaltrends2016.

25 Ibid.

26 "FRAN Quarterly: Quarter 1 – January–March 2016," Frontex, Frontex Risk Analysis Unit, 2016, http://FRONTEX.europa.eu/assets/Publications/Risk_Analysis/FRAN_Q1_2016_final.pdf.

27 "Mediterranean Migrant Arrivals Reach 314,003; Deaths at Sea: 3610," Missing Migrants, 7 October 2016, http://missingmigrants.iom.int/mediterranean-migrant-arrivals-reach-314003-deaths-sea-3610.

28 Jaume Castan Pinos, "Building Fortress Europe? Schengen and the Cases of Ceuta and Melilla" (working paper, Queen's University Belfast, Centre for International Borders Research, 2009), http://www.qub.ac.uk/research-centres/CentreforInternationalBordersResearch/Publications/WorkingPapers/CIBRWorkingPapers/Filetoupload,174398,en.pdf.

29 Daniel Nolan, "Hungary Orders 100-Mile Serbia Border Fence to Keep out Migrants," Telegraph, 17 June 2015, http://www.telegraph.co.uk/news/worldnews/europe/hungary/11680840/Hungary-orders-100-mile-Serbia-border-fence-to-keep-out-migrants.html.

30 "Hungary Starts Building Fence on Croatian Border," Deutsche Welle, 18 September 2015, http://www.dw.com/en/hungary-starts-building-fence-on-croatian-border/a-18721670.

31 "Migrant Crisis: Hungary's Closed Border Leaves Many Stranded," BBC
    News, 15 September 2015, http://www.bbc.co.uk/news/world-europe-
    34260071.

32 "Austria to Build Fence on Slovenia Border," Deutsche Welle, 15 September
    2015, http://www.dw.com/en/austria-to-build-fence-on-slovenia-border
    /a-18847582.

33 Caroline Mortimer, "Bulgaria Builds Final Part of Razor Wire Fence to Keep
    out Refugees," *Independent*, 4 August 2015, http://www.independent.co.uk
    /news/world/europe/bulgaria-builds-final-part-of-razor-wire-fence-to-keep-
    out-refugees-10437962.html.

34 "Protesters March Against Greece-Turkey Border Fence," *Kathimerini*, 24 Jan-
    uary 2016, http://www.ekathimerini.com/205366/article/ekathimerini/news
    /protesters-march-against-greece-turkey-border-fence.

35 John Hall, "European Refugee Crisis: Macedonia Builds 10-Foot High Razor-
    Topped Fence Along Greek Border," *International Business Times*, 10 January
    2016, http://www.ibtimes.co.uk/european-refugee-crisis-macedonia-builds-
    10-foot-high-razor-topped-fence-along-greek-border-1537078.

36 "Migrant Crisis: Slovenia Moves to 'Shut Down' Balkans Route," BBC News,
    9 March 2016, http://www.bbc.com/news/world-europe-35760534; and Bar-
    bara Surk, "Slovenia Builds Border Fence to Stem Flow of Migrants," *New
    York Times*, 11 November 2015, http://www.nytimes.com/2015/11/12/world
    /europe/slovenia-border-fence-migrants-refugees.html.

37 Bojan Pancevski, "Norway Builds Arctic Border Fence as It Gives Migrants
    the Cold Shoulder," *New York Times, Sunday Times*, 4 September 2016,
    http://www.thetimes.co.uk/article/norway-builds-arctic-border-fence-as-it-
    gives-migrants-the-cold-shoulder-hf37jlwqq.

38 Bianca Britton, "UK to Build 'Big New Wall' in Calais to Stop Migrants,"
    CNN, 7 September 2016, http://edition.cnn.com/2016/09/07/europe/calais-
    wall-migrants.

39 "Counting the Number of Migrants in the Calais 'Jungle,'" Full Fact, 31
    August 2016, https://fullfact.org/immigration/counting-number-migrants-
    calais-jungle.

40 "Worsening Conditions for Refugees in Hungary," European Council for
    Refugees and Exiles (ECRE), 17 June 2016, http://www.ecre.org/worsening-
    conditions-for-refugees-in-hungary.

41 "Refugee Law and Policy: Denmark," Library of Congress, 2016, accessed 14
    October 2016, https://www.loc.gov/law/help/refugee-law/denmark.php.

42 "20 July 2016: New Law That Affects Asylum Seekers and Their Families,"
    Migrationsverket, 20 July 2016, https://www.migrationsverket.se/English

/About-the-Migration-Agency/Legislative-changes-2016/Nyheter/2016-07-20-20-July-2016-New-law-that-affects-asylum-seekers-and-their-families.html.

43 Simon Bradley "Speedier Asylum Process Voted In," swissinfo.ch, http://www.swissinfo.ch/eng/speedier-process_should-asylum-procedures-once-again-be-reformed-/4220040.

44 "Managing Migration Better in All Aspects: A European Agenda on Migration," press release, European Commission, 13 May 2015, http://europa.eu/rapid/press-release_IP-15-4956_en.htm.

45 Ibid.

46 Ibid.

47 Ibid.

48 "Consolidated version of the Treaty on the Functioning of the European Union," EUR-Lex, Official Journal of the European Union, 2012/C 326/01, 6 October 2012, http://eur-lex.europa.eu/legal-content/EN/TXT/?uri=CELEX:12012E/TXT.

49 "Managing Migration Better in All Aspects," European Commission.

50 Ian Traynor, "EU Plans Migrant Quotas Forcing States to 'Share' Burden," *Guardian*, 10 May 2015, https://www.theguardian.com/world/2015/may/10/european-commission-migrant-quota-plan-mediterranean-crisis.

51 "Managing the Refugee Crisis: Commission Reports on Implementation of EU-Turkey Joint Action Plan," press release, European Commission, 10 February 2016, http://europa.eu/rapid/press-release_IP-16-268_en.htm.

52 Gerry Holt and Roland Hughes, "Failed Turkey Coup: A Summary of Today's Key Developments," BBC News, 15 July 2016, http://www.bbc.co.uk/news/live/world-europe-36811357.

53 "Back to Schengen: Commission Takes Next Steps Towards Lifting of Temporary Internal Border Controls," press release, European Commission, 4 May 2016, http://europa.eu/rapid/press-release_IP-16-1627_en.htm.

54 "Back to Schengen: Council Adopts Commission Proposal on Next Steps Towards Lifting of Temporary Internal Border Controls," press release, European Commission, 12 May 2016, http://europa.eu/rapid/press-release_IP-16-1723_en.htm.

55 "Completing the Reform of the Common European Asylum System: Towards an Efficient, Fair and Humane Asylum Policy," press release, European Commission, 13 July 2016, http://europa.eu/rapid/press-release_IP-16-2433_en.htm.

56 Ibid.

57 "The CEAS Reform Package: The Death of Asylum by a Thousand Cuts?," Jesuit Refugee Service Europe, Working Paper no. 6, 2017,

https://jrseurope.org/assets/Regions/EUR/media/files/JRS-EuropeCEASreform-WorkingPaper6.pdf.

58 "EU Agency for Asylum: Presidency and European Parliament Reach a Broad Political Agreement," European Council, Council of the European Union, 29 June 2017, http://www.consilium.europa.eu/en/press/press-releases/2017/06/29/eu-agency-for-asylum; and "About Us," European Asylum Support Office (EASO), https://www.easo.europa.eu/about-us.

59 "Completing the Reform of the Common European Asylum System," European Commission.

60 Ibid.

61 Ibid.

62 Ibid.

63 Ibid.

64 Constantin Hruschka, "Dublin Is Dead! Long Live Dublin! The 4 May 2016 Proposal of the European Commission," EU Immigration and Asylum Law and Policy, 17 May 2016, http://eumigrationlawblog.eu/dublin-is-dead-long-live-dublin-the-4-may-2016-proposal-of-the-european-commission.

65 Klen Jäärats, "How to Fix the Breaks in Europe's Asylum System," *Europe's World*, 23 June 2016, http://www.friendsofeurope.org/publication/how-fix-breaks-europes-asylum-system.

66 Roy Greenslade, "Sun and Mail Ignore the Economy to Push Migration Message on Brexit," *Guardian*, 21 June 2016, https://www.theguardian.com/media/greenslade/2016/jun/21/why-should-we-vote-to-leave-the-eu-its-migration-stupid.

67 "Brexit: Article 50 Has Been Triggered – What Now?," BBC News, 29 March 2017, http://www.bbc.co.uk/news/uk-politics-39143978.

68 Lisbon Treaty, Article 50, http://www.lisbon-treaty.org/wcm/the-lisbon-treaty/treaty-on-European-union-and-comments/title-6-final-provisions/137-article-50.html; "Consolidated Versions of the Treaty on European Union and the Treaty on the Functioning of the European Union," EUR-Lex, Official Journal of the European Union, 2012/C 326/01, 26 October 2012, http://eur-lex.europa.eu/legal-content/EN/TXT/?uri=celex%3A12012E%2FTXT.

69 European Union (Withdrawal) Bill (HL Bill 79), Parliament of the United Kingdom, https://publications.parliament.uk/pa/bills/lbill/2017-2019/0079/lbill_2017-20190079_en_2.htm#pb2-l1g6.

Beyond Context and Consequences: Countering the "Criminalization of Migration" through the Promotion of the Human Rights of Migrants

James C. Simeon and Idil Atak

The universal right to freedom of movement[1] is everywhere, noticeably, under siege as states, primarily in the Global North, impose restrictive measures on migration for all those seeking entry into their territory.[2] The concluding comments and reflections outlined here seek to map the way forward for the protection and advancement of the fundamental rights of migrants within a climate that is becoming constantly harsher toward all forms of migration, but especially for those who are forced to use irregular means to seek a life of freedom and opportunity, as is the birthright of us all by virtue of our humanity. Given the current trend of the criminalization of migration, or "crimmigration," the enormity of an undertaking of this nature cannot be overestimated. Stephen H. Legomsky has emphasized that, for the United States,

> Violations of the immigration laws trigger broader, harsher, and more frequent criminal consequences. Indeed, it is no longer rare for refugees seeking asylum to be criminally prosecuted for illegal entry. Conversely, Congress has steadily expanded the list of non-immigration-related crimes that trigger deportation and other adverse immigration consequences, and the sheer numbers of deportations on crime-related grounds have skyrocketed. The

underlying theories of deportation increasingly resemble those of criminal punishment. Preventive detention and plea bargaining, longstanding staples of the criminal justice system, have infiltrated the deportation process. Some of the same government actors, including federal sentencing judges and state and local police, are now frequently called upon to perform both criminal and immigration functions simultaneously.[3]

The process of the criminalization of migration has been accelerated by the coordinated terrorist attacks that took place in the United States on 11 September 2001, the worst terrorist attacks in modern history.[4] For the US, and to a lesser extent the rest of the world, 9/11 was, undoubtedly, a pivotal traumatizing and transformative event vis-à-vis migration. It has been noted that

> The very foundation of America's relationship to immigrants has shifted in the wake of new calls for protecting our borders, broader national security, and a resurgence of an "us" versus "them" mentality … This antipathy toward immigrants and discussions of national security have now extended to immigrant groups that have no history of engaging in terrorist acts. Calls to secure the United States/Mexico border have shifted from concern regarding the high numbers of undocumented immigrants to concern about national security and the infiltration of terrorists, vilifying the undocumented population even further.[5]

The impact of 9/11 was felt right across the globe, with everything from the so-called "War Against Terrorism" to the strengthening of intelligence and law enforcement organization by most member states of the United Nations. The focus on anti-terrorism and national security has been described by some as the "securitization of migration."[6] The criminalization of migration is, in part, a consequence of this securitization phenomenon.[7] Hence, the significance and importance of an edited collection that explores the criminalization of migration in Canada and abroad, through the conceptual lenses of both context and consequences.

The following reflections and conclusions are presented in three sections. The first section covers the all-important topic of how the criminalization of migration is defined in the literature on refugee and forced migration studies. This is reinforced with some recent illustrative examples of crimmigration in Canada, as well as in a number of other countries. The basic features and contours of the criminalization of migration are outlined within their contextual setting together with their consequences, which are oftentimes unintended. The second section discusses the durable solutions to "migration crises" and the mobilization of resistance to crimmigration, as well as the prevalent policy response by states to irregular migration. This section also reviews some of the key insights and findings of individual chapters in this collection that seek to reverse and overcome the "securitization of migration" through one of its principal means, criminalization – the central and overarching theme of this edited collection as a whole. The chapter concludes with reflections on charting the way forward by means of the "decriminalization of migration," or "decrimmigration," through the rigorous advancement of the human rights of migrants.[8] It identifies a number of promising avenues for achieving such an ambitious, yet exceedingly worthy, goal, including a new framework to deal with the "root causes" of forced migration, strategic litigation, political leadership that is prepared to develop innovative policies that protect the fundamental human rights of migrants, the progressive development of a new international migration regime that is premised on the protection and advancement of the human rights of migrants, and a vigilant and active civil society movement that transcends borders and is prepared to pressure policy makers to protect and advance the fundamental human rights of migrants and, in turn, each and every person by virtue of their humanity.

EXPLORING THE "CRIMINALIZATION OF MIGRATION" AND ITS CONTEXT AND CONSEQUENCES

Over the last three decades, various aspects of migration have been criminalized to such an extent that legal scholars have developed a new term to describe the phenomenon of the merging of criminal law and practice with immigration law and practice.[9] This term, crimmigration, has been defined in the following way:

Generally, "crimmigration law" refers to the intersection of criminal law and procedure with immigration law and procedure. This broad outline can be filled by the details of three trends that have dominated the evolution that criminal law and immigration law have undergone in recent years: criminal convictions now lead to immigration law consequences ever more often; violations of immigration law are increasingly punished through the criminal justice system; and law enforcement tactics traditionally viewed as parts of one or the other area of law have crossed into the other making enforcement of immigration law resemble criminal law enforcement and turning criminal law enforcement into a semblance of immigration law enforcement.[10]

Various notable features and trends in the criminalization of migration have been evident in Canada, the US, the UK, and elsewhere, for a considerable time.[11] Take, for instance, such measures as:

- the initial iteration of the 2012 Protecting Canada's Immigration System Act, which called for mandatory twelve-month detention without access to independent review for certain categories of arriving non-citizens;[12]
- the 2013 Faster Removal of Foreign Criminals Act, which denies permanent residents in Canada who are serving sentences of six months or more for "serious crimes" the right to appeal a deportation order;[13]
- the 1996 Illegal Immigration Reform and Immigrant Responsibility Act and the 1996 Antiterrorism and Effective Death Penalty Act, which have had a dramatic effect on the number of people who are eligible for detention and deportation in the United States. The two pieces of legislation made it so that "[r]elatively minor, nonviolent crimes – like burglary, tax evasion, and a broad number of drug offenses – were now considered 'aggravated felonies' in the administrative immigration context, even if those same crimes did not constitute felonies, aggravated or otherwise, under criminal law."[14]
- two packages of asylum laws passed in Germany in October 2015 and February 2016 that limited the benefits asylum seekers receive, expanded the list of safe countries, and put on hold the right of people with subsidiary protection status to reunite with their family members.[15] Following major electoral losses in German national elections in September 2017, Chancellor Angela Merkel agreed to try to limit the number of refugees arriving in Germany to 200,000, in a significant departure from her "open door immigration policy."[16]

The American Immigration Council's special report, "The Criminalization of Immigration in the United States," notes:

> In short, as U.S. immigration laws create more and more "criminal aliens," the machinery of detention and deportation grows larger as well, casting a widening dragnet over the nation's foreign-born population in search of anyone who might be deportable. With the technologically sophisticated enforcement systems in place today, being stopped by a police officer for driving a car with a broken tail light can culminate in a one-way trip out of the country if the driver long ago pled guilty to a misdemeanor that has since been defined as a deportable offense.[17]

Further, it is interesting to note that in the United States a wide range of migration-related activities were criminalized in the 1980s and 1990s. García Hernández points out that,

> [d]uring the 1980s, Congress also added new immigration-related crimes to the federal penal code. The Immigration Reform and Control Act of 1986 that famously provided legalization paths for millions of unauthorized migrants also made it a federal crime to hire unauthorized workers and increased the penalty for knowingly or recklessly smuggling people into the United States. Another statute enacted that year criminalized marrying solely for the purpose of obtaining an immigration benefit. Ten years later Congress created a host of crimes as part of the mammoth Illegal Immigration Reform and Immigrant Responsibility Act (IIRIRA). Falsely claiming to be a United States citizen, voting in a federal election, and participating in the false preparation of an immigration application were suddenly criminalized.[18]

In the UK, the 2016 Immigration Act has been criticized for "criminalizing immigrants without formal status by providing the possibility of jail time if they work illegally, and stiff penalties for those who employ them – policies that critics say will silence exploited workers and encourage ... immigrant-slavery situations."[19]

Further, according to the Canadian Civil Liberties Association (CCLA), "Numerous other new laws and policies have attempted to criminalize people (including refugees) who assist (other) refugees to enter Canada; created programs and legislation to restrict certain kinds of immigration; made certain immigrants more vulnerable; and treated certain immigrants, migrant workers and undocumented persons as if they were dangerous criminals."[20]

The prevailing trend in the Global North, as illustrated above, is the criminalization of migration that is characterized by the merging of immigration law and practice with criminal law and practice. For instance, Virginie Guiraudon has pointed out, from a comparative perspective, that

> as the East Sea episode [a freighter that was run aground on the French Riviera with some 900 Syrian Kurds on board in February 2001] has shown, policy instruments such as visas and carrier sanctions that seek to prevent "unwanted" migrants from reaching Europe's border have not stopped their arrival. They have instead criminalized the migration process itself, and raised the demand for smuggling networks and their lucre. France and the European Union today are witnessing the same perverse effects that the US experienced along its Mexican border, where new restrictions in some states only redirected flows to others, and raised the price of illegal passage.[21]

United Nations human rights bodies have also expressed a deep concern with the criminalization of migration. For instance, Emily Nagisa Keehn has stated the following:

> Certain U.N. human rights bodies have expressed concern with the increasing use of criminal law instead of administrative regulations to restrict migratory flows. These concerns span the criminalization of labor migration, of minors who undertake irregular border crossings, and of asylum seekers. They also give attention to attendant forms of criminalization such as punishing landlords who accommodate irregular migrants, or fishermen who rescue or inadvertently transport irregular migrants. Human rights abuses that are inherent in the criminal justice systems, such as inhumane conditions of detention, imprisonment of children, police harassment and violence, are also a concern as criminalized migration exposes migrants and asylum seekers to these forms of collateral consequences.[22]

In addition, the decriminalization of irregular migration has even come up at the recent consultations on the UN Migration Compact and the response was that the "decriminalization of irregular migration remains contentious."²³ Nonetheless, the UN Secretary-General's migration report, "Making Migration Work for All," released in advance of the Migration Compact negotiations, states:

> It is profoundly misguided, however, to treat migration itself as a threat. I am concerned that we have seen an increase in short-term and reactive security approaches to migration, such as setting up systems to detain migrants in transit countries, that are: (a) ill-advised and unsustainable; (b) put the safety of migrants in peril; and (c) risk being counter-productive on their own terms.
>
> Another symptom of this disturbing trend has been increased recourse to administrative detention of migrants as a measure with deterrent intent. This is often undertaken without adequate guarantees and at the expense of less coercive measures, resulting in migrants, including children, being exposed to arbitrary and punitive measures. Migrants in detention can be exposed to overcrowding, poor sanitary facilities and violence.²⁴

The Secretary-General's migration report urges member states to develop a strategy for dealing with large movements of migrants. The key elements of the strategy need to take into account the "humanitarian and human rights-based approach to assisting large movements of migrants,"²⁵ ensure that the appropriate mechanisms and resources are in place so that "the status of migrants in vulnerable situations can be determined individually, fairly and reliably;"²⁶ and ensure that migrants who do not qualify for international protection can be offered more credible pathways if faced with insurmountable obstacles to return to their countries of origin.²⁷

It is important and relevant to underscore, as brought in the UN Secretary-General's migration report, noted immediately above, that the phenomenon of the "securitization of migration" through "criminalization" also relies on both enforcement and detention, as both deterrent and compliance measures. The use of detention, and its privatization, has been most prevalent in the United States and Europe, but it has also made inroads in Canada.²⁸ According to the project Never Home: Legislating Discrimination in Canadian Immigration, organized by the advocacy group No One Is Illegal, between 2006 and 2014 the Canadian government detained some 87,317 migrants without charge, and spent more than a quarter of a billion dollars detaining migrants over a five-year period.[29] It is important to note that migrants are the only population within Canada that can be jailed simply on administrative grounds and without being charged with any criminal offence.[30] In fact, immigration detention is considered to be one of the fastest growing forms of incarceration in Canada. Over the last ten years, the Canadian government has detained an average of about 11,000 migrants per year, including some 807 children.[31] The United Nations High Commissioner for Human Rights Working Group on Arbitrary Detention strongly chastised the Canadian government for not adhering to international law relating to the detention of migrants in irregular situations.[32] With reference to a case involving someone who was in immigration detention for seven years, the Working Group noted: "It is also clearly established by other international bodies that the inability of a State party to carry out the expulsion of an individual does not justify detention beyond the shortest period of time or where there are alternatives to detention, and under no circumstances indefinite detention."[33] Never Home has asserted that

> Canada is one of the only "Western" countries to have indefinite detention, often with limited access to family, legal counsel and third-party monitoring agencies. The US and EU countries have a "presumptive period," meaning that if removal cannot happen within a certain number of days then detainees must be released. In the US, this period is 90 days. In Canada, some immigration detainees have been jailed for over ten years without charges or trial, including South African anti-apartheid icon Mbuyisa Makhubu.[34]

One of the principal features of crimmigration, evident in both immigration and criminal law and practice, is the emphasis on enforcement. Immigration enforcement is within the purview of the Canada Border Services Agency (CBSA), which is a relatively recent addition to the federal public bureaucracy that was established in 2003 as part of the institutional and structural reforms that emerged from the aftermath of the 11 September 2001 terrorist attacks in the United States.[35] The CBSA is part of the Public Safety Portfolio and reports directly to the minister of public safety.[36] It has a wide range of enforcement activities at the Canadian border and beyond, including a number relating to border crossings by migrants. With the establishment of the CBSA there has been a new focus on immigration enforcement. This can be seen across most of the Global North, especially after 9/11 with the new concentration of resources – financial, material, and human – on border security.[37] The advocacy group No One Is Illegal, among others, is explicitly pushing against this trend and asserting an alternative vision where freedom of movement is, no less, fully guaranteed, stating:

> Given that the detention and deportation of non-citizens is so readily accepted and unquestioned in society as the legitimate exercise of state sovereignty, we aim to make visible the material conditions and tangible practices of the detention and deportation of "undeserving" and "undesirable" non-citizens, who are essentially being criminalized for the mere act of migration. Rather, we aim for a world where freedom of movement and human mobility is guaranteed and the social control of migrants through the detention and deportation regime is abolished.[38]

One of the principal migration policy enforcement mechanism or instruments used by states is deportation.[39] The CBSA is the institution responsible for "carrying out arrests, detentions and removals of individuals who are not permitted in Canada."[40] According to the CBSA, "Removing individuals who do not have the right to enter or stay in Canada is essential to maintaining the integrity of our immigration program and to ensuring fairness for those who come to this country lawfully."[41]

Reports have indicated that Canada deports more than 10,000 people each year.[42] According to Never Home, Canada deports an average of thirty-five people per day, and a total of 117,531 people were deported between 2006 and 2014.[43] With a surge in refugee claims in Canada in 2016 to 2017, the deportation of migrants has increased as well.[44] In 2016, 7,357 people were deported, and it is estimated that the number of people deported in 2017 will have easily exceeded this.[45] A similar trend in the increase of the number of deportations and removals of foreign nationals was seen in other jurisdictions as well, such as the United States[46] and the United Kingdom.[47] The total number of removals in the United States in 2016 was 240,255.[48] The number of people who were removed or departed voluntarily in the United Kingdom was 39,626.[49]

Against this backdrop, this collection examines the phenomenon of the criminalization of migration in Canada and abroad through the central theme of context and consequences, and from four distinct viewpoints. First, it addresses the criminalization of migration from the lens of legal analogy, human smuggling, and trafficking. Part 1 includes a critical assessment of the "crimmigration" concept itself, while at the same time examining how it has been imbued with the judicial mentality or mind-set as the courts have applied and interpreted migration laws in various jurisdictions. How the courts, and especially the Supreme Court of Canada (scc), have recently dealt with the previous federal Conservative government's overly broad legislation seeking to clamp down on human smuggling is also thoroughly examined. The new policy and enforcement responses to human trafficking are also outlined and assessed in detail across all levels of the public policy spectrum in Canada. The second, in part 2 of the collection, considers the criminalization and exclusion of refugees under Article 1F of the 1951 *Convention Relating to the Status of Refugees* (the Refugee Convention).[50] Those who are responsible for serious criminality are deemed to be "undeserving" of refugee protection and are excluded from refugee status, despite the fact that they may have a well-founded fear of persecution on one of the five grounds of the 1951 Refugee Convention.[51] Part 2 of this collection deals with the criminalization of those who are alleged to have committed serious breaches in international and national criminal and/or humanitarian law. The issue concerns who ought to be held criminally liable for serious criminal offenses and, accordingly, deemed to be "undeserving" of international protection. The third viewpoint, found in part 3, examines the crimmigration response to "migration crises" from historical and/or comparative perspectives, and with Canada as the focus of the analysis. The tactic of "attrition through enforcement," a staple in the arsenal of crimmigration, can be seen most distinctly in the policies of the host states of Turkey and Jordan as they seek to cope with migrants who are being forcibly displaced due to the ever-escalating and protracted armed conflicts and violence raging in the Middle East. The "legalization" of the refugee status determination process in the United States is also considered – and thoroughly interrogated and scrutinized – as a method of erecting socio-legal barriers for those seeking asylum from Central and

South America along the southwestern US border. The "rhyme of history" is apparent in an examination of the mid-nineteenth-century Irish famine migration, with its politics of criminalization and marginalization of migrants, with clear echoes in the barriers being built today by jurisdictions in the Global North to keep people away from and outside their borders. Finally, the fourth viewpoint, in part 4, assesses the dynamics at play in the criminalization of refugees and other forced migrants, as well as possible challenges to this criminalization and prospects for the future, based on multiple aspects of recent history: the shifts in Canadian refugee policy over the last four decades; the growing sanctuary movement, which implicitly recognizes the human rights and dignity of all persons, irrespective of their legal status within the state and their entitlement to essential public services; and the emergence of and challenges to the Common European Asylum System across the European Union. Flashes of brilliance, observed repeatedly in the past, reveal the broad arc of history and a future that promises the progressive realization of the "freedom to move," regardless of volition, but most assuredly not without a constant and sustained struggle – indeed, not without a tremendous effort on the part of all those who are most desperate for a place of refuge.

The central theme of context, within which the criminalization of migration occurs, undoubtedly helps to shape and to mediate the resulting consequences, as is evident throughout each of the collection's contributions. But what is absolutely essential is the necessity to move beyond both context and its contingent consequences in an overall global sustaining effort to "decriminalize migration." What follows are a number of pathways to the realization of the fundamental human right to a "freedom of movement."

EXPLORING DURABLE SOLUTIONS TO "MIGRATION CRISES" WHILE RESISTING "CRIMMIGRATION"

This collection offers a series of lessons regarding the process of crimmigration, and some best practices to resist it. As such, it suggests both a rethinking of the role of states in the process of the criminalization of migration and, directly related to this, a consideration of the political ramifications of changing social, economic, and cultural attitudes towards migrants. Some of these lessons and best practices can be summarized as follows:

The Necessity of Addressing "Root Causes"
Rather than Just the "Symptoms"

The collection examines "migration crises" in some detail from the perspective of durable solutions and strategies for resisting "crimmigration." The major causes of refugees in the world are protracted armed conflict and persecution.[52] The *SAGE Encyclopedia of War* states the following regarding "War-Related Displacement and Flight":

> The phenomena of forced migration and displacement of civilians around the world are caused by multiple factors and a variety of extraordinary circumstances. These include, among others, natural disasters, development projects, and human trafficking. However, war was – and continues to be – one of the drivers of refugee creation. The great wars of the 20th century, as well as wars and other violent conflicts of recent decades, have produced a vast number of people who were forced to move away from their homes in search of safety.[53]

This driver, or "push factor," needs to be seriously addressed.[54] The most severe and deadly protracted armed conflict today is in Syria.[55] The others include conflicts in Afghanistan, Somalia, and South Sudan. Indeed, 55 per cent of the world's refugees come from only three countries: Syria, Afghanistan, and South Sudan.[56] All of these countries have been embroiled in protracted armed conflict for years. In fact, the top nine source countries for refugees have all been involved in brutal internal, protracted armed conflicts.[57]

Addressing the root causes of refugees requires a new protection orientation and framework that involves, as a minimum, the following four key reforms to the international refugee protection system. The first is a common definition for who is a refugee that includes "war refugees," such as that found in the 1984 Cartagena Declaration, the most progressive legal definition of who ought to be a refugee. The second is the adoption by the UN, and led by the UNHCR, of a global consultative process, like the Cartagena Declaration decennial consultative process, in order to come up with a comprehensive plan of action. The third is a greater ability and capacity for the UN to mediate and broker ceasefires and to negotiate peace agreements to stop protracted non-international armed conflict in order to prevent or to stop mass forced displacement, which is the principal consequence of these seemingly endless wars. The fourth required reform is the expansion of the Responsibility to Protect (R2P) doctrine to include mass forced displacement as an atrocity crime. This new protection orientation and framework is outlined in detail elsewhere.[58] The essential point here is that the Global North's preoccupation with the criminalization of migration does not address the root causes of refugee and other forced migrant movements, but rather only the symptoms of the mass production of refugees and other forced migrants.

The Role of the Judiciary

The courts have played a significant role in protecting the fundamental rights and freedoms of migrants, such as the labour rights of temporary foreign workers, and the provision of medical care for refugees and other forced migrants in Canada and some other countries. As well, court judgments have challenged the criminalization of asylum seekers, including their indefinite and arbitrary detention and the lack of appeal for some groups of refugee claimants and other migrants. The courts have also progressively clarified the scope of the 1951 Refugee Convention's exclusion clauses, limiting the overreach of decision makers in excluding some migrants.

A number of chapters in the collection draw attention to the role of the judiciary in promoting the human rights of migrants. For instance, Angus Grant offers a detailed analysis of the SCC's 2015 judgements whereby section 117 of the Immigration and Refugee Protection Act (IRPA) has been determined to be not applicable to persons who assist asylum seekers for humanitarian reasons or for reasons of mutual aid or family assistance.[59] Grant considers this to be a useful judicial contribution, particularly in light of people smuggling prosecutions taking place in numerous countries around the world, bringing as it does conceptual clarity to the different contexts of humanitarian assistance to refugees, and of extra-legal smuggling operations. Grant also points out the benefit of the judgements in dispelling the stigma attached to asylum seekers who travel with the assistance of smugglers.

Similarly, Graham Hudson highlights the important role played by the judiciary in Canada. He notes that even though superior courts do not have legislative jurisdiction over immigration proceedings per se, these courts are increasingly involved in immigration decisions. As an example, Hudson refers to cases in which migrants subject to lengthy or indefinite detentions were entitled constitutionally to apply for the right of *habeas corpus* through superior courts, bypassing the IRPA entirely. Hudson concludes that in these cases, courts saw no need to make formal distinctions between immigration law and criminal law, with the impact of detention on the physical, emotional, and psychological well-being of detainees being similar in both contexts.

The significant role of the courts in Canada, as well as in other states, in shaping the application and interpretation of migration law, is examined in the contributions of Nancy Weisman, Lorne Waldman and Warda Shazadi Meighen, and Joseph Rikhof, who examine in detail how the courts have defined who ought to be excluded from refugee protection under Article 1F of the 1951 Refugee Convention. Weisman considers the SCC's *Ezokola* judgement,[60] which established a new test for what constitutes exclusion from Convention refugee status under Article 1F(a), that is, for serious international crimes such as crimes against humanity and war crimes. The SCC judgement sought to update the test under Article 1F(a), given the developments in international criminal law with the Rome Statute and other supreme court judgements in other common law jurisdictions such as the UK and New Zealand. Likewise, Waldman and Shazadi Meighen do a close dissection of the SCC judgement in *Ezokola* and the UK Supreme Court judgement in *JS (Sri Lanka)*.[61] They argue that the higher standard of proof for exclusion is consistent with the nature of the criminality involved, for exclusion under Article 1F, and the recommendations of the UNHCR and legal scholars, who argue that the exclusion provisions of the 1951 Refugee Convention must be narrowly construed, interpreted, and applied. Rikhof considers Article 1F(b), of the so-called exclusion clauses, that eliminates all those who have committed a "serious non-political crime" prior to their arrival in their country of asylum. Rikhof finds that the courts have been generally consistent in their interpretation of these provisions and that Canada, in fact, has been at the forefront of the interpretation and application of Article 1F(b). What Weisman, Waldman and Shazadi Meighen, and Rikhof have amply demonstrated is that the highest courts in the Global North play a critical role in defining who ought to be excluded from refugee protection on the basis of serious criminality. Presumably, this is an ever-growing area of concern and interest, given the number of protracted armed conflicts and repressive non-democratic regimes in the world today.[62]

Finally, Dan Horner draws out insights from past practice on how, at the end of the 1840s, US Supreme Court decisions were instrumental in striking down repressive policies against migrants. He shows that these rulings led to a significant restructuring of transatlantic migration, with the flow of Irish migrants choosing to land in Boston and other American port cities, where the laws were more protective of their rights than in British North America.

The Importance of Advocacy.

Given the significant role of the courts in protecting the fundamental rights and freedoms of migrants, it stands to reason that refugee and migrant rights advocates ought to be taking their battles for advancing the protection and rights of refugees and migrants to the courts, and to the judicial system more broadly. In Canada, NGOs and advocacy groups are forming and organizing to protect the rights of all migrants, especially of refugees and other forced migrants – the most prominent among the long-standing organizations in this field being the Canadian Council for Refugees (CCR),[63] the Ontario Council of Agencies Serving Immigrants (OCASI),[64] and the Canadian Association of Refugee Lawyers (CARL).[65] The Canadian Association for Refugee and Forced Migration Studies (CARFMS) is also emerging as an important organization that brings together students, academics, practitioners, advocates, and policy makers in presenting the latest research findings and developments in Canada and abroad that deal with refugee and forced migrant rights, issues, and concerns.[66] Indeed, CARFMS is also contributing to raising the profile of some of the most important refugee and forced migration issues of the day.[67]

The importance of advocacy is highlighted in several chapters of this collection. Charity-Ann Hannan and Harald Bauder point to the role of NGOs, unions, and activist organizations in raising awareness about irregular migrant workers' employment and labour rights, and in providing support systems for enforcing these rights. They note that some of these actors played significant roles, both in Canada and the US, in conducting and disseminating research that raised awareness of employers' exploitation of migrant workers in irregular situations, as well as the need for support systems to help these workers enforce their rights, especially in the construction, food, and meat and poultry industries.

Likewise, in her first-hand account of the Central American refugee crisis in the United States, Galya Ben-Arieh underlines the efforts of volunteers coordinated by the American Immigration Lawyers Association. She notes that the American Immigration Council's Pro Bono Project (the Artesia Pro Bono Project) provided detained women and children refugee claimants with access to pro bono counsel in the Federal Law Enforcement Training Center detention facility in Artesia, New Mexico. Ben-Arieh's analysis clearly shows that without this help, the women detained in Artesia would have had little to no chance of lodging a refugee claim because of numerous policies that were part of the overall executive policy of "detain and deport."

Legal representation of refugees and other migrants is critical to advancing their claims to refugee protection. Initiatives led by advocacy groups, such as the Artesia Pro Bono Project, are a clear and obvious illustration of this within the context of special detention facilities for migrants apprehended while crossing the US border with Mexico. In addition, "strategic litigation" is an essential tool that the migrant advocacy community must fully embrace and use more effectively to ensure progressive social change for the entire community, including its most vulnerable members – refugees and other forced migrants – especially if they have arrived through irregular means. This appears to be one of the most efficacious routes to the decriminalization of migration. It relies on contestation and the assertion of universal human rights to meet the protection needs of migrants.

Local Governance and the Role of Cities

Key civic and political actors are increasingly looking for alternative ways to regulate migration and are developing concrete countermeasures to grant safety to people. The concept of the "sanctuary city" is one of these alternatives. Hannan and Bauder offer insight to how in these cities, municipal councils, and administrations resist national policies and practices of exclusion and seek to provide city services to all residents. Global cities here become the site of formal belonging. The notion of sanctuary is linked historically to churches offering irregular migrants protection from federal authorities in the US. The concept acquired a civic connotation within Canada in the mid-2000s, when community service organizations, human rights advocates, professionals (e.g., teachers, doctors, and lawyers), and migrants began mobilizing in the contexts of education and policing. This local, community-based initiative led to the passage of a sanctuary city policy in Toronto in 2013. The objective of Toronto's policy is to provide irregular migrants with a safe space, to engender civic engagement, to reduce socioeconomic marginalization, and to present victimization and exploitation.[68] Hamilton, Vancouver, Ajax, and London recently passed similar policies. As well, in February 2017, Montreal unanimously adopted a motion declaring itself a sanctuary city. This was largely a political response to the increasing number of asylum seekers illegally crossing the US border into the province of Quebec, following the announcement by the Trump administration that the Temporary Protected Status designation for Haitians in the US will come to an end in 2019.[69] Against this backdrop, the sanctuary city movement is attempting "to change the ways in which people interact with one another locally and to develop a shift in ideas around community and belonging."[70] Some scholars see sanctuary city policies as an opportunity to cultivate alternative conceptions of "urban citizenship," "urban belonging," or "citizenship-as-inhabitance."[71]

The Role of the Media

The role of mass media in projecting positive images of refugees and other forced migrants is equally important.[72] As such, refugee and migrant rights advocates should be developing comprehensive public media strategies to further a positive understanding and appreciation of the plight of refugees and other forced migrants and of their fundamental human rights in Canada and internationally. The UNHCR has taken a lead in this regard, but much more needs to be done at the state level among the NGO and advocacy community.[73] The same likely holds true for the use of modern digital technology in the form of social media, such as Facebook, Twitter, LinkedIn, and Instagram. All of these are most germane with the younger generation, who rely heavily on digital technologies for their information and means of communication.[74] Peter Goodspeed's chapter outlines the role the media coverage of the Indochinese refugee "crisis" in the mid-1970s played in establishing Canada's private sponsorship of refugees program. It also highlights the ways in which new digital technologies are affecting how people receive their news coverage.

A number of studies have indicated that the role of the media in projecting a positive image of refugees and other forced migrants are critical.[75] Joana Kosho has argued that the mainstream media has a direct impact on how migration issues and the migration crisis itself are perceived by the public and on political discourse and on international migration.[76] Kosho argues that the media affects public attitudes that effect public behaviour and that, then, puts pressure on decision makers and, in turn, shapes immigration and refugee public policies.[77] Victoria Danilova echoes this sentiment but also notes that the international community has recognized and acknowledged the importance of the media in combatting xenophobia and intolerance against migrants.[78] This all underscores the significance of the NGO and advocacy communities developing a comprehensive public media strategy to advance a positive image of refugees and other forced migrants in the general public's mind.

The Role of States and Civil Society
in International Solidarity and Responsibility Sharing

Several contributions in the collection point to the lack of international solidarity in terms of local integration and the resettlement of refugees. Petra Molnar shows, for instance, how difficult it is for Syrian refugees to integrate in Turkey and Jordan as their rising numbers affect the countries' ability to provide affordable legal, health, and social services. Indeed, a stronger commitment from states to the resettlement of refugees appears to be an effective solution to forced migration. Here again, the historical perspective is illuminating. Goodspeed reminds us that from 1979 to 1980, not only the Canadian government but also tens of thousands of individuals, families, churches, and neighbourhood groups in Canada rallied to resettle refugees from Vietnam, Laos, and Cambodia. Among the 60,000 Indochinese refugees resettled, approximately 26,000 were government assisted and 34,000 were privately sponsored.[79] As pointed out by Goodspeed, at the time, Operation Lifeline allowed the private sponsoring of thousands of refugees thanks to the remarkable leadership of politicians and the active involvement of Canadian citizens. Goodspeed further explains how the creation in 2015 of Lifeline Syria, a Toronto-based private sponsorship initiative, was inspired from the success of Operation Lifeline. Once again, retired civil servants, former politicians, social workers, academics, resettlement workers, and former activists from the Indochinese refugee crisis created Lifeline Syria. Launched on 17 June 2015, the initiative aimed to recruit, train, and assist private sponsors to support Syrian refugees to be resettled as permanent immigrants in the Greater Toronto Area.[80] Today, many Western countries are considering replicating Canada's private refugee sponsorship program.[81] The lesson of the private sponsorship program is that the public should be involved in the resettlement and integration of refugees and other forced migrants. Private sponsorship is a step in the right direction, but more systematic ways need to be devised for communities to be involved in the resettlement and the assistance of refugees and other forced migrants in their integration in their new host communities.[82] Further, as noted by Goodspeed in this collection, the processing of such a high number of refugees within a relatively short period of time in Canada has renewed scholarly research on questions of selection, resettlement, and integration, as well as on issues regarding the current asylum system in Canada and how it might be revised to ensure a fast and fair process that recognizes and upholds the rights of refugees.

The Crucial Role of Political Leadership

Leadership at the highest levels in government is crucial to protecting and advancing migrant rights. The resettlement in 2015 to 2016 of more than 26,000 Syrian refugees by the newly elected Liberal government of Justin Trudeau is a typical example of how political will and strong leadership can protect refugees and their human rights.[83] Canadians have taken in large numbers of refugees, who, rather than being a burden on the country, have consistently become enthusiastic contributors to Canada. At its core, private refugee sponsorship, as well as government sponsorship, is an exercise in nation building, in addition to rescuing refugees.[84]

The crucial role of sound political leadership is evident in other areas. Another example of the state's role in tackling forced migration can be found in Julie Kaye's chapter on one of the most important issues confronting the international community and Canada: human trafficking. This often takes the form of an international criminal activity that requires a proactive approach from states in order to be combatted effectively. Kaye's in-depth qualitative study focuses on law enforcement, along with the service agency personnel whose job is to provide the survivors of human trafficking with a path to human security and dignity. Kaye offers a set of lessons from state initiatives such as the National Action Campaign to Combat Human Trafficking in Canada.

As well, Judith Gleeson examines the historical development of the European Union, premised largely on the long-held vision of peaceful relationships among European states, and how Britain's withdrawal from the EU is detrimental to the protection of refugees and other forced migrants, as this decision diminishes the possibility of a meaningful Common European Asylum System (CEAS) within Europe. Gleeson shows that without progressive political leadership at the helm, further criminalization of migration is likely to take place. This, in turn, threatens the cause of creating a wider European community of "greater liberty, prosperity and security."

CHARTING THE WAY FORWARD
FOR THE DECRIMINALIZATION OF MIGRATION

Overall, this collection serves as a plea for states to address the infringement of the human rights of migrants, including the freedom of movement, through the growing trend of the criminalization of migration.[85] Today, migration and asylum policies are dominated by the concerns of states over the security of their borders, domestic political sensitivities, and their short-term economic interests. In a globalizing world, it is paradoxical that the freedom of movement of a significant number of migrants remains restricted. As a result, a considerable number of migrants endure human rights violations. As has been mentioned by the United Nations Human Rights Council, given the global character of the migratory phenomenon, the human rights of migrants need to be protected, particularly at a time in which the increased regional and global mobility of persons and the structural changes in the global economy generate new opportunities and challenges for origin, transit, and destination countries.[86] In this context, migrants' awareness of their rights and their access to available domestic and international legal remedies are of critical importance.

As mentioned previously, it is also important not to lose sight of the "root causes" of forced migration – principally, wars and protracted armed conflict, overwhelmingly in the form of protracted non-international armed conflict.[87] These "root causes" are well known to the international community, which has been unable, or in some instances even unwilling, to address them effectively.[88] Clearly, addressing the "root causes" of forced migration is an enormous undertaking that cannot be overestimated, but it is essential to fully comprehending the nature of the problem and effectively addressing its consequences. Many reforms and solutions have been raised over the years, including a complete reconsideration of the international refugee protection regime itself. Ideally, any thoughtful new international refugee protection regime or international migration regime would not only provide meaningful protection alternatives to the world's refugees and other forced migrants but protect the human rights of all migrants.[89] It is also clear that states must fulfil their obligations to protect the human rights and dignity of all people, especially those who are the most vulnerable: refugees and other forced migrants.[90] This would imply, of course, that states, both individually and collectively, must uphold not only the fundamental human right of asylum but also the universal human right of freedom of movement.

All of this requires that states and other actors must move away from the securitization of migration through its criminalization. In summary, the most promising avenues at present appear to be a new framework to deal with the "root causes" of forced migration, strategic litigation, political leadership that is prepared to develop innovative policies that protect the fundamental human rights of migration, the progressive development of a new international migration regime premised on the protection and advancement of the human rights of migrants, and a vigilant and active civil society movement that transcends borders and is prepared to pressure policy makers to protect and advance the fundamental human rights of migrants. These avenues, along with other strategies and possible solutions discussed in this collection, would help build a process for decriminalizing migration, while at the same time enhancing the security of all states through the protection and enhancement of the human rights of migrants, rather than the infringement and restriction of these rights. In short, a rigorous and universal application of the fundamental human rights of migrants, especially refugees and other forced migrants, is crucial for the "decriminalization of migration." We must move beyond the particular contextual circumstances or situation and their varying consequences through "decrim-migration" to help realize one of the most fundamental of all human rights, the freedom of movement.

The collection of strategies and possible solutions outlined here are simple enough, but their exercise is extremely difficult, as it requires the concerted effort of progressive individuals, organizations, and institutions at all levels of society, nationally, regionally, and internationally. Such a gargantuan undertaking must begin with a firm and dedicated commitment at the individual level from each of us. The first step must begin with empathy and understanding, which often commences through education. This edited collection is one small contribution towards such an individual commitment, which, hopefully, will lead to the effective protection of the human rights of all migrants.

NOTES

1 Universal Declaration of Human Rights, 10 December 1948, United Nations General Assembly, A/RES/3/217 A. Article 13, states "(1) Everyone has the right to freedom of movement and residence within the borders of each state; (2) Everyone has the right to leave any country, including his own, and to return to his country." Section 6 (1) of the Canadian Charter of Rights and Freedoms, Mobility Rights, states: "Every citizen of Canada has the right to enter, remain in and leave Canada." The privileges and immunities clause of the US Constitution, Article 4, Section 2 – "the citizens of each state shall be entitled to all privileges and immunities of citizens in several states" – has been interpreted by the US Supreme Court in a series of leading cases, including *Corfield v. Coryell*, 6 Fed. Cas. 546 (1823); *Paul v. Virginia*, 75 US 168 (1869); and *Ward v. Maryland*, 79 US 418 (1871), that freedom of movement is a fundamental constitutional right.

2 Thomas Gammeltoft-Hansen and Nikolas F. Tan, "The End of the Deterrence Paradigm?" *Journal of Migration and Human Security*, 5, no. 1 (2017): 28–56; Catherine Morris, "Myanmar: International Law Duties of Neighbouring States to Refugees and Asylum Seekers – Briefing Note," Lawyers' Rights Watch Canada, 11 November 2017, https://www.lrwc.org/myanmar-international-law-duties-of-neighbouring-states-to-refugees-and-asylum-seekers-briefing-note; "EU Policies Put Refugees at Risk: An Agenda to Restore Protection," Human Rights Watch, 23 November 2016, https://www.hrw.org/news/2016/11/23/eu-policies-put-refugees-risk; and Niels Frenzen, "NATO Expands Aegean Sea Migrant Patrols into Turkish and Greek Territorial Waters – Rescued Migrants to Be Automatically Returned to Turkey," Migrants at Sea, 7 March 2016, https://migrantsatsea.org/tag/push-back-practice.

3 Stephen H. Legomsky, "The New Path of Immigration Law: Asymmetric Incorporation of Criminal Justice Norms," *Washington and Lee Law Review* 64, no. 2 (2007): 471, https://scholarlycommons.law.wlu.edu/wlulr /vol64/iss2/3.

4 "Worst Terrorist Attacks in World History," World Atlas, https://www.world atlas.com/articles/worst-terrorist-attacks-in-history.html.

5 Rich Furman, Alissa R. Ackerman, Melody Loya, Susanna Jones, and Nalinin Egi, "The Criminalization of Immigration: Value Conflicts for the Social Work Profession," *Journal of Sociology and Social Welfare* 39, no. 1 (2012): 169–85. https://www.ncbi.nlm.nih.gov/pmc/articles/PMC5614495.

6 Andreas Themistocleous, "Securitizing Migration: Aspects and Critiques," GW Post, 16 May 2013, accessed 27 December 2017, https://thegwpost.com /2013/05/16/securitizing-migration-aspects-and-critiques; Philippe Bourbeau, *The Securitization of Migration: A Study of Movement and Order* (London: Routledge, 2011); Vicki Squires, "The Securitization of Migration: An Absent Presence?" in *The Securitisation of Migration in the EU: Debates Since 9/11*, eds. Gabriella Lazaridis and Khursheed Wadia (London: Palgrave Macmillan, 2015), https://link.springer.com/chapter/10.1057/9781137480583 _2 (accessed 27 December 2017); and Valeria Bello, "The Securitisation of Migration in the EU: Debates Since 9/11." *Global Affairs* 2, no. 2 (2016): 233–4.

7 Alison Gerard and Sharon Pickering, "Crimmigration: Criminal Justice, Refugee Protection and the Securitisation of Migration," in *The Routledge Handbook of International Crime and Justice Studies*, eds. Heather Bersot and Bruce Arrigo (London: Routledge, 2013); and Philippe Bourbeau, ed., *Handbook on Migration and Security* (Cheltenham: Edward Elgar, 2017).

8 James C. Simeon, "Asserting Universal Human Rights to Decriminalize Migration," CARFMS/ACERMF Blog, 22 August 2017, accessed 26 December 2017, http://carfms.org/blog/asserting-universal-human-rights-to-decriminal-ize-migration-by-james-c-simeon; Jennifer M. Chacón, "Overcriminalizing Immigration," *Journal of Criminal Law and Criminology* 102, no. 3 (2012); and Emily Nagisa Keehn, "Decriminalization and the UN Human Rights Bodies," (Harvard Law School Human Rights Program research working paper series, HRP 18-002), 2018, accessed 10 May 2018, http://hrp.law .harvard.edu/wp-content/uploads/2018/03/Emily-Keehn_HRP-18_002.pdf.

9 César Cuauhtémoc García Hernández, *Crimmigration Law* (ABA Book Publishing, 2015).

10 Ibid., 3.

11 Wendy Chan, "Are We All Frauds Now? The Ongoing Criminalization of Immigration in Canada," Border Criminologies Blog, 3 November 2014,

https://www.law.ox.ac.uk/research-subject-groups/centre-criminology/centre border-criminologies/blog/2014/11/are-we-all-frauds; Sula Sidnell-Greene, "Bill C-24 and the Ongoing Criminalization of Migrants in Canada," *Shameless*, 30 October 2015, http://shamelessmag.com/blog/entry/bill-c-24-and-the-ongoing-criminalization-of-migrants-in-canada; James Gacek, "Canadian Crimmigration: How Ill-Perceived Presumptions and Threats Shape Migrant Detention," Robson Crim Legal Blog, 1 June 2017, https://www .robsoncrim.com/single-post/2017/06/01/Canadian-Crimmigration-How-Ill-Perceived-Presumptions-and-Threats-Shape-Migrant-Detention; and Petra Molnar and Stephanie Silverman, "Cracks Where the Light Gets In: Recent Legal Breakthroughs in Detention and Crimmigration in Canada," *Metropolitics*, 7 December 2016, http://www.metropolitiques.eu/Cracks-Where-the-Light-Gets-in.html.

12 http://laws-lois.justice.gc.ca/eng/AnnualStatutes/2012_17/page-1.html.

13 Faster Removal of Foreign Criminals Act, SC 2013, ch. 16, http://laws-lois .justice.gc.ca/eng/annualstatutes/2013_16/page-1.html.

14 Aviva Stahl, "How a Clinton-Era Law Is Still Criminalizing Immigrants Today," Vice, 17 October 2016, https://www.vice.com/en_ca/article/7bmxye /how-a-20-year-policy-is-still-criminalizing-immigrants-today.

15 Victoria Rietig and Andreas Müller, "The New Reality: Germany Adapts to Its Role as a Major Migrant Magnet," Migration Policy Institute, 31 August 2017, https://www.migrationpolicy.org/article/new-reality-germany-adapts-its-role-major-migrant-magnet.

16 Judith Vonberg, "Merkel Changes Tune on German Refugee Cap," CNN, 9 October 2017, http://www.cnn.com/2017/10/09/europe/germany-upper-limit-refugees/index.html.

17 Walter Ewing, Daniel E. Martínez, Rubén G. Rumbaut, "The Criminalization of Immigration in the United States," 13 July 2015, American Immigration Council, https://www.americanimmigrationcouncil.org/research /criminalization-immigration-united-states.

18 Hernández, *Crimmigration Law*, 11.

19 Dylan Waisman, "Britain's Harsh New Immigration Law Turns Refugees into Criminals," *National Observer*, 8 December 2015, http://www.national observer.com/2015/12/08/opinion/britains-harsh-new-immigration-law-turns-refugees-criminals.

20 "Equality: Immigration and Refugees," Canadian Civil Liberties Association, accessed 2 August 2017, https://ccla.org/focus-areas/equality/immigration-and-refugees.

21 Virginie Guiraudon, "Immigration Policy in France," *Brookings*, 1 July 2001, https://www.brookings.edu/articles/immigration-policy-in-france.

22 Keehn, "Decriminalization and the UN."

23 Nathalie Risse, "UN Launches Consultation Phase for Migration Compact," SDG Knowledge Hub, International Institute for Sustainable Development, 11 May 2017, accessed 10 May 2018, http://sdg.iisd.org/news/un-launches-consultation-phase-for-migration-compact.

24 "Making Migration Work for All: Report of the Secretary-General," United Nations General Assembly (A/72/643), 12 December 2017, 10–11.

25 Nathalie Risse, "UN Secretary-General Launches Migration Report Ahead of Compact Negotiations," SDG Knowledge Hub, International Institute for Sustainable Development, 16 January 2018, accessed 11 May 2018, http://sdg.iisd.org/news/un-secretary-general-launches-migration-report-ahead-of-compact-negotiations.

26 Ibid.

27 Ibid.

28 Stephanie Silverman, "In the Wake of Irregular Arrivals: Changes to the Canadian Immigration Detention System," *Refuge* 30, no. 2 (2014): 27–34, https://refuge.journals.yorku.ca/index.php/refuge/article/viewFile/39616/35895; Hanna Gros and Paloma van Groll, "'We Have No Rights': Arbitrary Imprisonment and Cruel Treatment of Migrants with Mental Health Issues in Canada," University of Toronto, Faculty of Law, International Human Rights Program, 2015, https://www.law.utoronto.ca/utfl_file/count/media/ihrp_we_have_no_rights_report_web_version_final_170615.pdf.

29 "Nearly 100,000 Migrants in Canada Jailed Without Charge," Never Home, n.d., accessed 3 August 2017, http://www.neverhome.ca/detention.

30 Ibid.

31 Ibid.

32 UN General Assembly, Human Rights Council, Working Group on Arbitrary Detention, "Opinions Adopted by the Working Group on Arbitrary Detention at its sixty-ninth session (22 April–1 May 2014), No. 15/2014 (Canada)," A/HRC/WGAD/2014/15, 23 July 2014, https://documents-dds-ny.un.org/doc/UNDOC/GEN/G14/093/42/PDF/G1409342.pdf?OpenElement.

33 Ibid., para. 23.

34 "Nearly 100,000 Migrants in Canada," Never Home.

35 Ibid.; Government of Canada, Canada Border Services Agency, "About the CBSA: CBSA Heraldry," 2015, accessed 4 August 2017, http://www.cbsa-asfc.gc.ca/agency-agence/herald-armoiries-eng.html; and "2007 October Report of the Auditor General of Canada: Chapter 5 – Keeping the Border Open and Secure – Canada Border Services Agency," Office of the Auditor General of Canada, 2007, http://www.oag-bvg.gc.ca/internet/English/parl_oag_200710_05_e_23829.html; and "Canada 150 at the CBSA: Our People,"

Canada Border Services Agency, https://www.cbsa-asfc.gc.ca/multimedia
/canada150/menu-eng.html

36 Government of Canada, Canada Border Services Agency, "About the CBSA:
    Who We Are," 2011, accessed 4 August 2017, http://www.cbsa-
    asfc.gc.ca/agency-agence/who-qui-eng.html.

37 Patrick Lennox, "From Golden Straitjacket to Kevlar Vest: Canada's Trans-
    formation to a Security State," *Canadian Journal of Political Science* 40, no. 4
    (2007): 1017–38; Jennifer Hyndman and Allison Mountz, "Refuge or Exclu-
    sion: The Geography of Exclusion," in *Violent Geographies: Fear, Terror and
    Political Violence*, eds. Derek Gregory and Allen Pred (New York: Routledge,
    2007), 77–92; Eleanor Acer, "Refuge in an Insecure Time: Seeking Asylum in
    the Post-9/11 United States," *Fordham International Law Journal*, 28 (2004):
    1361; and Anna Pratt, "Between a Hunch and a Hard Place: Making Suspi-
    cion Reasonable at the Canadian Border," *Social and Legal Studies* 19, no. 4
    (2010): 461–80.

38 "Detention and Deportation," No One Is Illegal – Toronto, accessed 2
    August 2017, http://toronto.nooneisillegal.org/node/376.

39 Dennis Molinaro, "Deportation from Canada," *Canadian Encyclopedia*,
    accessed 28 December 2017, http://www.thecanadianencyclopedia.ca/en
    /article/deportation.

40 Government of Canada, Canada Border Services Agency, "Arrests, Deten-
    tions and Removals," 2017, accessed 28 December 2017, http://www.cbsa-
    asfc.gc.ca/security-securite/arr-det-eng.html.

41 Ibid.

42 "Canada Deports More Than 10,000 Each Year, Some to Wars and Repres-
    sive Regimes," *Toronto Metro*, 20 August 2014, http://www.metronews.ca
    /news/canada/2014/08/20/canada-deports-more-than-10000-each-year-some-
    to-wars-and-repressive-regimes.html.

43 "'Back to Where You Came From': Canada Deports 35 Daily," Never Home,
    n.d., accessed 28 December 2017, http://www.neverhome.ca/deportation.

44 "Canada Ramping up Deportations of Asylum Seekers, Government Data
    Shows," Global News, 24 August 2017, https://globalnews.ca/news/3694772
    /canada-deporting-asylum-seekers; and Nathan Vanderklippe, "Canada
    Deports Hundreds to China Each Year with No Treatment Guarantee,"
    Globe and Mail, 3 April 2017, https://www.theglobeandmail.com/news
    /world/canada-deports-hundreds-to-china-each-year-with-no-treatment-
    guarantee/article34558610.

45 Ibid.

46 "Deportations/Removals," Migration Policy Institute, n.d., accessed 28

December 2017, https://www.migrationpolicy.org/topics/deportations removals.

47 Government of the United Kingdom, Home Office, "National Statistics, Removals and Voluntary Departures," updated 3 March 2016, accessed 28 December 2017, https://www.gov.uk/government/publications/immigration-statistics-october-to-december-2015/removals-and-voluntary-departures.

48 Department of Homeland Security, US Immigration and Customs Enforcement, "FY 2016 ICE Immigration Removals," updated 12 May 2017, accessed 28 December 2017, https://www.ice.gov/removal-statistics/2016.

49 "Deportations, Removals and Voluntary Departures from the UK," The Migration Observatory, University of Oxford, 4 October 2017, accessed 28 December 2017, http://www.migrationobservatory.ox.ac.uk/resources /briefings/deportations-removals-and-voluntary-departures-from-the-uk.

50 UN General Assembly, *Convention Relating to the Status of Refugees*, 28 July 1951, United Nations, Treaty Series, vol. 189, 137.

51 UNHCR, *Handbook and Guidelines on the Procedures and Criteria for Determining Refugee Status: Under the 1951 Convention and the 1967 Protocol Relating to the Status of Refugees*, reissued, Geneva, 2011, ch. 4, Exclusion Clauses, para. 140, http://www.unhcr.org/publications/legal/3d58e13b4/handbook-procedures-criteria-determining-refugee-status-under-1951-convention .html.

52 "'Unprecedented' 65 Million People Displaced by War and Persecution in 2015 – UN," UN News, 20 June 2016, https://news.un.org/en/story/2016/06 /532532-unprecedented-65-million-people-displaced-war-and-persecution-2015-un; Zack Beauchamp, "9 Maps and Charts That Explain the Global Refugee Crisis," Vox, 30 January 2017, https://www.vox.com/world/2017/1/30 /14432500/refugee-crisis-trump-muslim-ban-maps-charts; and "What's Driving the Global Refugee Crisis," International Crisis Group, 15 September 2016, accessed 7 August 2017, https://www.crisisgroup.org/global/what-s-driving-global-refugee-crisis.

53 Paul Joseph, ed., *The SAGE Encyclopedia of War: Social Science Perspectives*. "Migration" (Thousand Oaks: SAGE Publications, 2016), 1061.

54 Tom Clark and James C. Simeon, "War, Armed Conflict, and Refugees: The United Nations Endless Battle for Peace," *Refugee Survey Quarterly* 35, no. 3 (2016): 35–70.

55 "World Report 2017 – Syria: Events of 2016," Human Rights Watch, 2017, https://www.hrw.org/world-report/2017/country-chapters/syria; and Jean-Marie Guéhenno, "10 Conflicts to Watch in 2017," *Foreign Policy*, 5 January 2017, http://foreignpolicy.com/2017/01/05/10-conflicts-to-watch-in-2017.

56 "Global Trends: Forced Displacement 2016," United Nations High Commissioner for Refugees, 2017, http://www.unhcr.org/globaltrends2016.
57 Ibid. See "Where do the refugees come from?"
58 James C. Simeon, "A New Protection Orientation and Framework for Refugees and Other Forced Migrants." *Laws* 6, 4 (2017): 30, http://www.mdpi.com/2075-471X/6/4/30.
59 *R. v. Appulonappa*, [2015] 3 SCR 754, 2015 SCC 59 (CanLII); and *Boio v. Canada (Citizenship and Immigration)*, [2015] 3 SCR 704, 2015 SCC 58 (CanLII).
60 *Ezokola v. Canada (Citizenship and Immigration)*, [2013] 2 SCR 678, 2013 SCC 40 (CanLII).
61 *R (on the application of JS) (Sri Lanka) (Respondent) v. Secretary of State for the Home Department (Appellant)* [2010] UKSC 15.
62 Uppsala Universitet, Department of Peace and Conflict Research, Charts, Graphs, and Maps, Map of the World's Conflicts, "Organized Violence in 2016," Uppsala Conflict Data Program, Uppsala University, Department of Peace and Conflict Research, n.d., accessed 28 December 2017, http://www.pcr.uu.se/digitalAssets/667/c_667494-l_1-k_map16.png. According to the UCDP/PRIO Armed Conflict Dataset there were 39 state-based armed conflicts in the world in 2016. See Marie Allansson, Erik Melander, and Lotta Themnér, 2017. "Organized Violence, 1989–2016," *Journal of Peace Research* 54, no. 4: 574–87; and "Worst of the Worst 2012: The World's Most Repressive Societies," Freedom House, 2012, https://freedomhouse.org/report/special-reports/worst-worst-2012-worlds-most-repressive-societies.
63 Canadian Council for Refugees (CCR), https://www.canadahelps.org/en/charities/canadian-council-for-refugees.
64 Ontario Council of Agencies Serving Immigrants (OCASI), http://www.ocasi.org.
65 Canadian Association of Refugee Lawyers (CARL), http://www.carl-acaadr.ca.
66 Canadian Association for Refugee and Forced Migration Studies (CARFMS), http://carfms.org.
67 CARFMS/ACERFM Blog, http://carfms.org/blog.
68 Toronto City Council Decision, "Undocumented Workers in Toronto," CD 18.5, 20 February 2013, http://app.toronto.ca/tmmis/viewAgendaItemHistory.do?item=2013.CD18.5.
69 Miriam Jordan, "Trump Administration Ends Temporary Protection for Haitians," *New York Times*, 20 November 2017.
70 Jean McDonald, "Migrant Illegality, Nation Building, and the Politics of Regularization in Canada," *Refuge* 26, no. 2 (2009): 65–77.

71 Harald Bauder, "Possibilities of Urban Belonging," *Antipode* 48, no. 2 (2016): 252–71.

72 Helen Dempster and Karen Hargrave, "Understanding Public Attitudes Towards Refugees and Migrants" (Chatham House, The Royal Institute of International Affairs, working paper 512), 2017, accessed 11 May 2018, https://www.odi.org/sites/odi.org.uk/files/resource-documents/11600.pdf; and "Media Coverage and Public Perceptions of Refugees and Migrants," Ethical Journalism Network, 3 May 2017, accessed 11 May 2018, https://ethicaljournalismnetwork.org/media-coverage-public-perceptions-refugees-migrants.

73 "#WithRefugees, Coalition," United Nations High Commissioner for Refugees, n.d., accessed 5 August 2017. See also "Positive Images Project – Understanding Refugees," Global Dimension, 2017, accessed 5 August 2017, https://globaldimension.org.uk/casestudy/positive-images-project-under-standing-refugees.

74 Cléa Desjardins, "Fear-Mongering or Friendly: How Social Media Shapes Attitudes Towards Refugees," Concordia News, 14 September 2016, http://www.concordia.ca/cunews/main/releases/2016/09/14/fear-mongering-or-friendly-how-social-media-shapes-attitudes-towards-refugees.html; Giovanna Coppola, "5 Examples of How Social Media Helps the Refugee Crisis," Creative Connection, 28 August 2016, http://creativeconnection.co.uk/social-media-refugee-crisis; and Victoria M. Esses, Stelian Medianu, and Andrea S. Lawson, "Uncertainty, Threat, and the Role of the Media in Promoting the Dehumanization of Immigrants and Refugees," *Journal of Social Issues* 69, no. 3 (2013): 518–36, http://onlinelibrary.wiley.com/doi/10.1111/josi.12027/full.

75 Esses, Medianu, and Lawson, "Uncertainty, Threat, and the Role of the Media"; and "Study Shows Media Play Role in Dehumanizing Immigrants and Refugees," Phy.org, University of Western Ontario, 23 September 2013, accessed 11 May 2018, https://phys.org/news/2013-09-media-role-dehumaniz-ing-immigrants-refugees.html.

76 Joana Kosho, "Media Influence on Public Opinion Attitudes Towards the Migration Crisis," *International Journal of Scientific and Technology Research* 5, no. 5 (2016), http://www.ijstr.org/final-print/may2016/Media-Influence-On-Public-Opinion-Attitudes-Toward-The-Migration-Crisis.pdf.

77 Ibid.

78 Victoria Danilova, "Media and Their Role in Shaping Public Attitudes Towards Migrants," United Nations University, Institute on Globalization, Culture and Mobility, 16 July 2014, accessed 11 May 2018,.

https://gcm.unu.edu/publications/articles/media-and-their-role-in-shaping-public-attitudes-towards-migrants.html.

79 Michael M. Molloy and James C. Simeon, eds., "The Indochinese Refugee Movement and the Launch of Canada's Private Sponsorship Program," special issue, *Refuge* 32, no. 2 (2016), https://refuge.journals.yorku.ca/index.php/refuge/issue/view/2311.

80 Lifeline Syria, http://lifelinesyria.ca.

81 Maria Teresa Rojas and Alyssa Ross, "How Private Sponsorship Programs Could Help Resettle Refugees," 16 December 2015, Open Society Foundations, https://www.opensocietyfoundations.org/voices/how-private-sponsorship-programs-could-help-resettle-refugees; Esmat Jeraj, "Full Community Sponsorship of Refugees Launched in the UK: First Refugees Expected to Arrive in Weeks," Citizens UK, 19 July 2016, accessed 11 May 2018, http://www.citizensuk.org/full_community_sponsorship_of_refugees; Judith Kumin, "Welcoming Engagement: How Private Sponsorship Can Strengthen Refugee Resettlement in the European Union," Migration Policy Institute, 2015, http://www.migrationpolicy.org/research/welcoming-engagement-how-private-sponsorship-can-strengthen-refugee-resettlement-european.

82 Ibid.

83 Government of Canada, Immigration and Citizenship, "#WelcomeRefugees: Key Figures," 2016, accessed 5 August 2017, http://www.cic.gc.ca/english/refugees/welcome/milestones.asp. According to Government of Canada statistics, as of 29 January 2017, 40,081 Syrian refugees have been welcomed to Canada.

84 Jennifer Hyndman and Michaela Hynie, "From Newcomer to Canadian: Making Refugee Integration Work," *Policy Options*, 17 May 2016, http://policyoptions.irpp.org/magazines/may-2016/from-newcomer-to-canadian-making-refugee-integration-work.

85 In the context of the US, see Jennifer M. Chacón, "Criminalizing Immigration," in *Reforming Criminal Justice – Volume 1: Introduction and Criminalization*, ed. Erik Luna (Phoenix, AZ: Academy of Justice, 2017), 205–28, accessed 11 May 2018, http://academyforjustice.org/wp-content/uploads/2017/10/Reforming-Criminal-Justice_Vol_1.pdf.

86 United Nations General Assembly, Human Rights Council, "Human Rights of Migrants," Preamble, A/HRC/23/L.12, 7 June 2013.

87 Volker Türk, Alice Edwards, Cornelis Wouters, eds., *In Flight from Conflict and Violence: UNHCR's Consultations on Refugee Status and Other Forms of International Protection* (Cambridge: Cambridge University Press, 2017).

88 Dinoj K. Upadhyay, "Migrant Crisis in Europe: Causes, Responses, Complex-
    ities," Indian Council of World Affairs, 26 April 2016, http://www.icwa.in/pdfs
    /guestcolumn/2014/MigrantCrisisinEurope26042016.pdf.

89 For instance, one example of a comprehensive reform proposal can be
    found in James C. Hathaway, "A Global Solution to a Global Refugee Cri-
    sis," *RefLAW, a project of the University of Michigan Law School*, 29 February
    2016, http://www.reflaw.org/a-global-solution-to-a-global-refugee-crisis. See
    also Alex Neve, "Refugee Reform Must Become a Global Project," 1 March
    2016, openDemocracy, https://www.opendemocracy.net/openglobalrights
    /alex-neve/refugee-reform-must-become-global-project. For the entire collec-
    tion of these articles, see, "The Future of Refugee Protection: What New
    Approaches to Meet a Growing Crisis?" openDemocracy, https://www.open
    democracy.net/openglobalrights/future-of-refugee-protection.

90 François Crépeau, "A New Agenda for Facilitating Human Mobility After
    the UN Summits on Refugees and Migrants," openDemocracy, 24 March
    2017, https://www.opendemocracy.net/beyondslavery/safepassages/fran-ois-
    cr-peau/new-agenda-for-facilitating-human-mobility-after-un-summits-
    on-refuge.

Contributors

IDIL ATAK is an associate professor and the graduate program director in the Department of Criminology at Ryerson University. She received her PhD from the Université de Montréal's Faculty of Law. Atak is the editor-in-chief of the *International Journal of Migration and Border Studies*. She is a member of the International Association for the Study of Forced Migration's (IASFM) executive committee, the past president of the Canadian Association for Refugee and Forced Migration Studies (CARFMS), and a research associate at Hans and Tamar Oppenheimer Chair in Public International Law (McGill University).

HARALD BAUDER is a professor in the Department of Geography and Environmental Studies and the director of the graduate program (MA) in Immigration and Settlement Studies (ISS) at Ryerson University. From 2011 to 2015 he served as the founding academic director of the Ryerson Centre for Immigration and Settlement (RCIS). His recent books include *Migration Borders Freedom* (Routledge 2017), *Immigration Dialectic: Imagining Community, Economy, and Nation* (University of Toronto Press 2011), and *Labor Movement: How Migration Regulates Labor Markets* (Oxford University Press, 2006). In 2015, he received the Konrad Adenauer Research Award from the Royal Society of Canada and the Alexander von Humboldt Foundation for his lifetime achievement in promoting academic interchange between Canada and Germany.

GALYA BEN-ARIEH, JD, PhD, is professor of instruction in political science and the founding director of the Center for Forced Migration Studies at the Buffett Institute for Global Studies, Northwestern University. Through grants and fellowships from the Käte Hamburger Kolleg/Centre for Global Cooperation Research (University of Duisburg-Essen), the National Science Foundation, the Social Science Research Council, and the Kellogg Center for Dispute Resolution, and private funding to launch a research program on refugee resettlement, she has developed programs and research to better understand the condition and realities of refugee movement across state borders to avoid the risk of harm and settlement in host countries. Ben-Arieh has conducted field research in the Great Lakes region of Eastern Africa, Germany, and the US, and has published widely, with a recent book, *Adjudicating Refugee and Asylum Status: The Role of Witness, Expertise, and Testimony* (coedited with Benjamin Lawrance), Cambridge University Press (2015). She serves on the executive committee of the International Association for the Study of Forced Migration, and has worked as an immigration attorney representing political asylum claimants both as a solo-practitioner and as a pro bono attorney.

FRANÇOIS CRÉPEAU, OC, FRSC, AdE, fellow of the Trudeau Foundation, is a full professor and holds the Hans and Tamar Oppenheimer Chair in Public International Law at the Faculty of Law of McGill University. He served as the United Nations Special Rapporteur on the Human Rights of Migrants from 2011 to 2017. He is a fellow of the Royal Society of Canada. In August 2015, he became director of McGill's Centre for Human Rights and Legal Pluralism for a three-year mandate. Crépeau was also 2016 Robert F. Drinan Visiting Professor of Human Rights at Georgetown University. The focus of his current research includes migration control mechanisms, the rights of foreigners, the interface between security and migration, and the interface between the rule of law and globalization.

JUDITH GLEESON is an Upper Tribunal judge. She read law at Lady Margaret Hall, Oxford and was a Wiener-Anspach scholar on the Diploma in Civil and Community Law in 1975 at the Université libre de Bruxelles before qualifying as a solicitor of the Supreme Court in 1981. She became a judge in 1993 and a vice-president of the United Kingdom's Immigration and Asylum Tribunal in 2002, and has been an Upper Tribunal judge in the Immigration and Asylum Chamber since 2010. Judge Gleeson is the author of a number of leading country guidance decisions, which are cited in English-speaking jurisdictions worldwide. Judge Gleeson is a Council member of the International Association of Refugee and Migration Judges and speaks on refugee law around the world.

PETER GOODSPEED is a retired Canadian journalist who spent thirty years working as a foreign correspondent for the *Toronto Star* and the *National Post*. He was the 2014 recipient of the Atkinson Foundation's annual Journalism Fellowship and produced a series of stories, "The Politics of Compassion: Canada and the Syrian Refugee Crisis," for the *Toronto Star* in September 2014. He served as a founding board member and volunteer with Lifeline Syria.

ANGUS GRANT is a Canadian lawyer, academic, and commentator on immigration and refugee law. As a lawyer with a practice focused exclusively on constitutional, immigration, and refugee law, Grant has become recognized as a leading expert in the field and has represented individuals and organizations at every level of court in Canada. Most recently, Grant represented the Canadian Council for Refugees before the Supreme Court of Canada in *R. v. Appulonappa* and *B010 v. Canada (Citizenship and Immigration)*, two ground-breaking cases on the Canadian approach to combatting human smuggling in both criminal and immigration law contexts. After completing his doctorate in law at Osgoode Hall Law School of York University, Grant has been a visiting professor of law at Osgoode since 2017. Grant lives in Toronto, Canada.

CHARITY-ANN HANNAN is a PhD candidate in Policy Studies at Ryerson University. Before starting her PhD, Hannan was a research associate at the Diversity Institute at Ryerson, where she was involved with many research projects that examined the employment experiences of immigrants, the social mobility of immigrants, the employment advancement of racialized minorities, and the representation of racialized minorities in positions of leadership across multiple sectors. For her dissertation, she is examining the representation of racialized minorities in the Canadian policy process. Her research interests include (im)migration, (im)migrants, labour, employment, exploitation, inequality, employment equity, illegalized migrants, resistance, sanctuary cities, research methods, quantitative analysis, critical discourse analysis, and the policy process.

DAN HORNER is an assistant professor in the Department of Criminology at Ryerson University. He is an historian of public life, politics, and culture in nineteenth-century Canada. He has published a number of articles on topics such as migration, public health, and political violence in mid-nineteenth-century Montreal, and has recently begun a new project that examines how ideas about public order circulated throughout the North Atlantic world during this period. His first monograph, entitled *Taking to the Streets: Crowds, Politics and Identity in Mid-Nineteenth-Century Montreal*, is under contract with McGill-Queen's University Press. He is a member of the Montreal History Group/Groupe d'histoire de Montréal, a research collective of Quebec historians who work on issues of race, gender, and class.

GRAHAM HUDSON is an associate professor in the Department of Criminology at Ryerson University. He holds a BA (Hons) in history and philosophy from York University, a JD from the University of Toronto, an LLM from Queen's University, and a PhD from Osgoode Hall Law School. His current research interests include the sanctuary city movement in Canada and abroad, the criminalization of migration, security studies, and legal theory.

JULIE KAYE is an assistant professor in the Department of Sociology at the University of Saskatchewan. Working in the areas of critical criminology, community research, and organizing, and feminist, decolonial scholarship, Kaye's research examines settler-colonialism and Indigenous-led responses to varying forms of colonial gender violence and criminalization, as well as harm reduction, consent, self-determination, and body sovereignty. Through CIHR and SSHRC-funded research projects, she works alongside sex workers and harm reduction agencies to explore anti-violence strategies. Her work is widely available, including through publications in the *New York Times*, the *Toronto Star*, and the *Edmonton Journal*, and a number of community mobilization activities, such as the community-based artistic work "Our Breaking Point: Canada's Violation of Rights in Life and Death." Her book, *Responding to Human Trafficking: Dispossession, Colonial Violence, and Resistance among Indigenous and Racialized Women*, published by University of Toronto press, examines anti-trafficking responses in the context of settler-colonialism.

PETRA MOLNAR is a human rights and refugee lawyer in Toronto, Canada, and a research associate at the International Human Rights Program, University of Toronto Faculty of Law. She holds an MA in social anthropology from York University, a JD from the University of Toronto, and is an LLM candidate at the University of Cambridge. Molnar writes about the discourses that shape the relationship between law, society, and culture, and the politics of refugee, immigration, and international human rights law.

JOSEPH RIKHOF has received a BCL from the University of Nijmegen, the Netherlands; an LLB from McGill University; a diploma in air and space law from McGill University; and a PhD from the Irish Centre for Human Rights. He teaches International Criminal Law at the University of Ottawa. Until February 2017 he was the senior counsel, manager of the law with the War Crimes and Crimes Against Humanity section of Canada's Department of Justice. He was a visiting professional with the International Criminal Court in 2005 while also serving as special counsel and policy advisor to the Modern War Crimes section of Canada's Department of Citizenship and Immigration between 1998 and 2002. His expertise lies with the law related to organized crime, terrorism, genocide, war crimes, and crimes against humanity, especially in the context of immigration and refugee law. He has written over forty-five articles, as well as *The Criminal Refugee: The Treatment of Asylum Seekers with a Criminal Background in International and Domestic Law*, exploring these research interests, and has lectured on the same topics around the world. In addition, he is co-author, with Robert Currie, of the book *International and Transnational Criminal Law* (2nd ed.), as well as a faculty member of the Philippe Kirsch Institute.

WARDA SHAZADI MEIGHEN is a refugee and immigration lawyer in Toronto and teaches refugee law at the University of Toronto's Faculty of Law. She holds an MSc in refugee studies from the University of Oxford. Shazadi Meighen is on the Human Rights Watch's Canada Committee and has also served as the coeditor-in-chief for the *Oxford Monitor of Forced Migration*, where she managed a team of ten editors tasked with publishing scholarship that reflects the global state of forced migration. Warda was co-counsel to the British Columbia Civil Liberties Association in *R. v. Tran* at the Supreme Court of Canada.

JAMES C. SIMEON, LLM (Cantab), PhD (York University), is an associate professor in the School of Public Policy and Administration (SPPA) at York University. He is a member-at-large of the executive of the Canadian Association for Refugee and Forced Migration Studies (CARFMS) and a past-president of CARFMS. He also serves as the coordinator of the International Association of Refugee and Migration Judges' (IARMJ) Inter-Conference Working Party Process. Before joining the faculty at York University he served as the IARMJ's first executive director, and prior to that he was a member and coordinating member of the Immigration and Refugee Board of Canada (IRB).

LORNE WALDMAN has been practicing exclusively in the area of immigration and refugee law since 1979 at his own firm, Waldman & Associates. He is the author and editor of *Immigration Law and Practice* (Butterworths Canada 1992). He has appeared as counsel in many of the key Canadian refugee jurisprudence, including at the Supreme Court of Canada. He has taught in law schools throughout Canada. He consistently ranks as one of Canada's most influential lawyers. Waldman was counsel for the UNHCR in Ezokola at the Supreme Court of Canada. He is currently faculty at the Philippe Kirsch Institute and an adjunct professor at Osgoode Hall Law School.

NANCY WEISMAN is senior counsel to the Immigration Division at the Immigration and Refugee Board of Canada (IRB). Weisman has an LLB from Osgoode Hall Law School and a BA from the University of Manitoba. She is a member of the Law Society of Upper Canada. Weisman has lectured extensively on issues pertaining to immigration and refugee law, in particular on war crimes and crimes against humanity, at various conferences throughout Canada and at Osgoode Hall Law School and at the Law Society of Upper Canada. She has also published in the *International Journal of Refugee Law*.

Index